Kitchen Princess

4

Manga by Natsumi Ando

Story by Miyuki Kobayashi

Translated by Satsuki Yamashita

Adapted by Nunzio DeFilippis and Christina Weir

Lettered by North Market Street Graphics

Ballantine Books · New York

Kitchen Princess volume 4 is a work of fiction. Names, characters, places, and incidents are the products of the author's imagination or are used fictitiously. Any resemblance to actual events, locales, or persons, living or dead, is entirely coincidental.

A Del Rey Manga/Kodansha Trade Paperback Original

Published in the United States by Del Rey Books, an imprint of The Random House Publishing Group, a division of Random House, Inc., New York.

Publication rights arranged through Kodansha Ltd.

First published in Japan in 2006 by Kodansha Ltd., Tokyo

ISBN 978-0-345-49830-4

Printed in the United States of America

www.delreymanga.com

9 8 7 6

Translator: Satsuki Yamashita
Adaptor: Nunzio DeFilippis and Christina Weir
Lettering: North Market Street Graphics
Original cover design by Akiko Omo

Contents

Honorifics Explained

Throughout the Del Rey Manga books, you will find Japanese honorifics left intact in the translations. For those not familiar with how the Japanese use honorifics and, more important, how they differ from American honorifics, we present this brief overview.

Politeness has always been a critical facet of Japanese culture. Ever since the feudal era, when Japan was a highly stratified society, use of honorifics—which can be defined as polite speech that indicates relationship or status—has played an essential role in the Japanese language. When addressing someone in Japanese, an honorific usually takes the form of a suffix attached to one's name (example: "Asuna-san"), is used as a title at the end of one's name, or appears in place of the name itself (example: "Negi-sensei," or simply "Sensei!").

Honorifics can be expressions of respect or endearment. In the context of manga and anime, honorifics give insight into the nature of the relationship between characters. Many English translations leave out these important honorifics, and therefore distort the feel of the original Japanese. Because Japanese honorifics contain nuances that English honorifics lack, it is our policy at Del Rey not to translate them. Here, instead, is a guide to some of the honorifics you may encounter in Del Rey Manga.

-san: This is the most common honorific and is equivalent to Mr., Miss, Ms., or Mrs. It is the all-purpose honorific and can be used in any situation where politeness is required.

-sama: This is one level higher than "-san" and is used to confer great respect.

-dono: This comes from the word "tono," which means "lord." It is an even higher level than "-sama" and confers utmost respect.

-kun: This suffix is used at the end of boys' names to express familiarity or endearment. It is also sometimes used by men among friends, or when addressing someone younger or of a lower station.

-chan: This is used to express endearment, mostly toward girls. It is also used for little boys, pets, and even among lovers. It gives a sense of childish cuteness.

Bozu: This is an informal way to refer to a boy, similar to the English terms "kid" and "squirt."

Sempai/
Senpai: This title suggests that the addressee is one's senior in a group or organization. It is most often used in a school setting, where underclassmen refer to their upperclassmen as "sempai." It can also be used in the workplace, such as when a newer employee addresses an employee who has seniority in the company.

Kohai: This is the opposite of "sempai" and is used toward underclassmen in school or newcomers in the workplace. It connotes that the addressee is of a lower station.

Sensei: Literally meaning "one who has come before," this title is used for teachers, doctors, or masters of any profession or art.

[blank]:   This is usually forgotten in these lists, but it is perhaps the most significant difference between Japanese and English. The lack of honorific means that the speaker has permission to address the person in a very intimate way. Usually, only family, spouses, or very close friends have this kind of permission. Known as *yobisute*, it can be gratifying when someone who has earned the intimacy starts to call one by one's name without an honorific. But when that intimacy hasn't been earned, it can be very insulting.

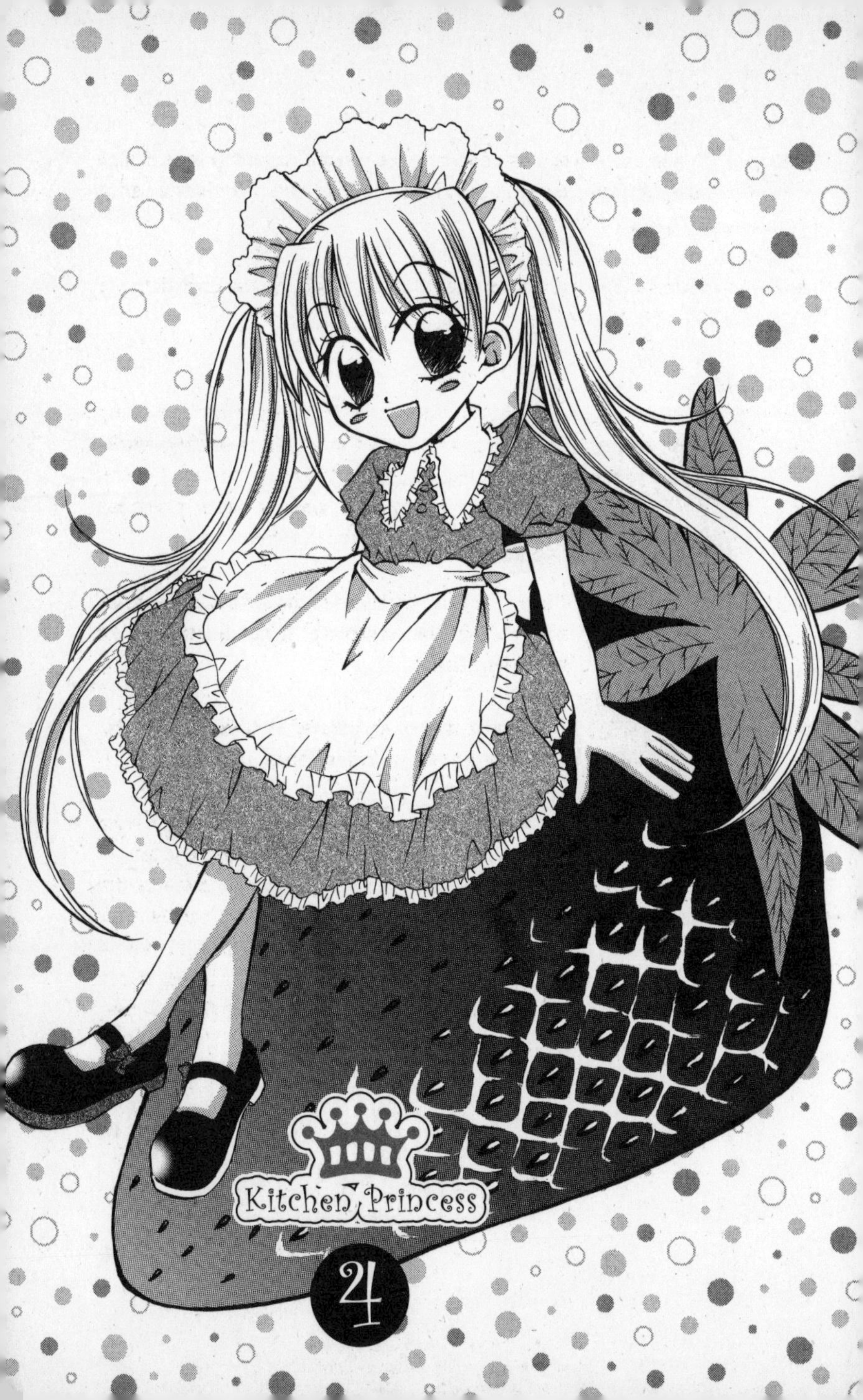
Kitchen Princess
4

Kitchen Princess

Table of Contents

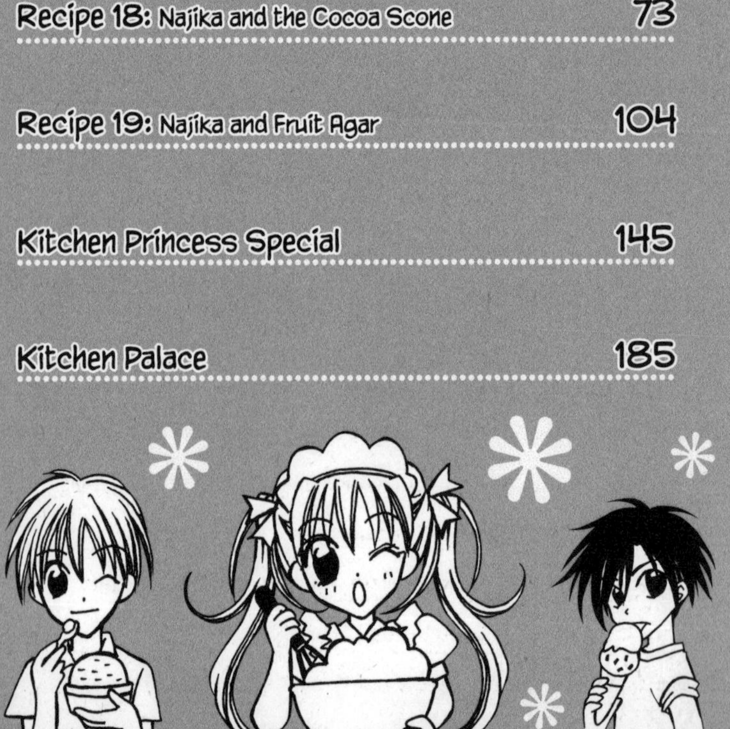

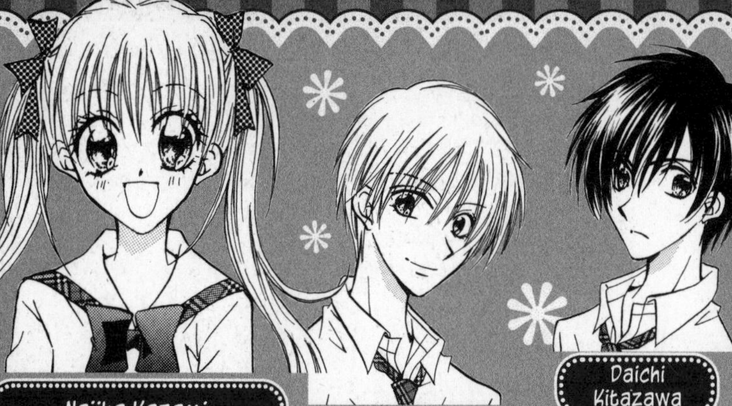

Najika Kazami

The cheerful main character who loves to eat and cook. She is in 7th grade. She has an absolute sense of taste.

Sora Kitazawa

Daichi's older brother and student body president. He is also temporarily serving as the director of the academy.

Daichi Kitazawa

The first boy Najika met when she came to Seika Academy. He doesn't get along with his older brother Sora and therefore lives in the dorms.

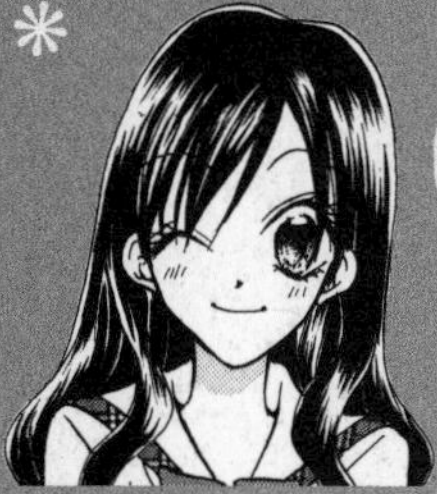

Akane Kishida

A teen model who is popular in the fashion magazines. She did not think highly of Najika, but...?

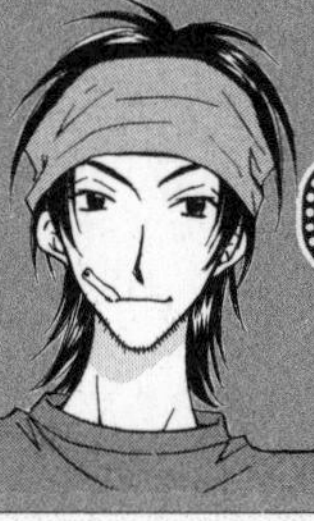

Fujita-san

He is the lazy chef at the Fujita Diner. But in actuality, he is a highly skilled chef.

The Story So Far...

Kitchen Princess

Najika lost her parents when she was young and lived in "Lavender House," an orphanage in Hokkaido. She joined Seika Academy in Tokyo to find her Flan Prince, a boy who saved her from drowning when she was young. At the academy, Najika overcame a cooking showdown and the closing of the Fujita Diner. Najika is slowly becoming attracted to Sora. And for some reason this irritates Daichi. One day, Daichi noticed Najika's watch was cracked and he bought her a new one. But Akane took it before Najika found it. She lied to Daichi and said that Najika gave it to her...

Kitchen Princess

4 Panel Manga #1

If the Kitazawa brothers were on good terms...
Daichi, you must be hungry after basketball.
Take my food.
What are you saying?
You're so busy with student body work.
You eat my food!!
Oh!
CLANG
Daichi!!
Are you okay, Daichi?
As long as you're okay, nothing else matters.
Onii-san...
Yeah... but onii-san, your food...
But it was food I cooked.

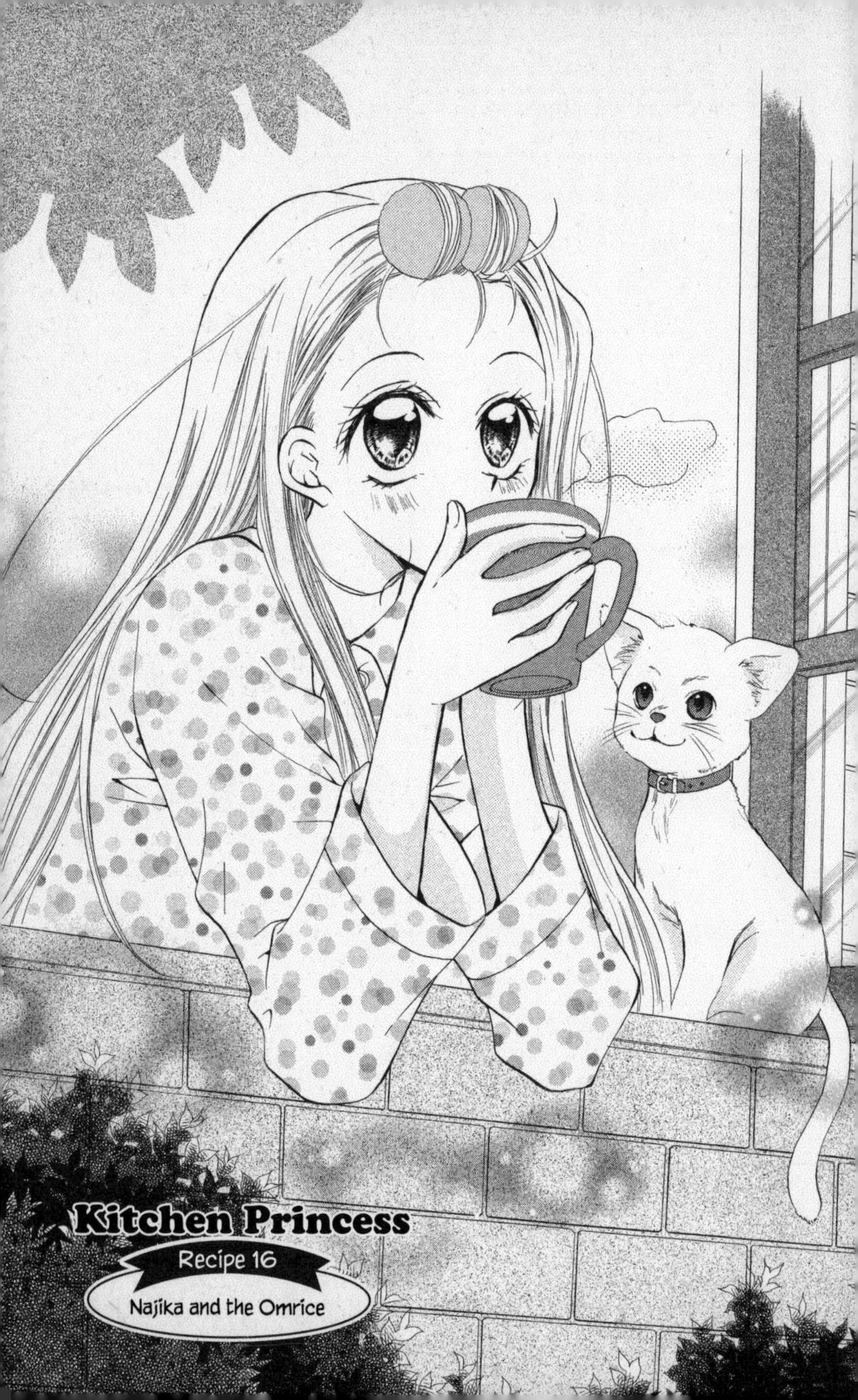
Kitchen Princess
Recipe 16
Najika and the Omrice

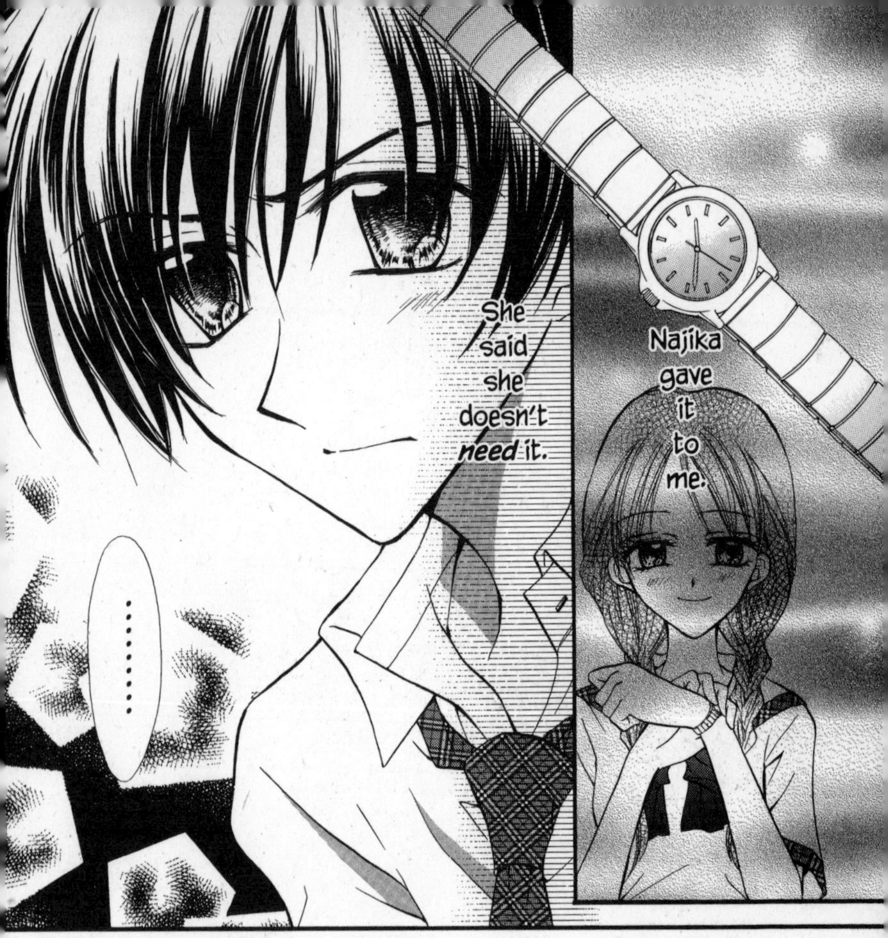
Najika gave it to me.
She said she doesn't need it.
......

About Recipe 16's Splash Page

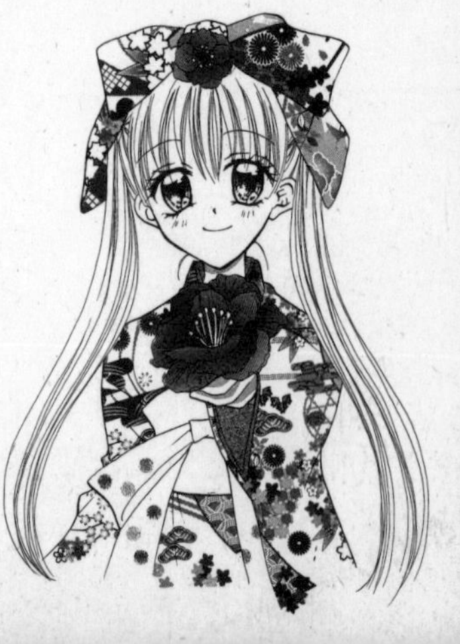

I don't know why I put in a cat...

Najika is in a tough situation in this chapter, so I wanted to let her relax a little on the splash page.

She's drinking hot chocolate.

I love polka dots and I have a lot of clothes with polka-dot patterns, but I don't have polka-dot pajamas. So maybe I gave them to Najika as a way of expressing my desire to have them.

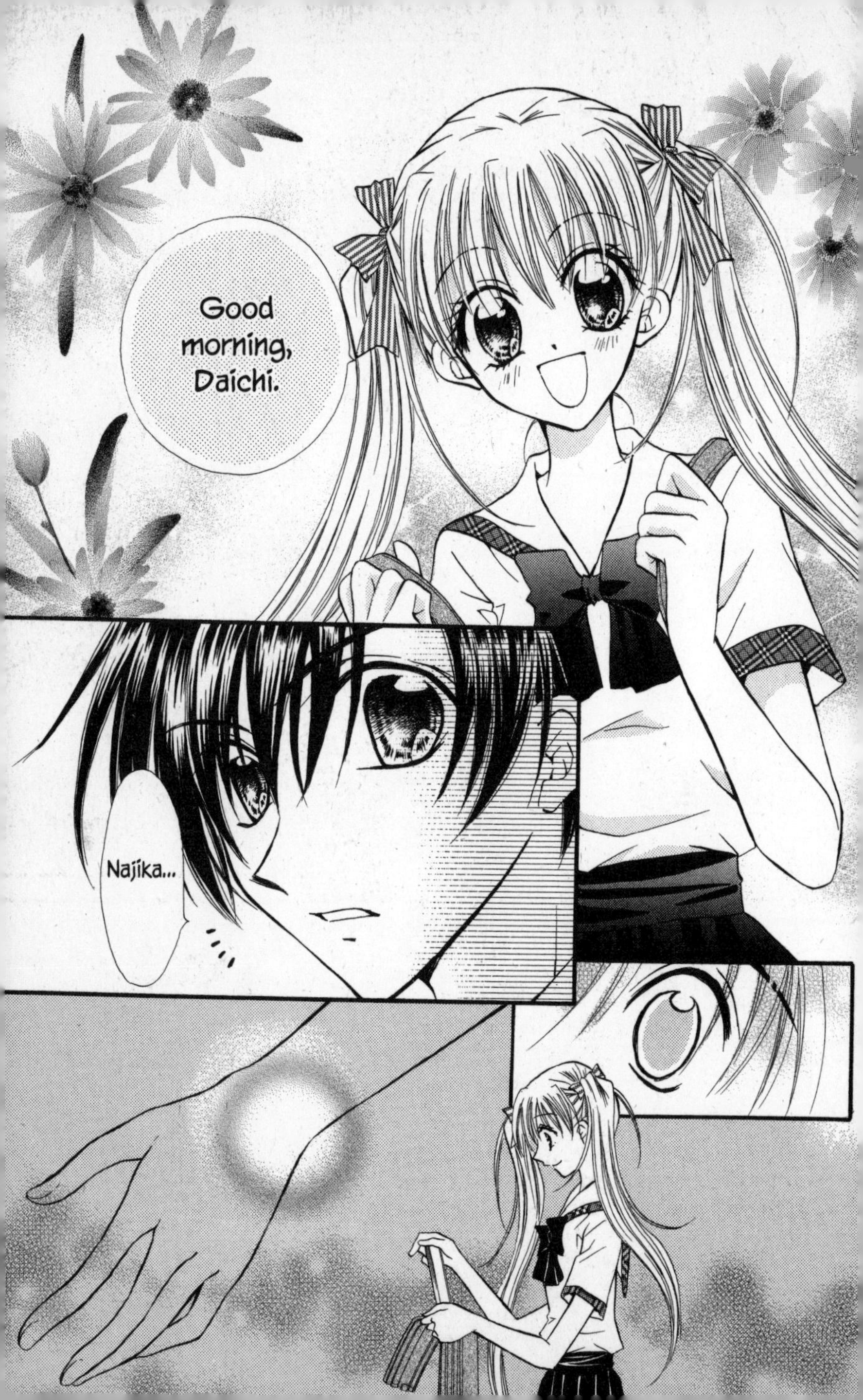
Good morning, Daichi.
Najika...

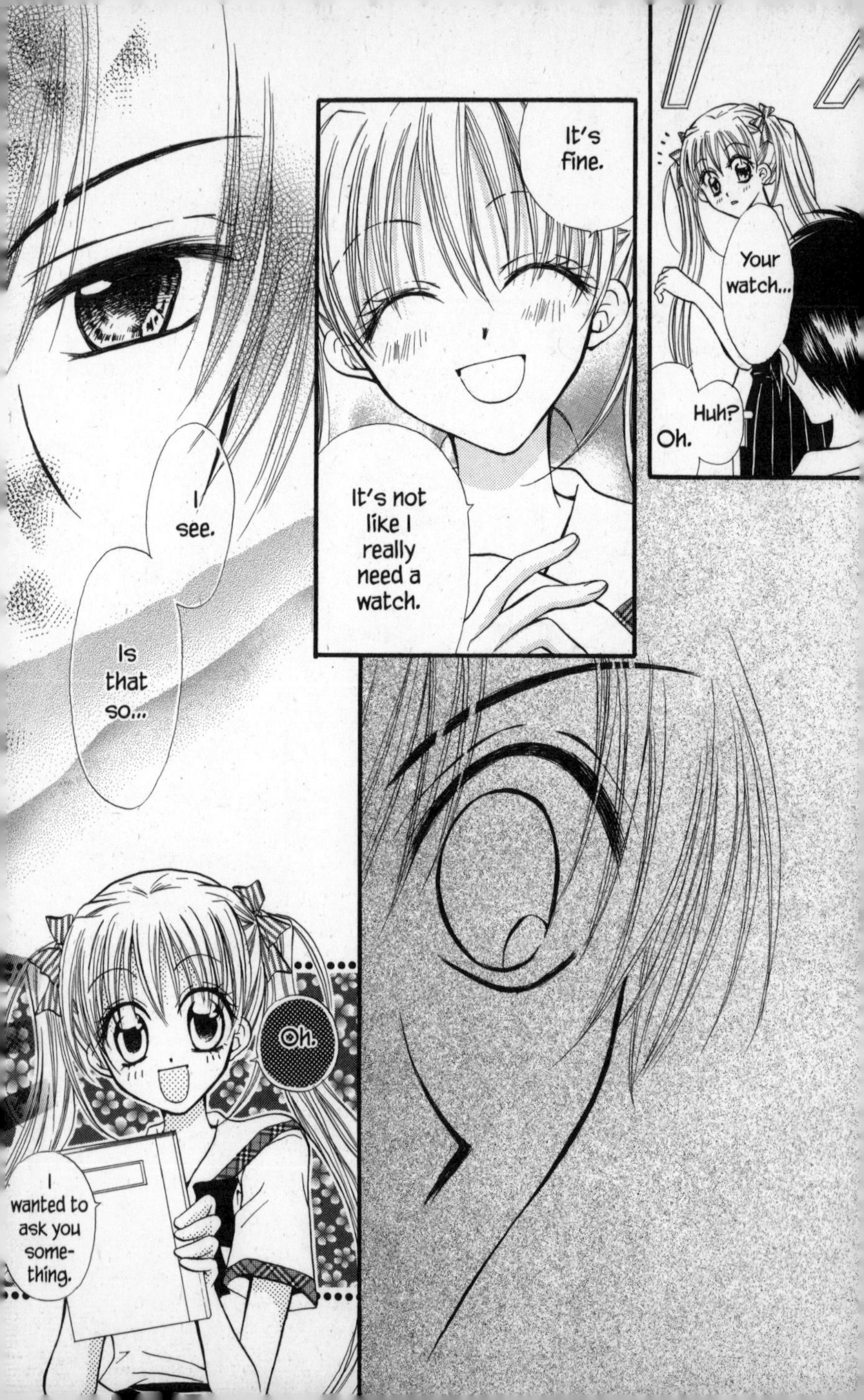

Your watch...
Huh? Oh.
It's fine.
It's not like I really need a watch.
I see.
Is that so...
Oh.
I wanted to ask you some-thing.

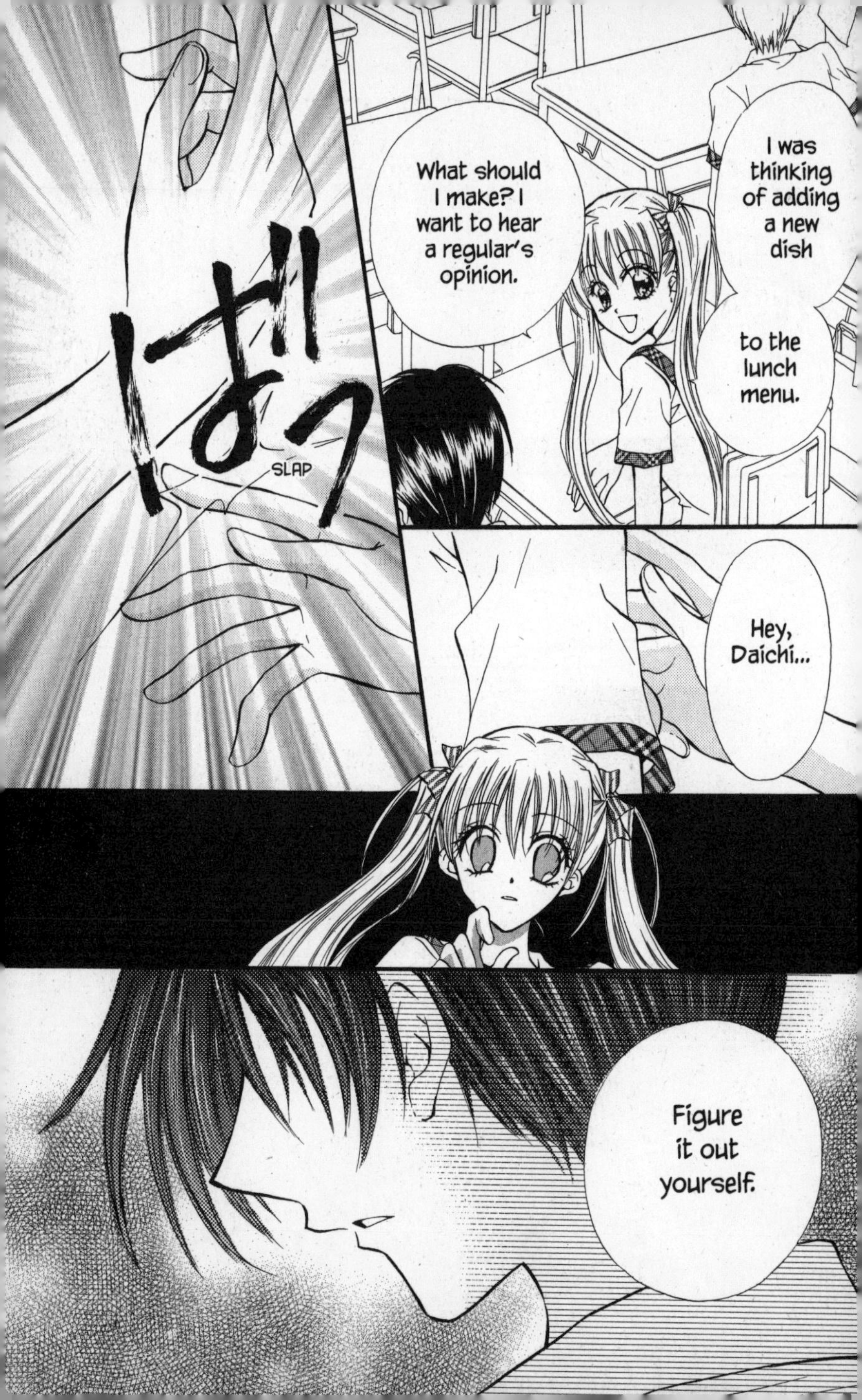
I was thinking of adding a new dish
to the lunch menu.
What should I make? I want to hear a regular's opinion.
Hey, Daichi...
はっ
SLAP
Figure it out yourself.

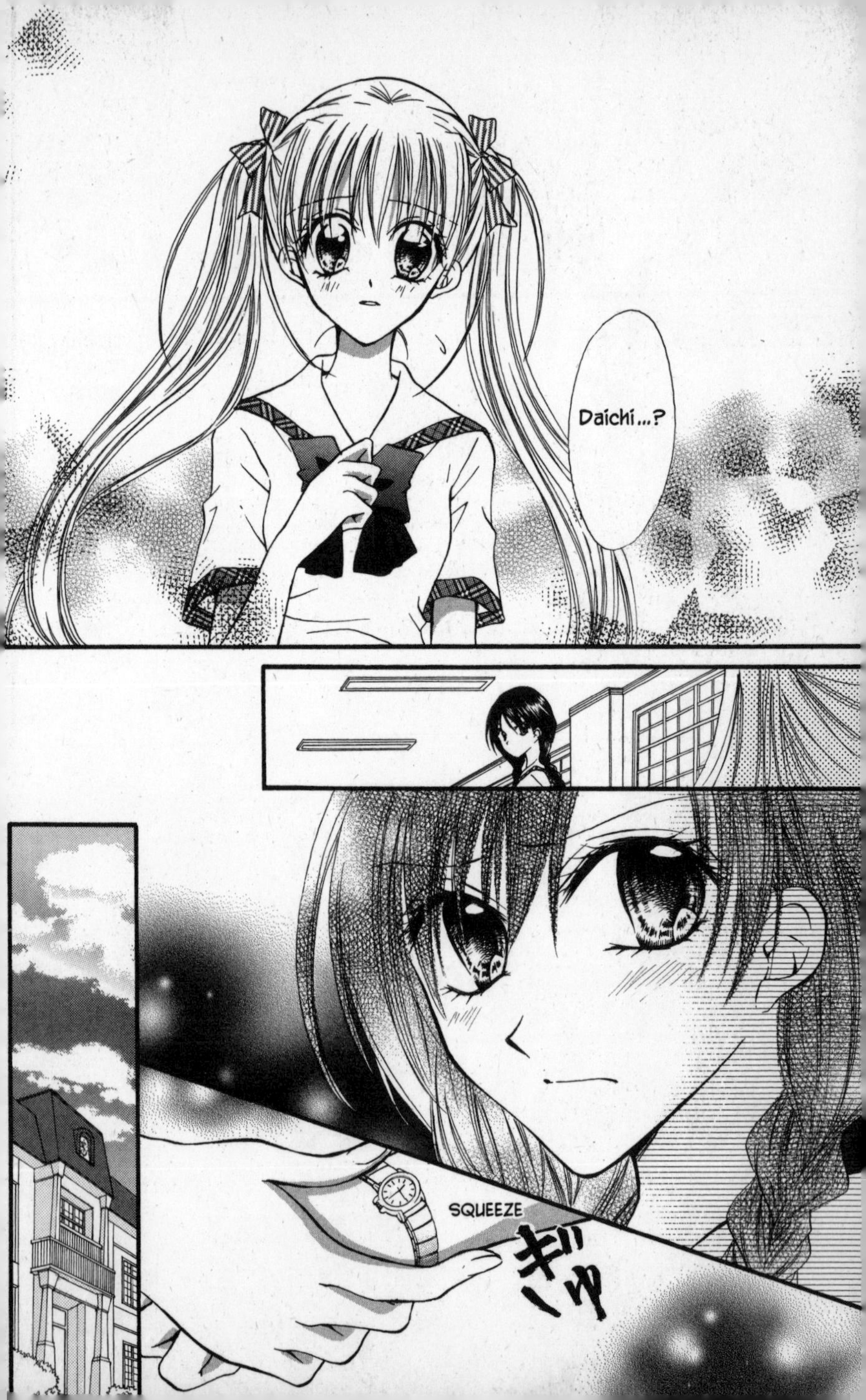
Daichi...?
SQUEEZE
ぎゅ

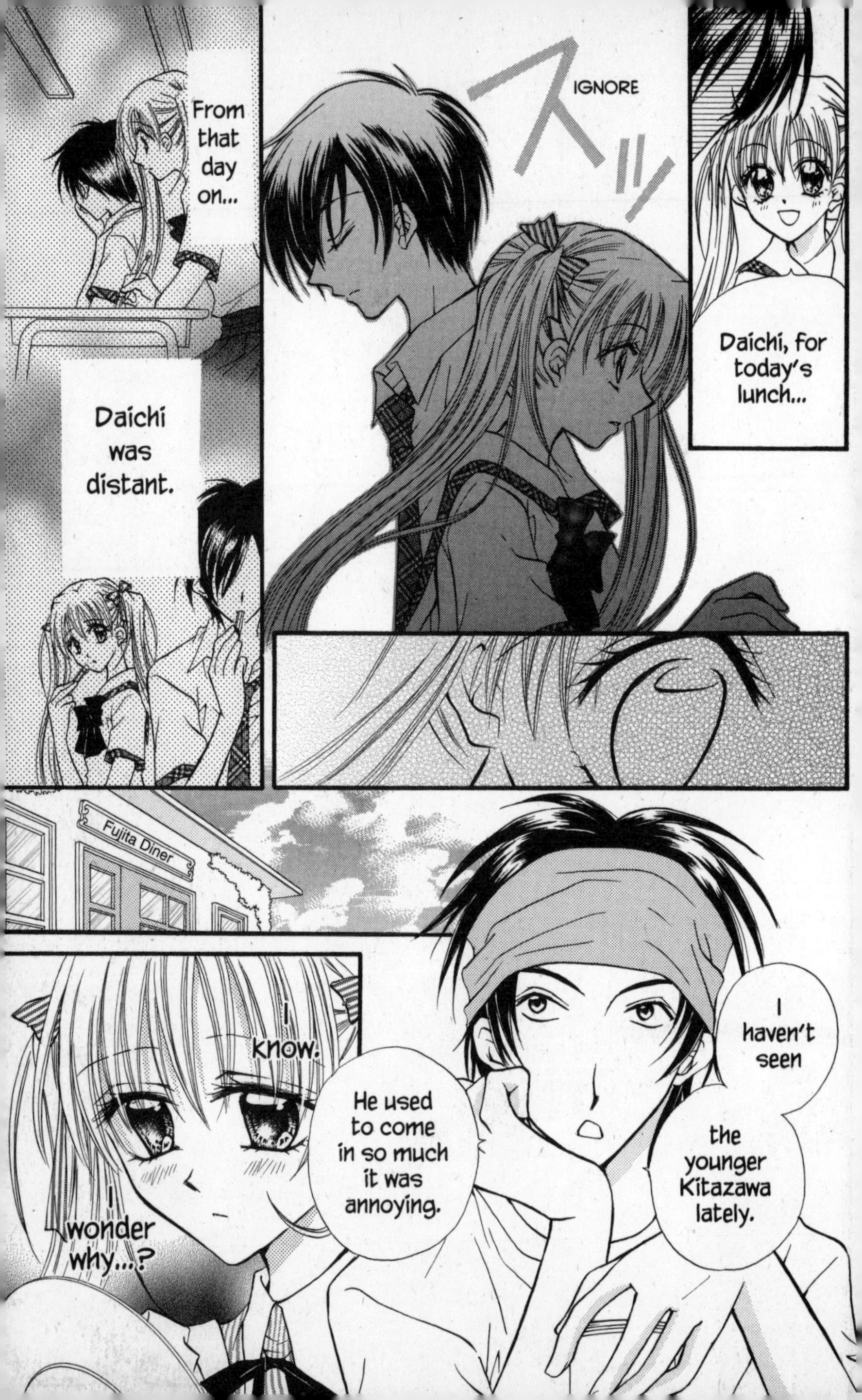

Daichi, for today's lunch...
IGNORE
From that day on...
Daichi was distant.
Fujita Diner
I haven't seen
the younger Kitazawa lately.
He used to come in so much it was annoying.
I know.
I wonder why...?

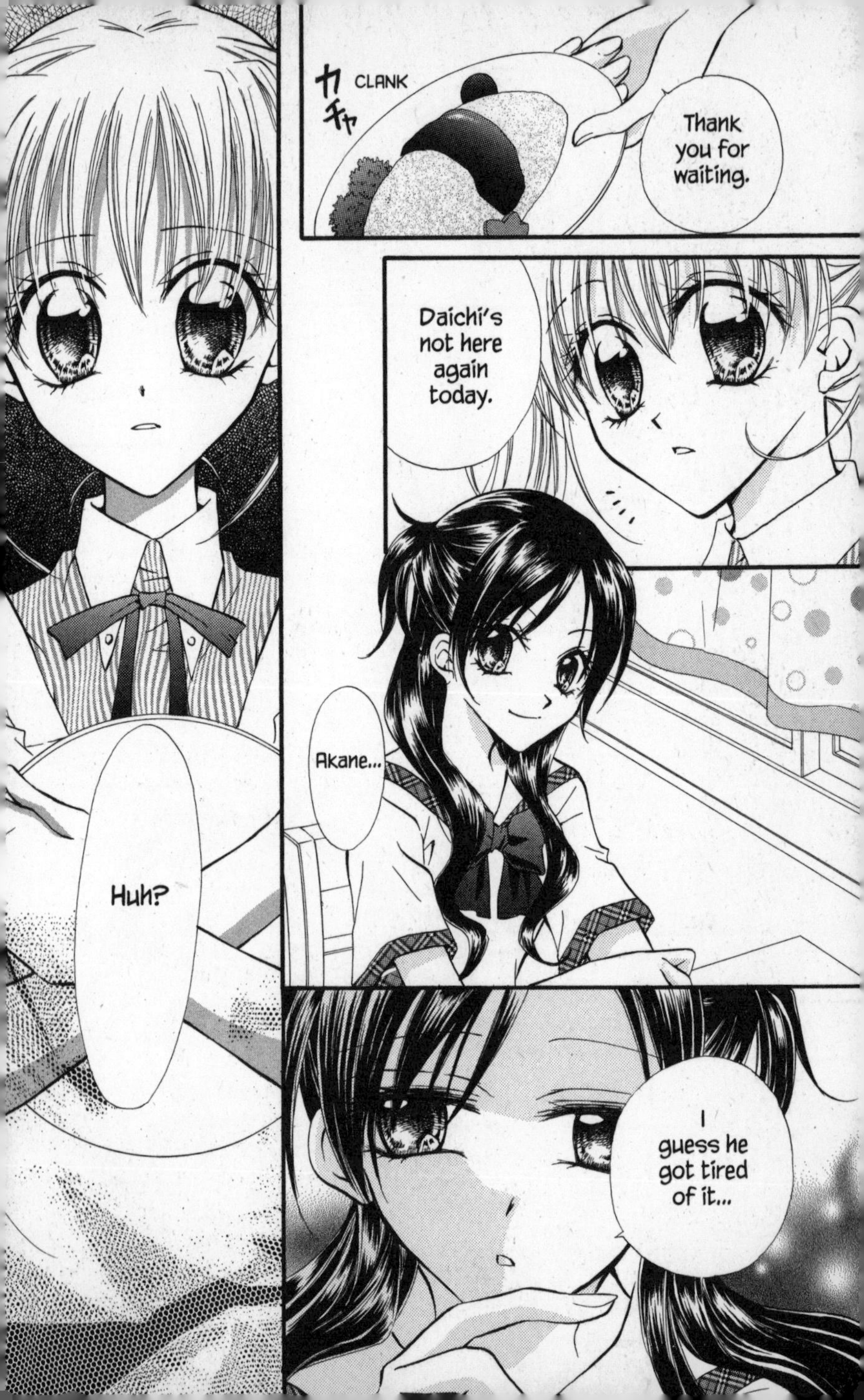
カチャ
CLANK
Thank you for waiting.
Daichi's not here again today.
Akane...
I guess he got tired of it...
Huh?

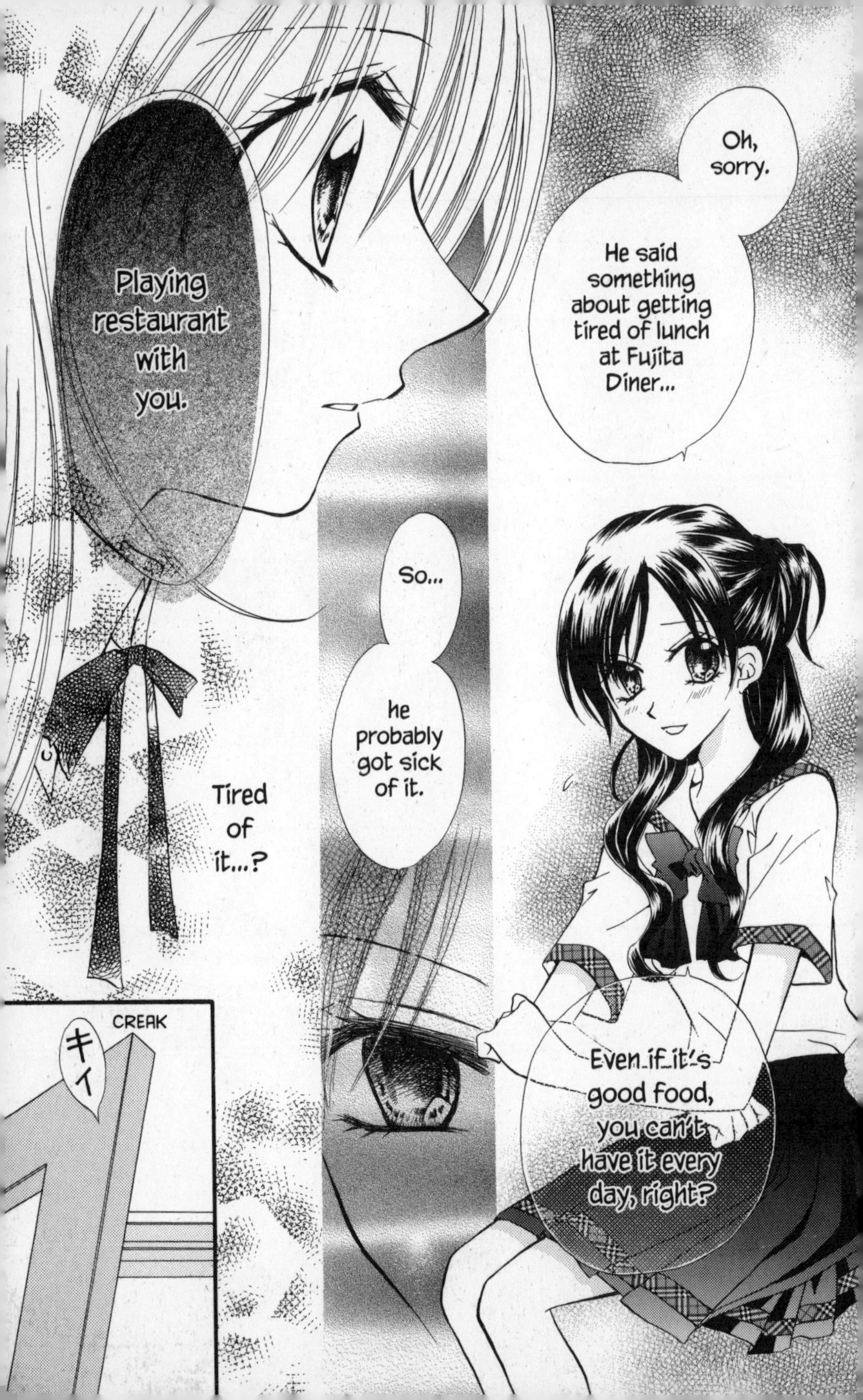
Oh, sorry.
He said something about getting tired of lunch at Fujita Diner...
Even if it's good food, you can't have it every day, right?
So...
he probably got sick of it.
Playing restaurant with you.
Tired of it...?
キイ
CREAK

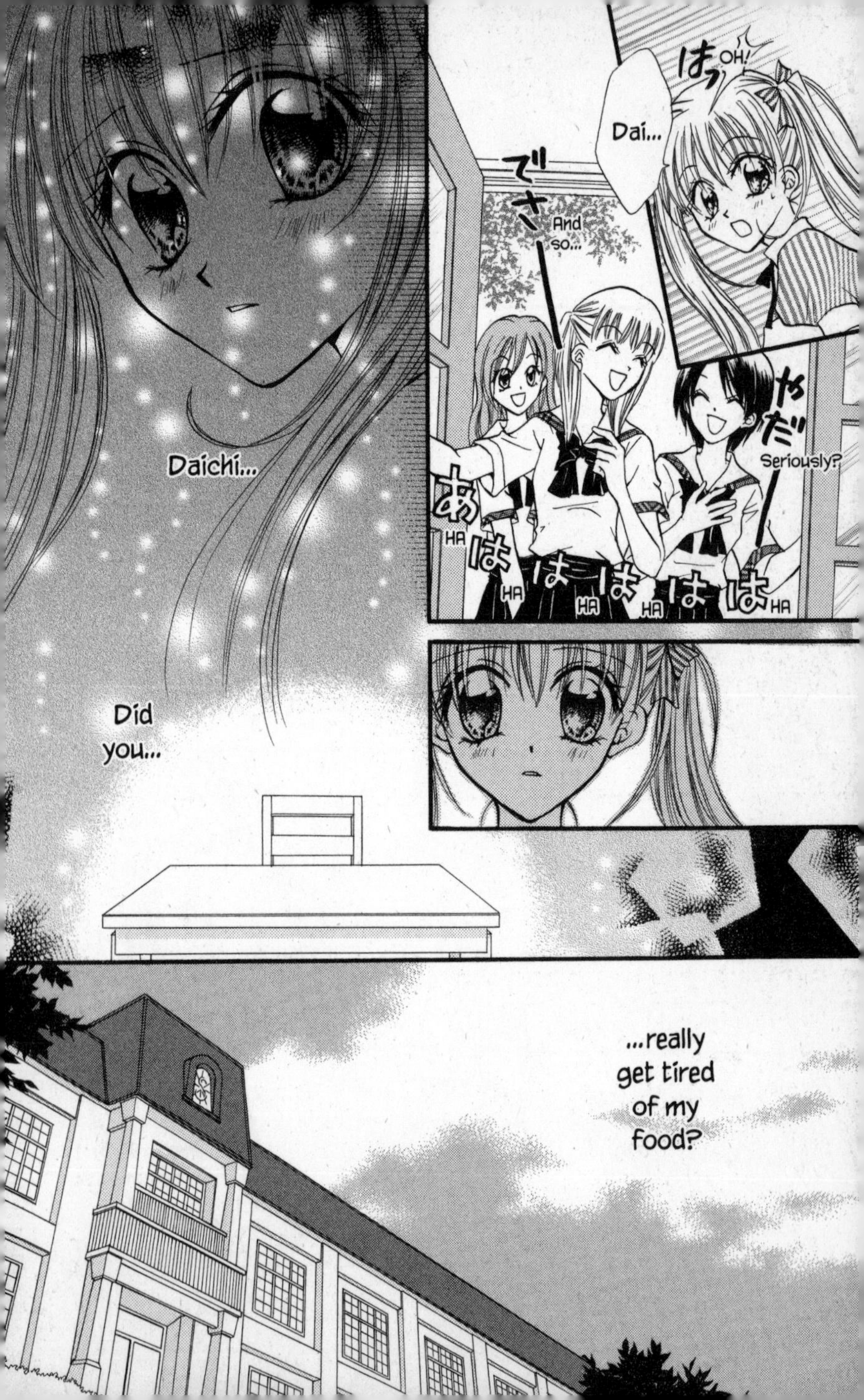

は OH!
Dai...
でさ And so...
やだ Seriously?
あははははは HA HA HA HA HA
Daichi...
Did you...
...really get tired of my food?

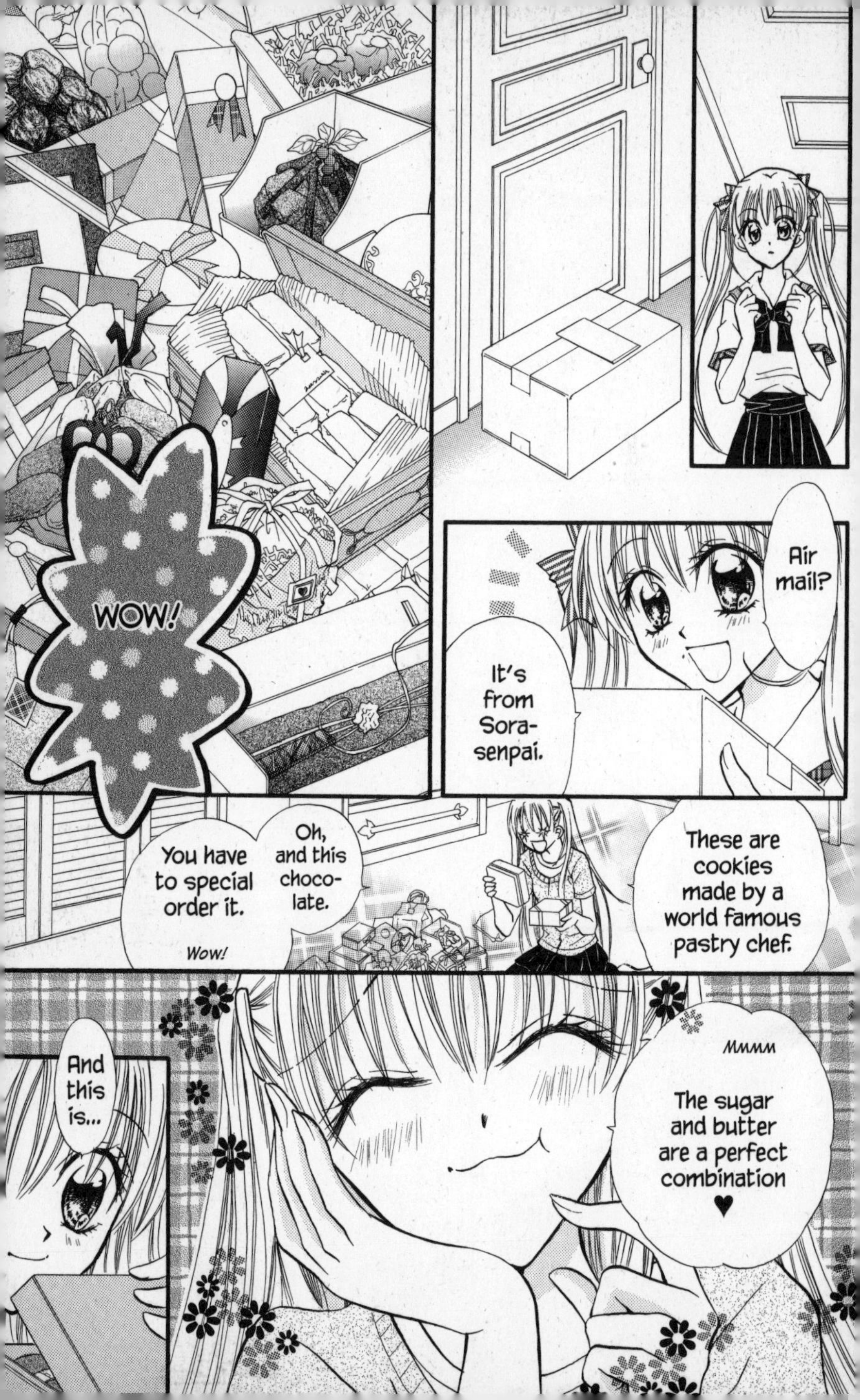

Air mail?
It's from Sora-senpai.
WOW!
These are cookies made by a world famous pastry chef.
Oh, and this choco-late.
You have to special order it.
Wow!
Mmmm
The sugar and butter are a perfect combination ♥
And this is...

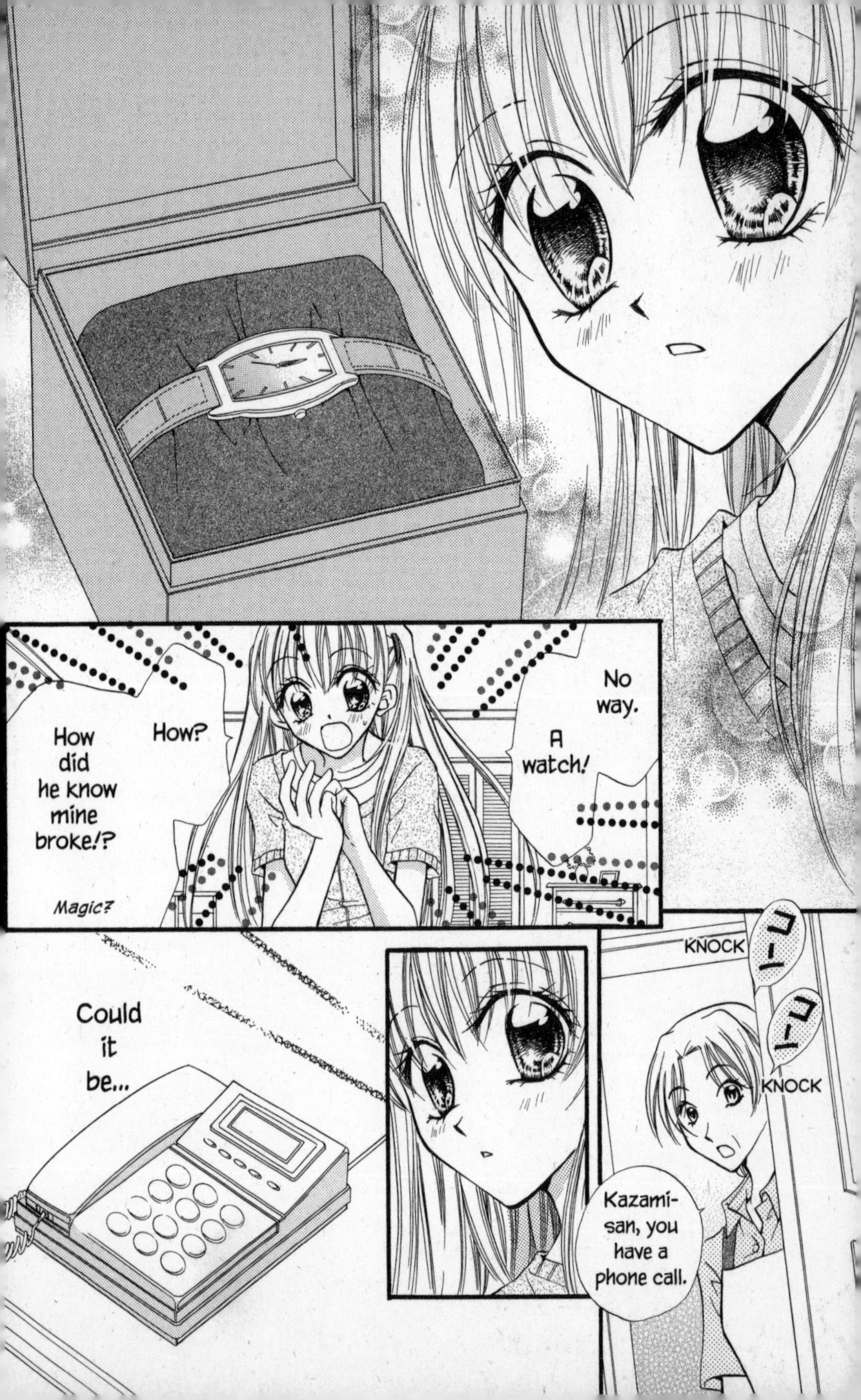

No way.
A watch!
How?
How did he know mine broke!?
Magic?
KNOCK
KNOCK
Kazami-san, you have a phone call.
Could it be...

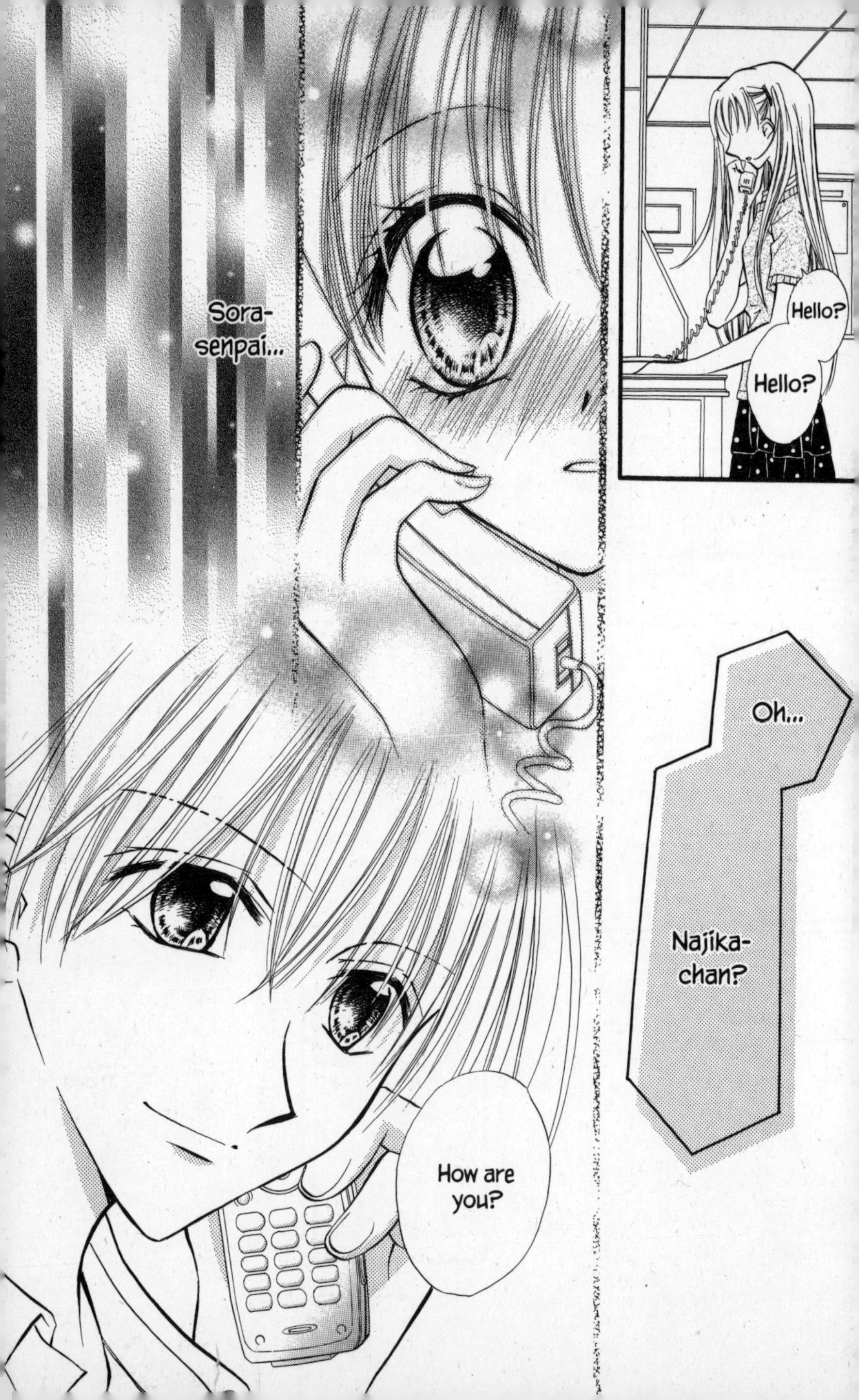
Hello?
Hello?
Oh...
Najika-chan?
Sora-senpai...
How are you?

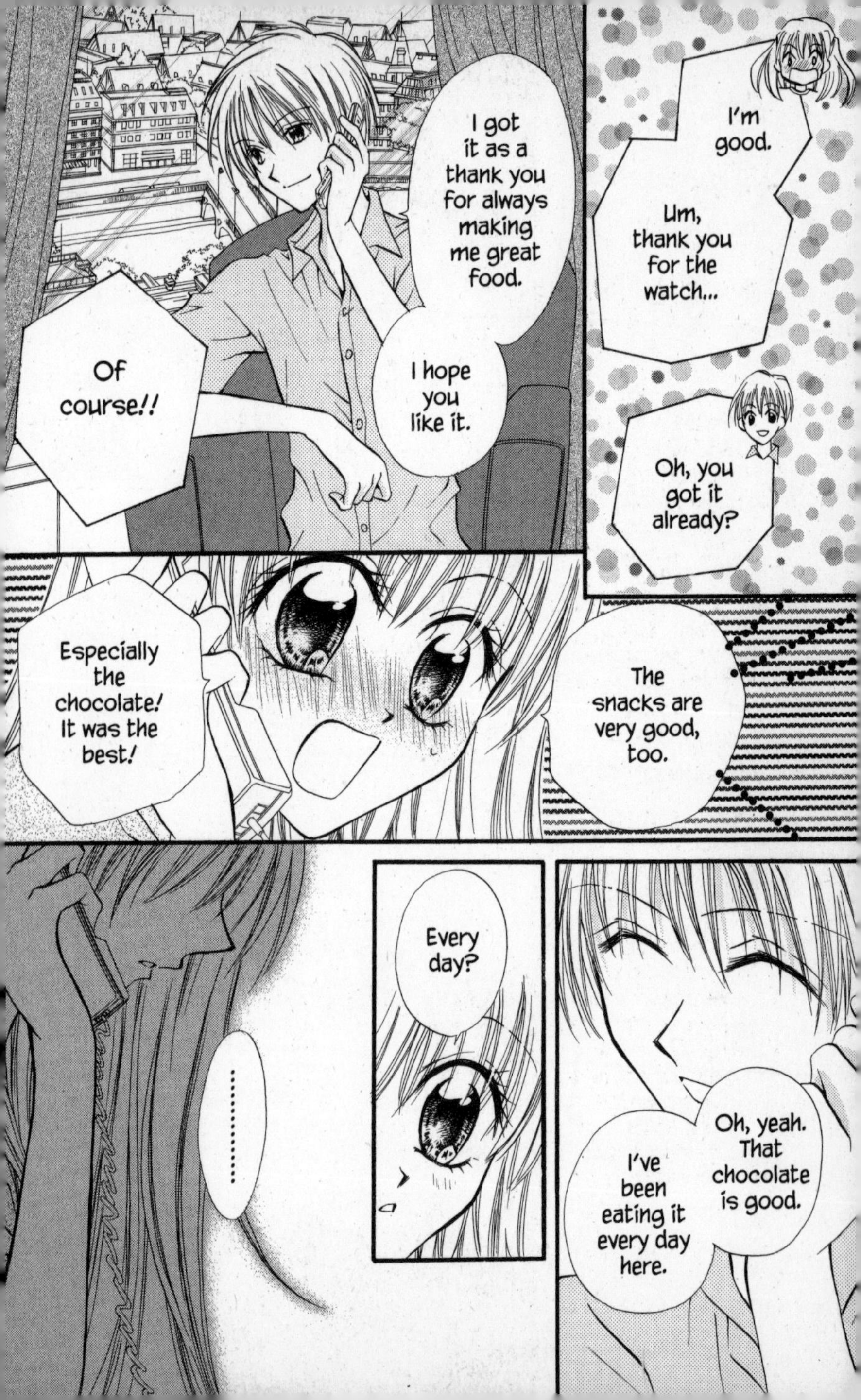
I'm good.
Um, thank you for the watch...
Oh, you got it already?
I got it as a thank you for always making me great food.
I hope you like it.
Of course!!
The snacks are very good, too.
Especially the chocolate! It was the best!
Oh, yeah. That chocolate is good.
I've been eating it every day here.
Every day?
......

Hello

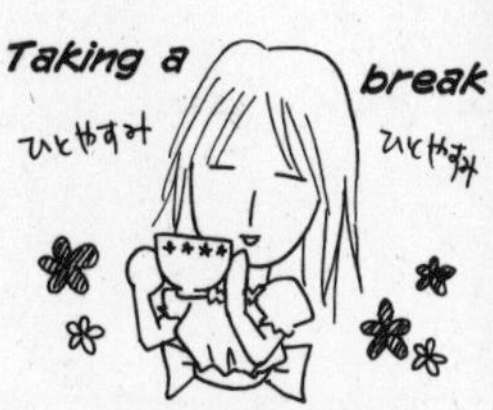
Taking a
break
ひとやすみ
ひとやすみ

Hi there. (bow) Lately I've been looking for good bakeries and trying out all of their cakes. So I can never forget to do my stretches every day!! Then I will go back to talking about my memories of each chapter!!

Recipe 16

When I eat omrice, I like the rice to be chicken rice ♥ And if the egg is half cooked, it's the best! There's a really good restaurant near my house, and I so wanted to go while I was working on this chapter. Come to think of it, I haven't gone in a while...

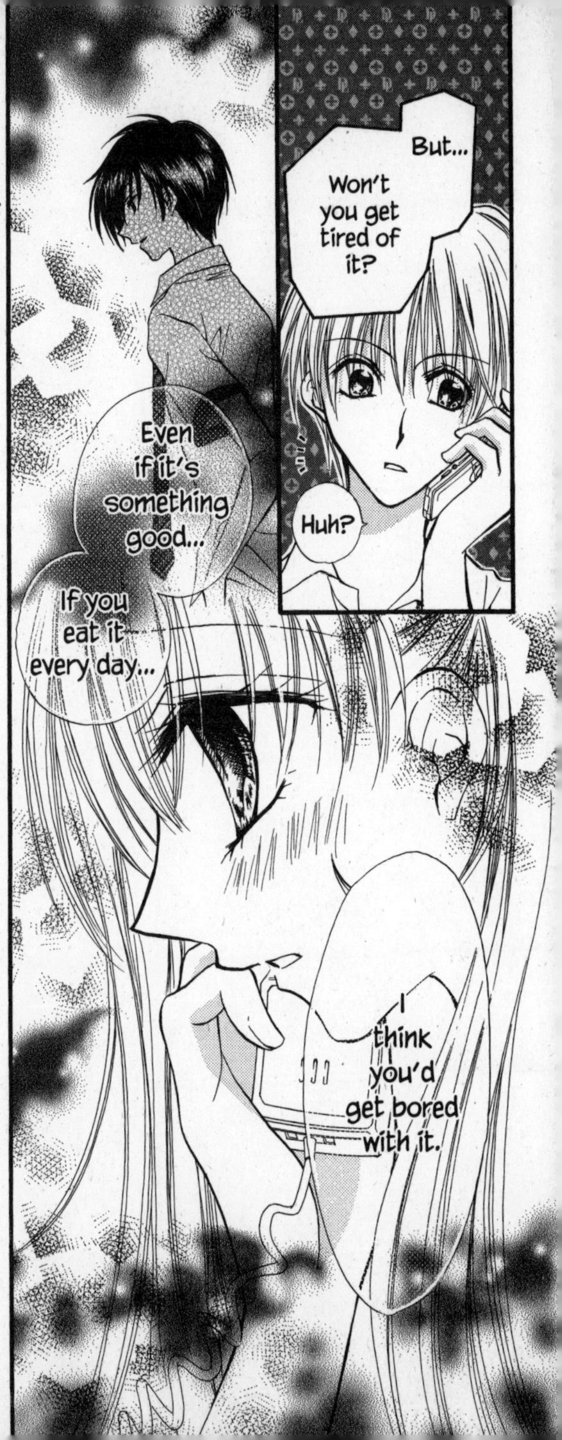
But...
Won't you get tired of it?
Huh?
Even if it's something good...
If you eat it every day...
I think you'd get bored with it.

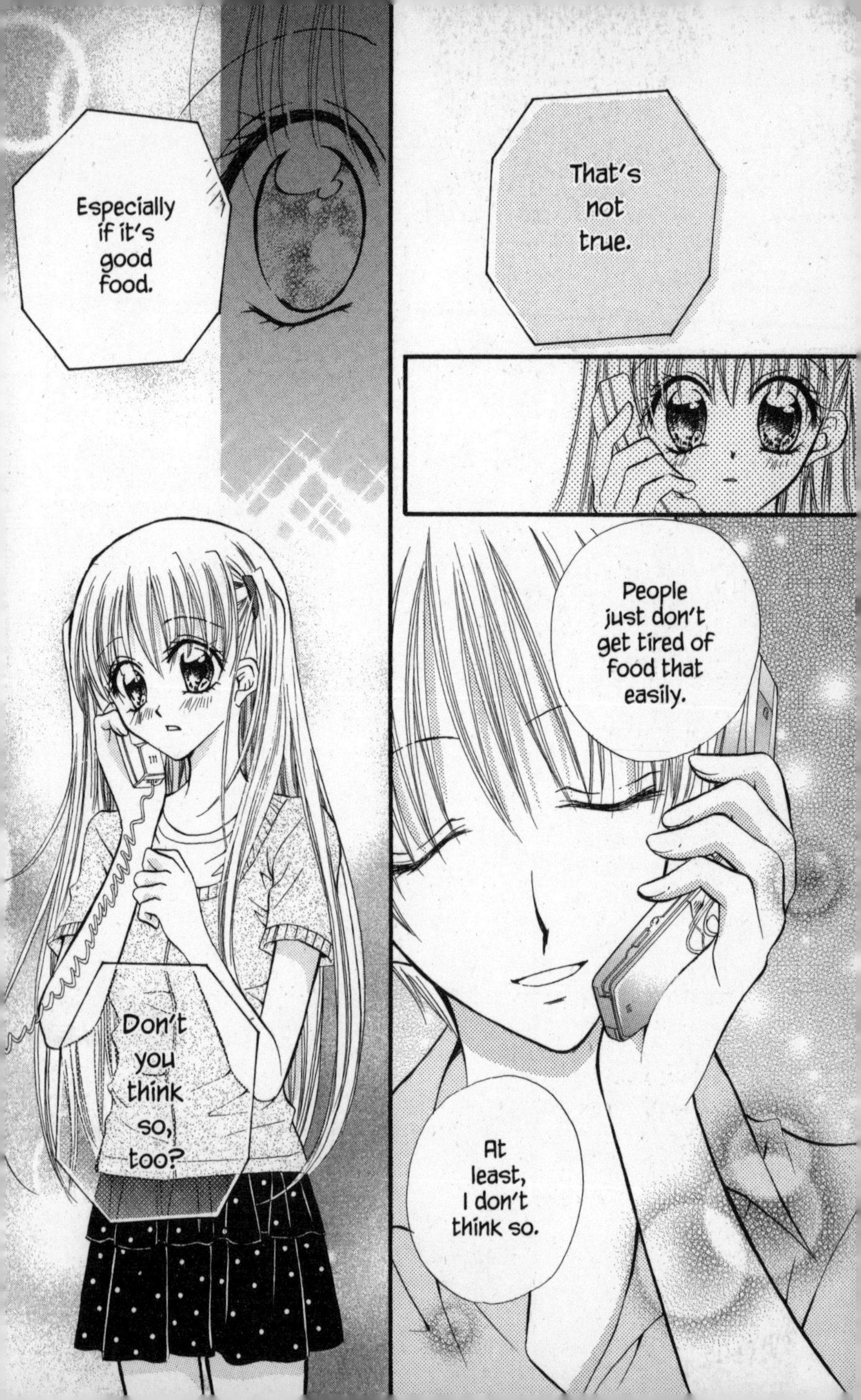
That's not true.
People just don't get tired of food that easily.
At least, I don't think so.
Especially if it's good food.
Don't you think so, too?

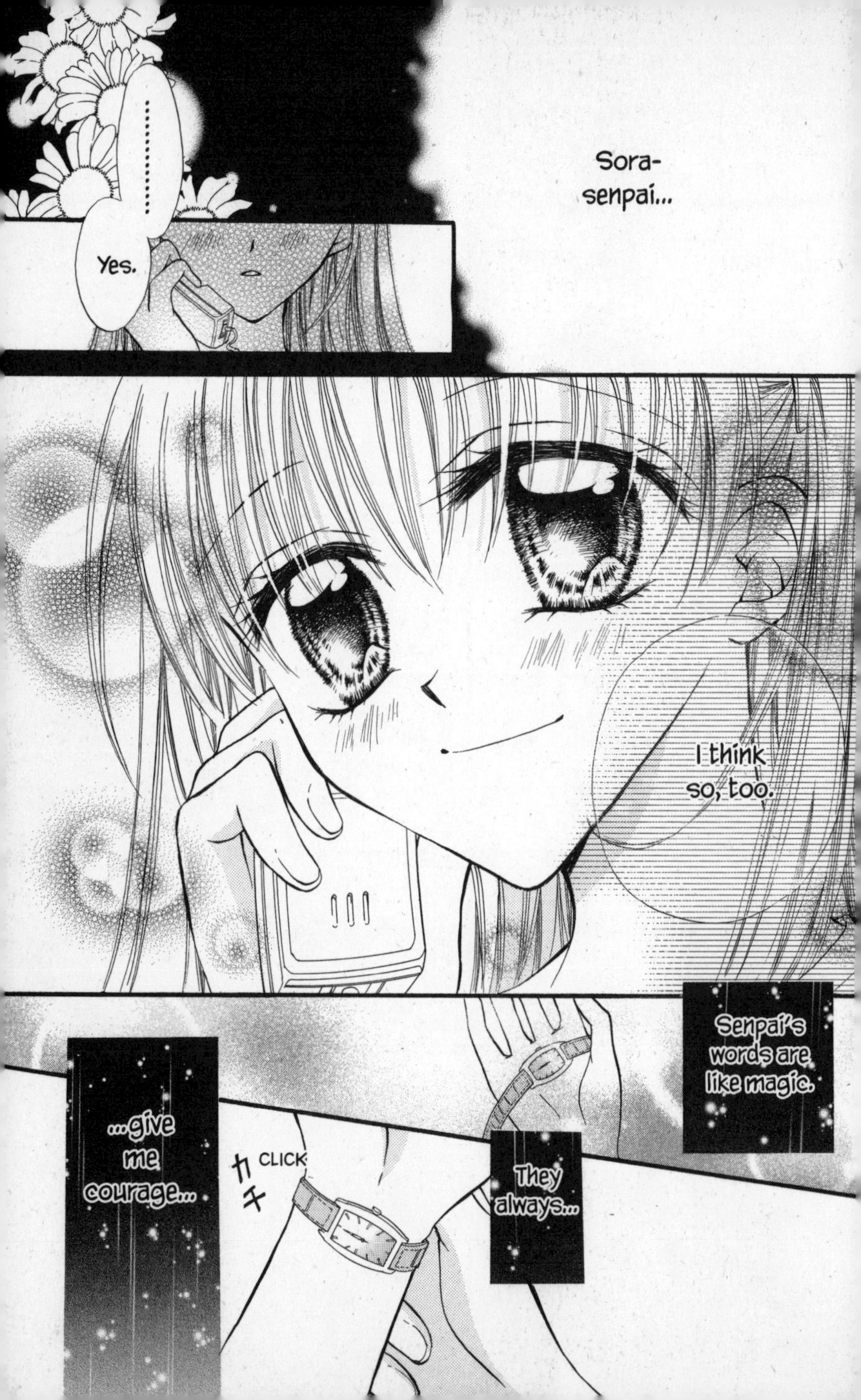
Sora-senpai...
......
Yes.
I think so, too.
Senpai's words are like magic.
They always...
カチ CLICK
...give me courage...

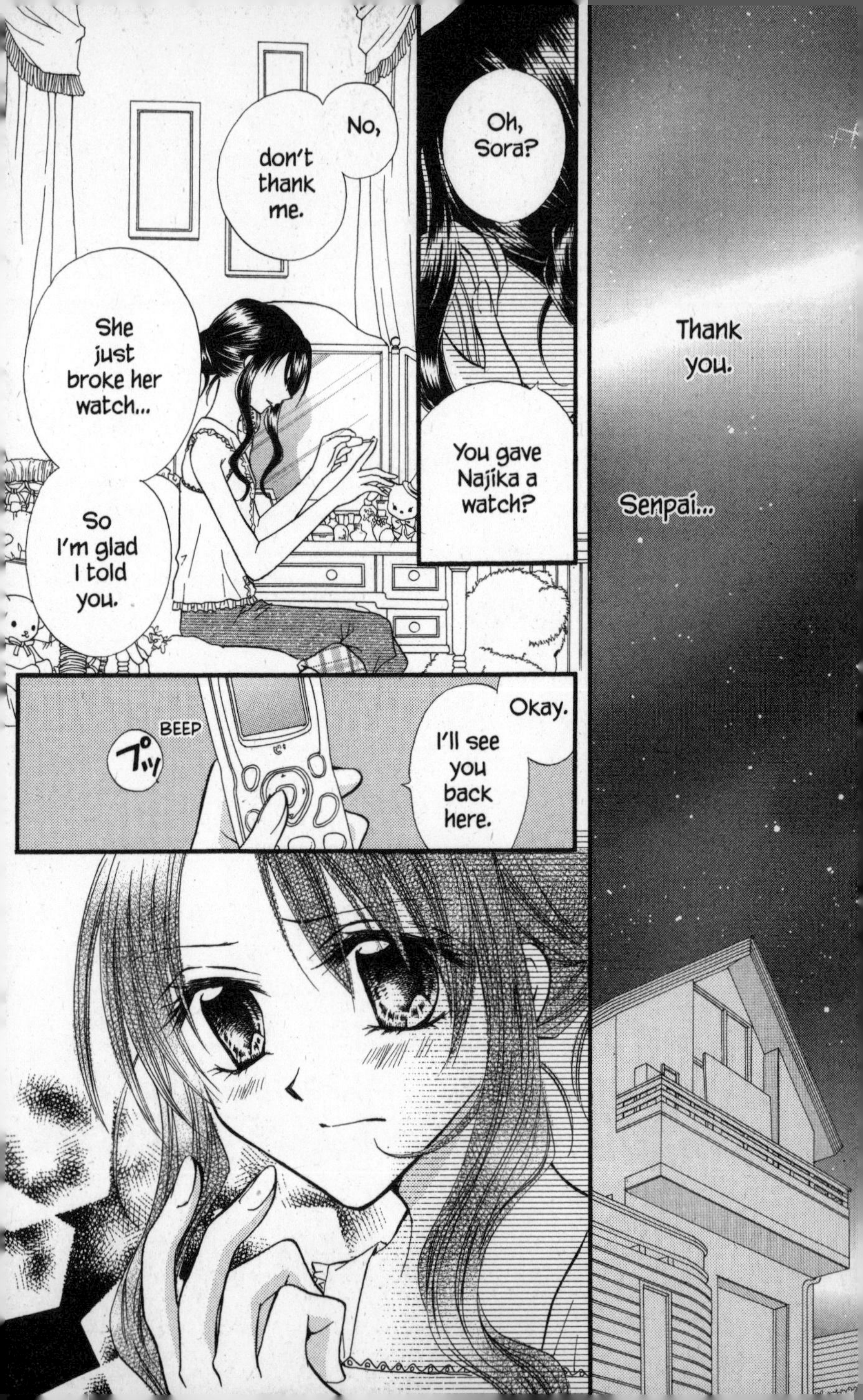
Thank you.
Senpai...
Oh, Sora?
You gave Najika a watch?
No, don't thank me.
She just broke her watch...
So I'm glad I told you.
Okay. I'll see you back here.
BEEP
プッ

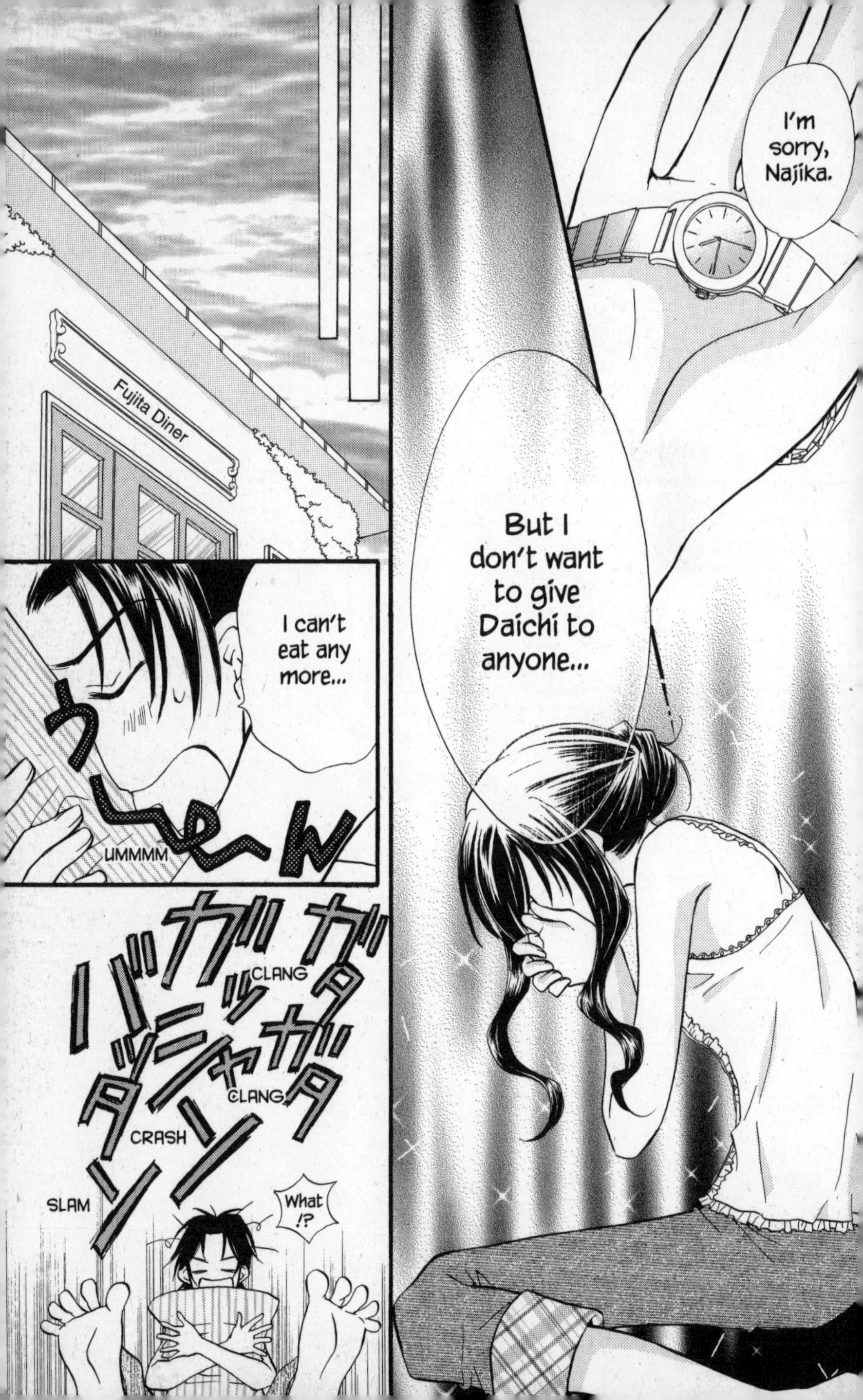
I'm sorry, Najika.
But I don't want to give Daichi to anyone...
Fujita Diner
I can't eat any more...
UMMMM
CLANG
CLANG
CRASH
SLAM
What!?

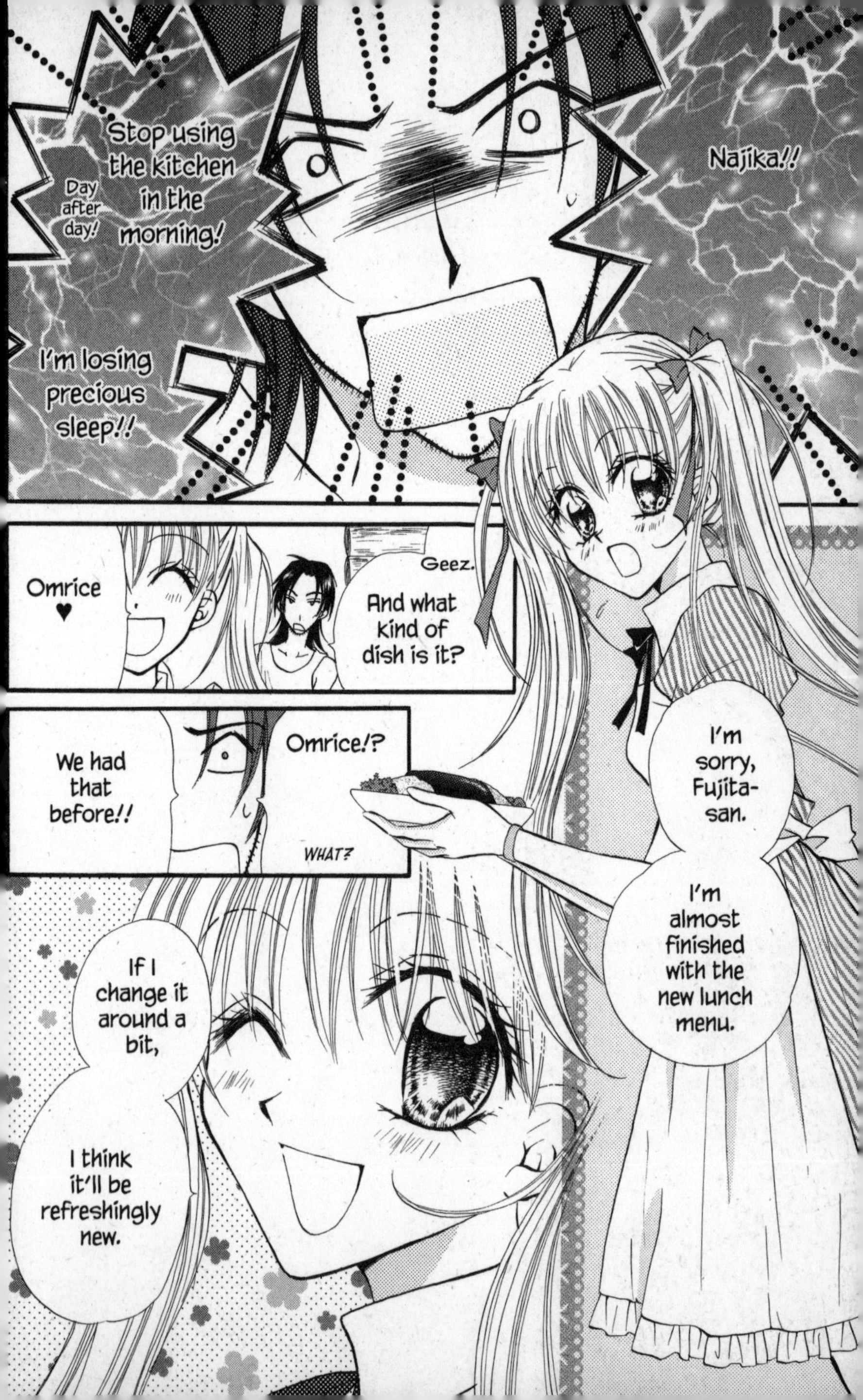
Najika!!
Stop using the kitchen in the morning!
Day after day!
I'm losing precious sleep!!
I'm sorry, Fujita-san.
I'm almost finished with the new lunch menu.
Geez.
And what kind of dish is it?
Omrice ♥
Omrice!?
WHAT?
We had that before!!
If I change it around a bit,
I think it'll be refreshingly new.

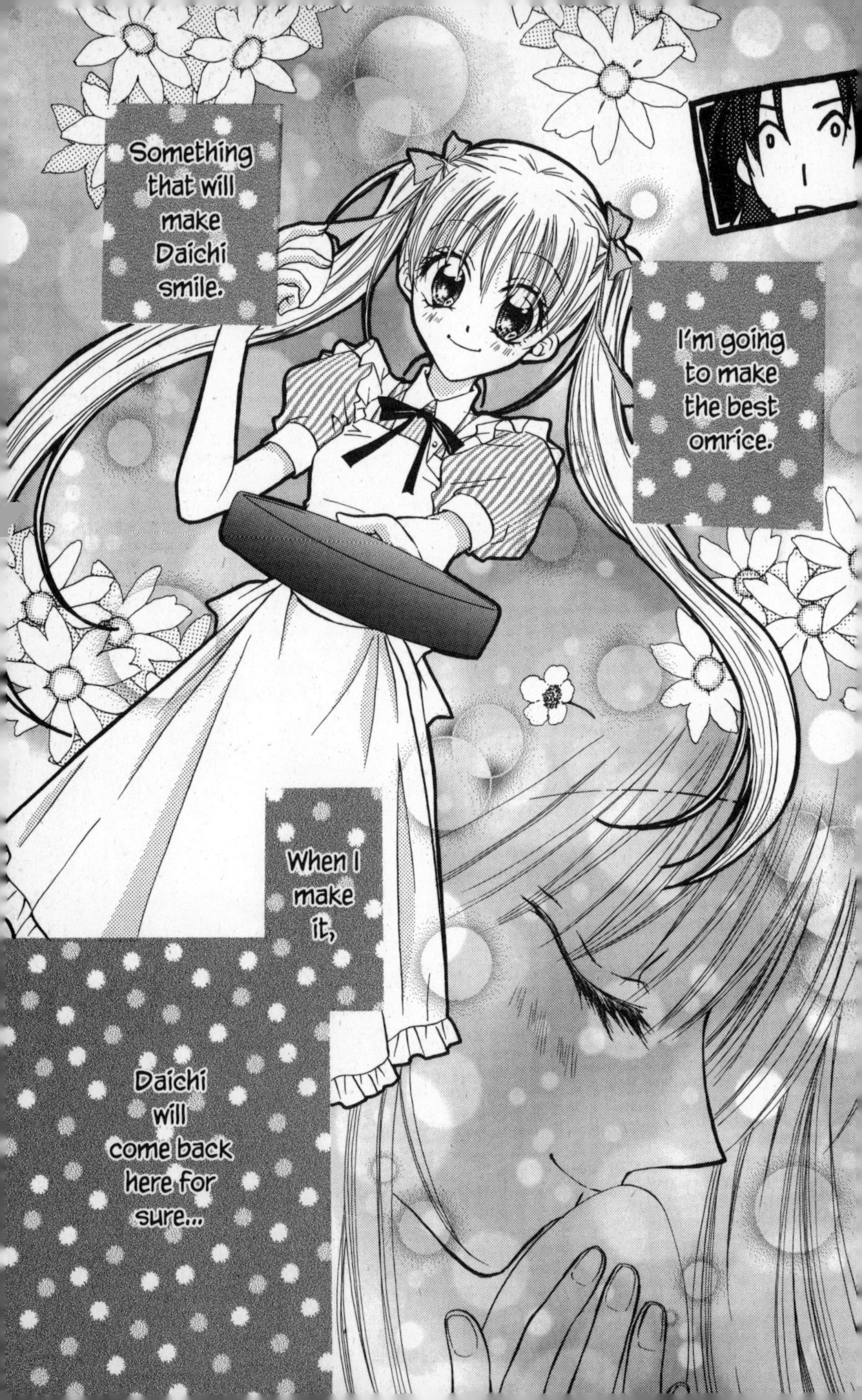
Something that will make Daichi smile.
I'm going to make the best omrice.
When I make it,
Daichi will come back here for sure...

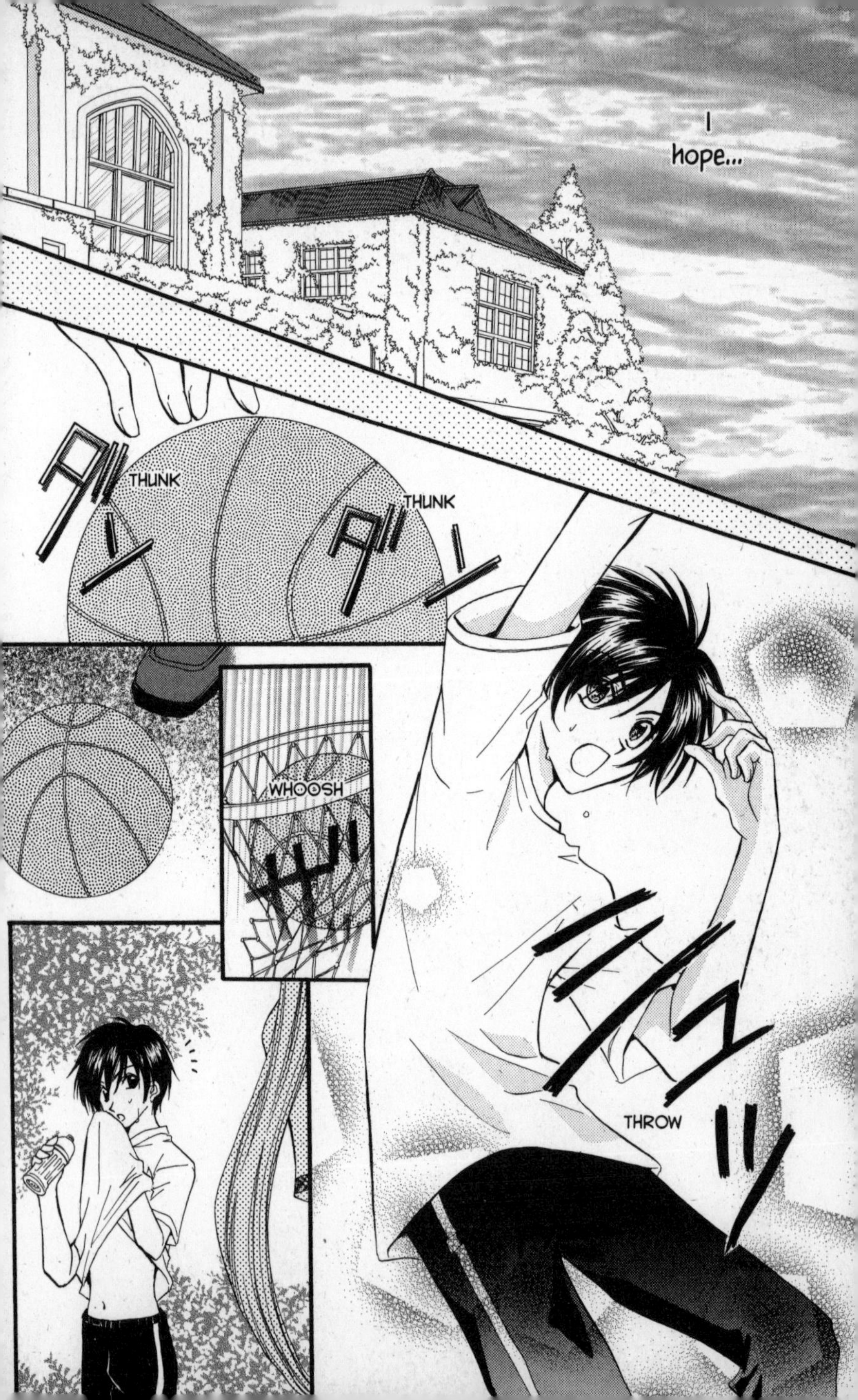
I hope...
THUNK
THUNK
THROW
WHOOSH

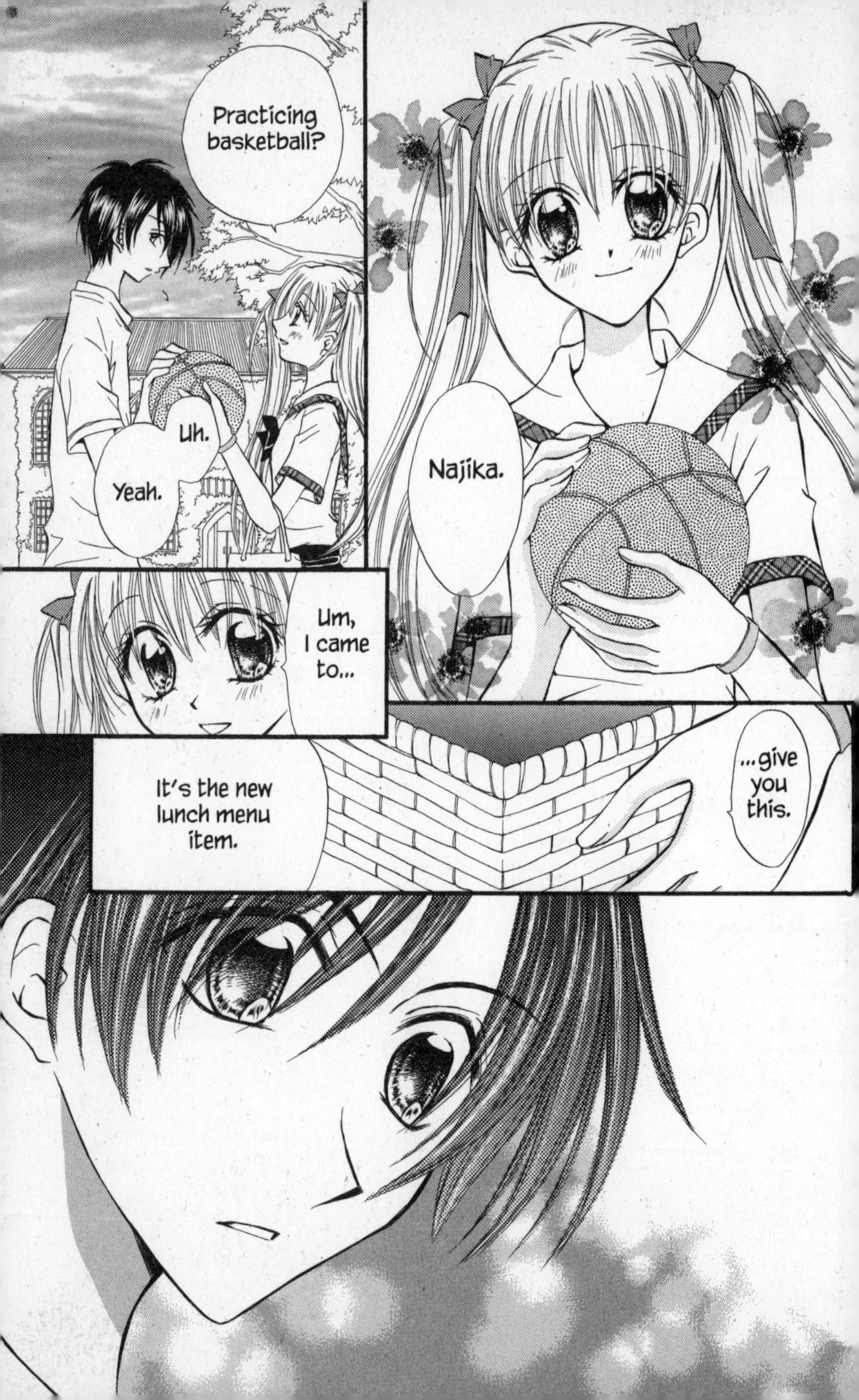
Najika.
Practicing basketball?
Uh.
Yeah.
Um, I came to...
...give you this.
It's the new lunch menu item.

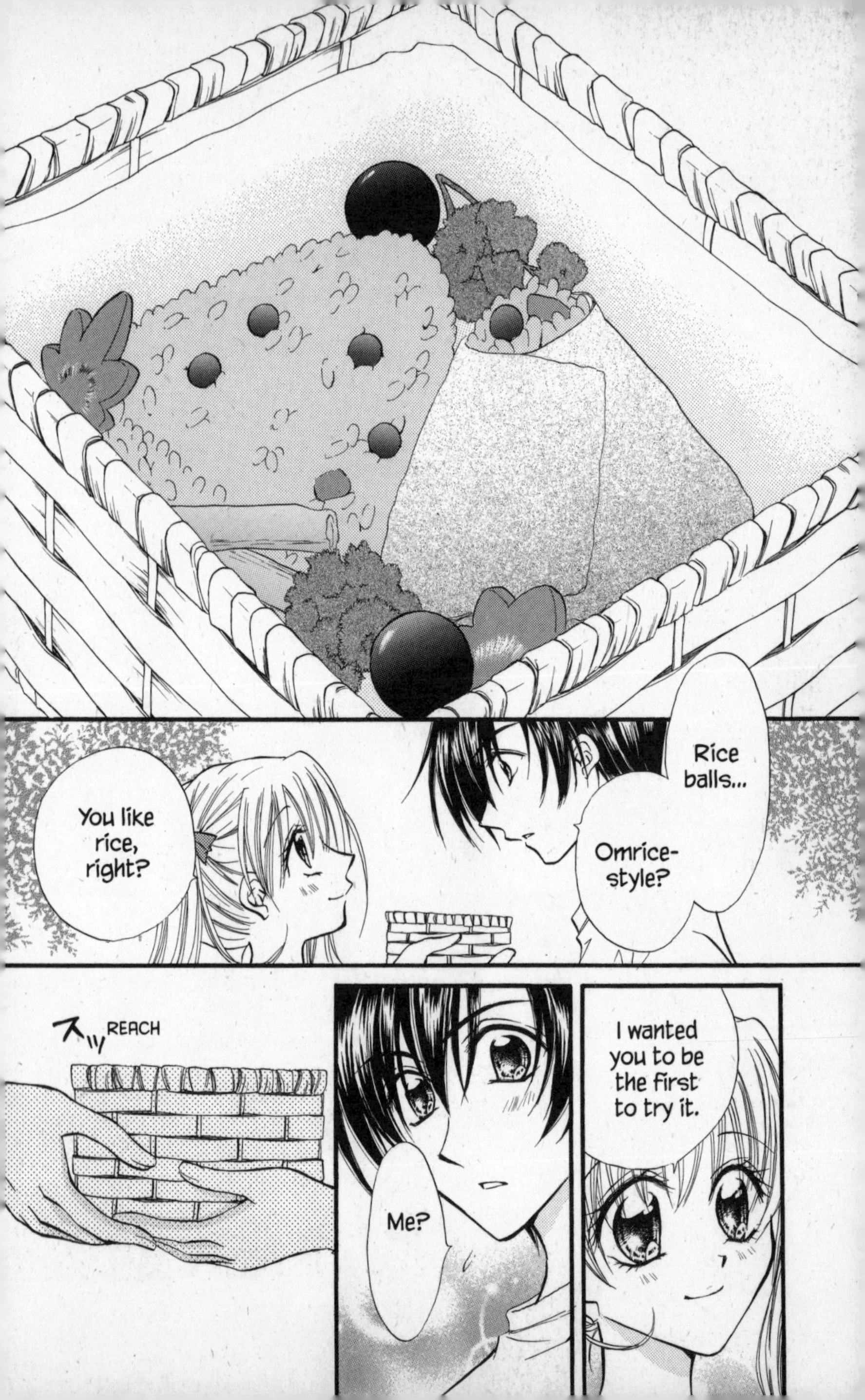
Rice balls...
Omrice-style?
You like rice, right?
I wanted you to be the first to try it.
Me?
スッ REACH

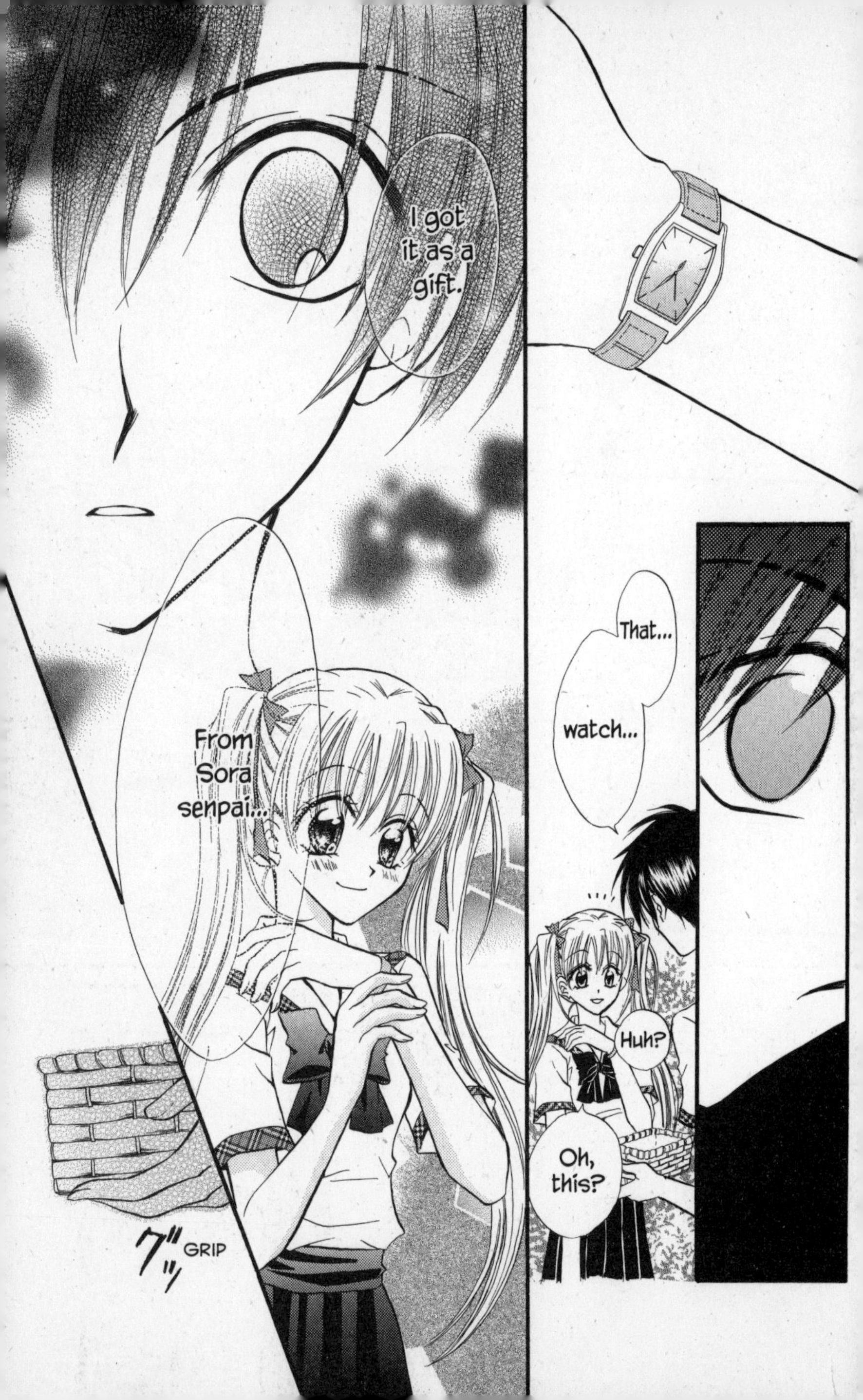
That...
watch...
Huh?
Oh, this?
I got it as a gift.
From Sora senpai...
グッ
GRIP

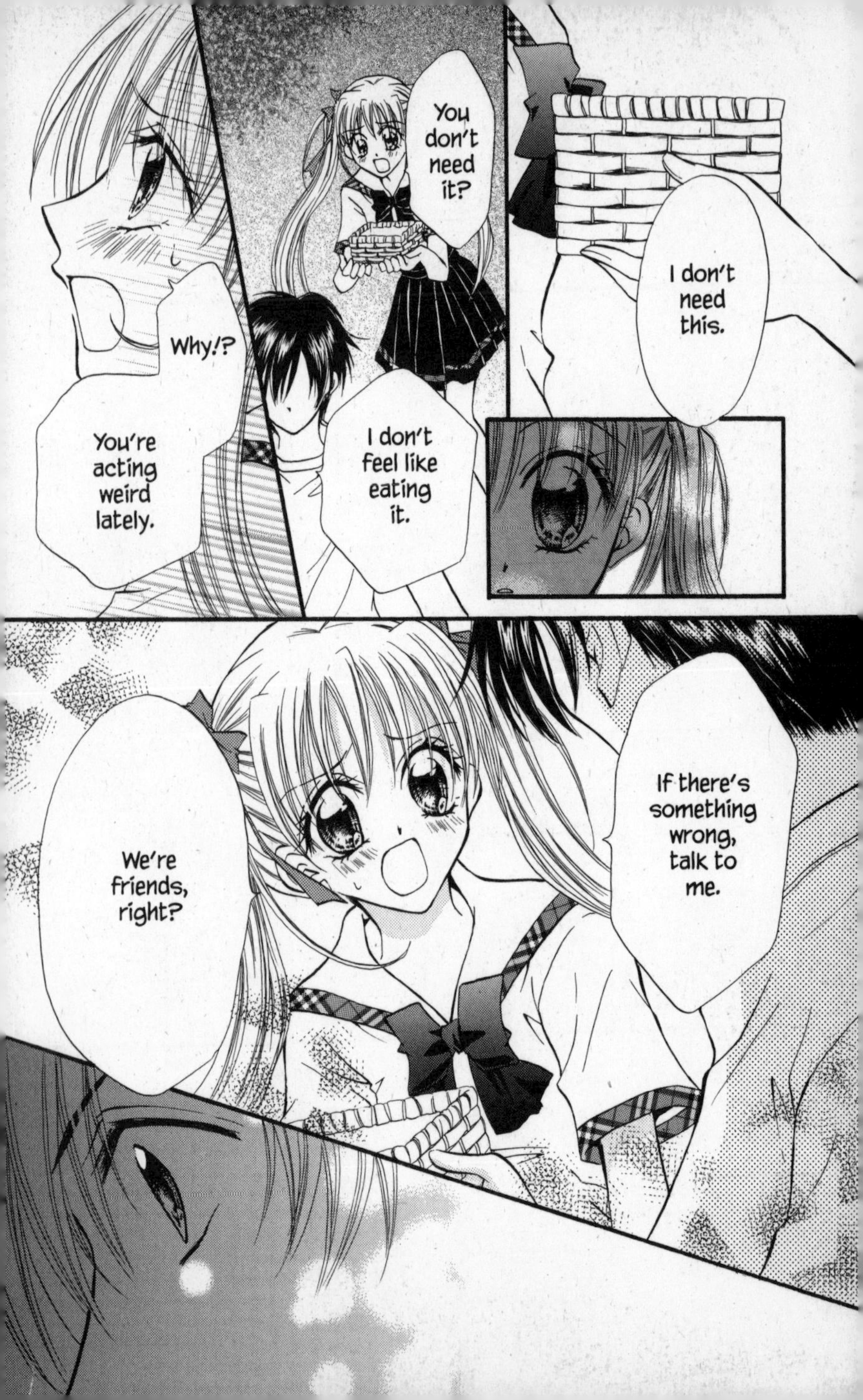
I don't need this.
You don't need it?
I don't feel like eating it.
Why!?
You're acting weird lately.
If there's something wrong, talk to me.
We're friends, right?

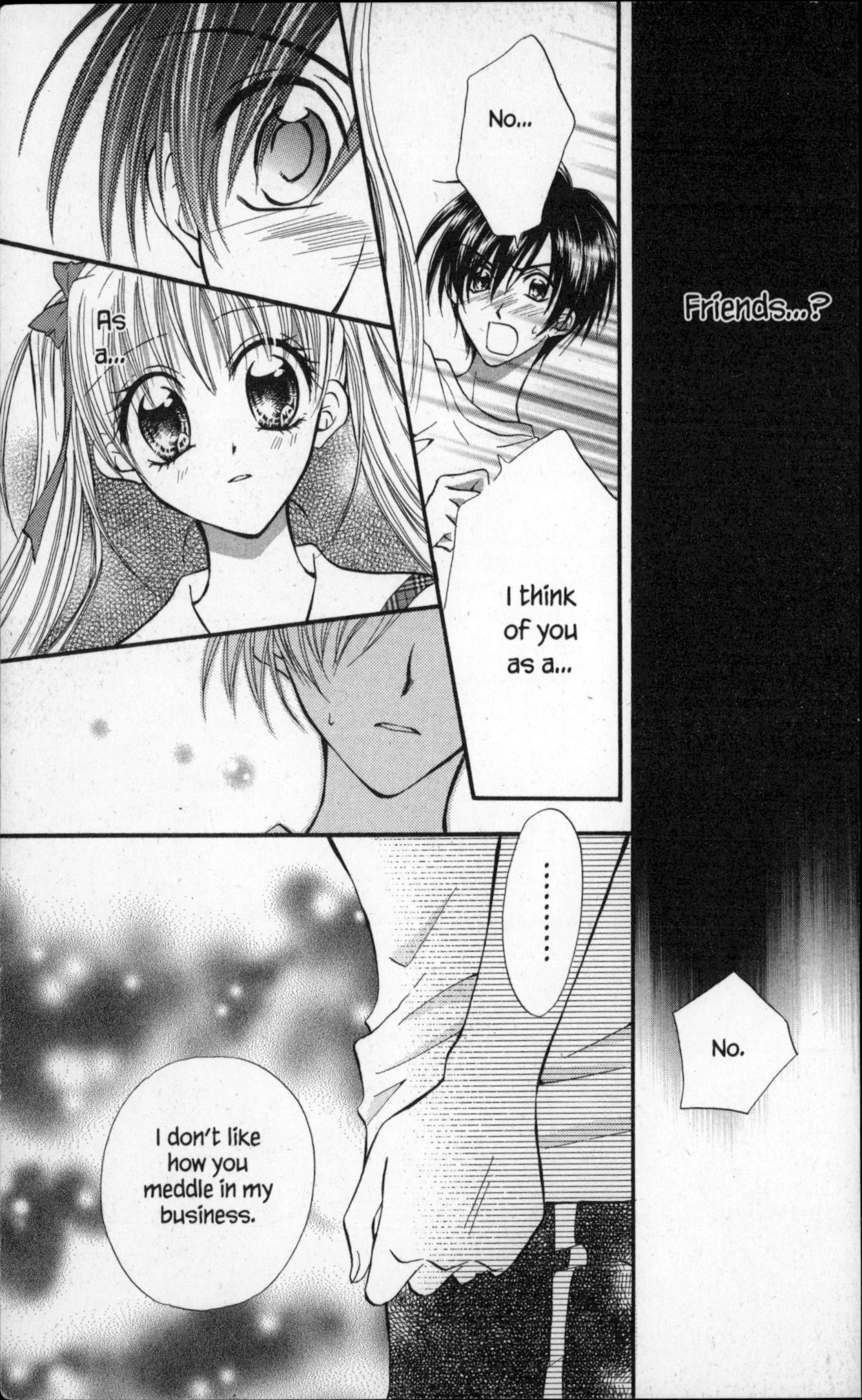
Friends...?
No.
No...
As a...
I think of you as a...
....
I don't like how you meddle in my business.

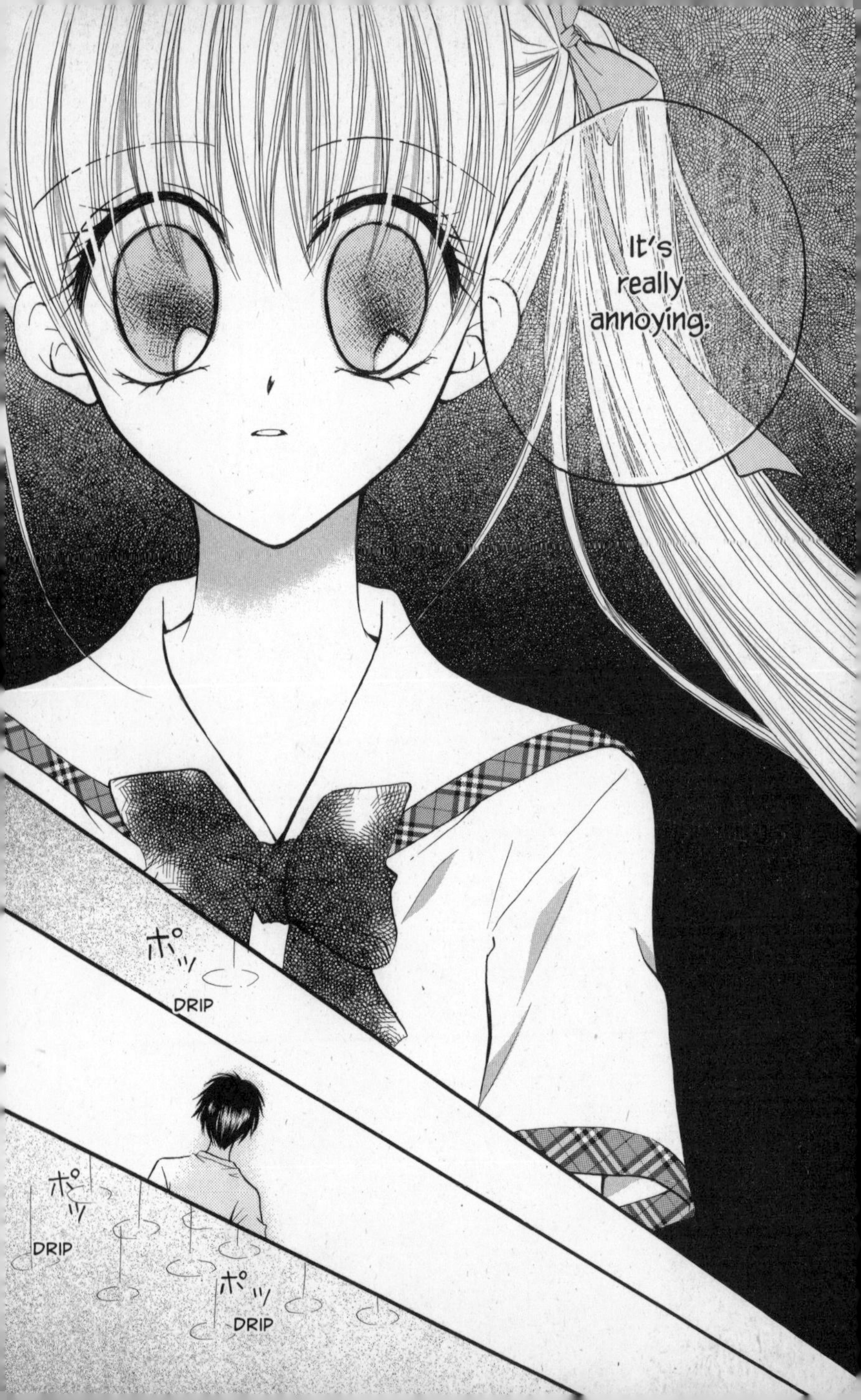
It's really annoying.
ポッ
DRIP
ポッ
DRIP
ポッ
DRIP

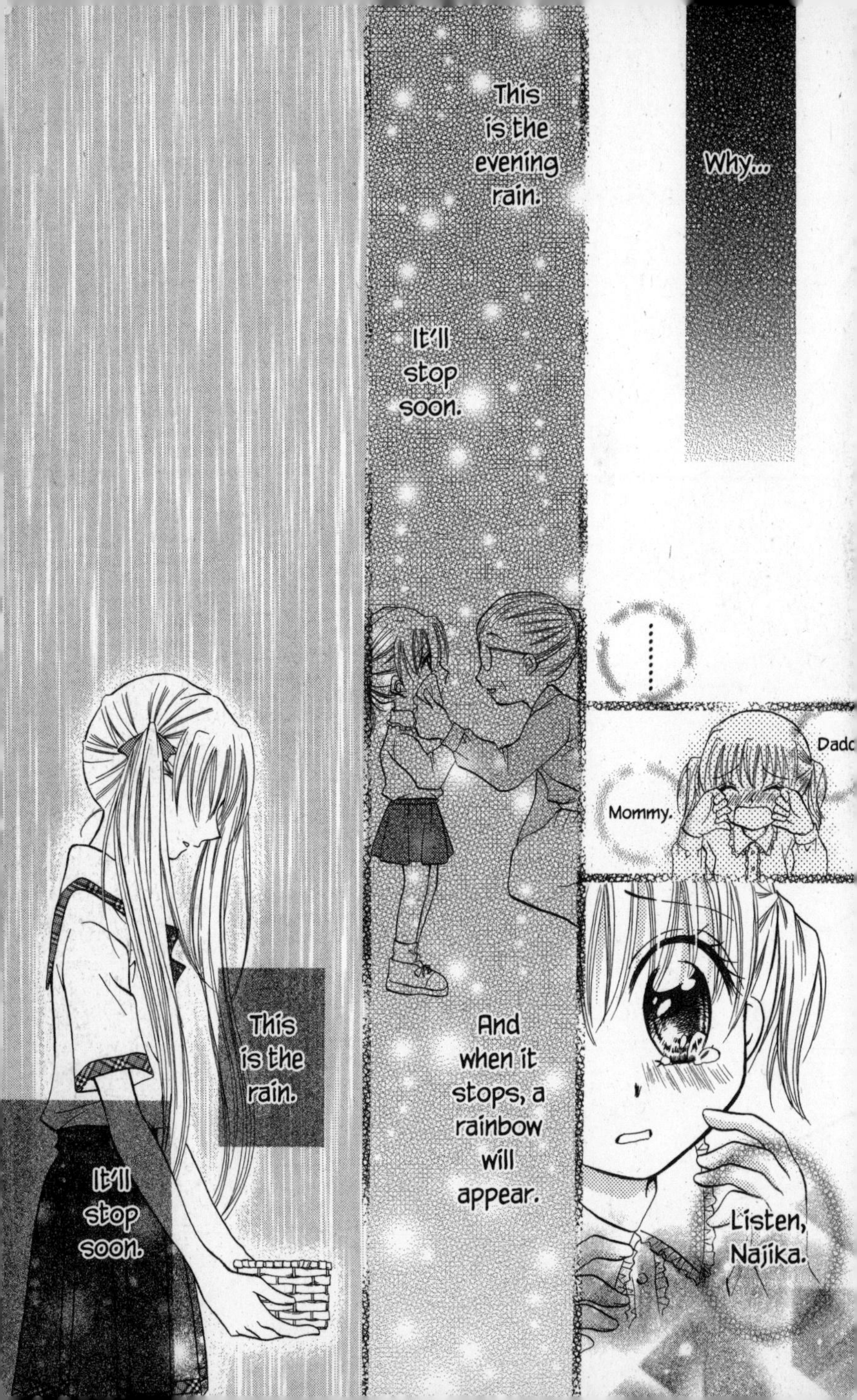
Why...
......
Dadd
Mommy.
Listen, Najika.
This is the evening rain.
It'll stop soon.
And when it stops, a rainbow will appear.
This is the rain.
It'll stop soon.

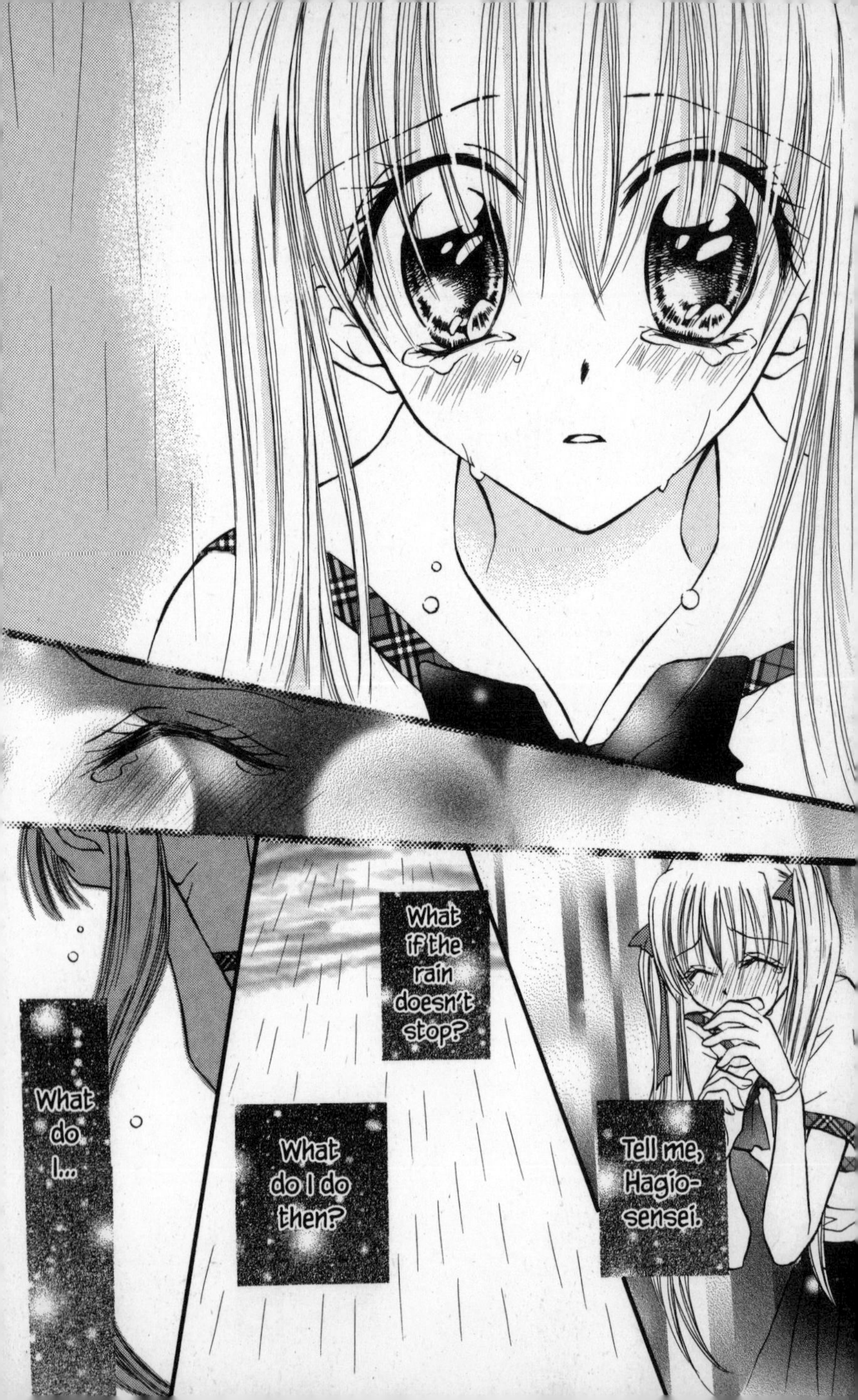
Tell me, Hagio-sensei.
What if the rain doesn't stop?
What do I do then?
What do I...

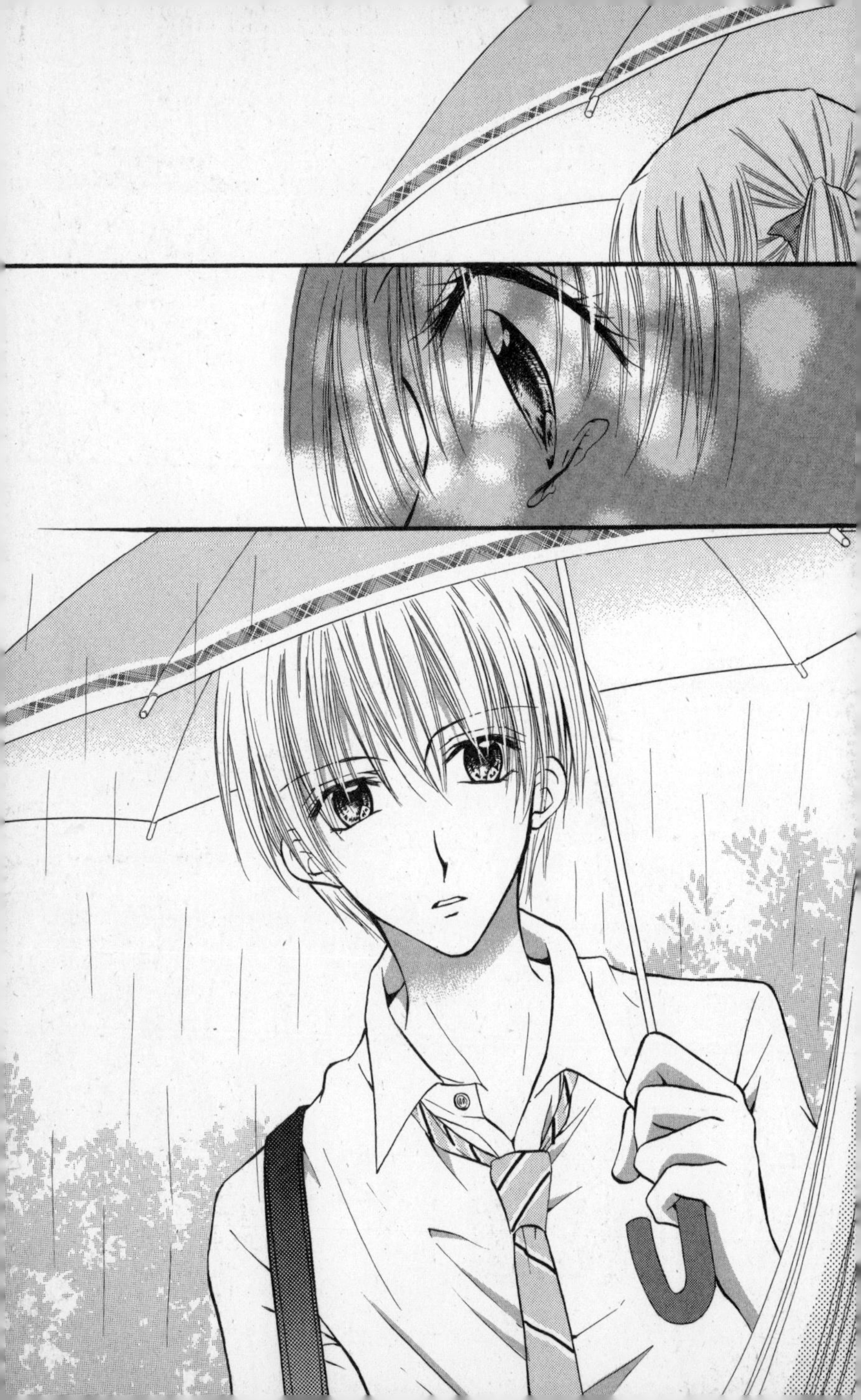

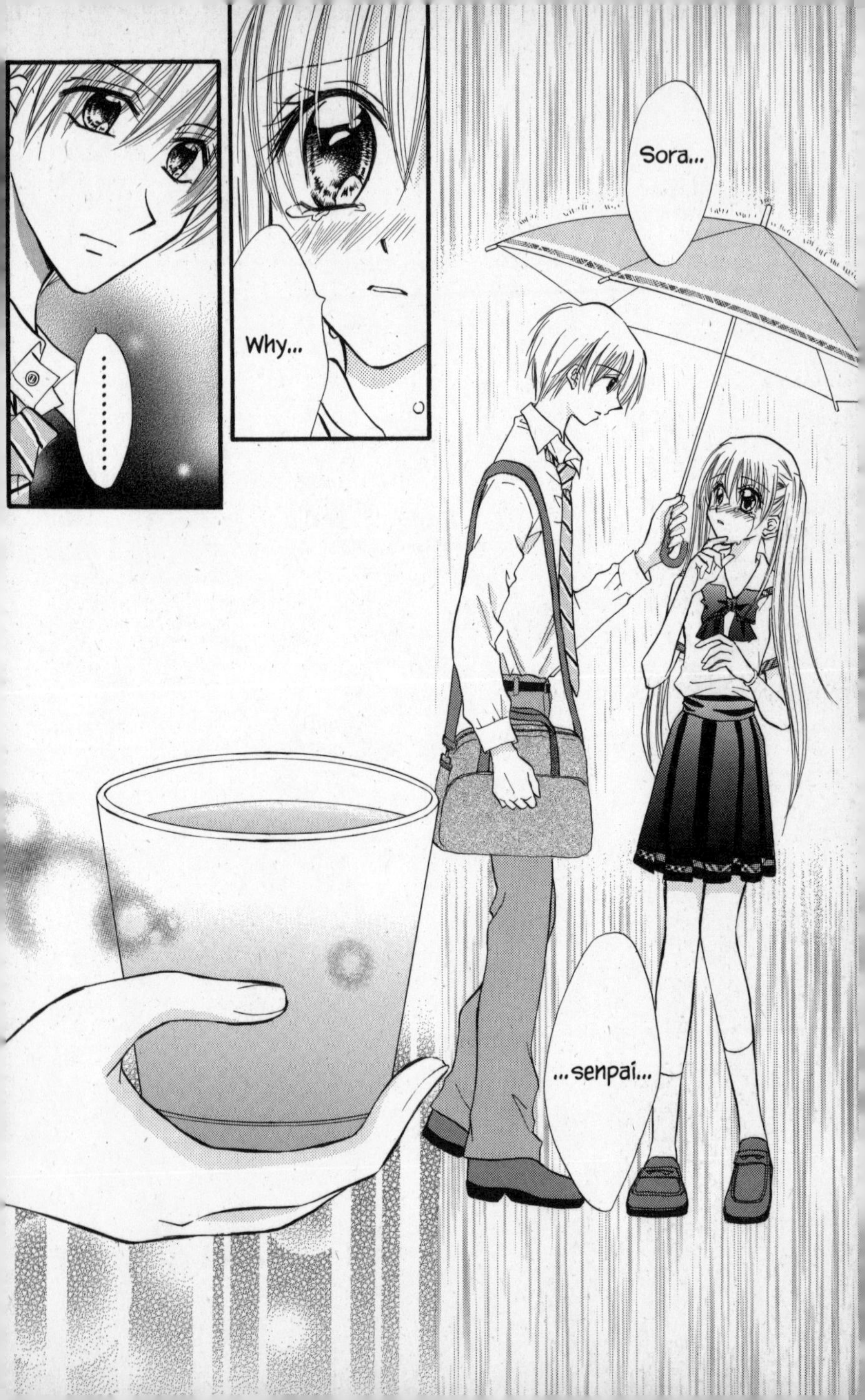
Sora...
...senpai...
Why...
....

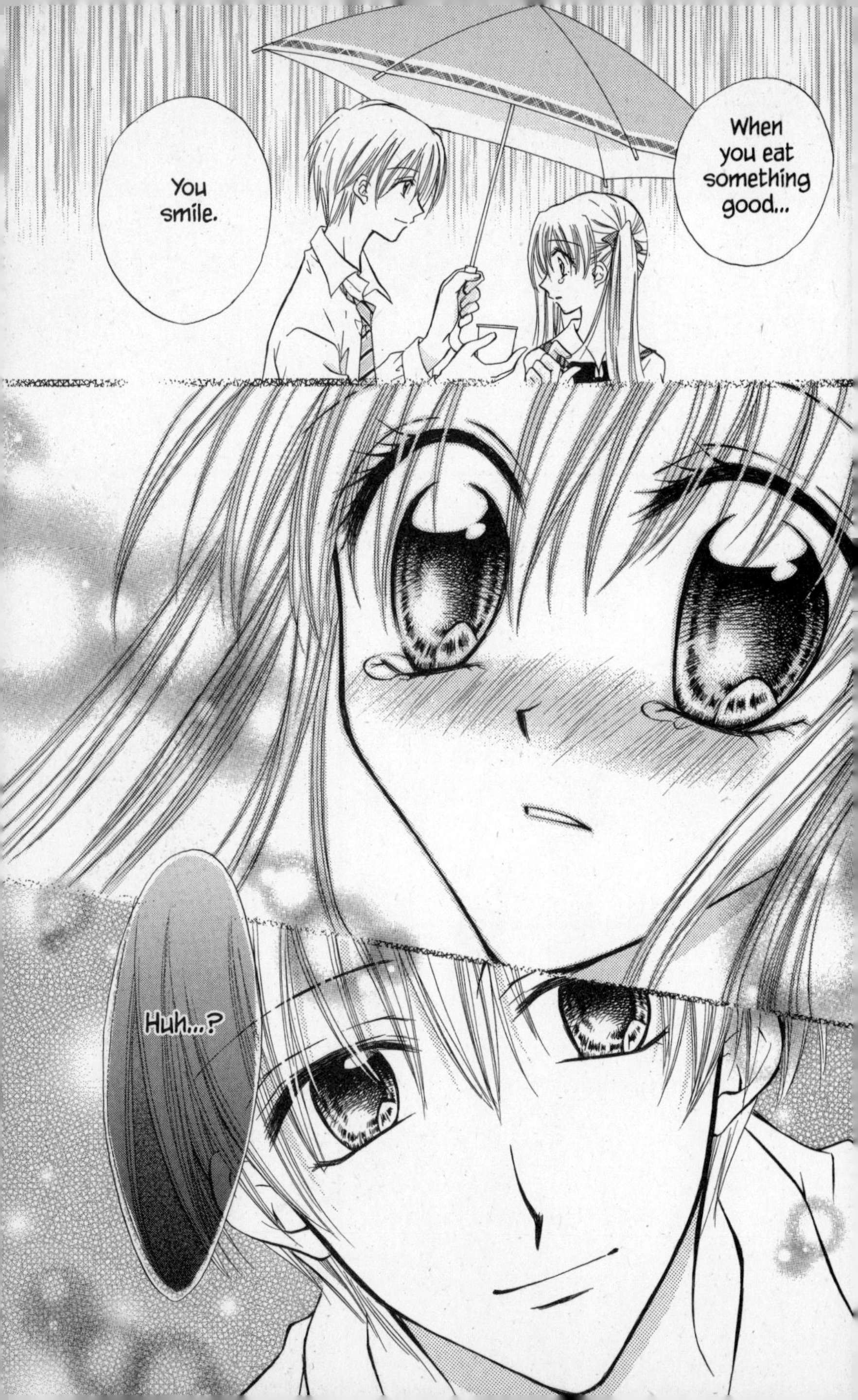
When you eat something good...
You smile.
Huh...?

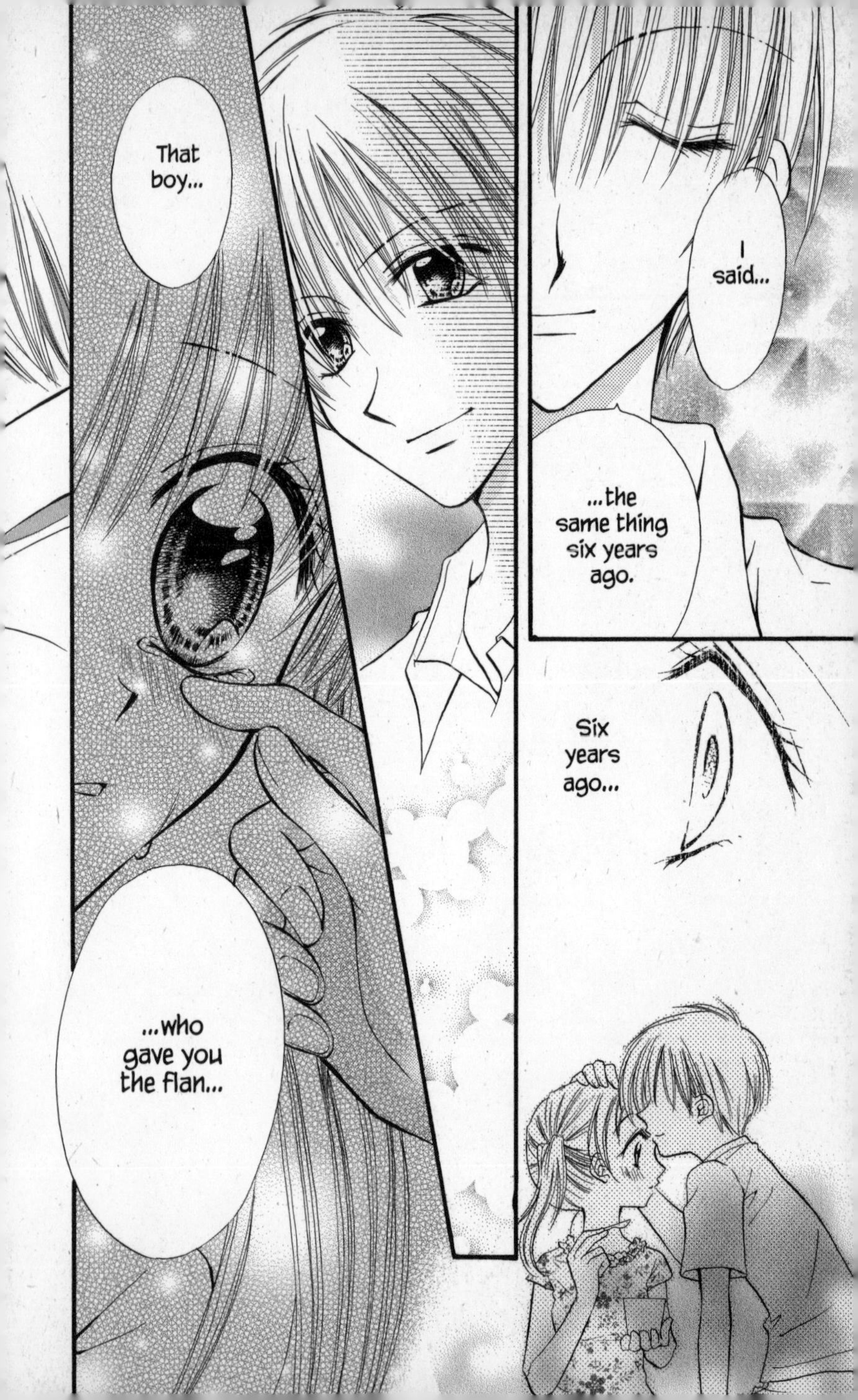
I said...
...the same thing six years ago.
Six years ago...
That boy...
...who gave you the flan...

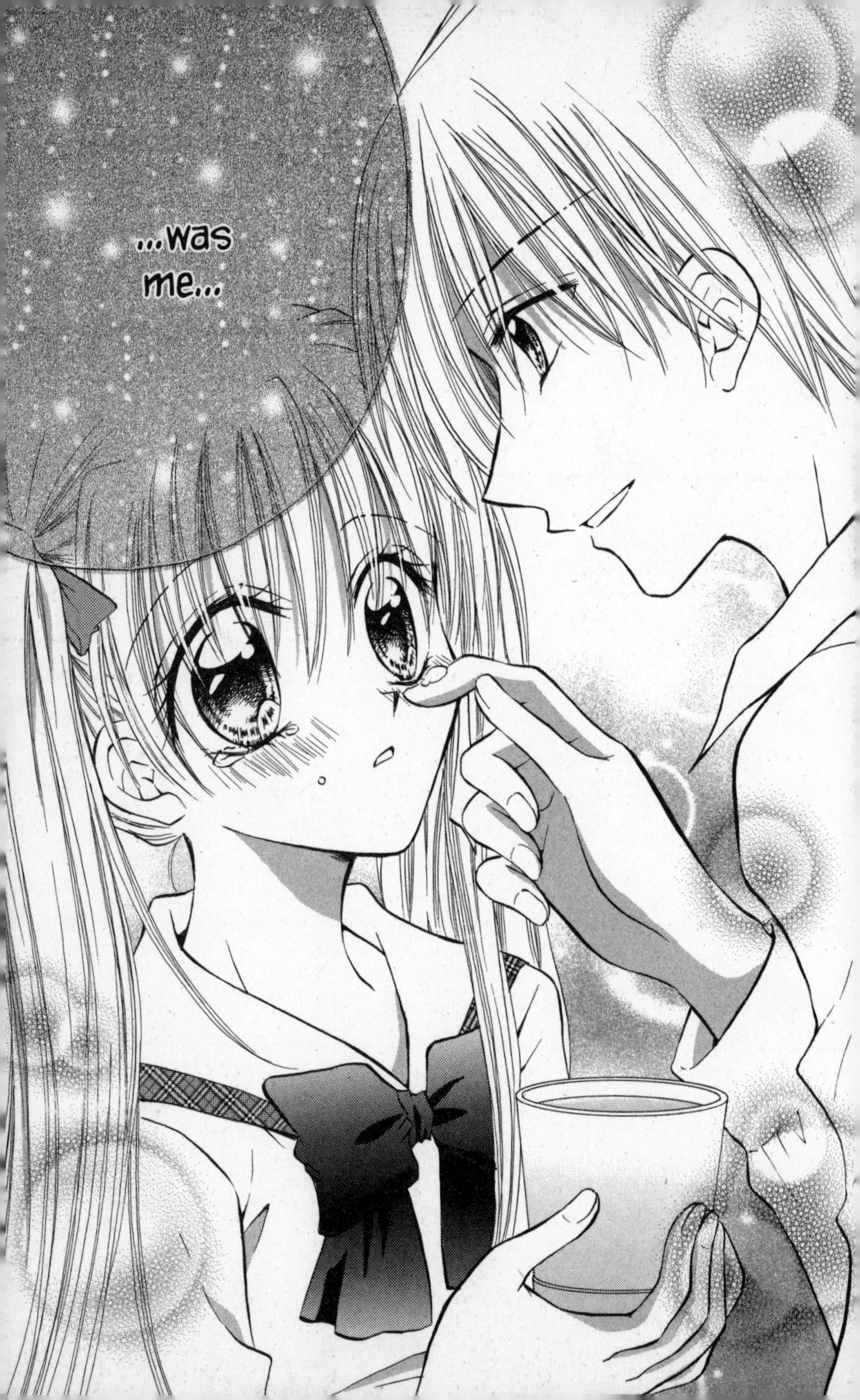
...was me...

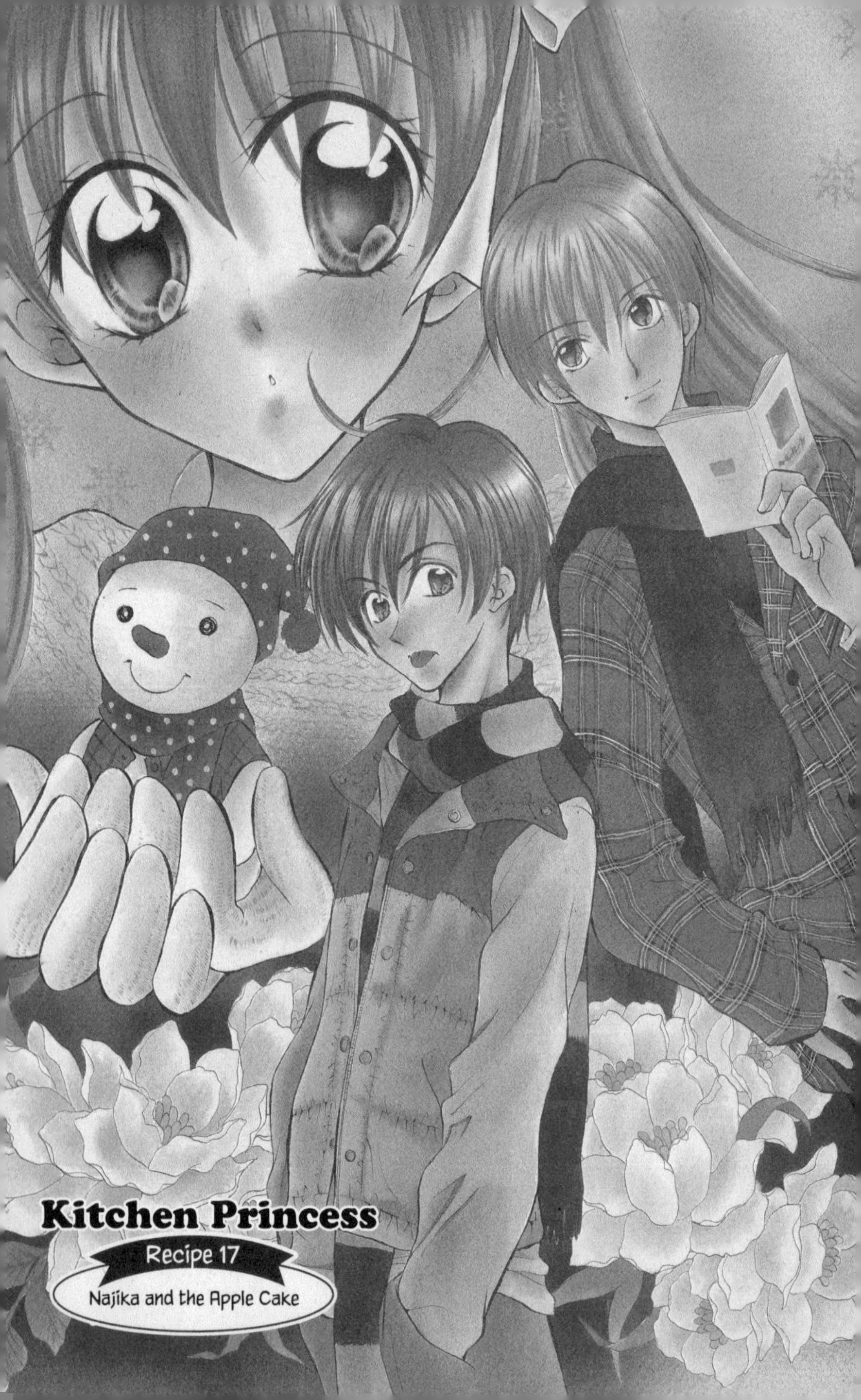
Kitchen Princess
Recipe 17
Najika and the Apple Cake

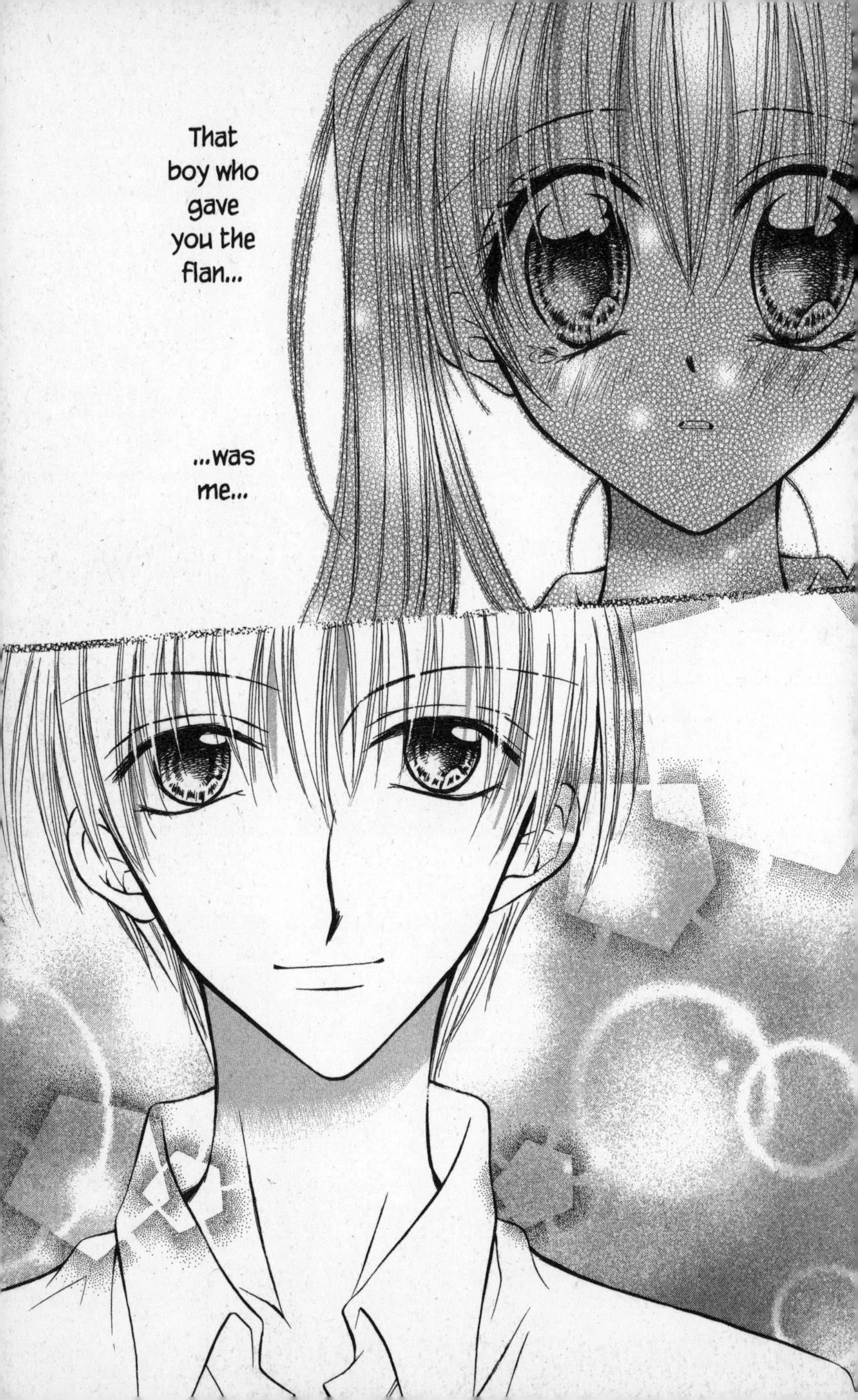
That boy who gave you the flan...
...was me...

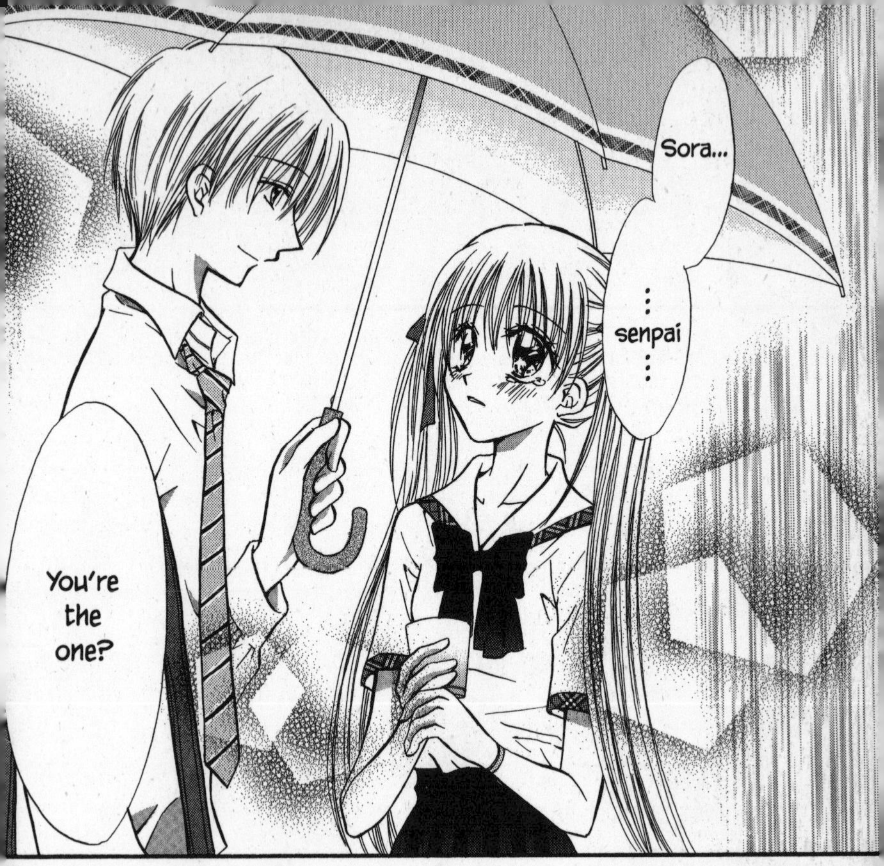
Sora...
...senpai...
You're the one?

About Recipe 17's Splash Page

The story is set in the summer, but the magazine came out right in the middle of the winter! So I drew snow and scarves. Sora and Daichi have different taste in clothes, so it's fun to dress them. ♫ Daichi likes shirts with hoods, and Sora has a lot of sweaters. To draw the snowflakes, I used a stamp and silver ink. It came out well, even when it was printed, so I was very happy.

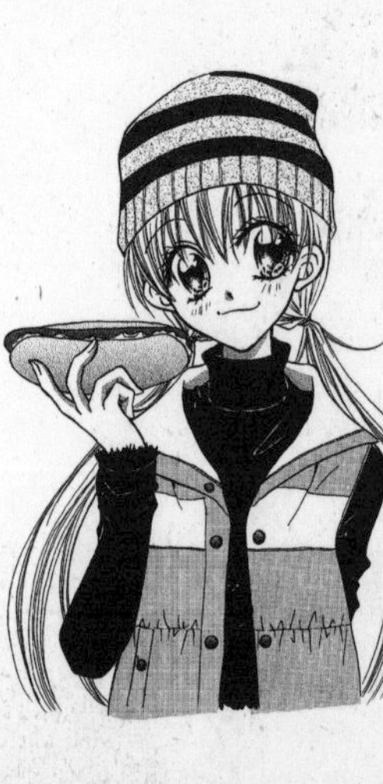

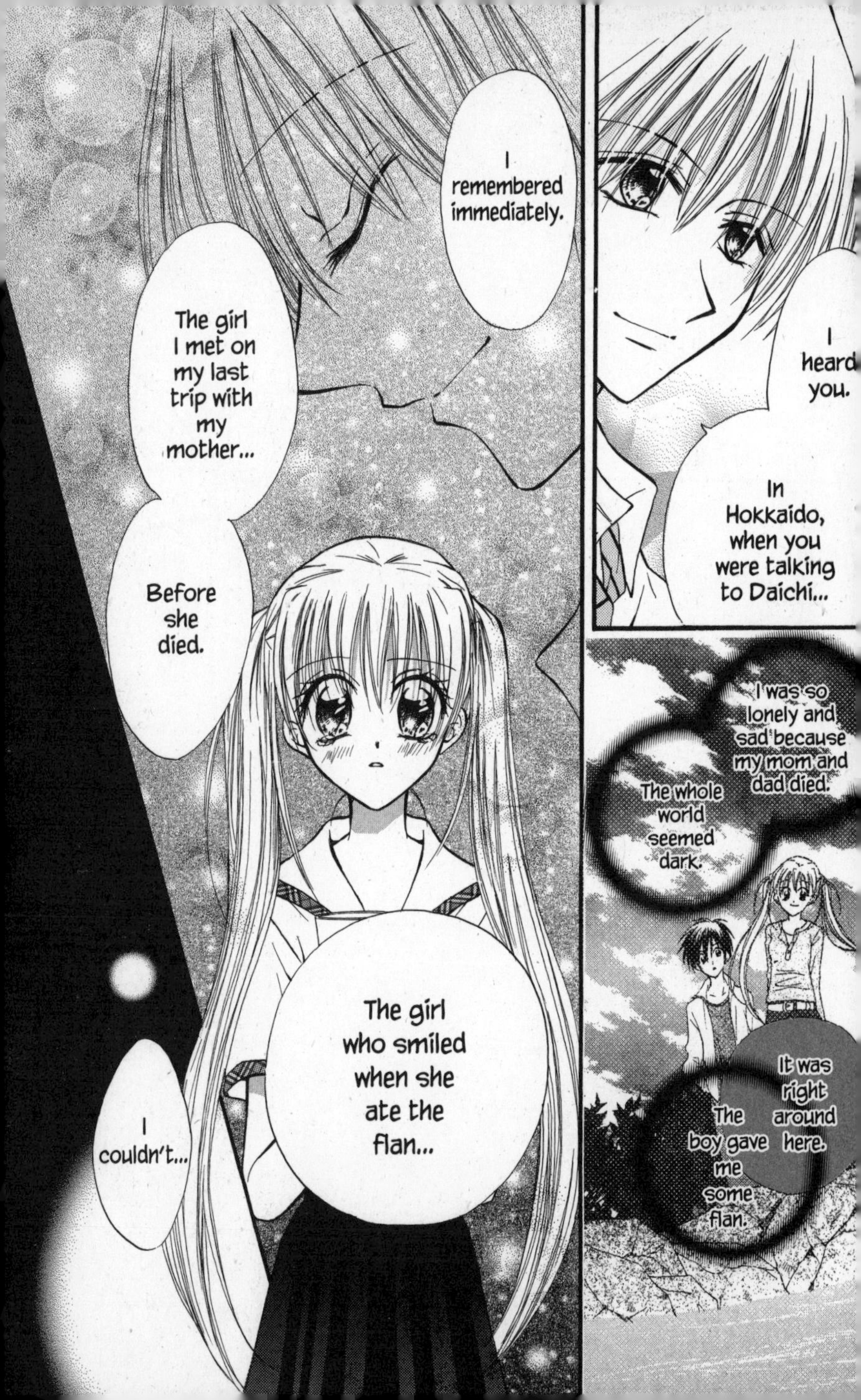
I heard you.
In Hokkaido, when you were talking to Daichi...
I was so lonely and sad because my mom and dad died.
The whole world seemed dark.
It was right around here.
The boy gave me some flan.
I remembered immediately.
The girl I met on my last trip with my mother...
Before she died.
The girl who smiled when she ate the flan...
I couldn't...

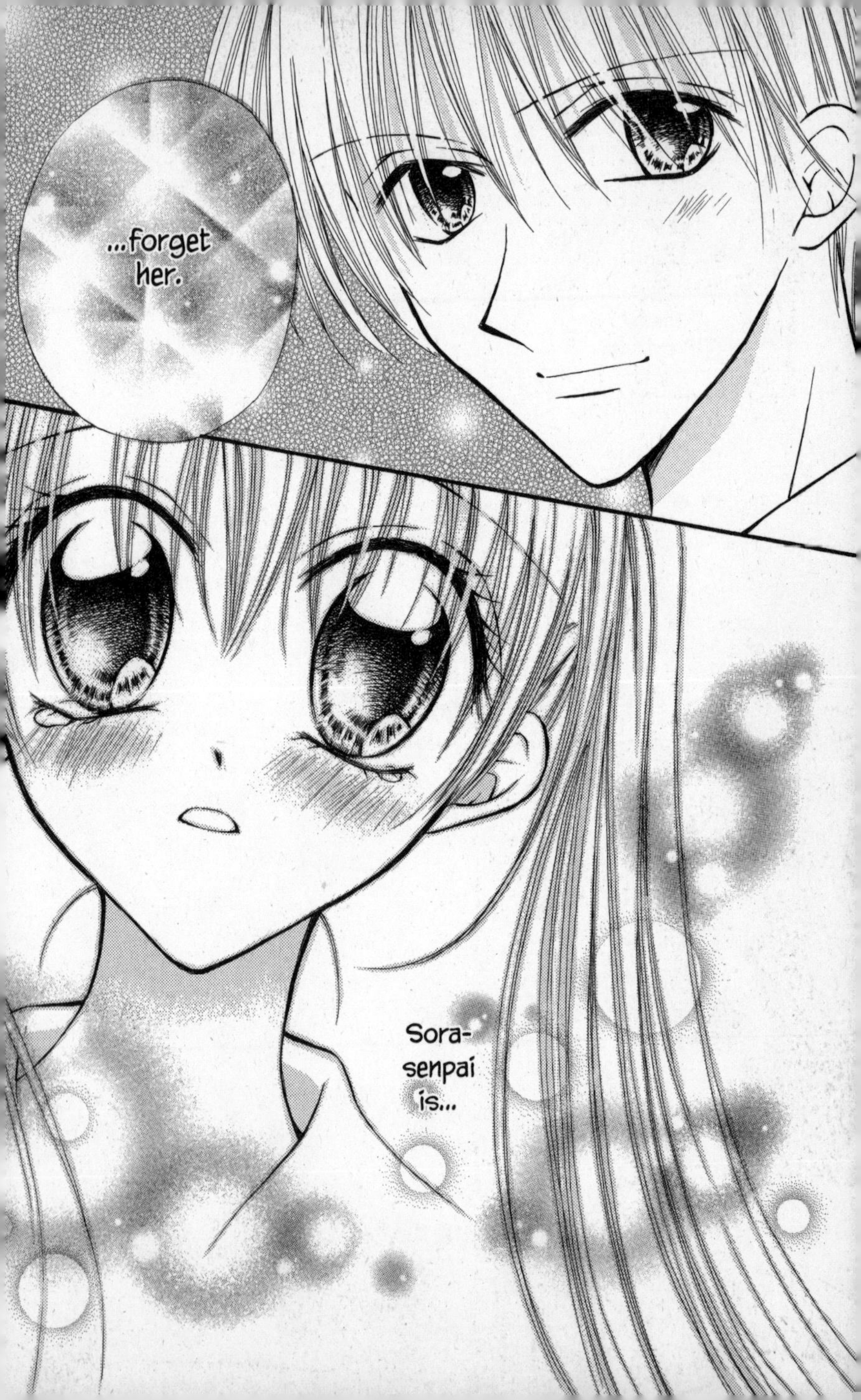
...forget her.
Sora-senpai is...

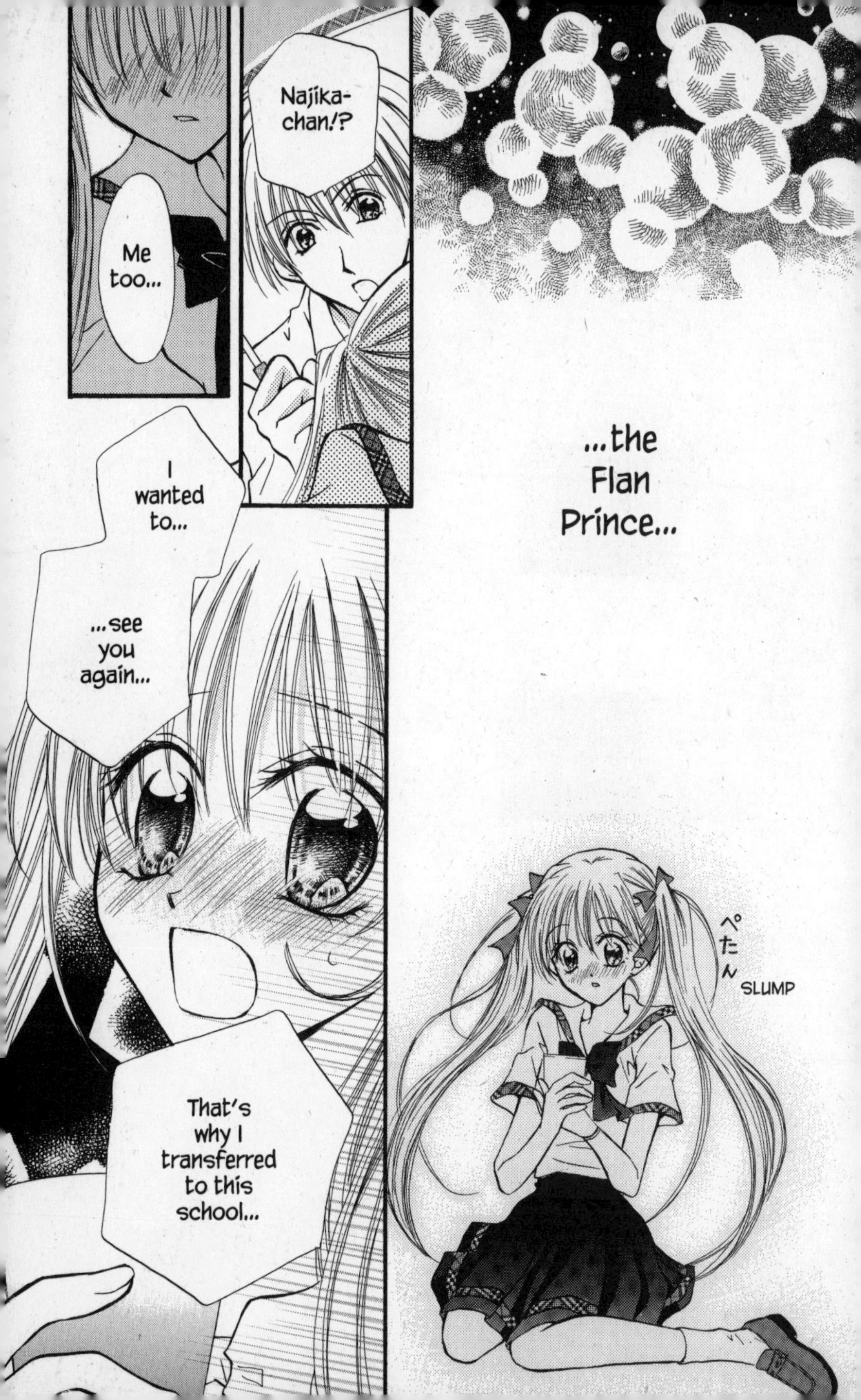
...the Flan Prince...
ぺたん
SLUMP
Najika-chan!?
Me too...
I wanted to...
...see you again...
That's why I transferred to this school...

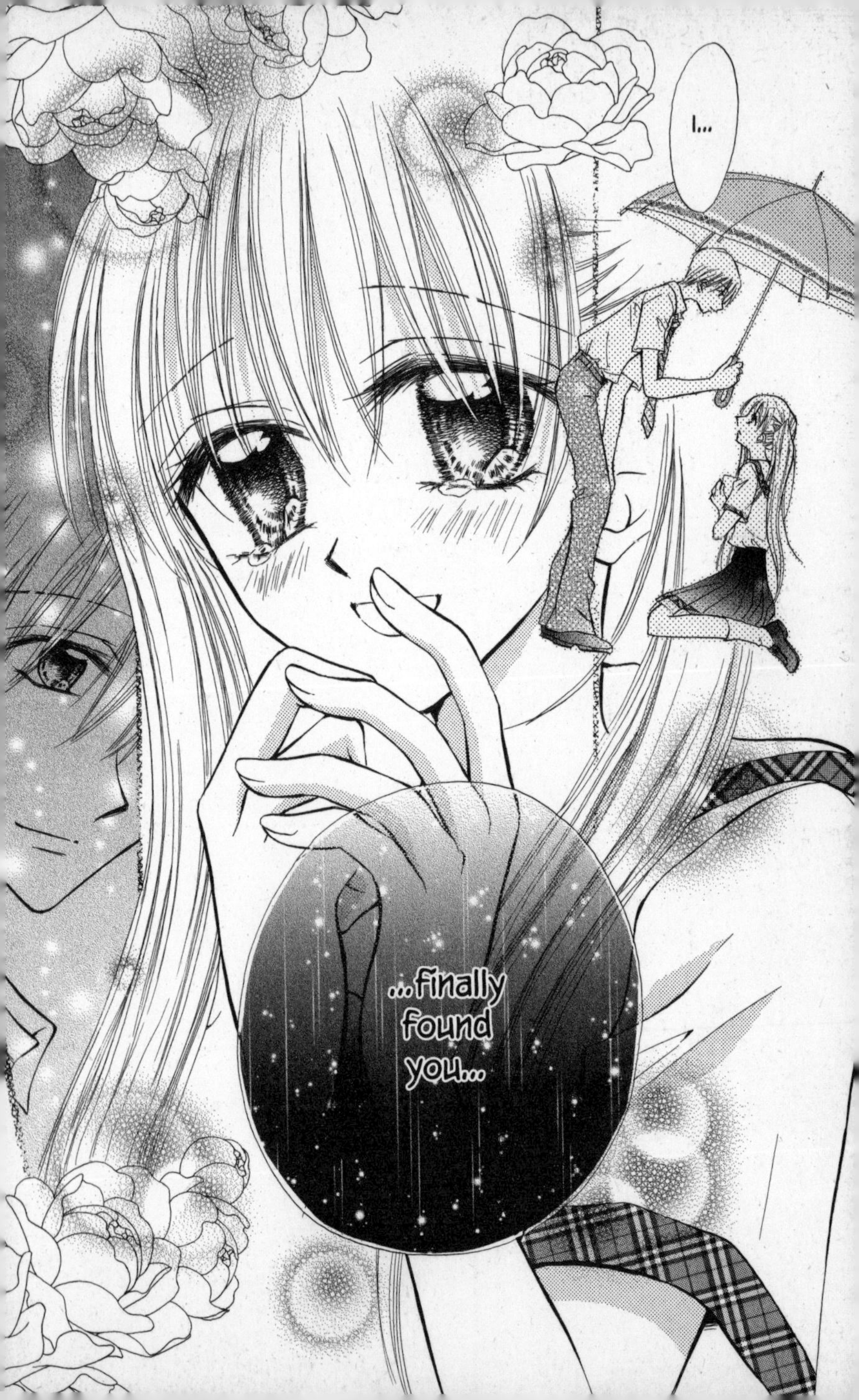
I...
...finally found you...

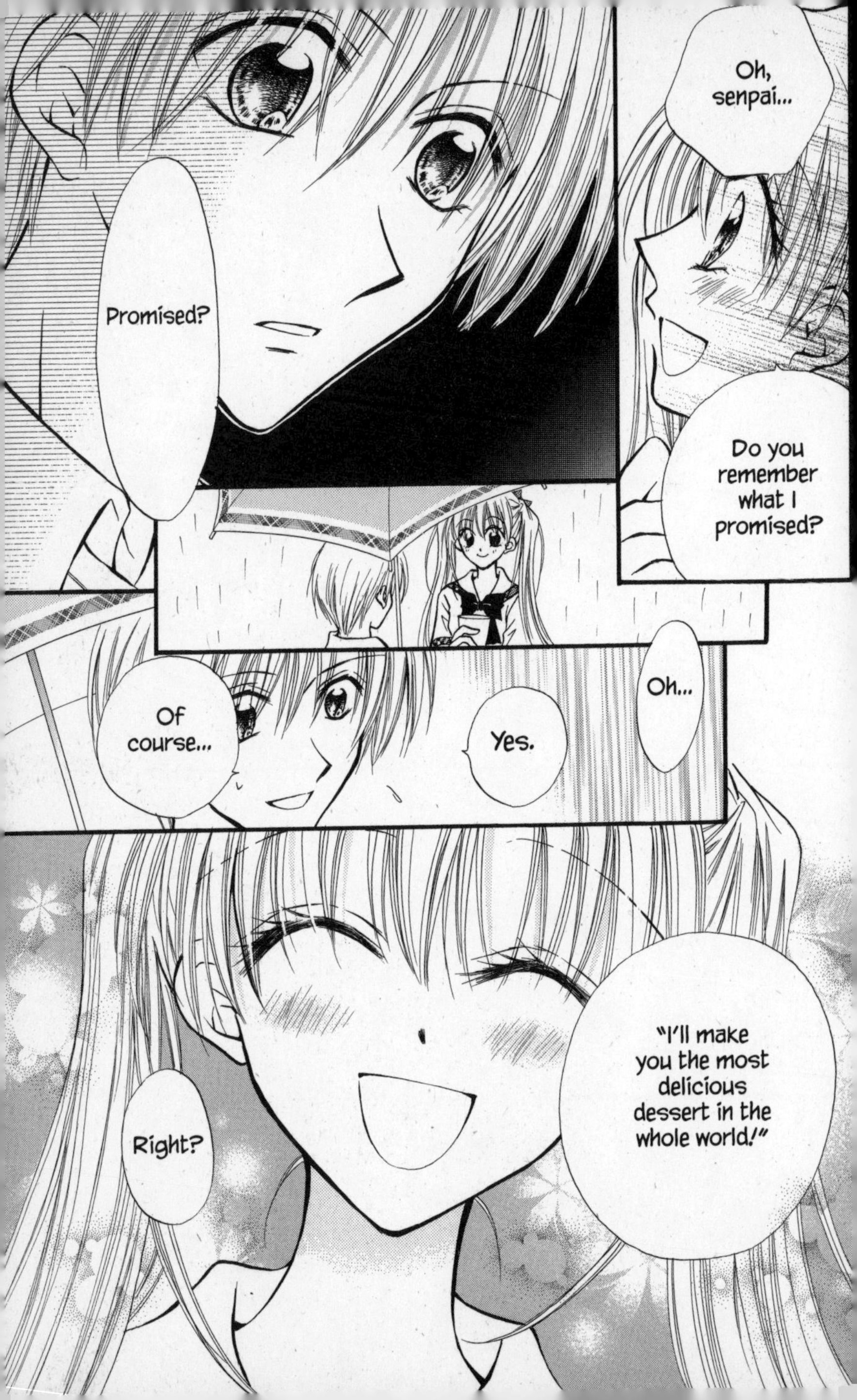
Oh, senpai...
Do you remember what I promised?
Promised?
Oh...
Yes.
Of course...
"I'll make you the most delicious dessert in the whole world!"
Right?

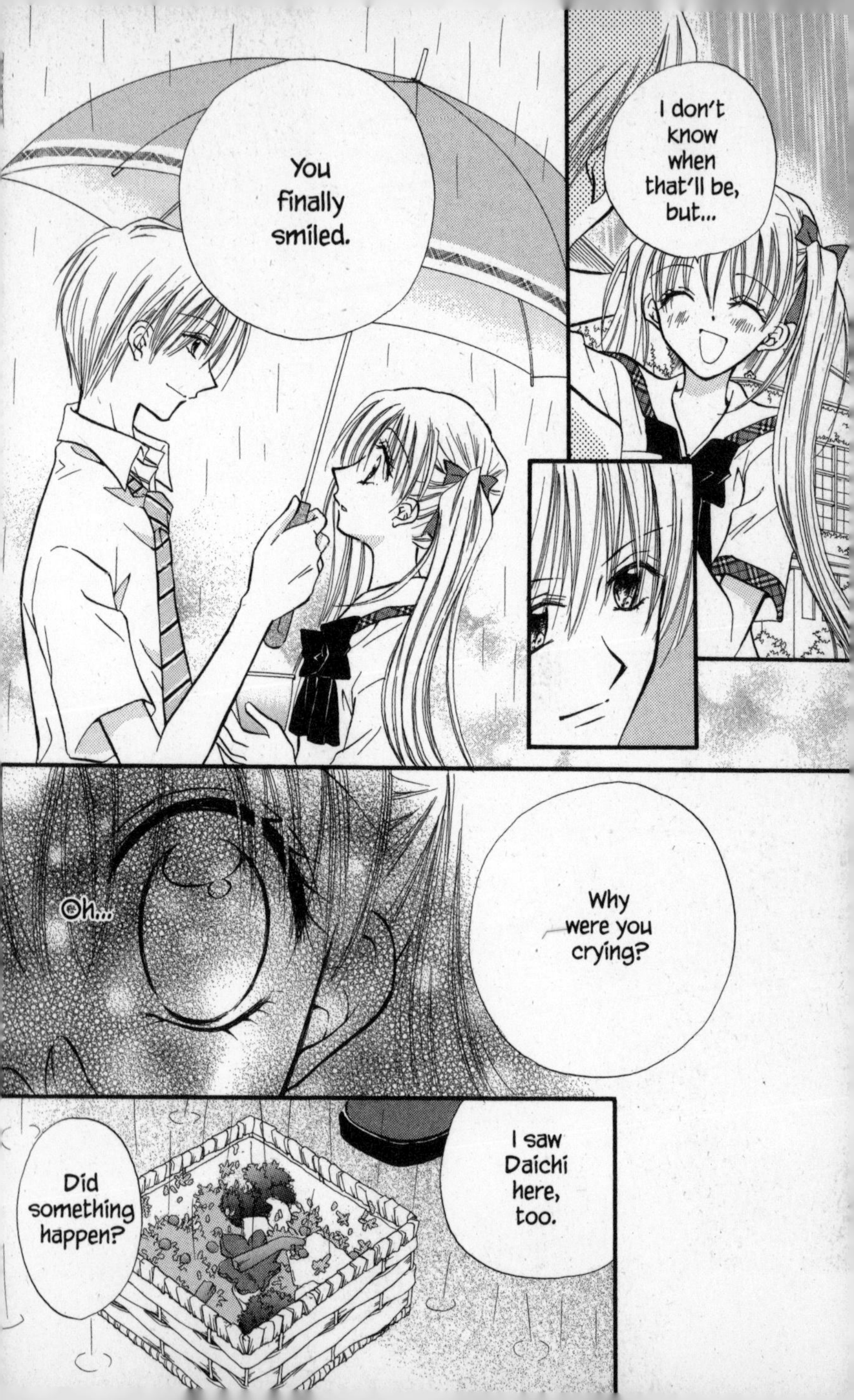
I don't know when that'll be, but...
You finally smiled.
Why were you crying?
Oh...
I saw Daichi here, too.
Did something happen?

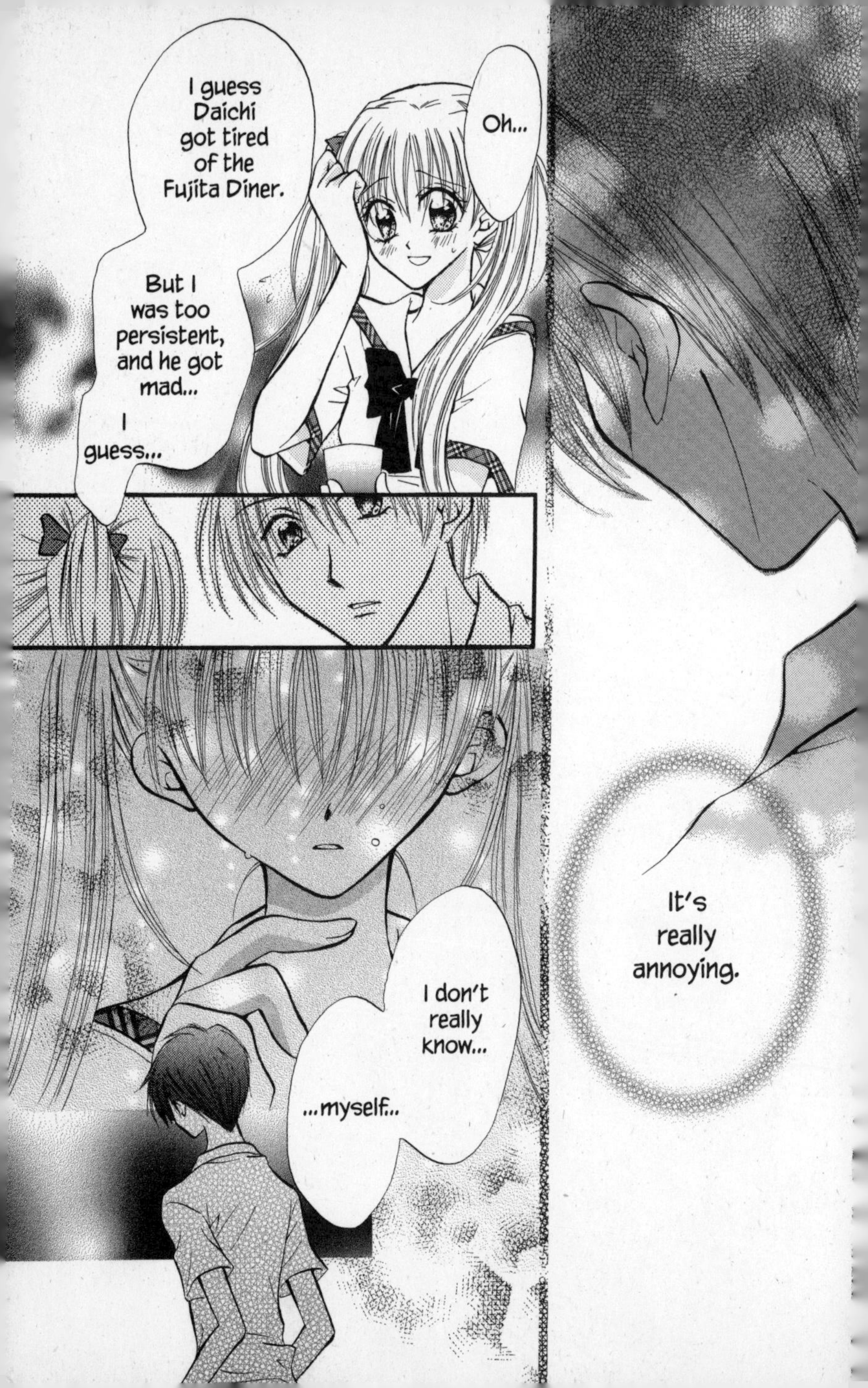

It's really annoying.
Oh...
I guess Daichi got tired of the Fujita Diner.
But I was too persistent, and he got mad...
I guess...
I don't really know...
...myself...

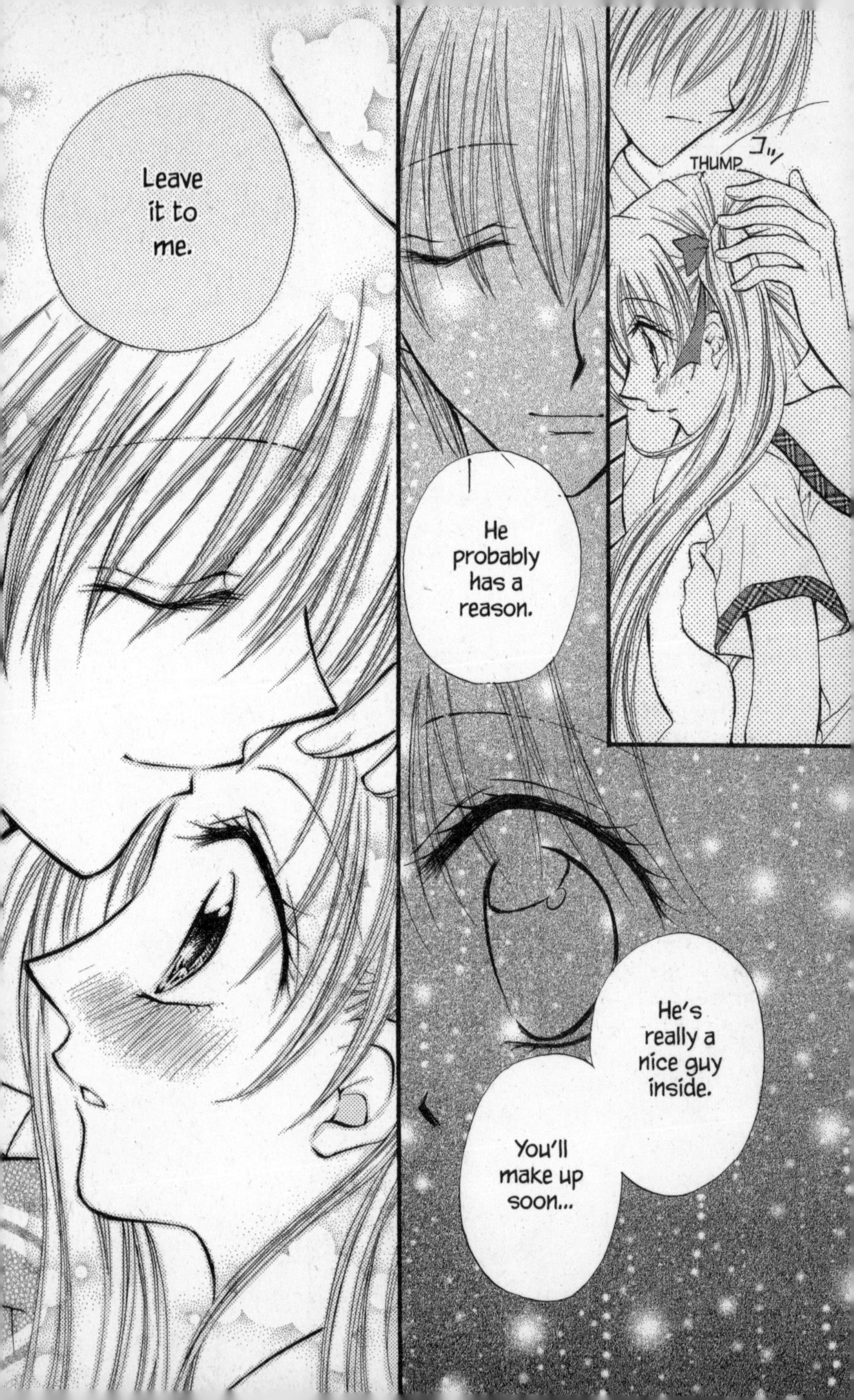
THUMP
ゴッ
He probably has a reason.
He's really a nice guy inside.
You'll make up soon...
Leave it to me.

Recipe 17

The apple cake in this chapter was the one I ate when I went to Miyuki sensei's house. (Please check Volume 3 for more information. ♥) She made it especially for me. It was really good and I wanted to eat more! I think she saw my aura of greed and gave me some to take home, too. ♥ Thank you very much!!

Recipe 18

Najika and Akane have a fight... They got to say what they wanted, and it felt good drawing them. I love the scones from Starbucks Coffee! They are so big, they fill me up. ♫ I eat them often for breakfast. I prefer the flavored ones to the plain ones. Especially the ones with chocolate in them.

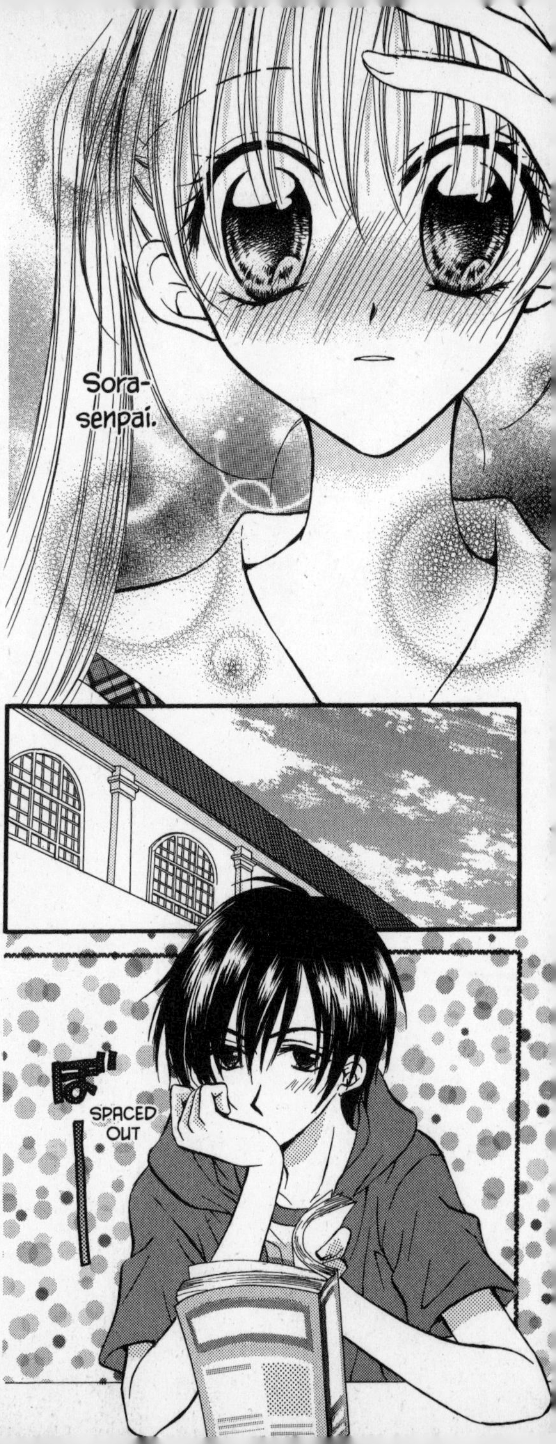
Sora-senpai.
SPACED OUT

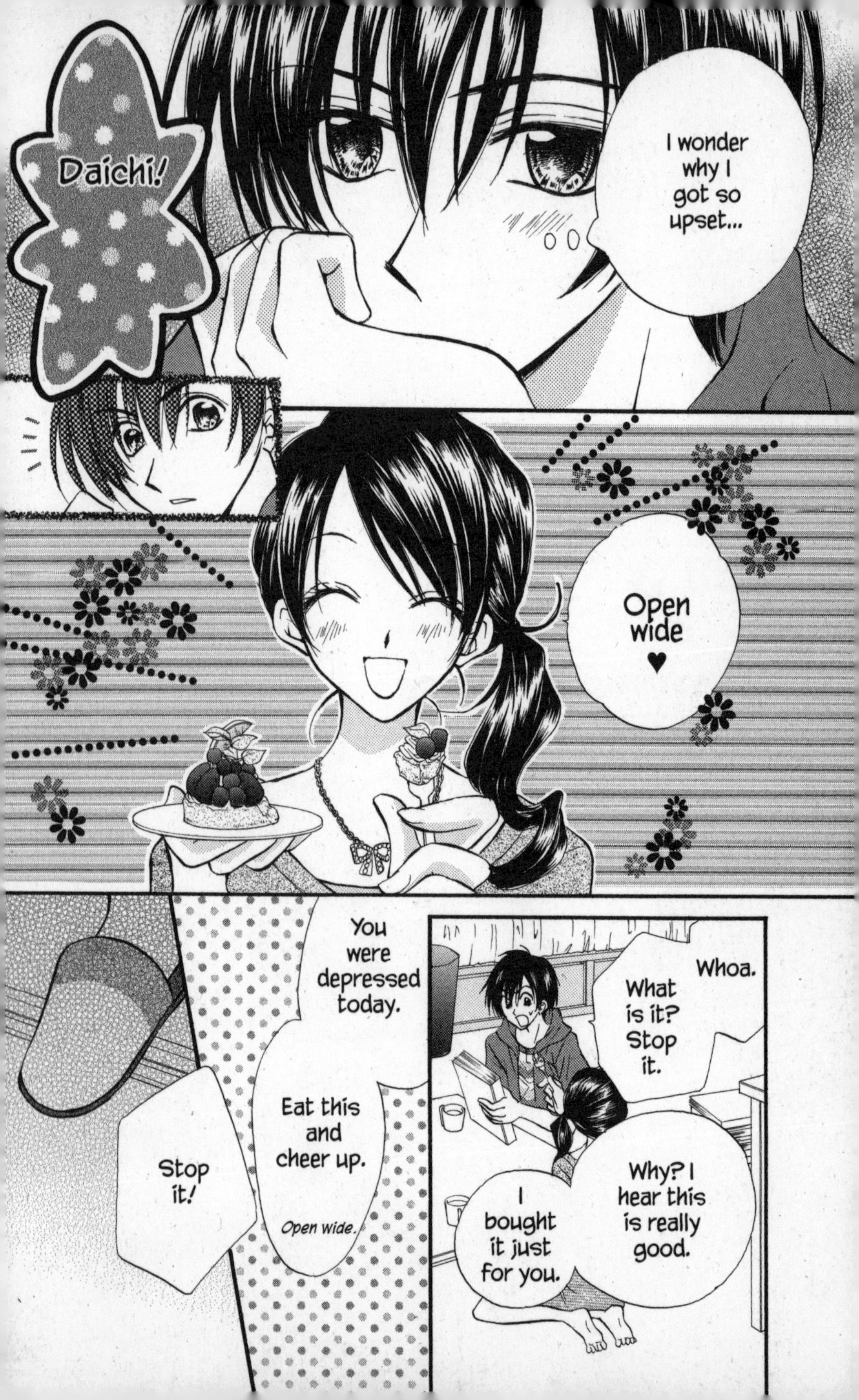
I wonder why I got so upset...
Daichi!
Open wide ♥
Whoa.
What is it? Stop it.
Why? I hear this is really good.
I bought it just for you.
You were depressed today.
Eat this and cheer up.
Open wide.
Stop it!

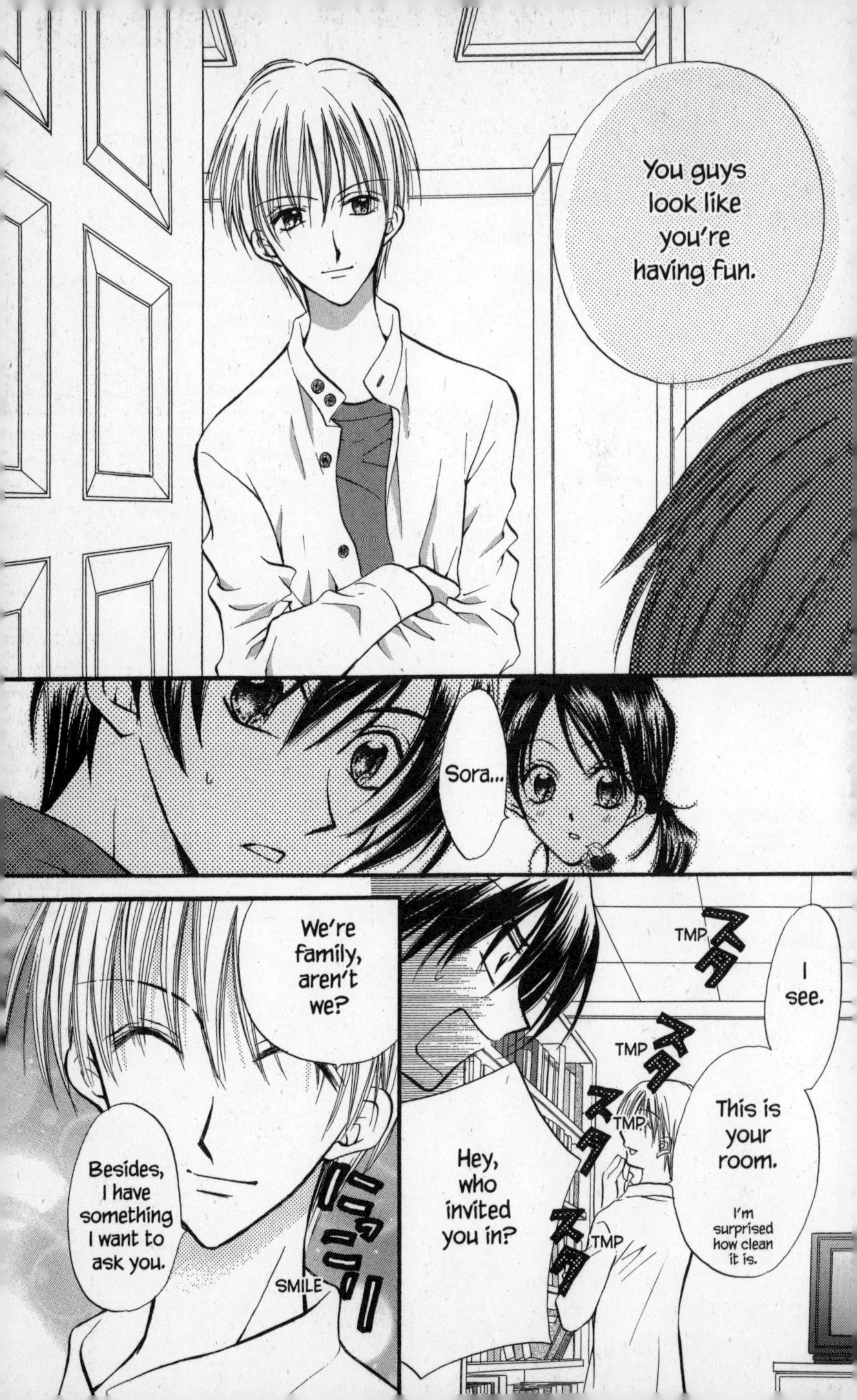
You guys look like you're having fun.
Sora...
I see.
TMP
TMP
TMP
TMP
This is your room.
I'm surprised how clean it is.
Hey, who invited you in?
We're family, aren't we?
Besides, I have something I want to ask you.
SMILE

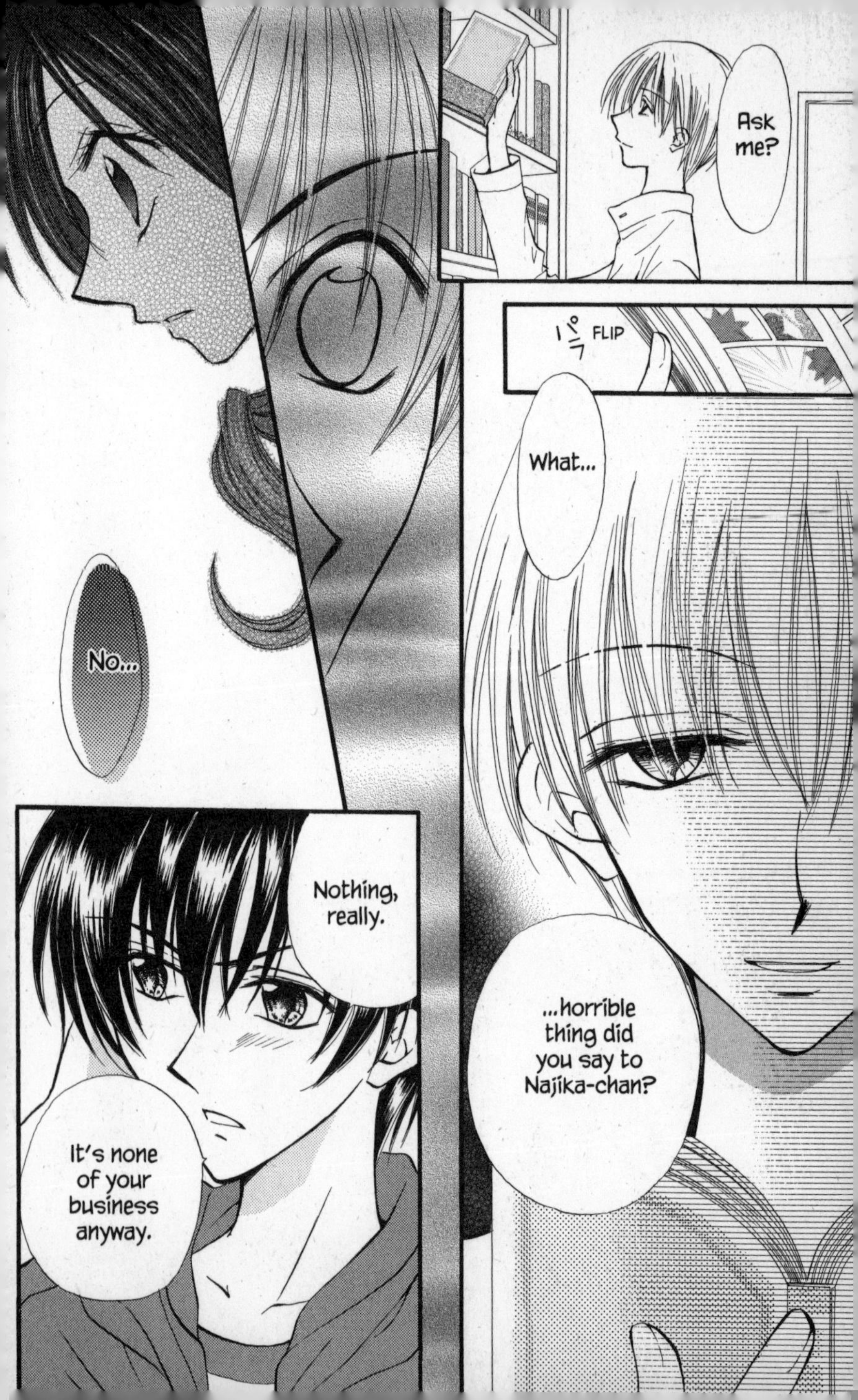
Ask me?
パラ FLIP
What...
...horrible thing did you say to Najika-chan?
No...
Nothing, really.
It's none of your business anyway.

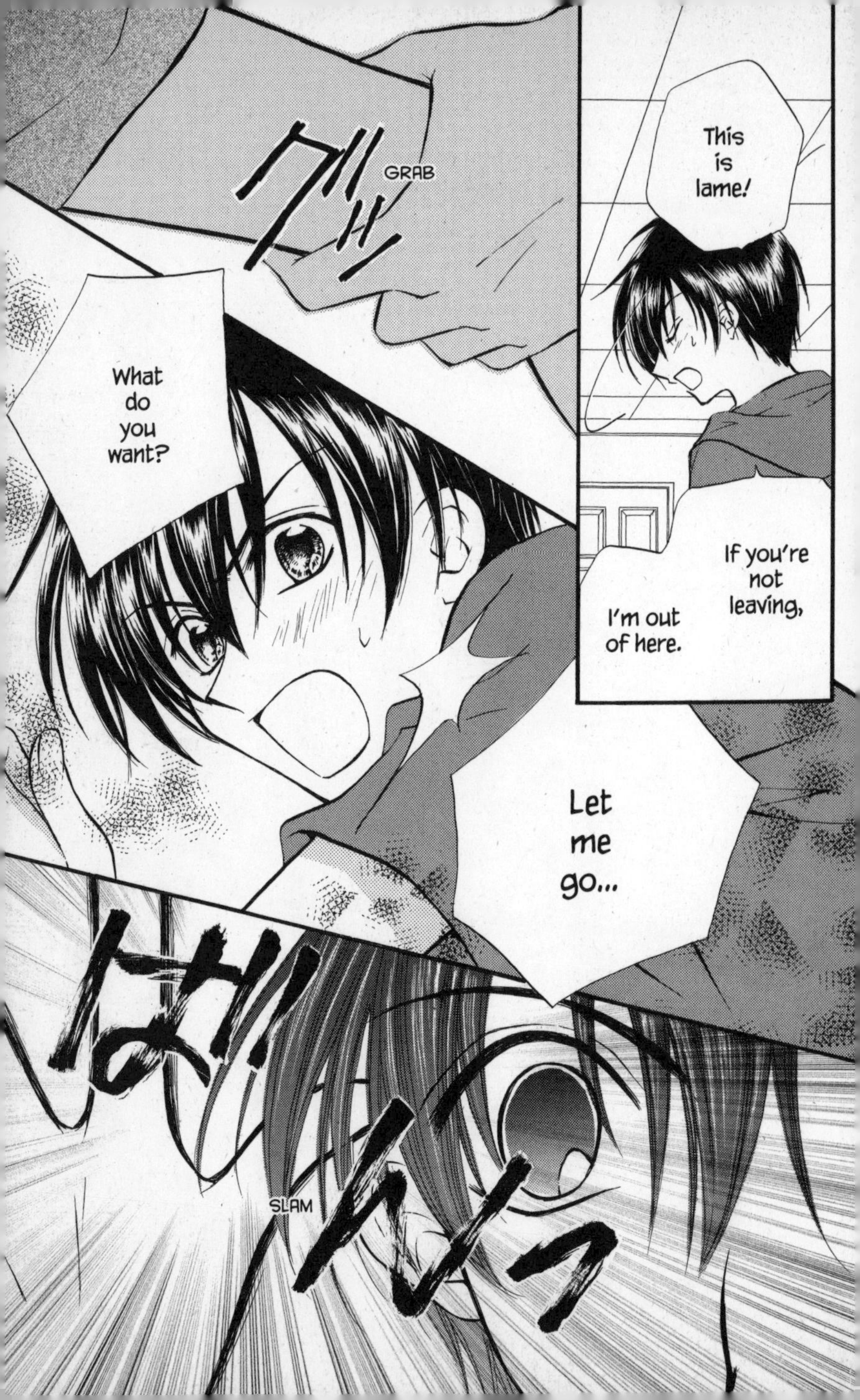
This is lame!
If you're not leaving,
I'm out of here.
GRAB
What do you want?
Let me go...
SLAM

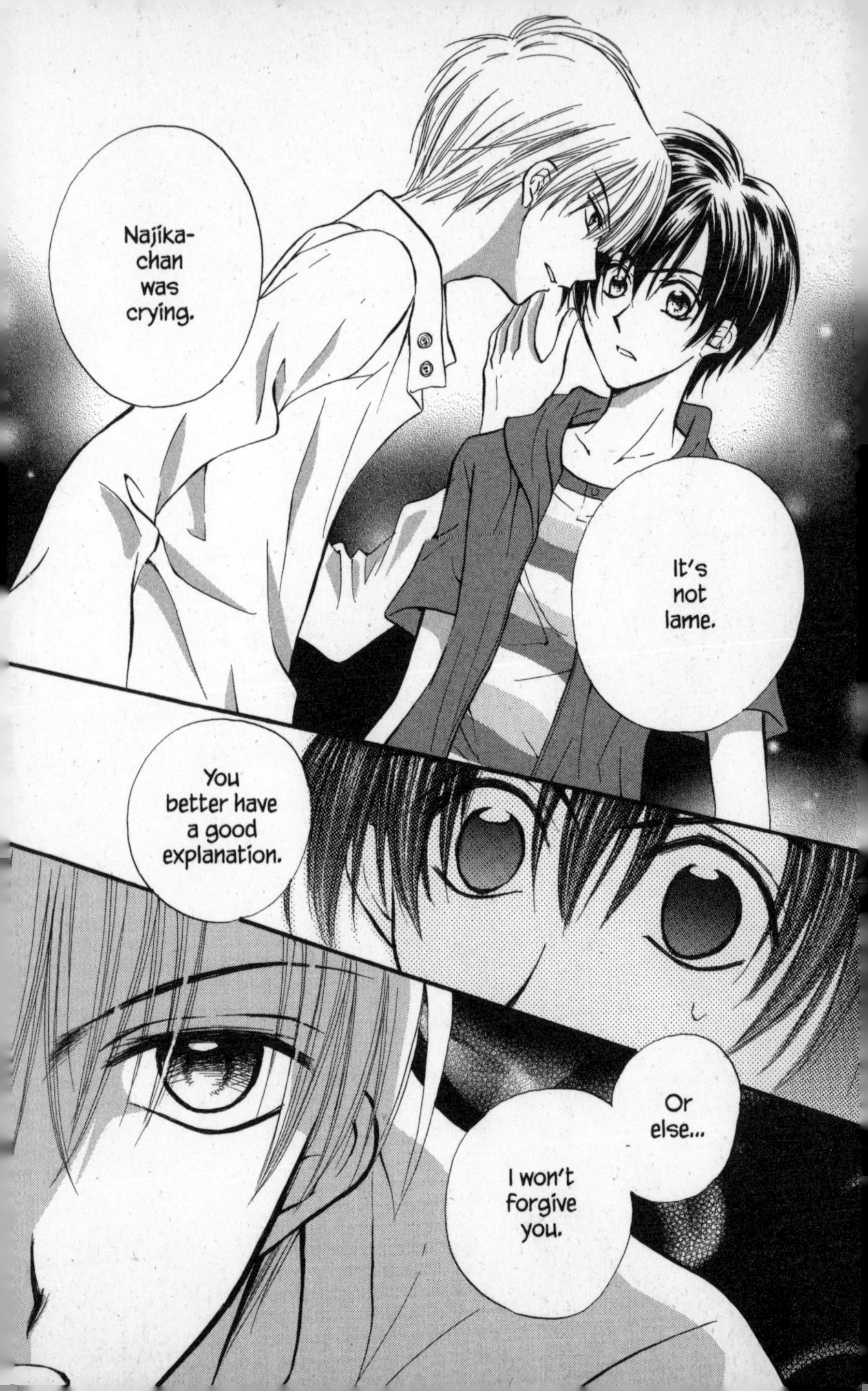
Najika-chan was crying.
It's not lame.
You better have a good explanation.
Or else...
I won't forgive you.

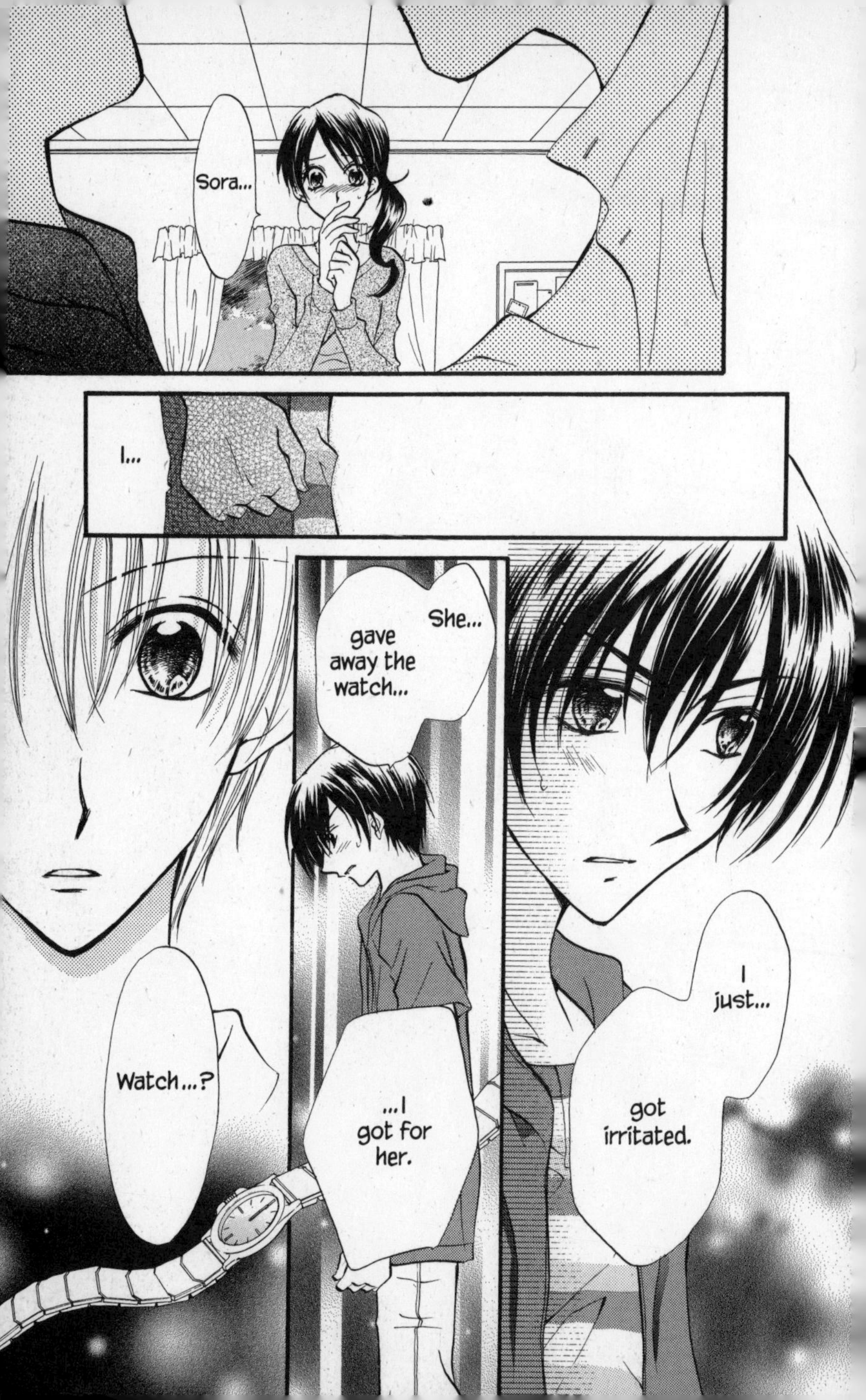
Sora...
I...
She...
gave away the watch...
...I got for her.
I just...
got irritated.
Watch...?

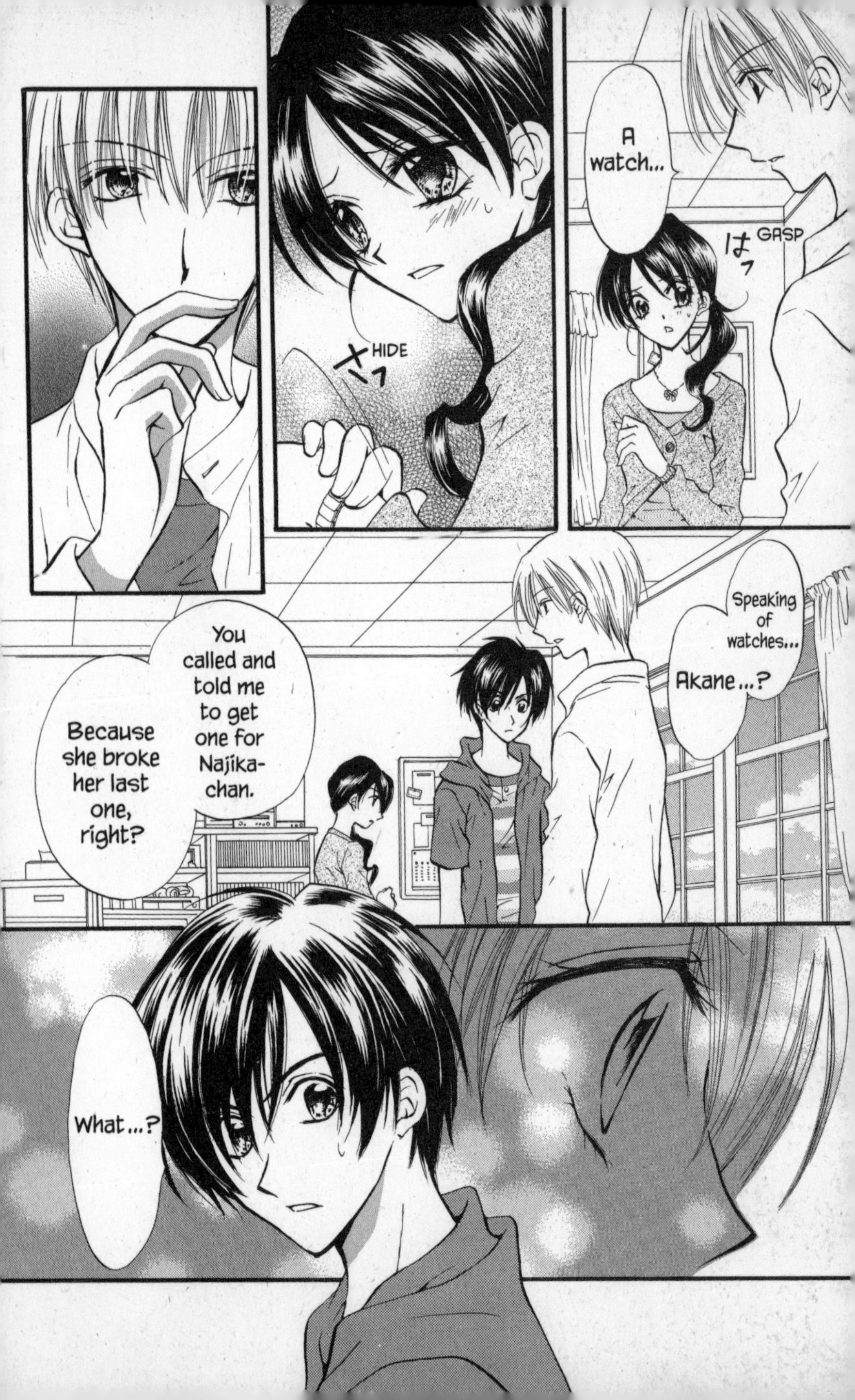
A watch...
は GASP
さ HIDE
Speaking of watches...
Akane...?
You called and told me to get one for Najika-chan.
Because she broke her last one, right?
What...?

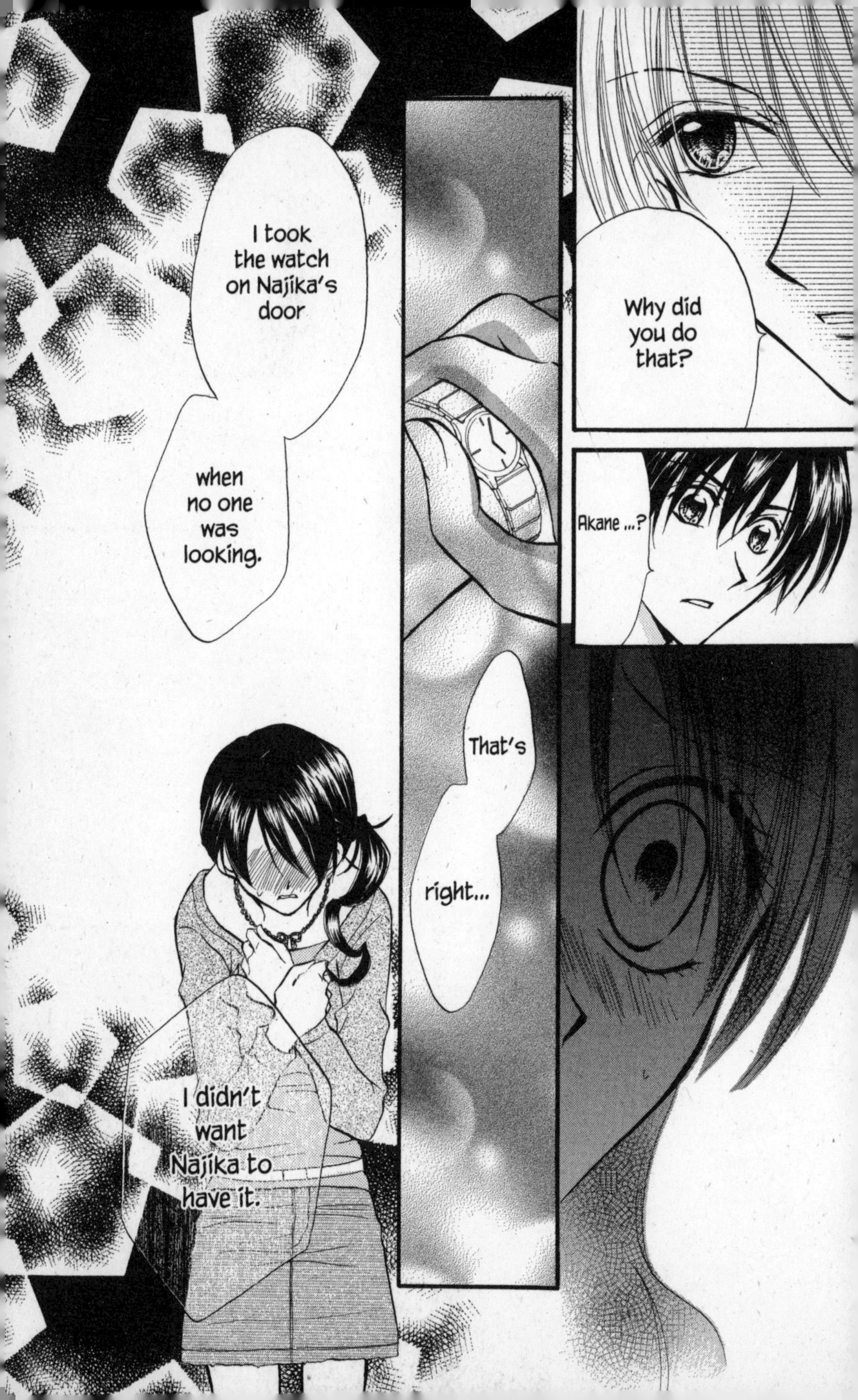
Why did you do that?
Akane ...?
That's right...
I took the watch on Najika's door
when no one was looking.
I didn't want Najika to have it.

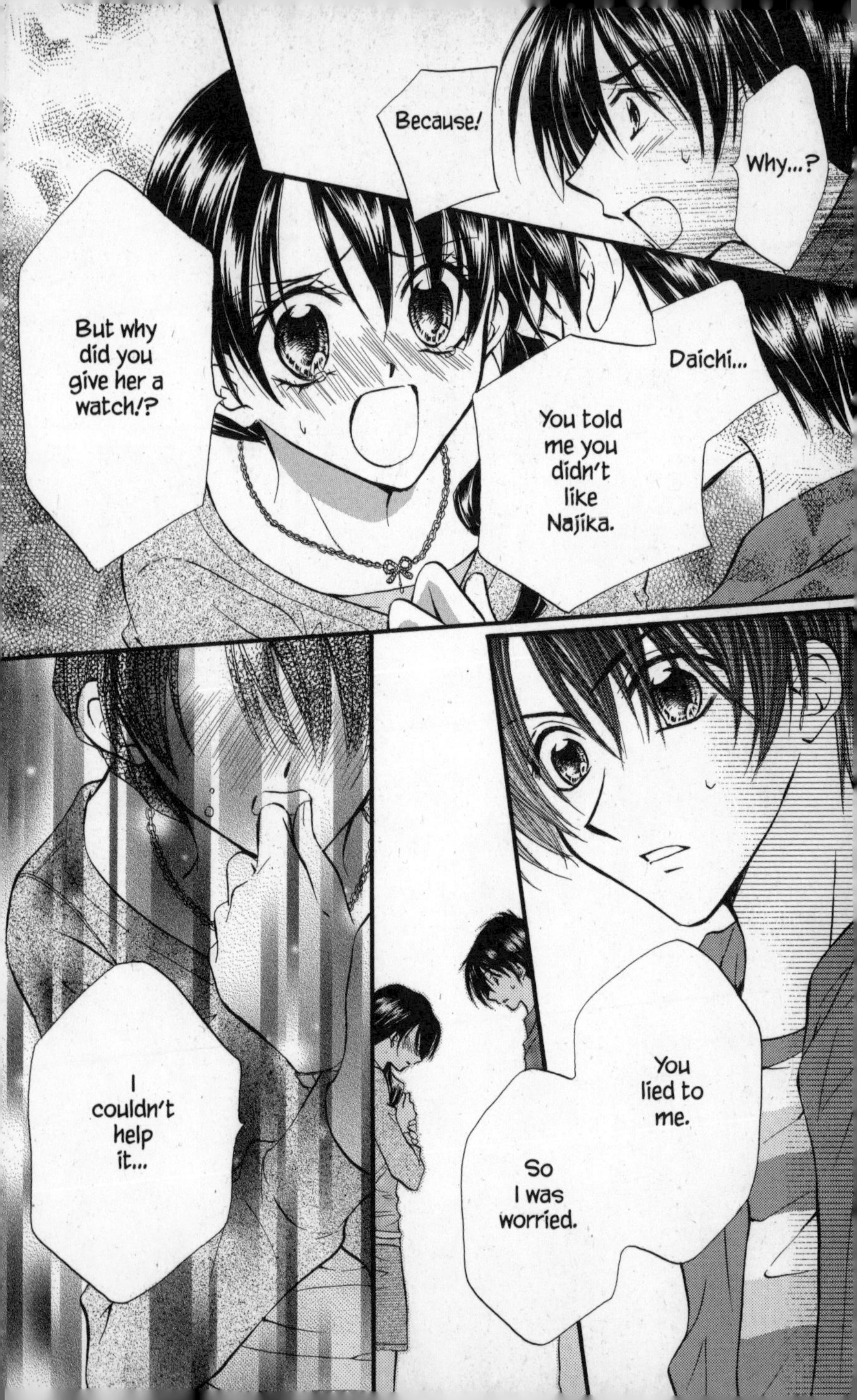
Why...?
Because!
Daichi...
You told me you didn't like Najika.
But why did you give her a watch!?
You lied to me.
So I was worried.
I couldn't help it...

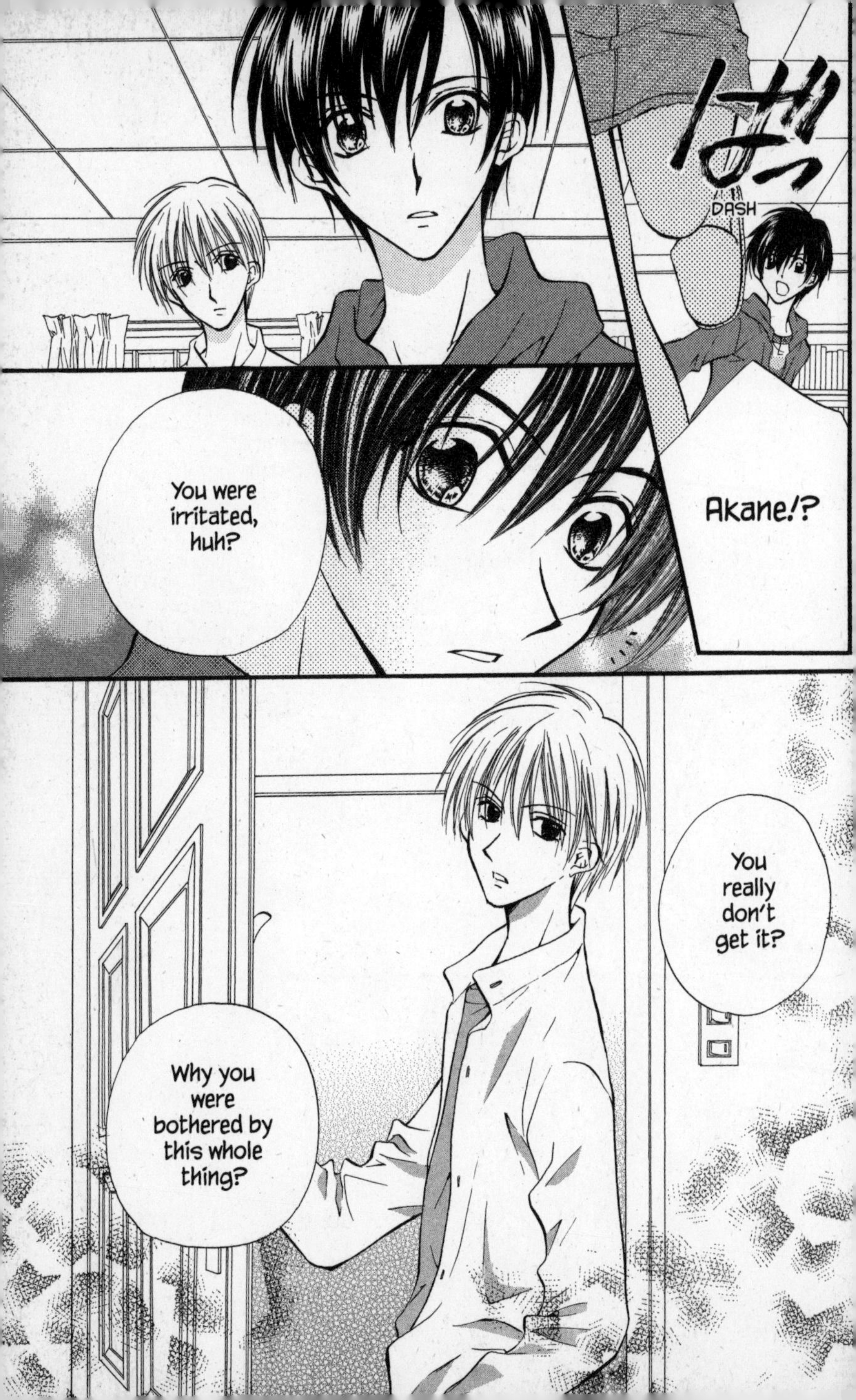
ぱっ
DASH
Akane!?
You were irritated, huh?
You really don't get it?
Why you were bothered by this whole thing?

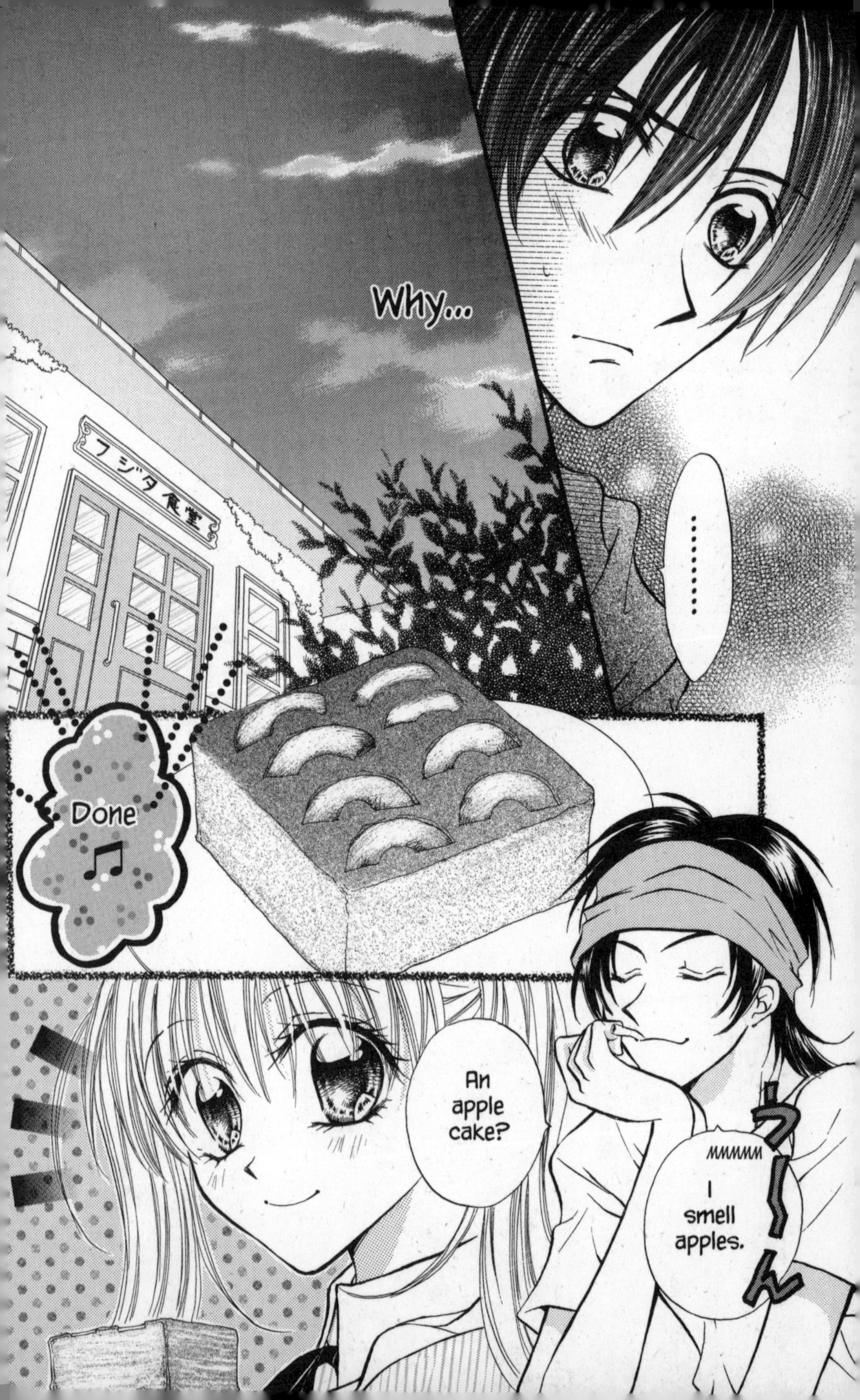
Why...
......
フジタ食堂
Done ♫
うーん
MMMMMM I smell apples.
An apple cake?

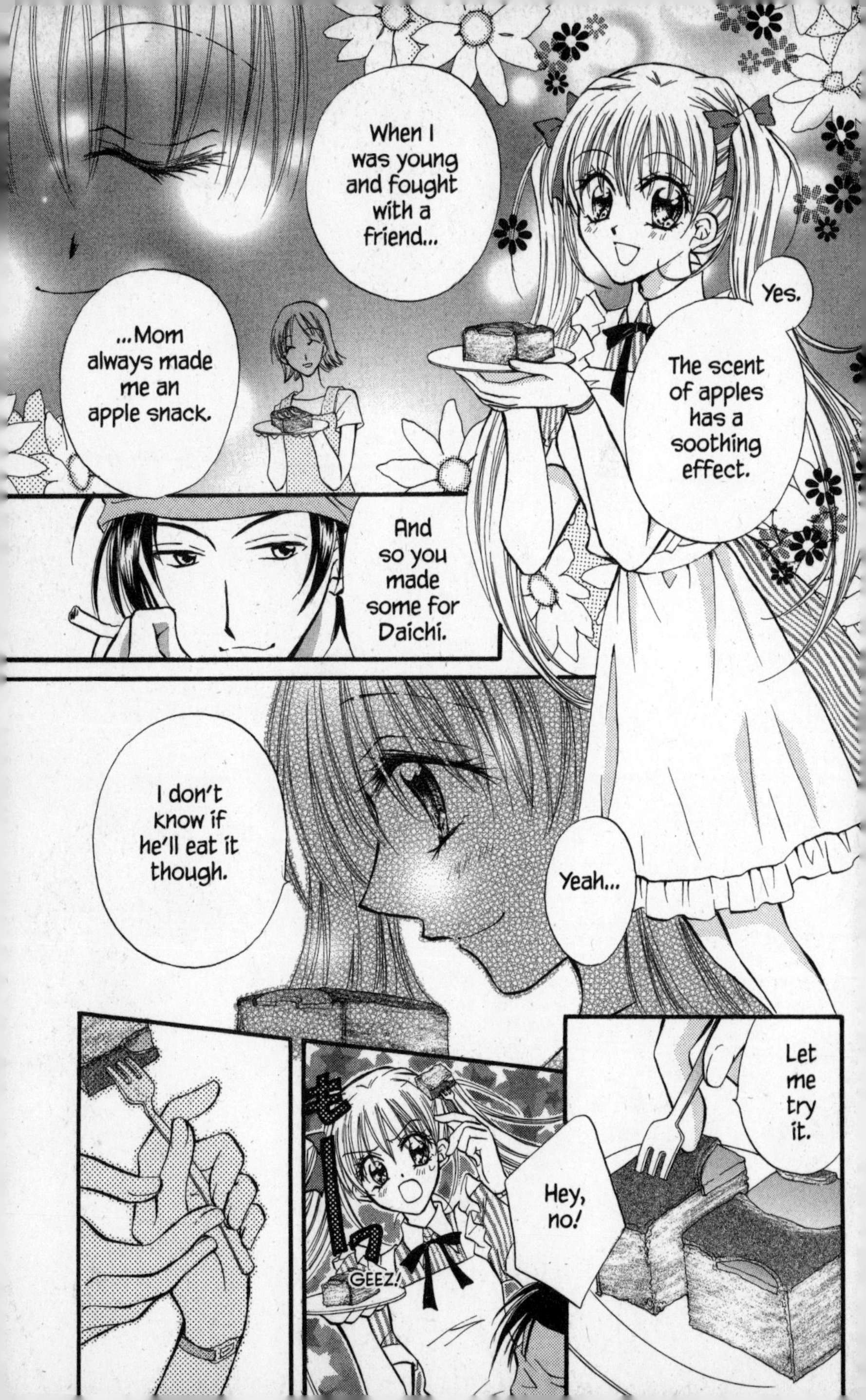
When I was young and fought with a friend...
...Mom always made me an apple snack.
Yes.
The scent of apples has a soothing effect.
And so you made some for Daichi.
I don't know if he'll eat it though.
Yeah...
Let me try it.
Hey, no!
GEEZ!

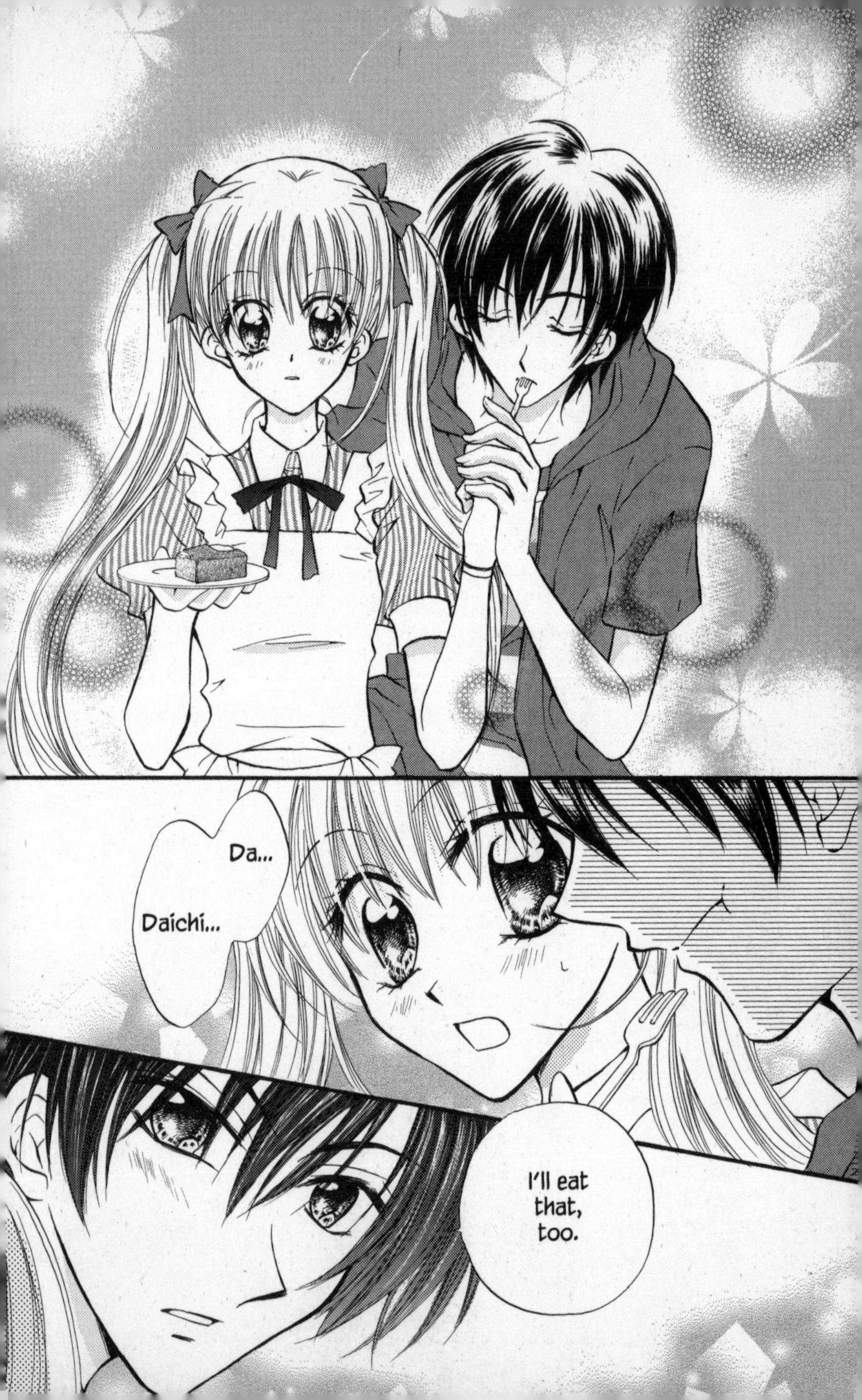
Da... Daichi...
I'll eat that, too.

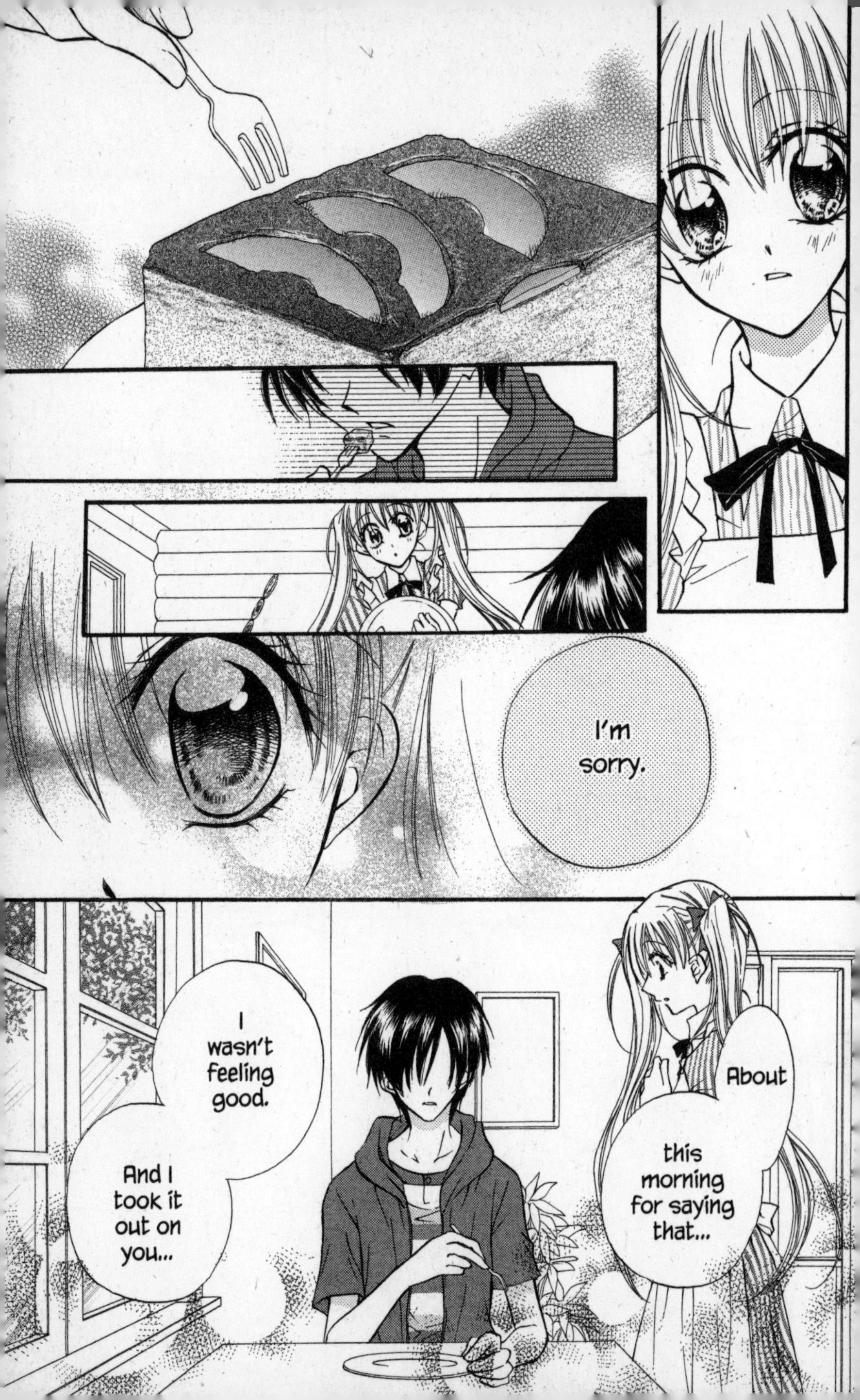
I'm sorry.
About
this morning for saying that...
I wasn't feeling good.
And I took it out on you...

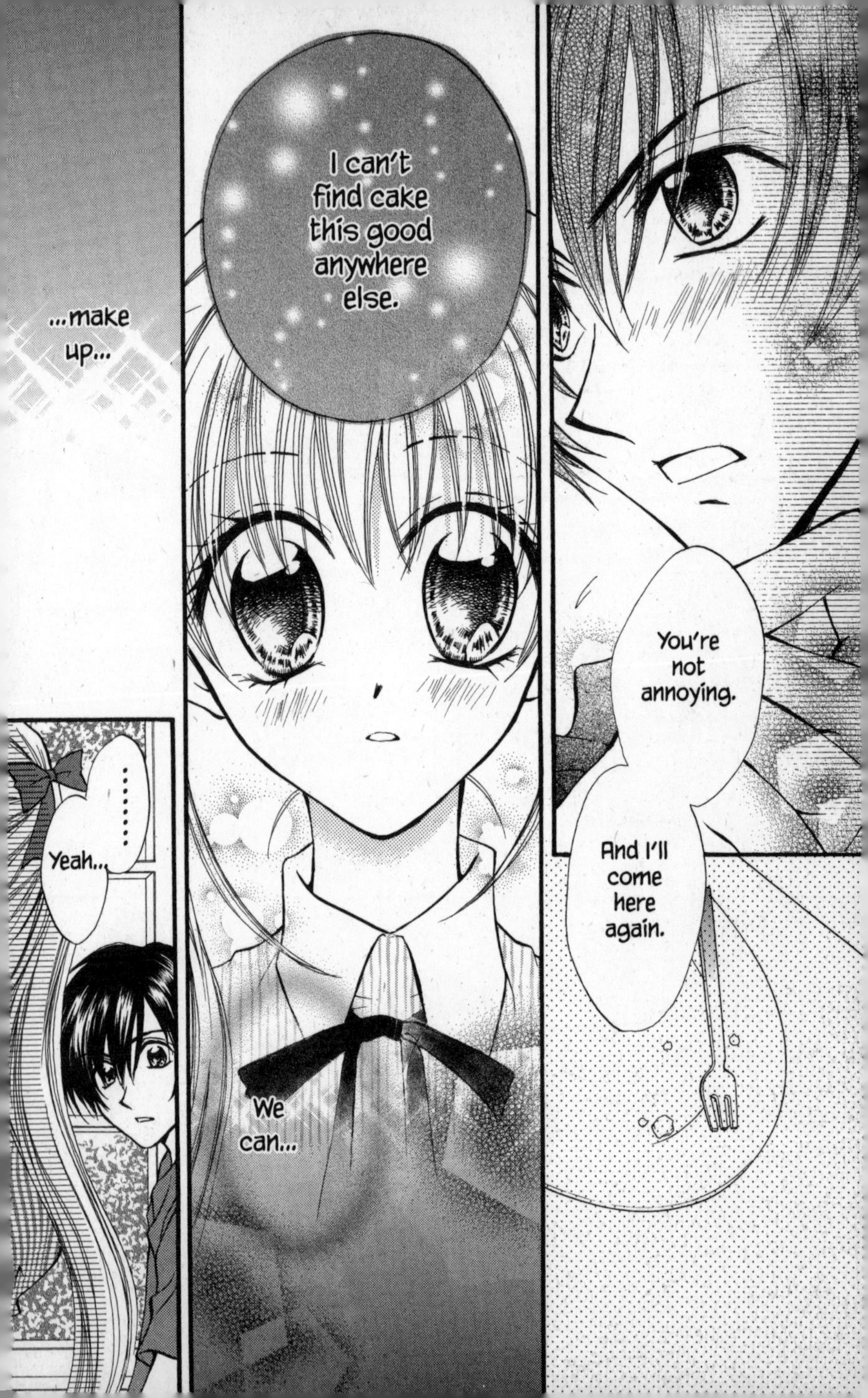
You're not annoying.
And I'll come here again.
I can't find cake this good anywhere else.
We can...
...make up...
......
Yeah...

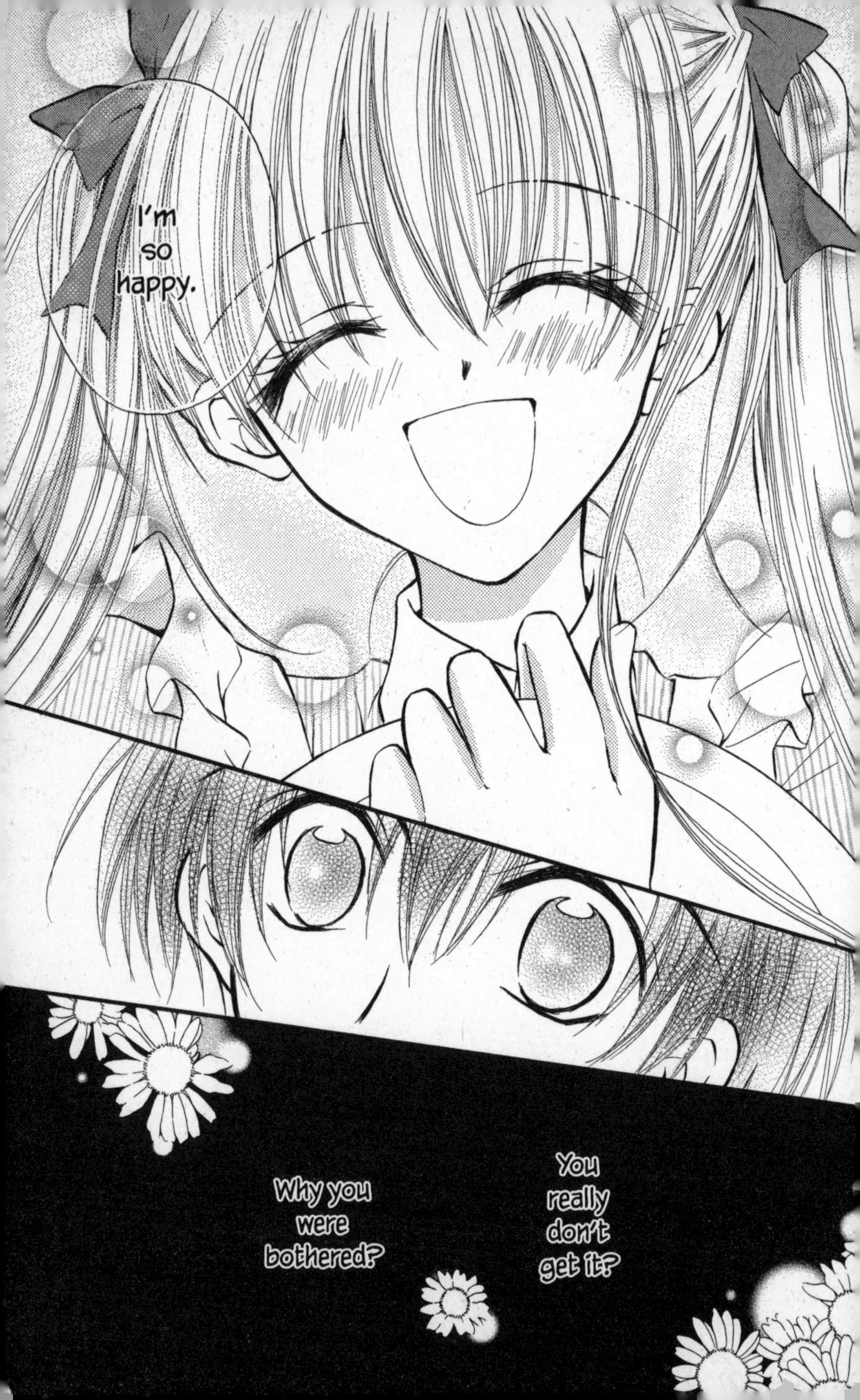
I'm so happy.
You really don't get it?
Why you were bothered?

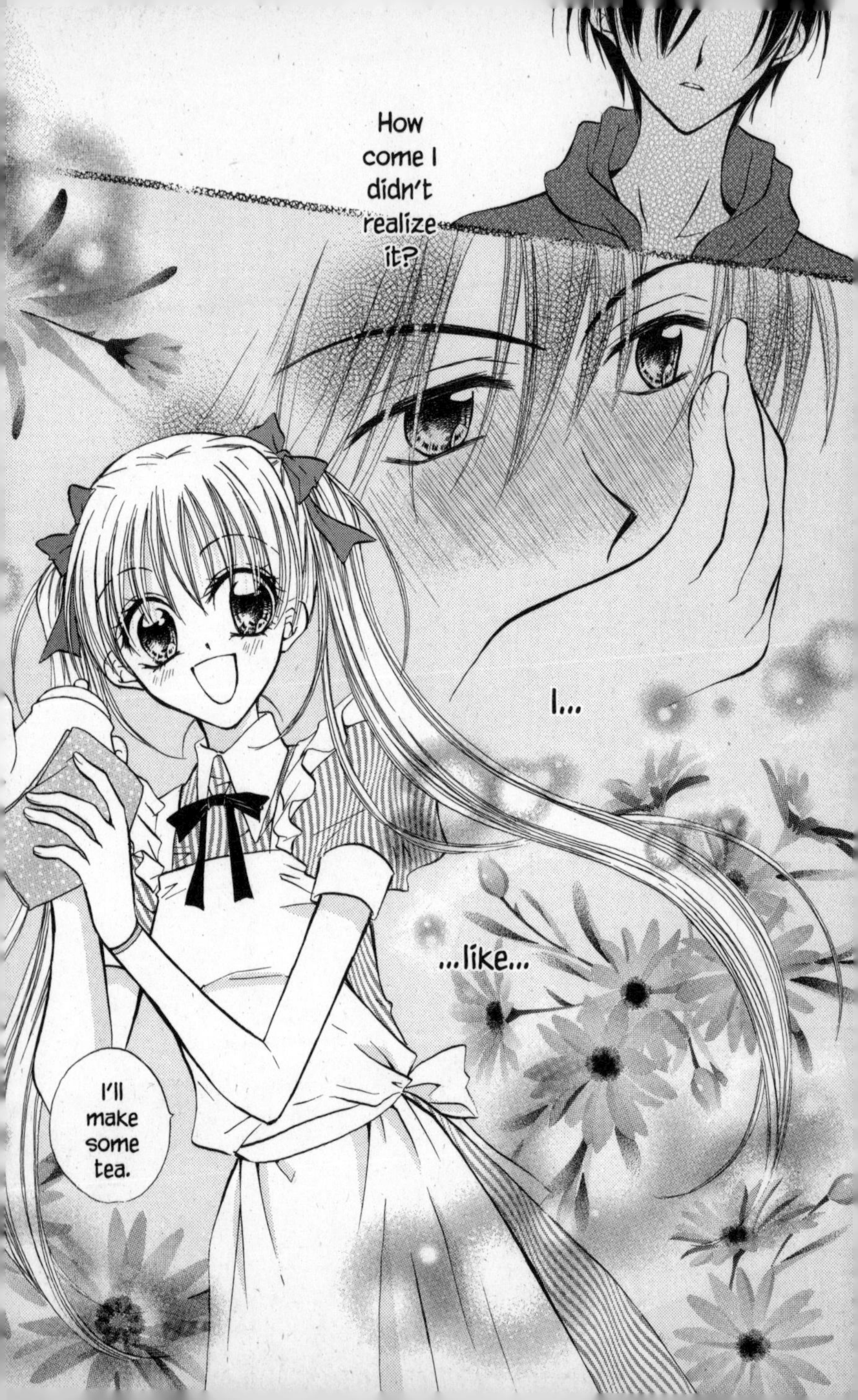
How come I didn't realize it?
I...
...like...
I'll make some tea.

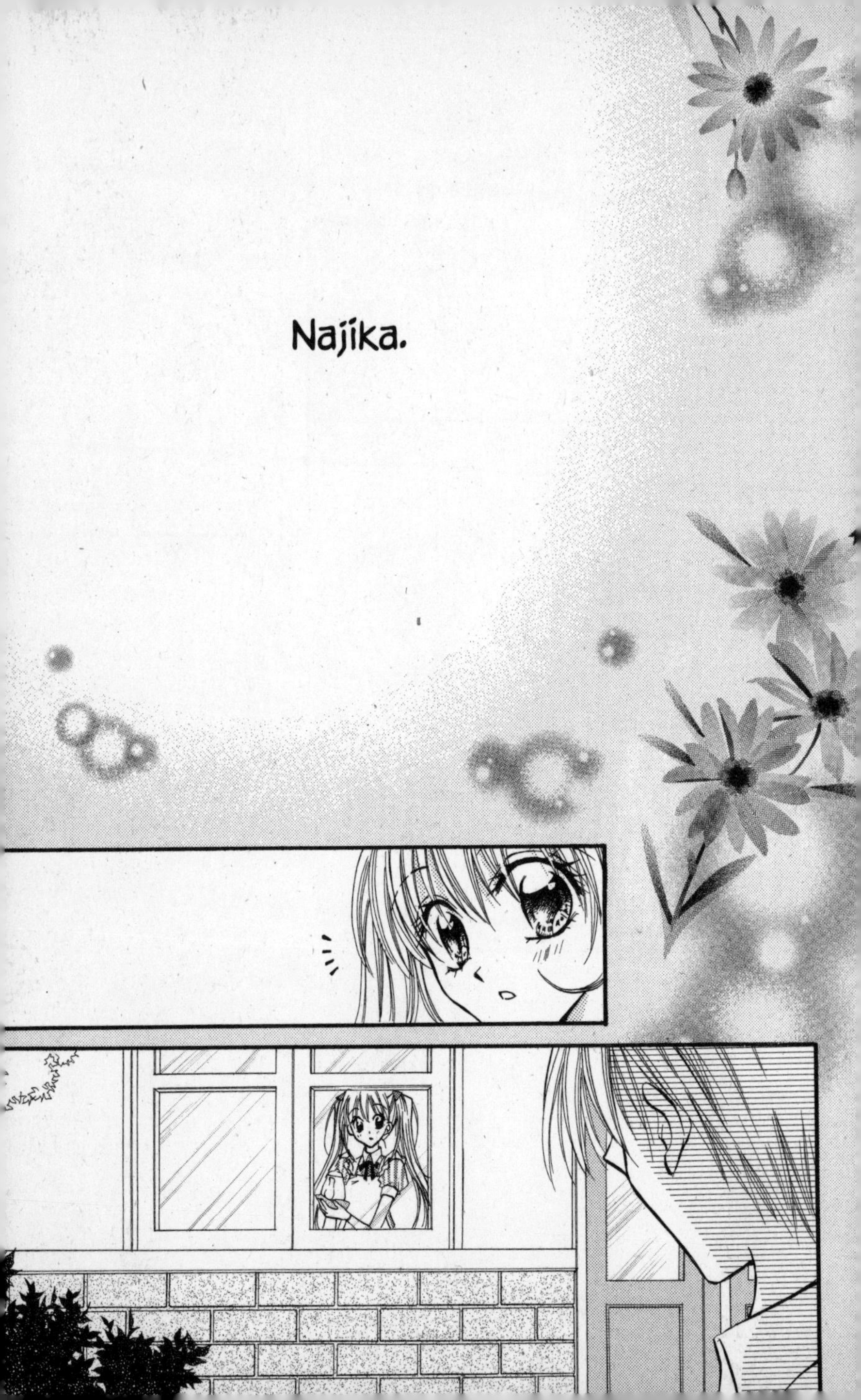
Najika.

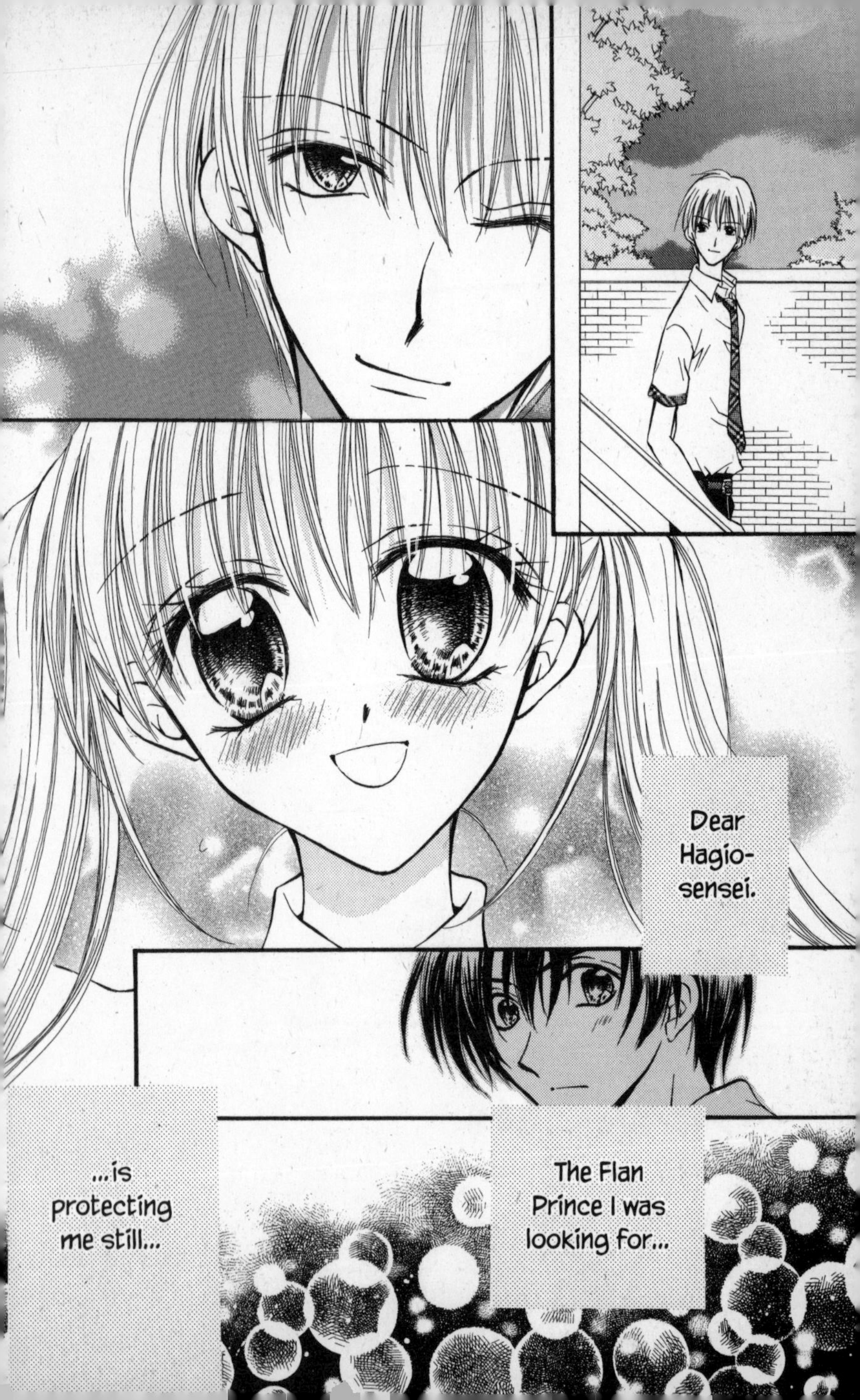
Dear Hagio-sensei.
The Flan Prince I was looking for...
...is protecting me still...

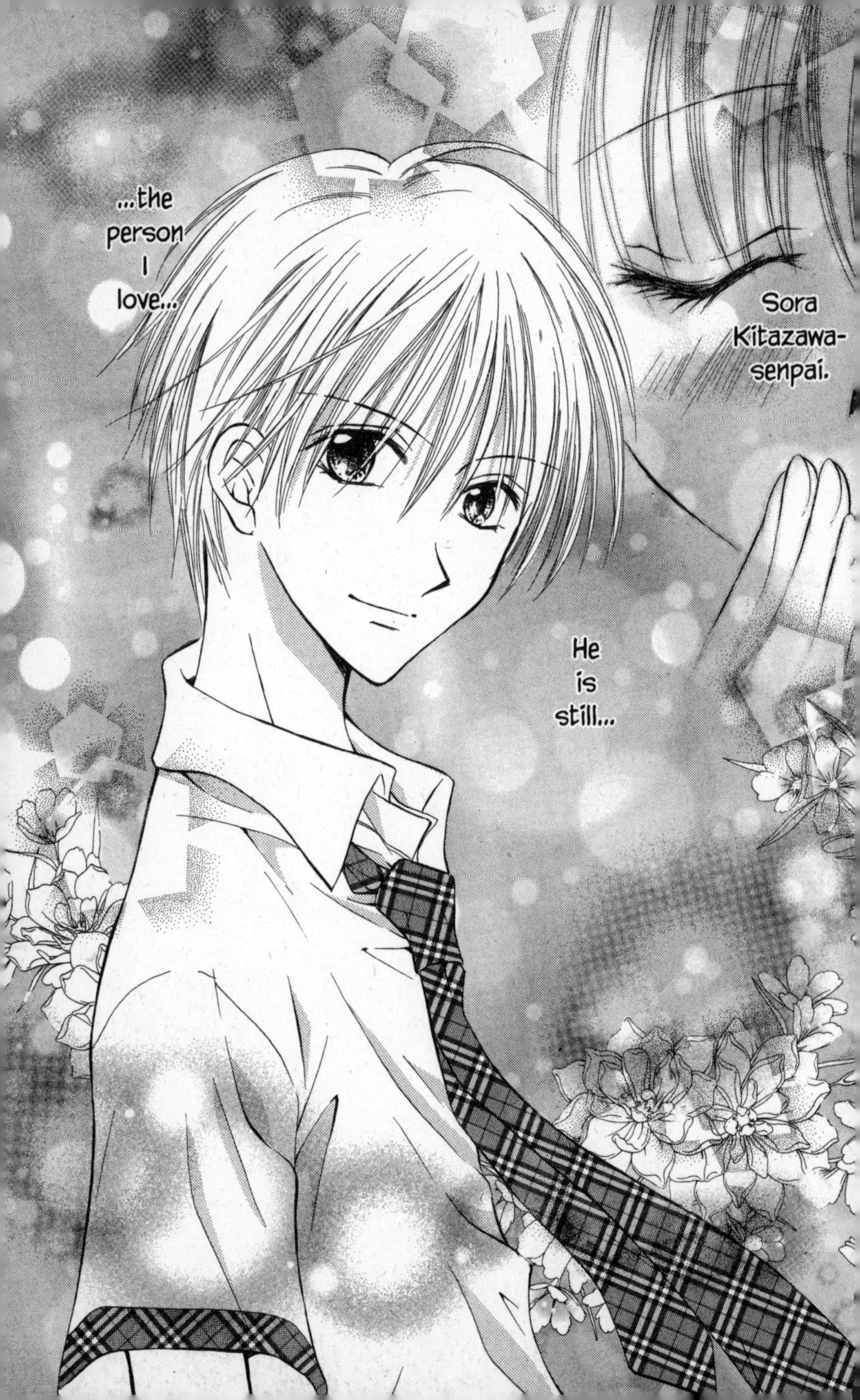
He is still...
...the person I love...
Sora Kitazawa-senpai.

Kitchen Princess

4 Panel Manga #2

If Najika Were a Snob...
What?
You want me to cook?
I guess I have to.
I'll use foie gras and caviar.
I need golden knives, too.
Oh my!
Oil splashed on my Chanel apron!
Here you go, one plate is 1,000,000 yen.*
MURKY
I'm not gonna eat that!

*$10,000

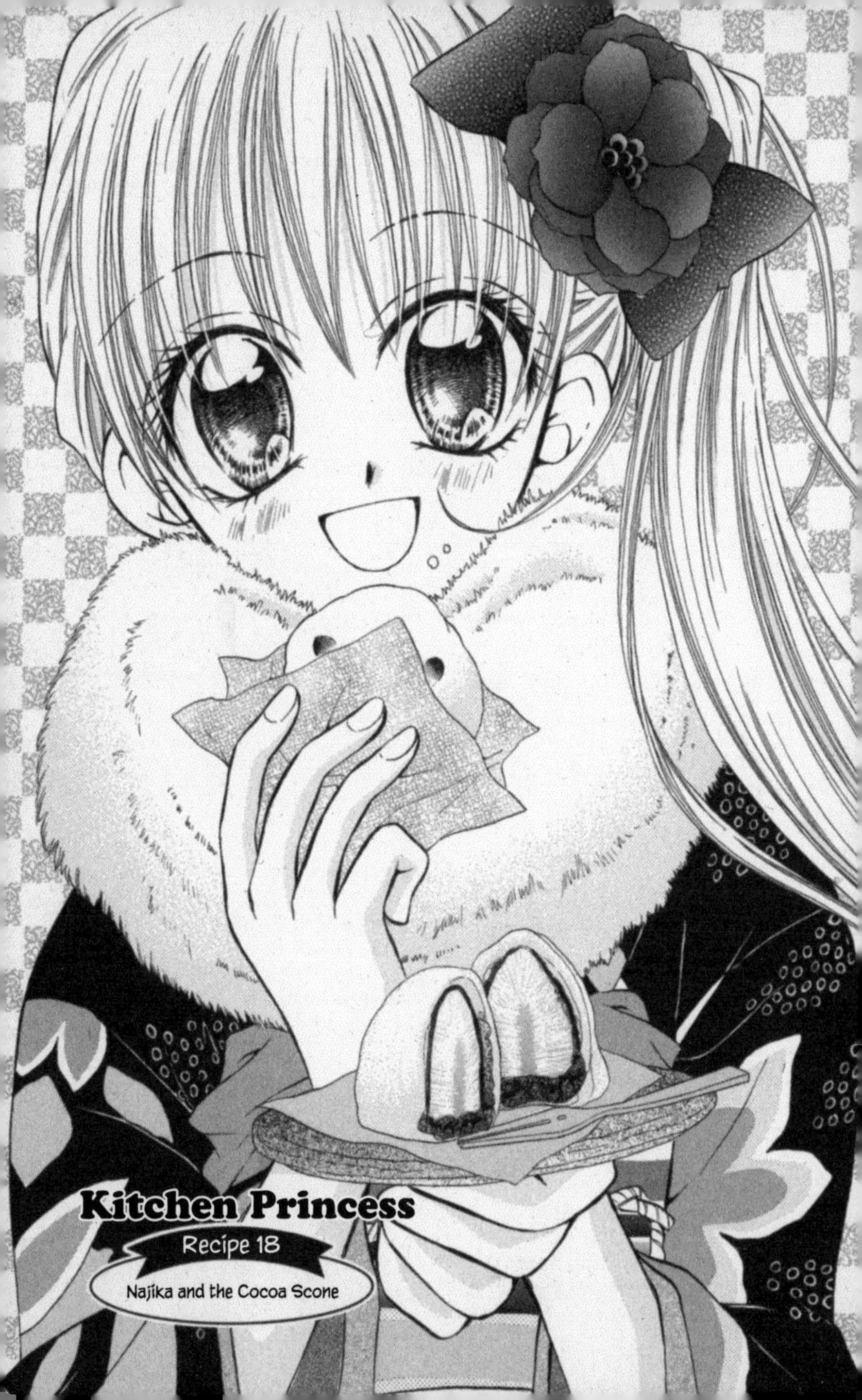
Kitchen Princess
Recipe 18
Najika and the Cocoa Scone

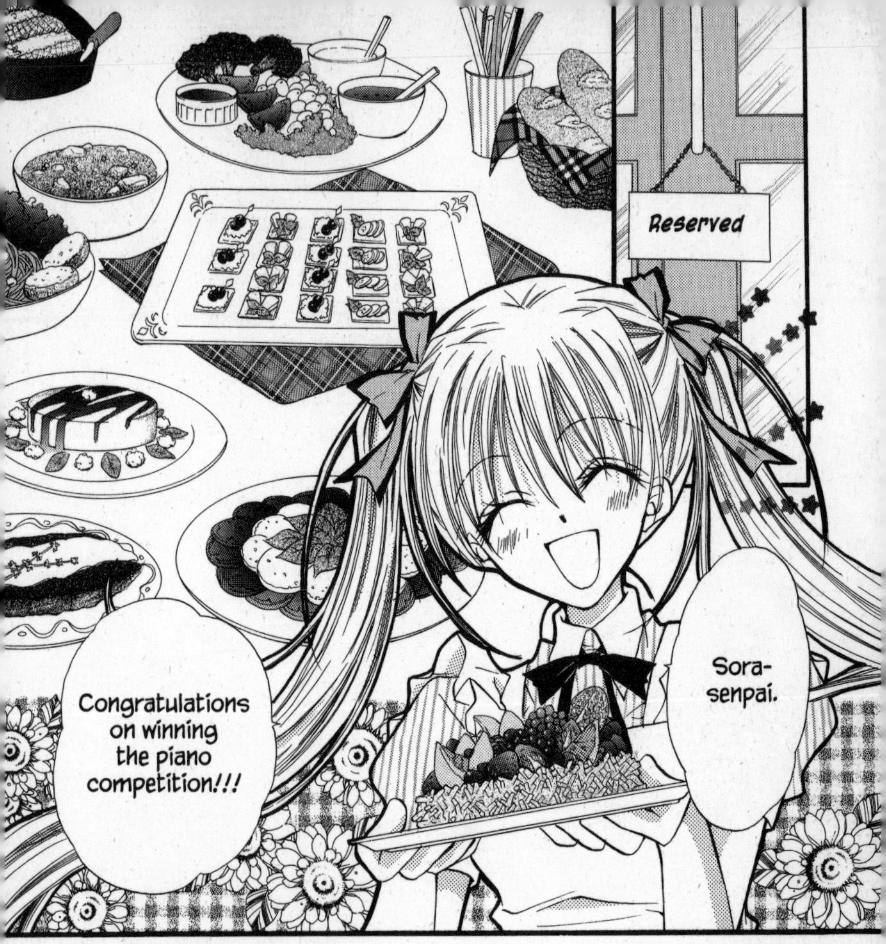
Reserved
Sora-senpai.
Congratulations on winning the piano competition!!!

About Recipe 18's Splash Page

Since the magazine was released for New Year's, I drew Najika wearing a kimono. And I wanted her to eat something (because it's a cooking manga). So I thought "Then I must have her eat something Japanese!" I was looking through a cookbook and the strawberry rice cake looked so good, I decided on that!! I was drawing some other food before that, but now I can't remember what it was...

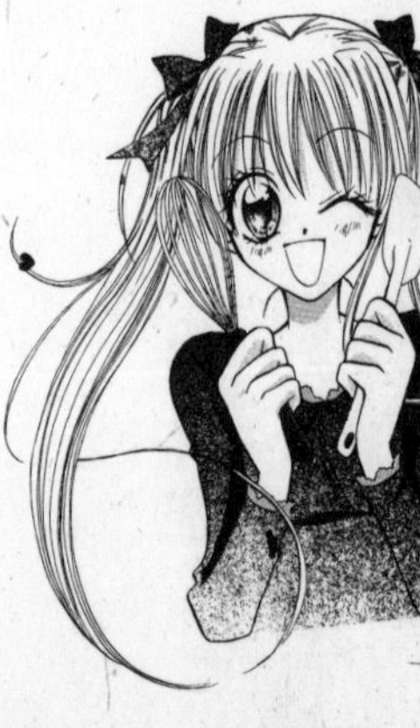

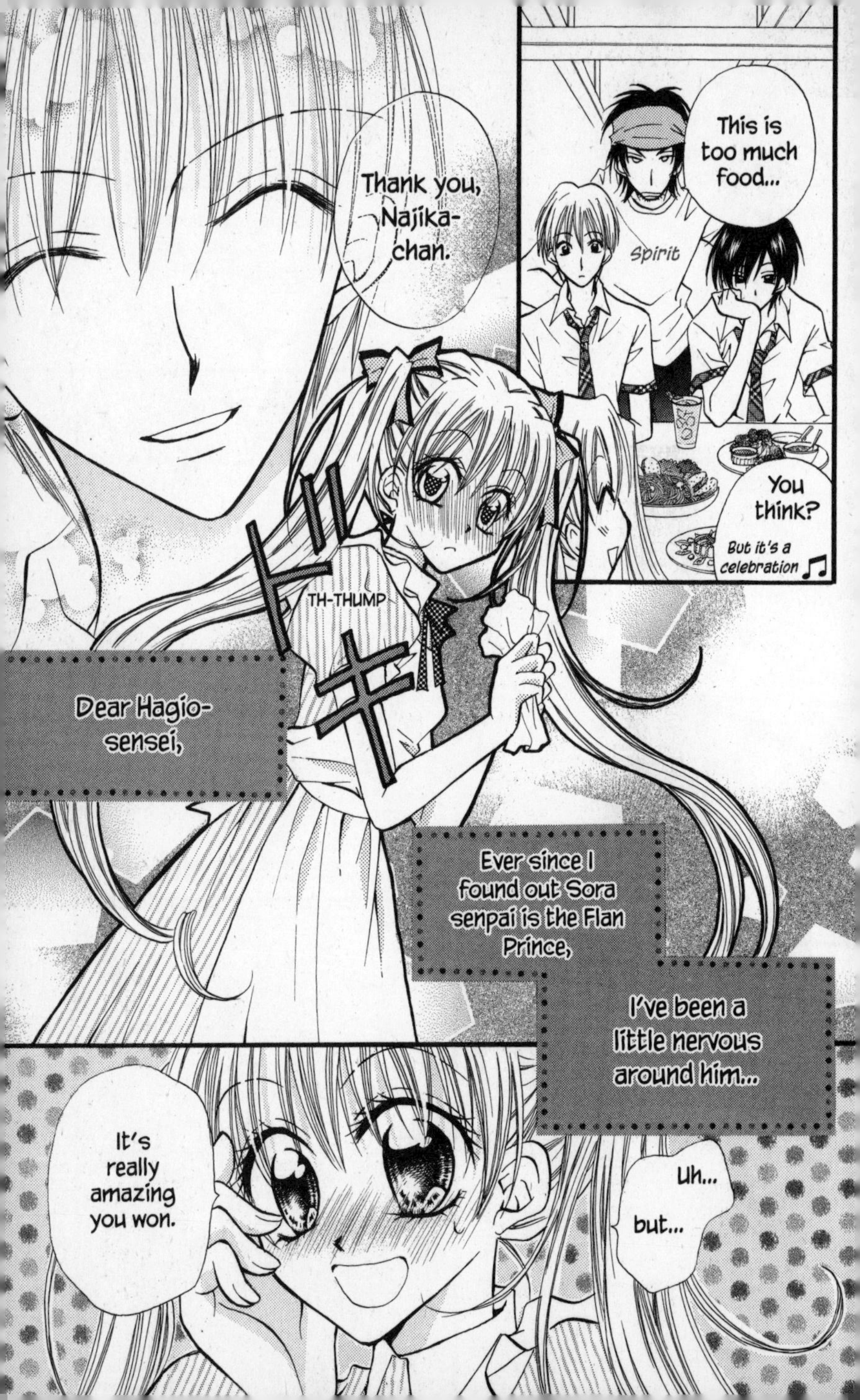
This is too much food...
You think?
But it's a celebration ♫
Thank you, Najika-chan.
TH-THUMP
Dear Hagio-sensei,
Ever since I found out Sora senpai is the Flan Prince,
I've been a little nervous around him...
Uh...
but...
It's really amazing you won.

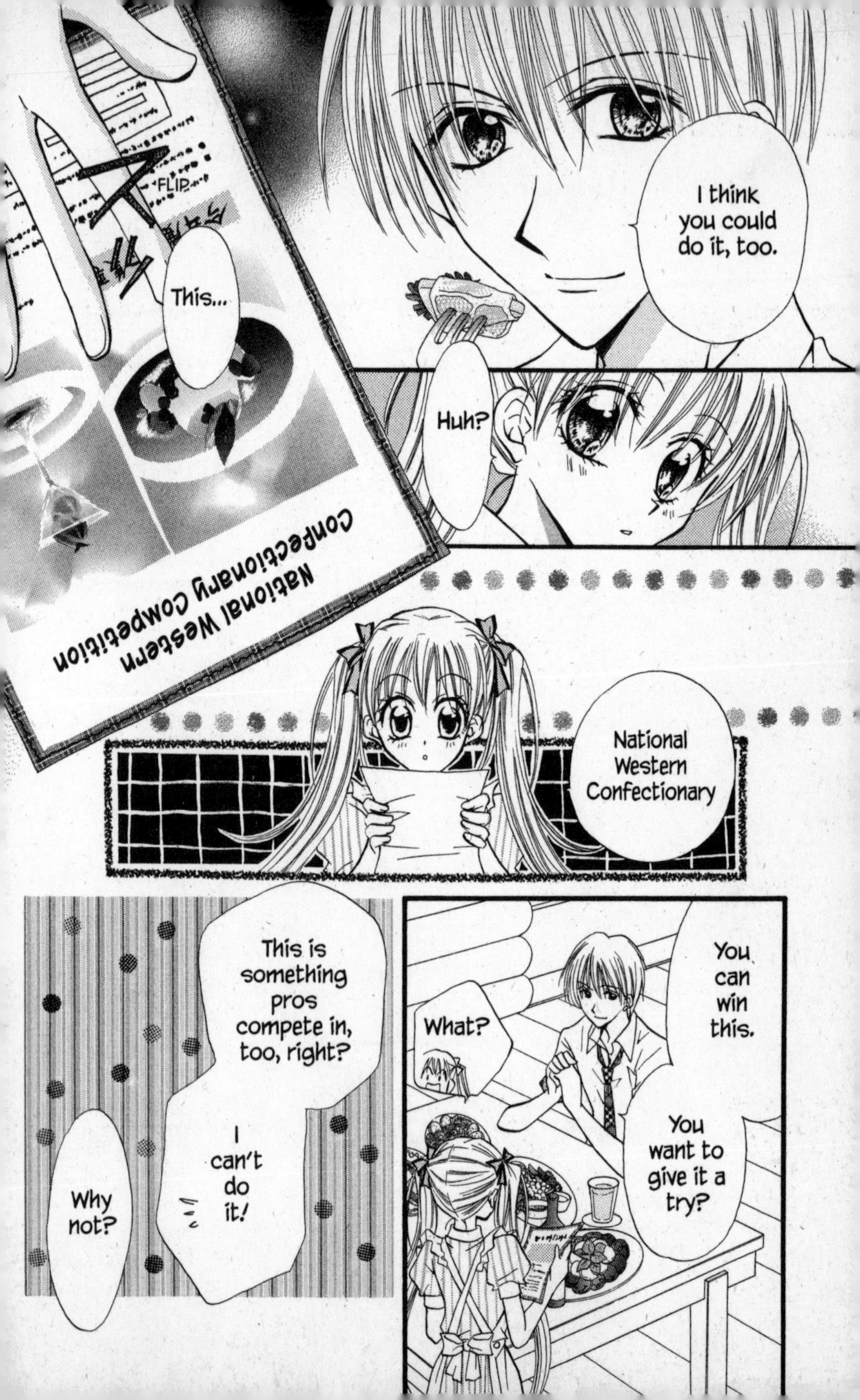
I think you could do it, too.
Huh?
FLIP
This...
National Western Confectionary Competition
National Western Confectionary
You can win this.
What?
You want to give it a try?
This is something pros compete in, too, right?
I can't do it!
Why not?

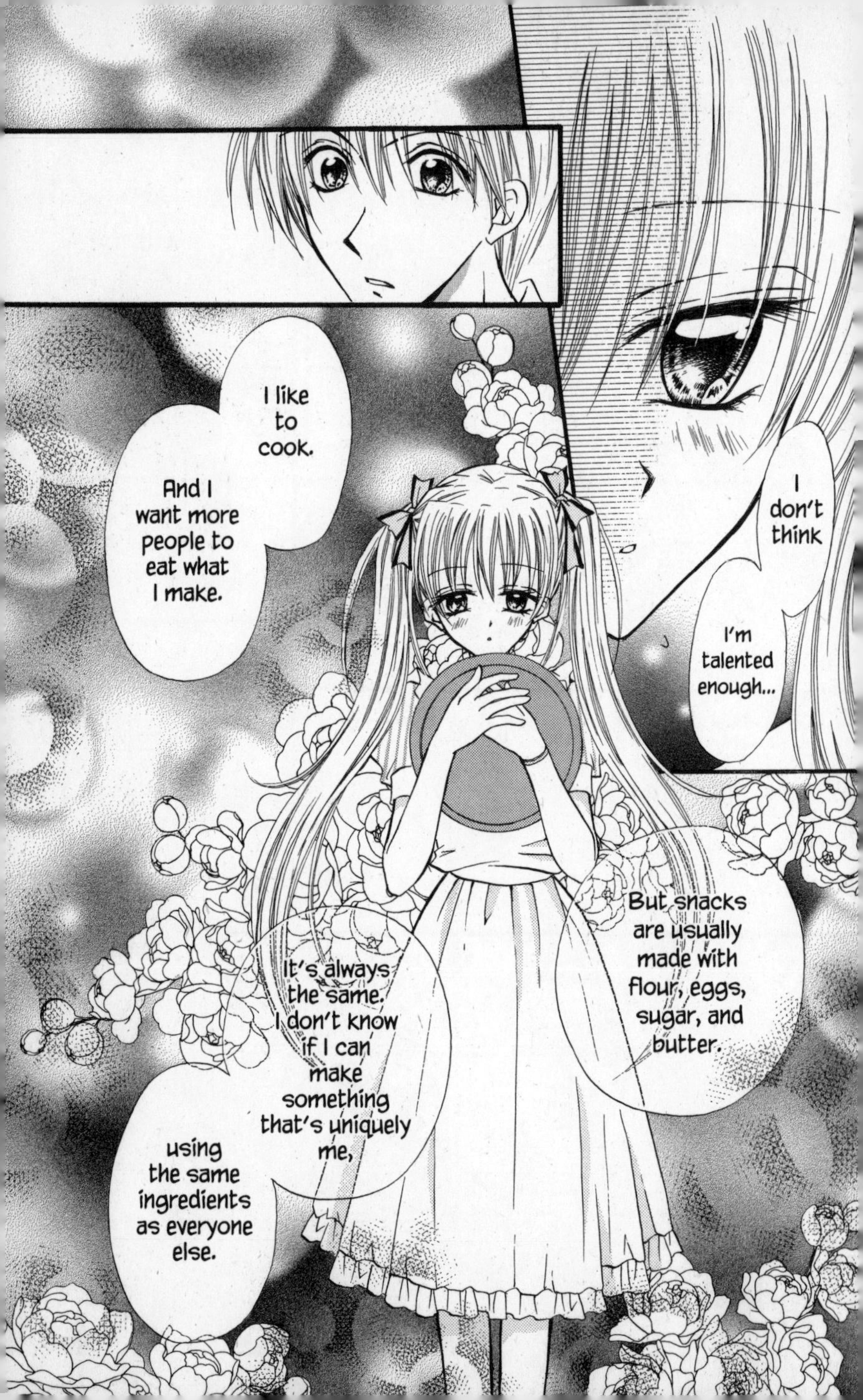
I don't think
I'm talented enough...
I like to cook.
And I want more people to eat what I make.
But snacks are usually made with flour, eggs, sugar, and butter.
It's always the same. I don't know if I can make something that's uniquely me,
using the same ingredients as everyone else.

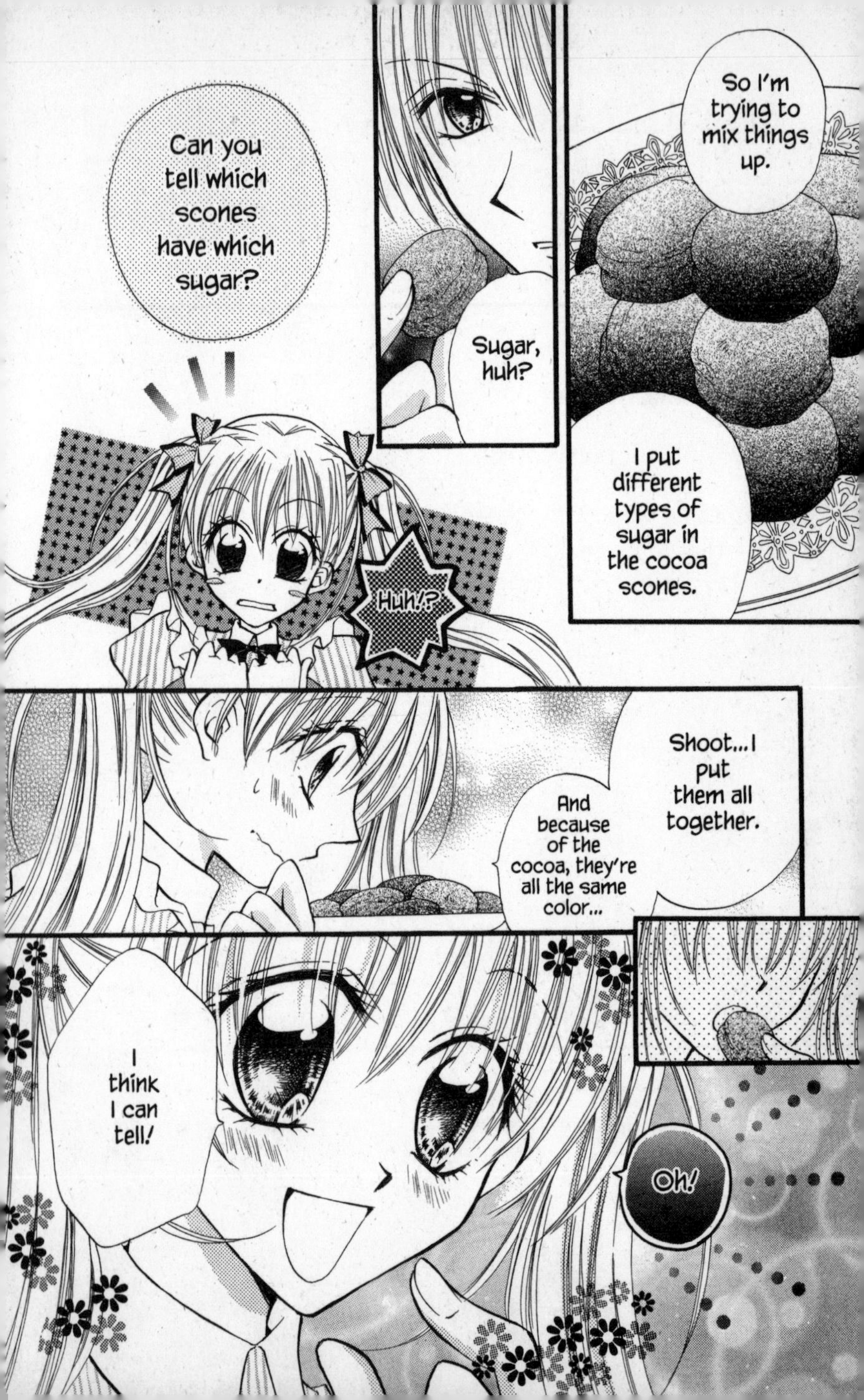
So I'm trying to mix things up.
I put different types of sugar in the cocoa scones.
Sugar, huh?
Can you tell which scones have which sugar?
Huh!?
Shoot...I put them all together.
And because of the cocoa, they're all the same color...
Oh!
I think I can tell!

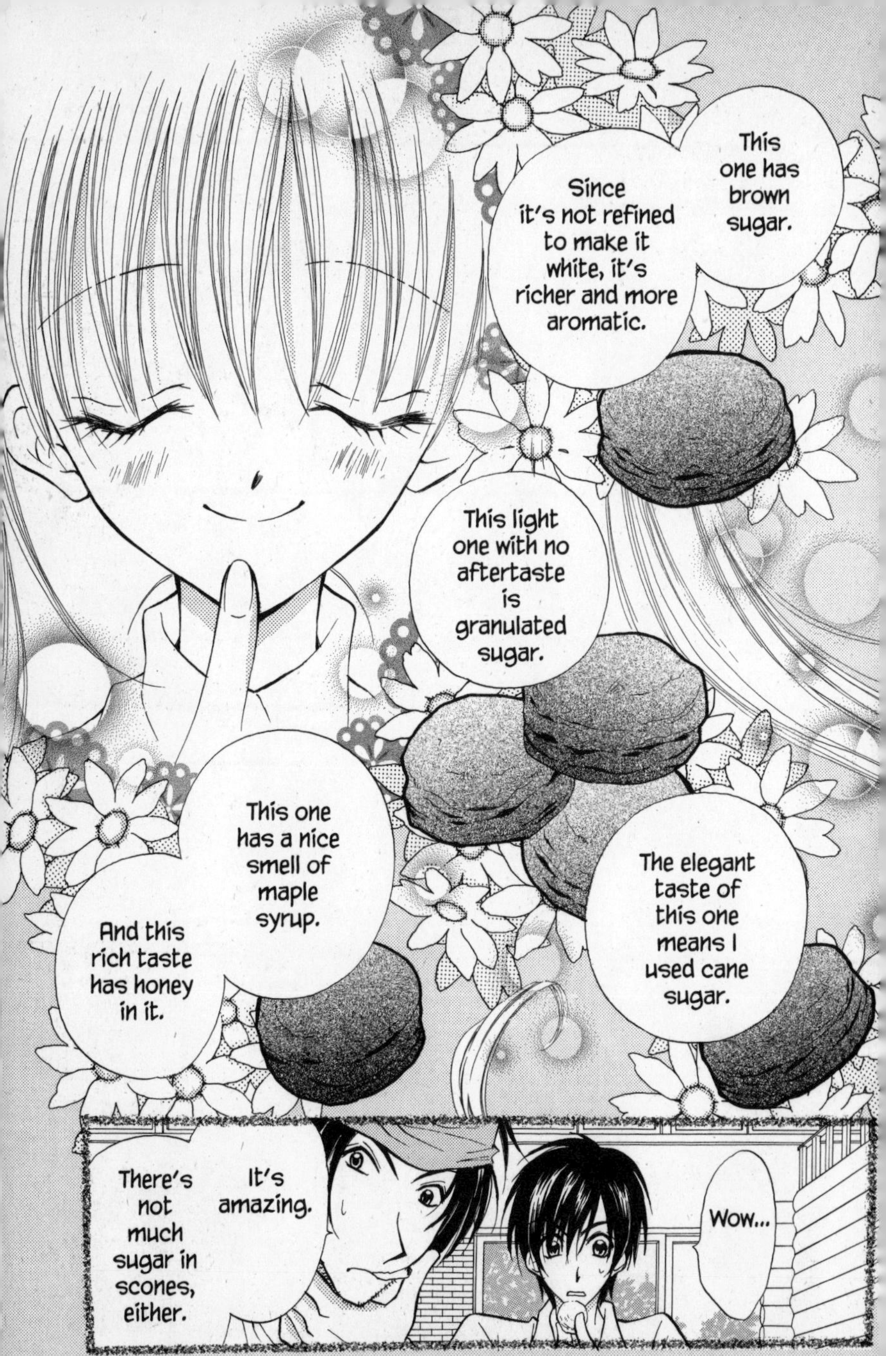
This one has brown sugar.
Since it's not refined to make it white, it's richer and more aromatic.
This light one with no aftertaste is granulated sugar.
The elegant taste of this one means I used cane sugar.
This one has a nice smell of maple syrup.
And this rich taste has honey in it.
Wow...
It's amazing.
There's not much sugar in scones, either.

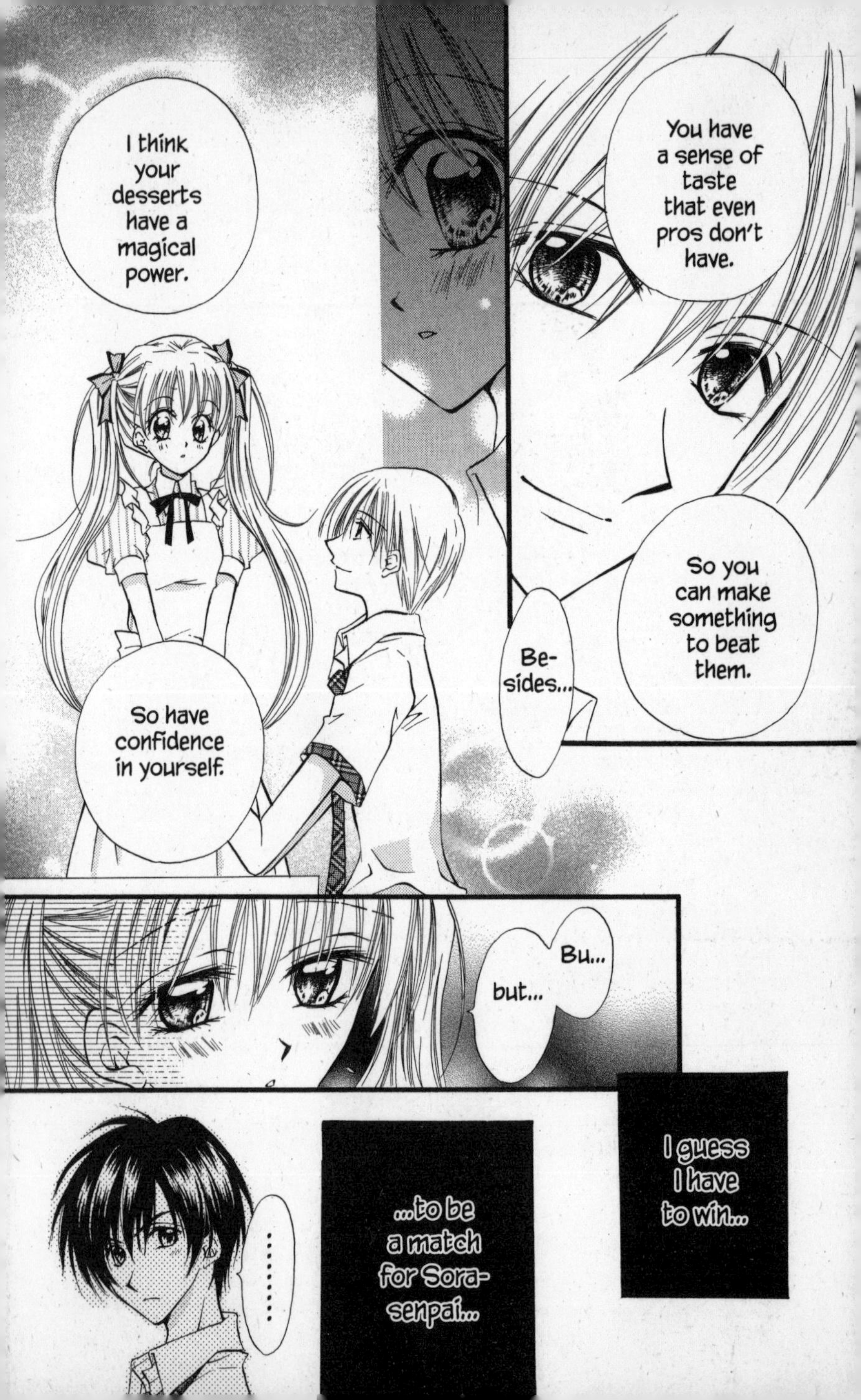

You have a sense of taste that even pros don't have.
So you can make something to beat them.
Be-sides...
I think your desserts have a magical power.
So have confidence in yourself.
Bu... but...
I guess I have to win...
...to be a match for Sora-senpai...
......

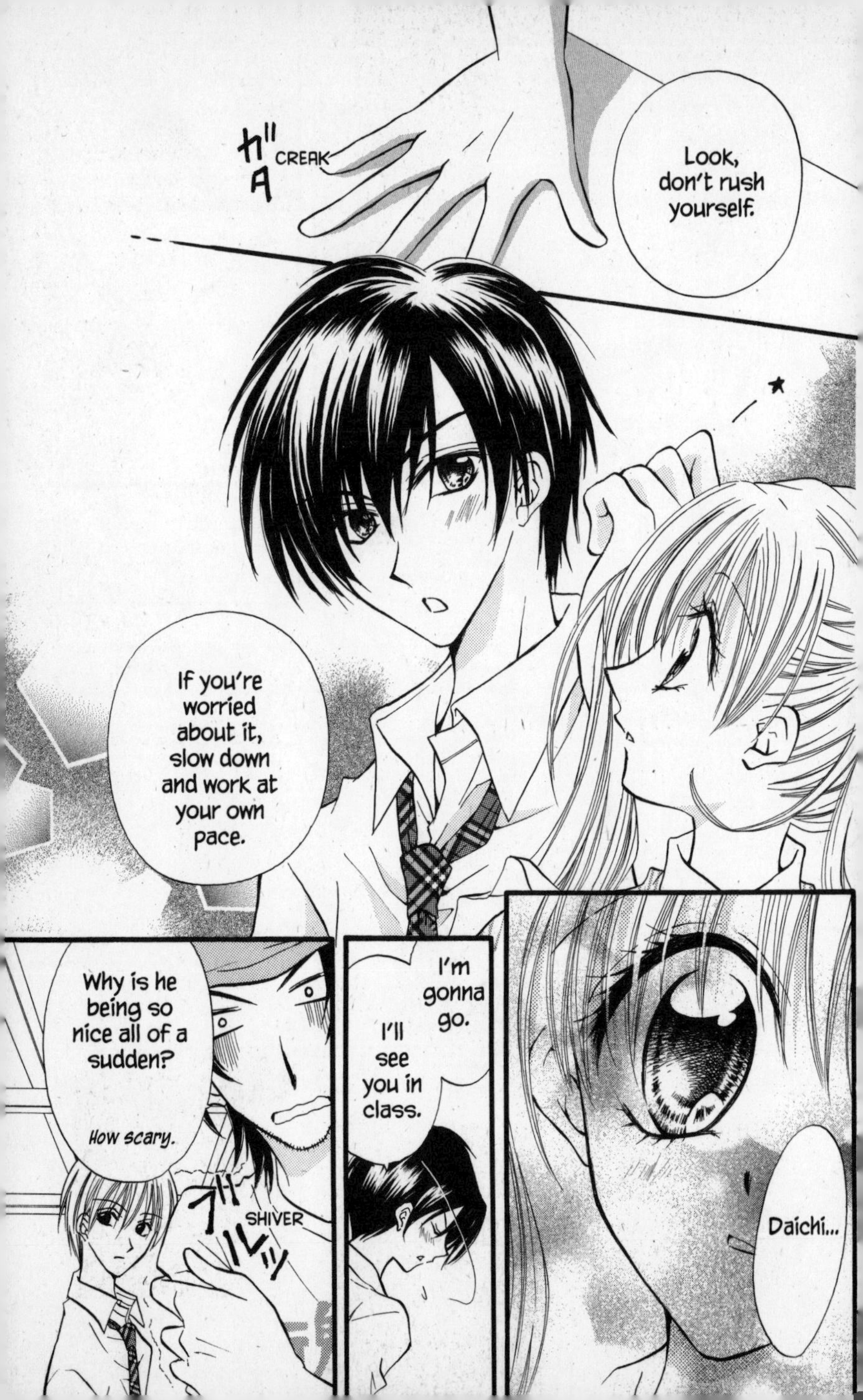
ガタ
CREAK
Look, don't rush yourself.
If you're worried about it, slow down and work at your own pace.
Daichi...
I'm gonna go.
I'll see you in class.
Why is he being so nice all of a sudden?
How scary.
ブルルッ
SHIVER

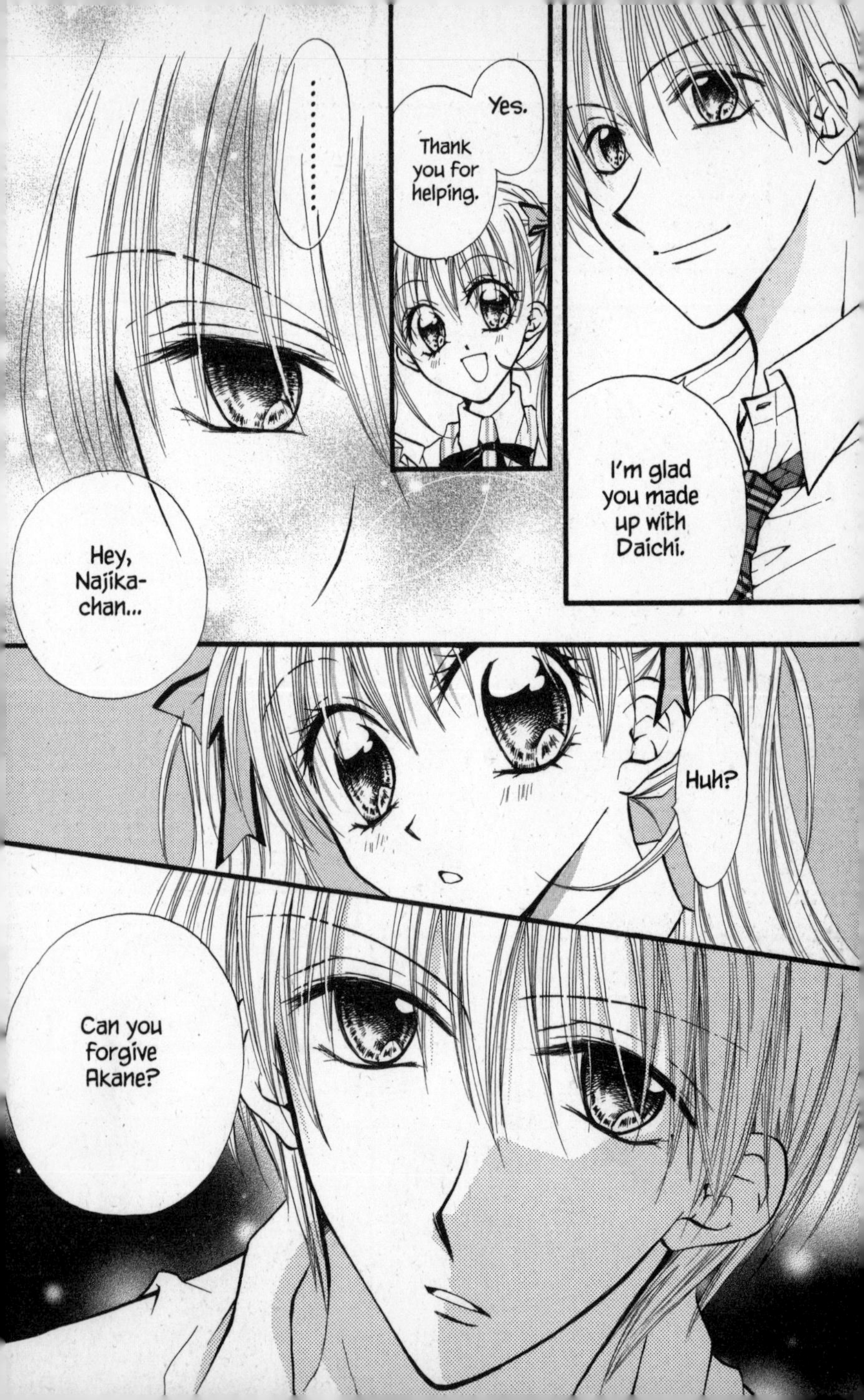
I'm glad you made up with Daichi.
Yes.
Thank you for helping.
......
Hey, Najika-chan...
Huh?
Can you forgive Akane?

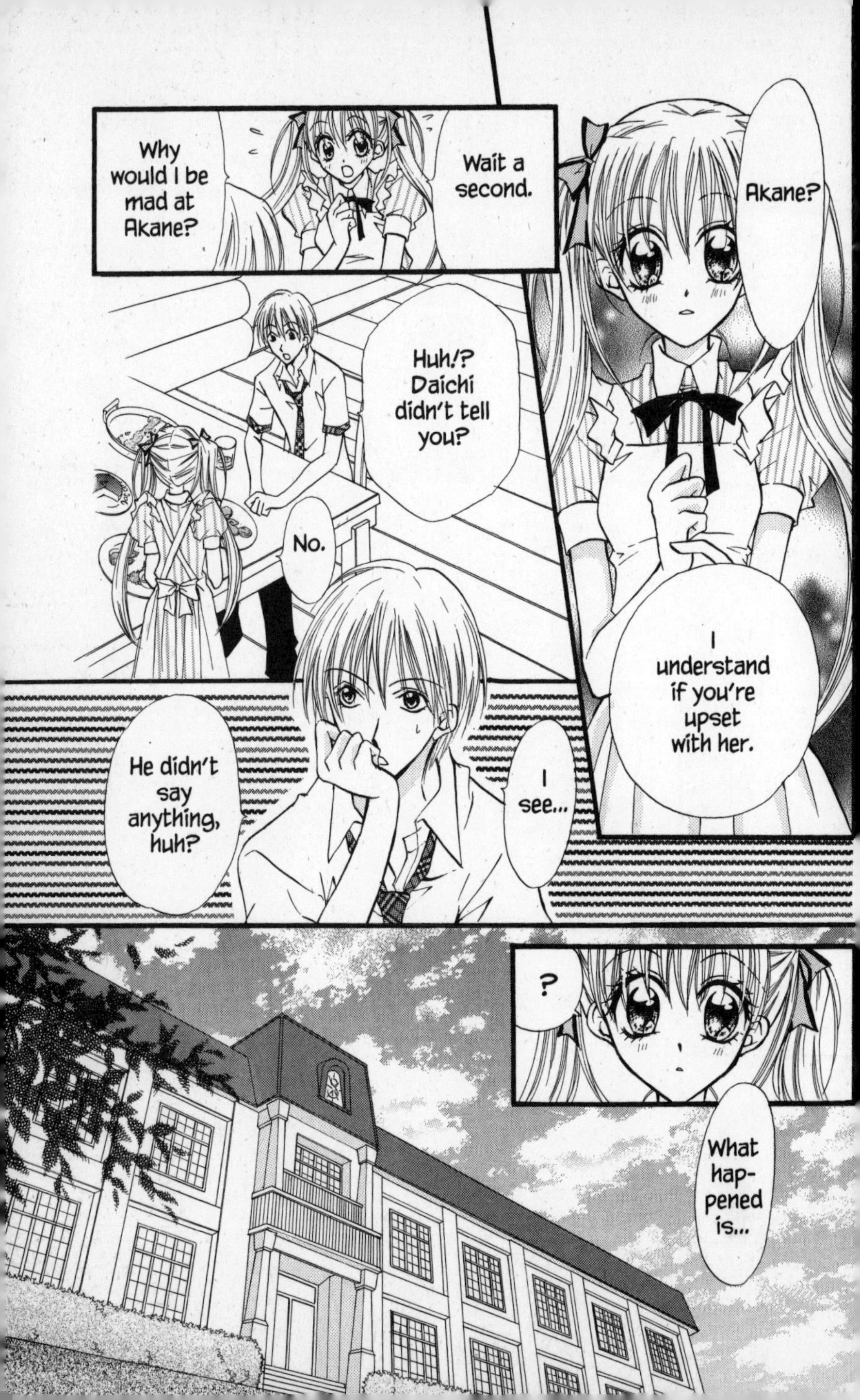
Akane?
I understand if you're upset with her.
Wait a second.
Why would I be mad at Akane?
Huh!? Daichi didn't tell you?
No.
I see...
He didn't say anything, huh?
?
What hap-pened is...

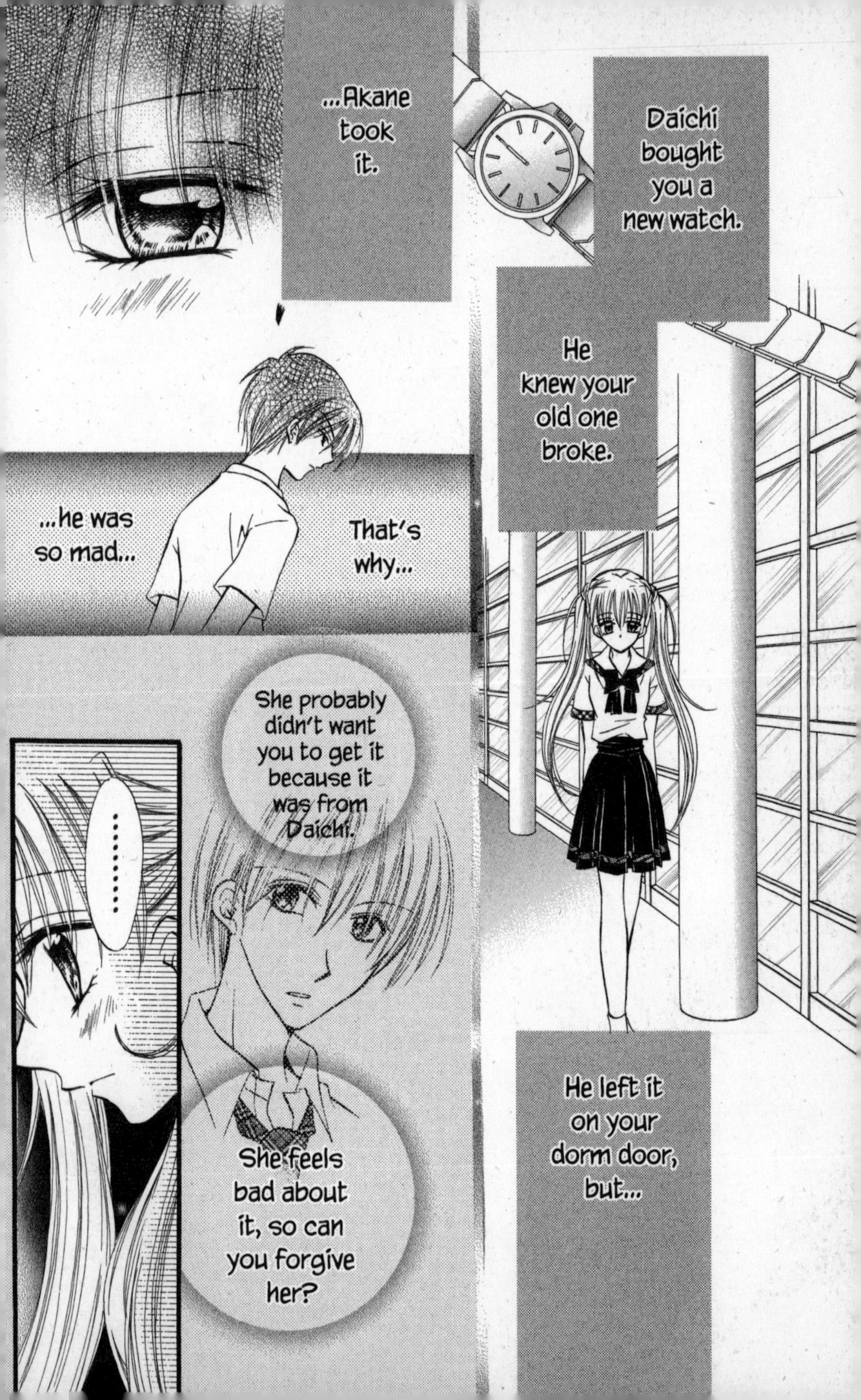
Daichi bought you a new watch.
He knew your old one broke.
He left it on your dorm door, but...
...Akane took it.
That's why...
...he was so mad...
She probably didn't want you to get it because it was from Daichi.
......
She feels bad about it, so can you forgive her?

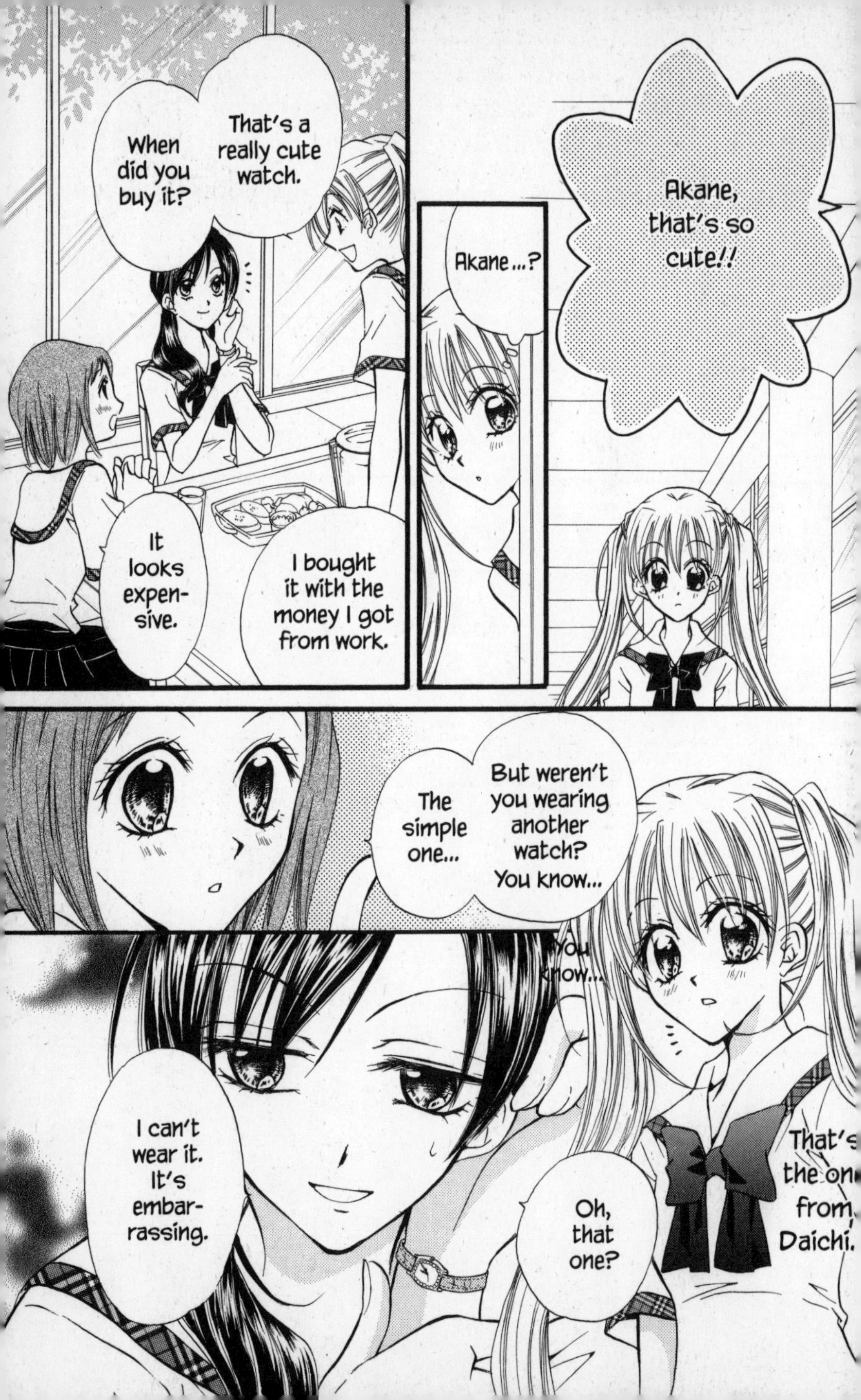
Akane, that's so cute!!
Akane...?
That's a really cute watch.
When did you buy it?
I bought it with the money I got from work.
It looks expensive.
But weren't you wearing another watch? You know...
The simple one...
You know...
That's the one from Daichi.
Oh, that one?
I can't wear it. It's embarrassing.

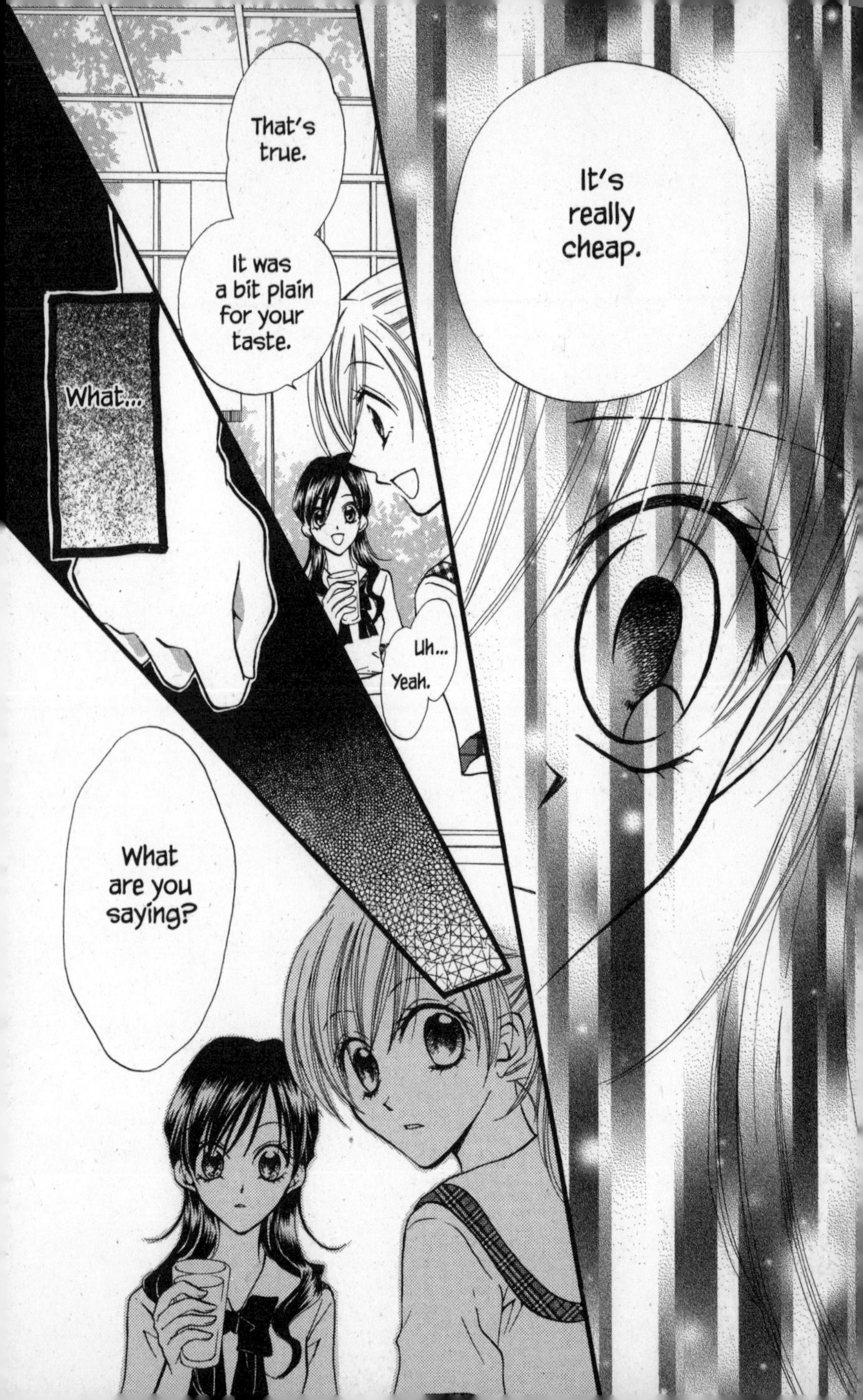
That's true.
It was a bit plain for your taste.
Uh... Yeah.
It's really cheap.
What...
What are you saying?

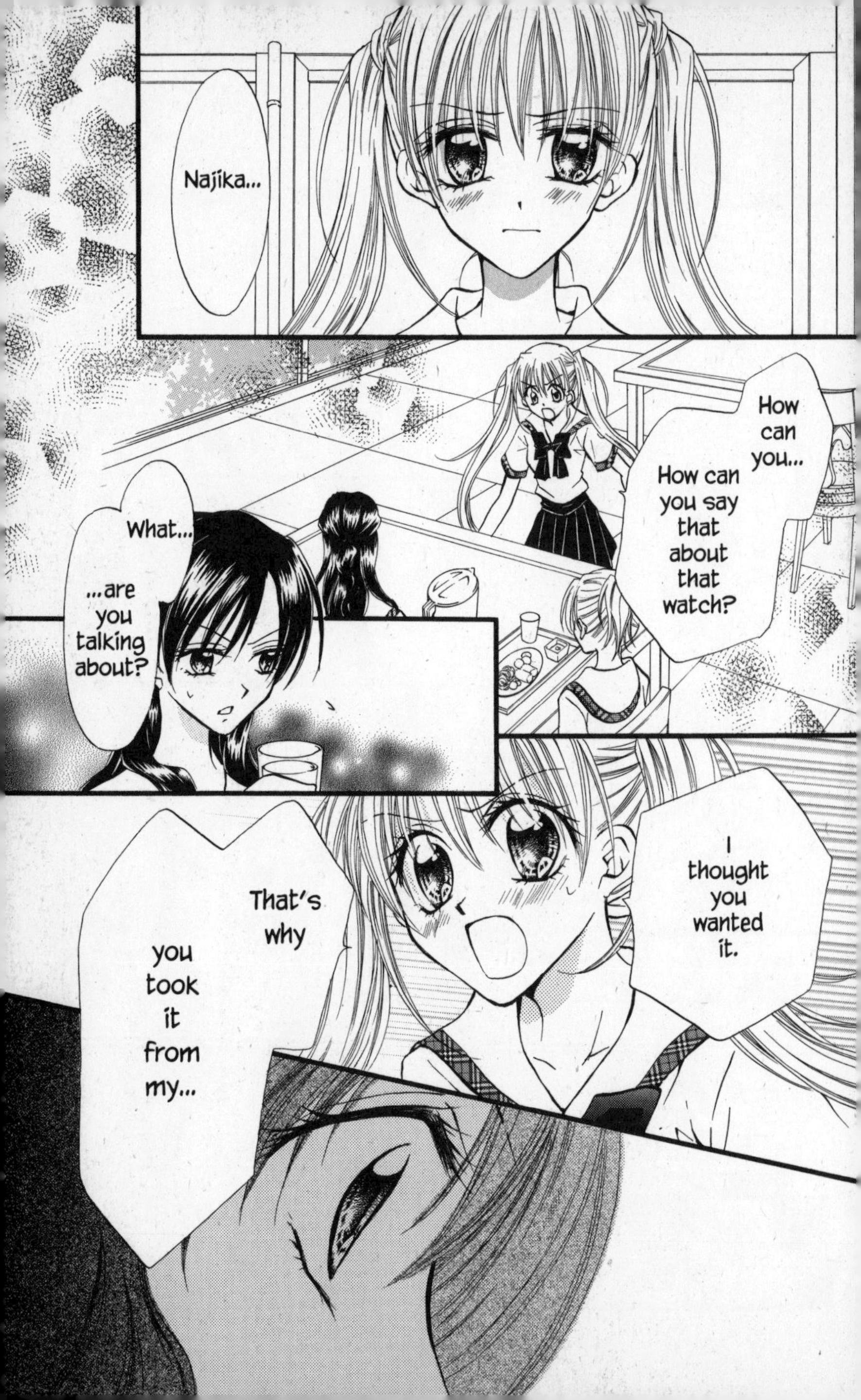
Najika...
How can you...
How can you say that about that watch?
What...
...are you talking about?
I thought you wanted it.
That's why you took it from my...

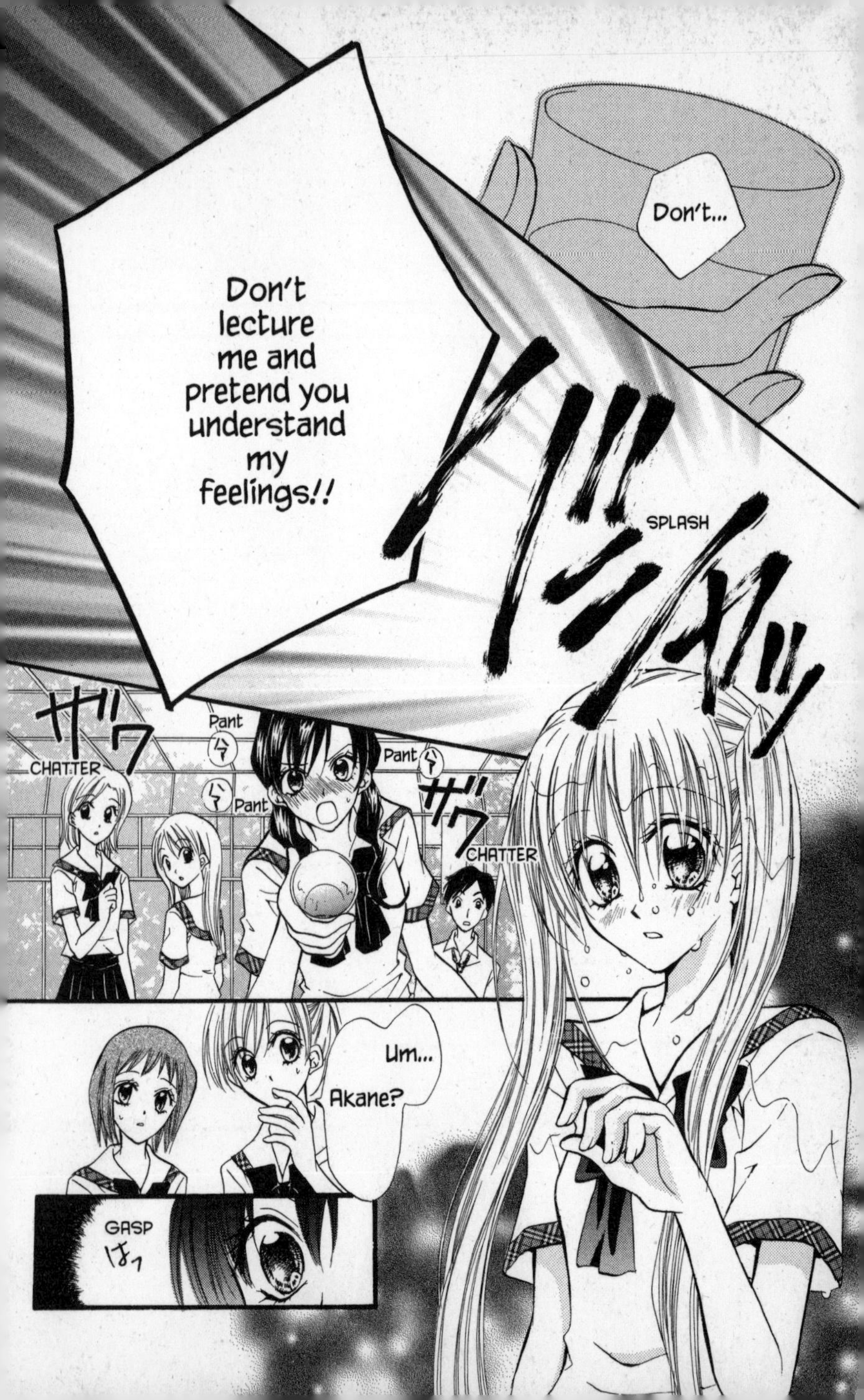
Don't...
Don't lecture me and pretend you understand my feelings!!
SPLASH
ザワ
CHATTER
Pant
Pant
Pant
ザワ
CHATTER
Um...
Akane?
GASP
はっ

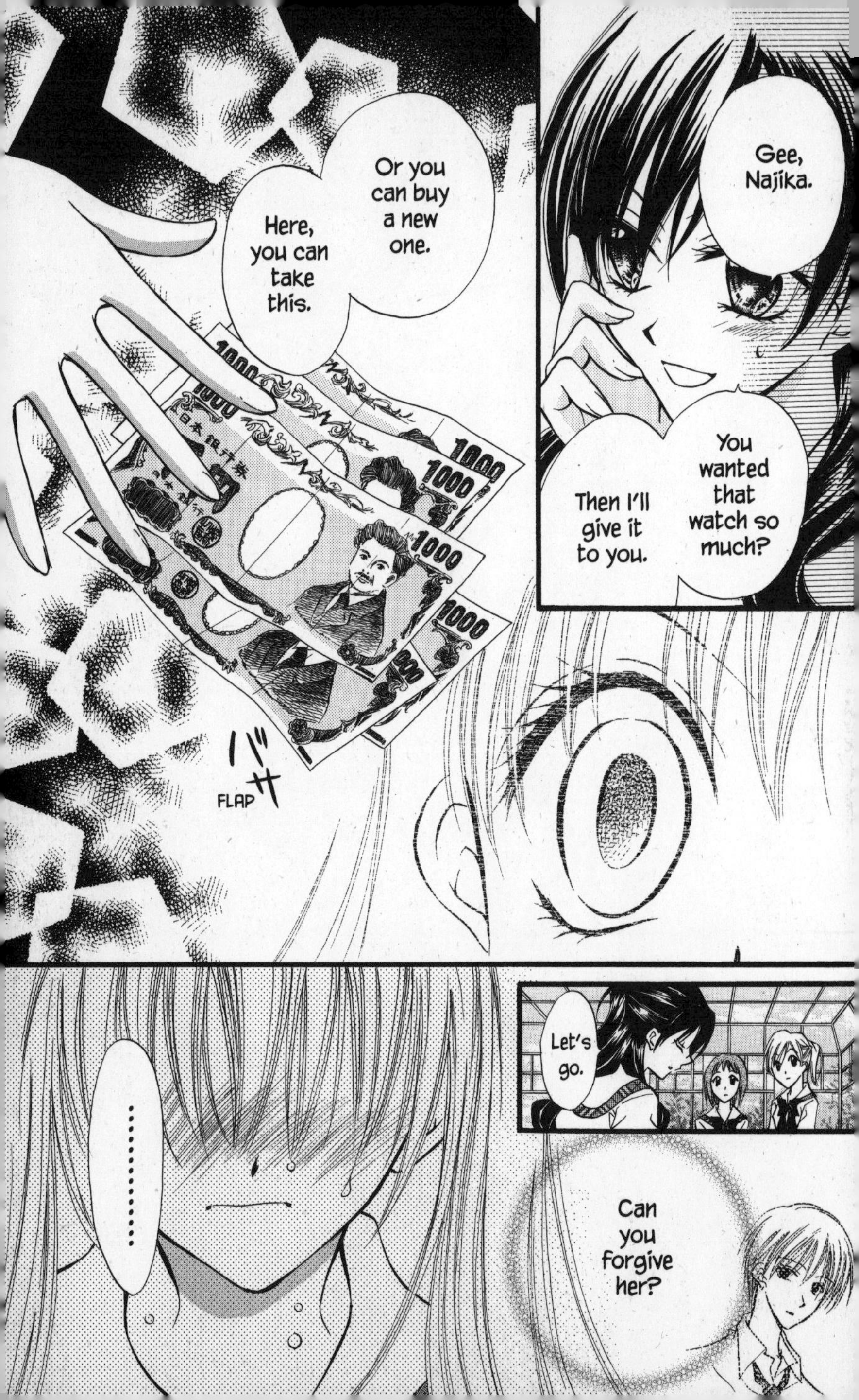

Gee, Najika.
You wanted that watch so much?
Then I'll give it to you.
Or you can buy a new one.
Here, you can take this.
バサ
FLAP
Let's go.
Can you forgive her?
......

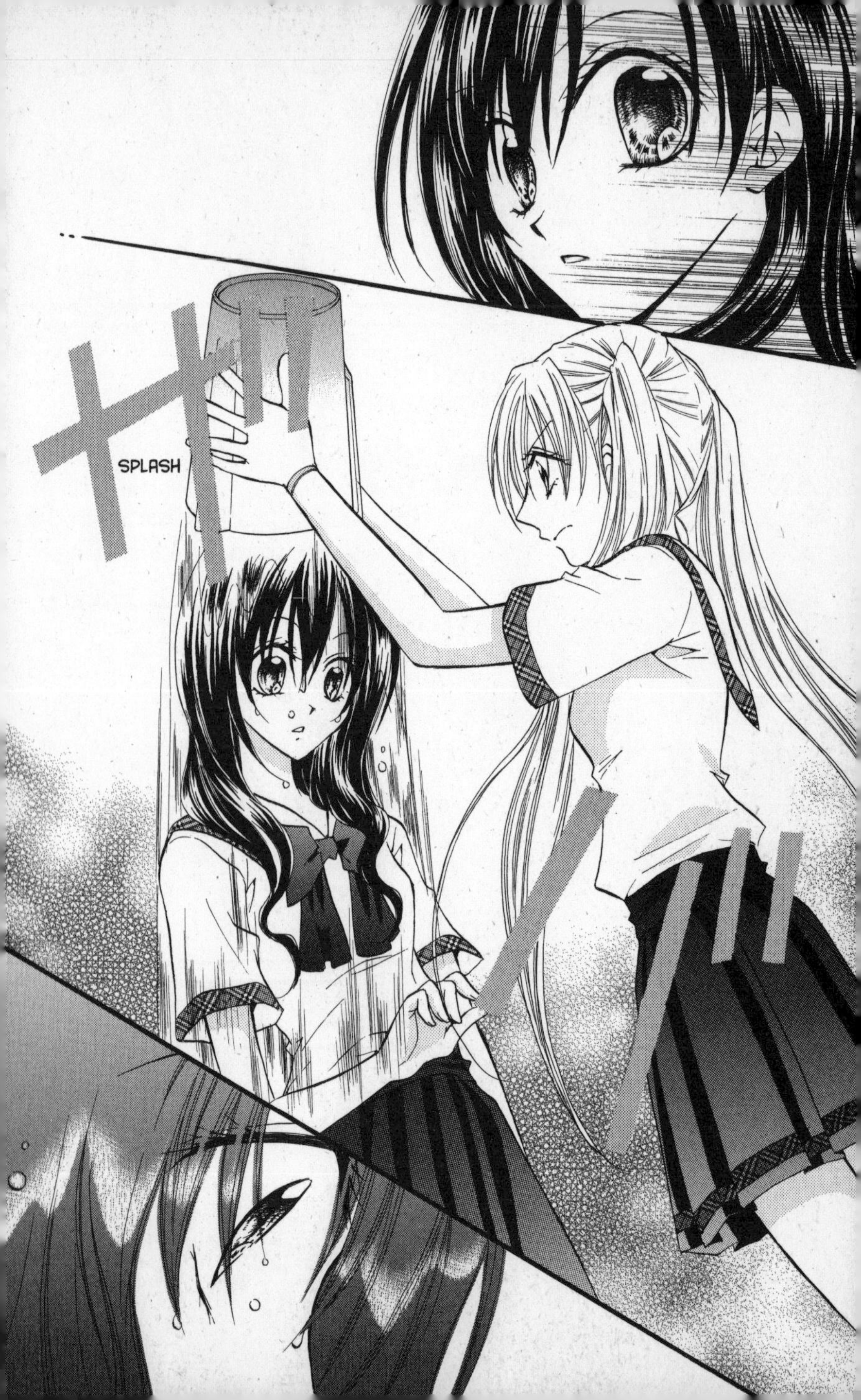

SPLASH

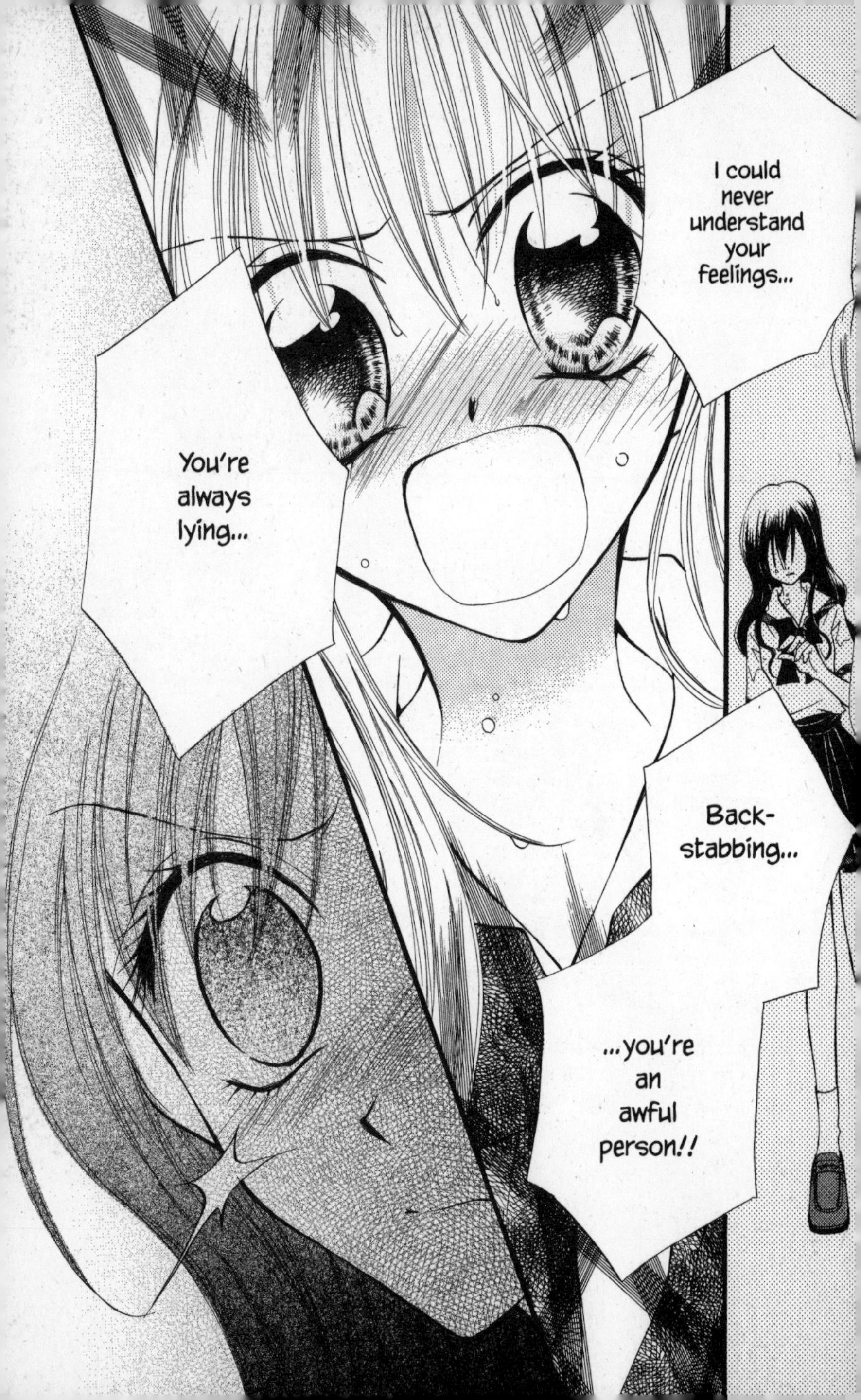
I could never understand your feelings...
You're always lying...
Back-stabbing...
...you're an awful person!!

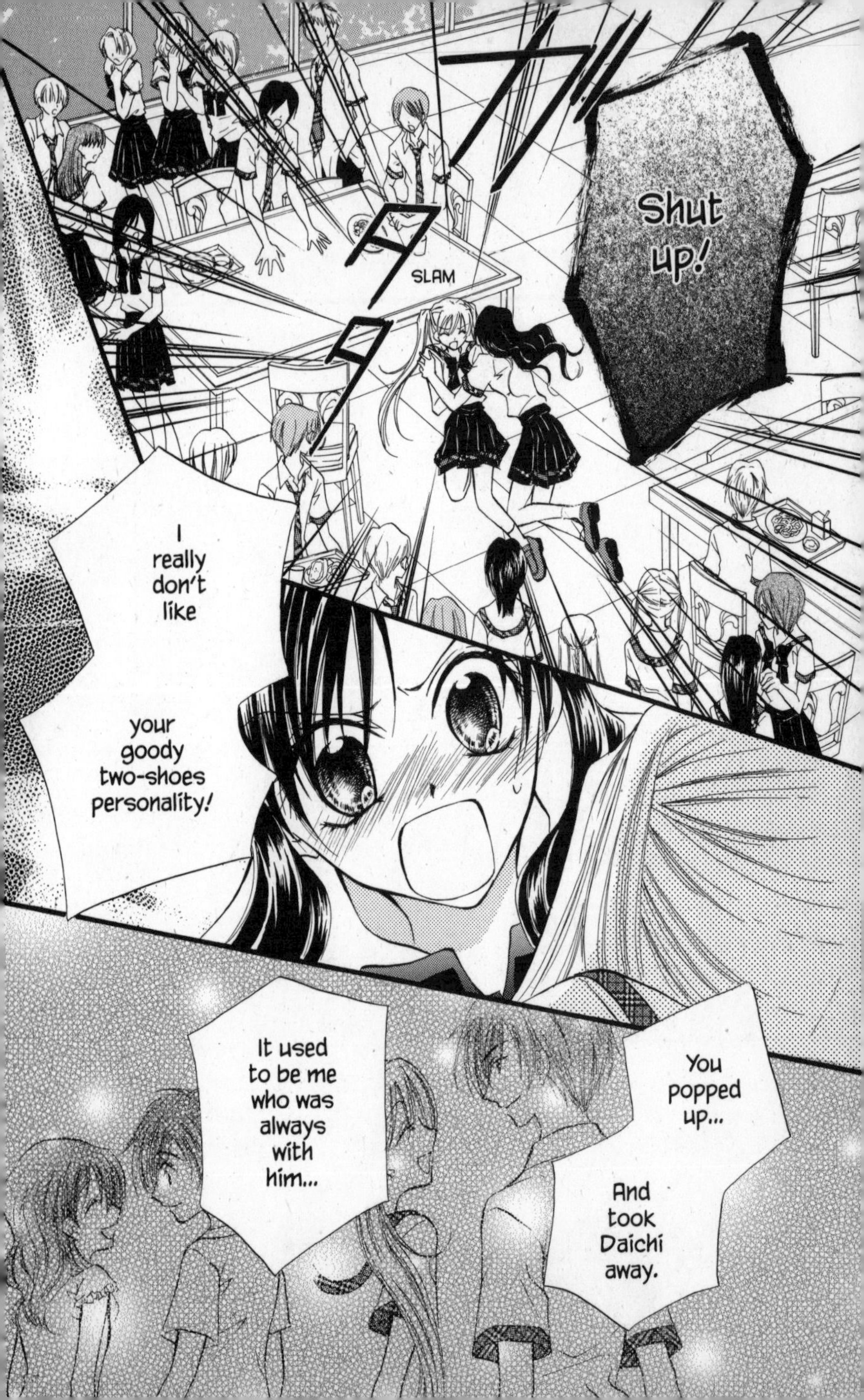
Shut up!
SLAM
I really don't like
your goody two-shoes personality!
You popped up...
And took Daichi away.
It used to be me who was always with him...

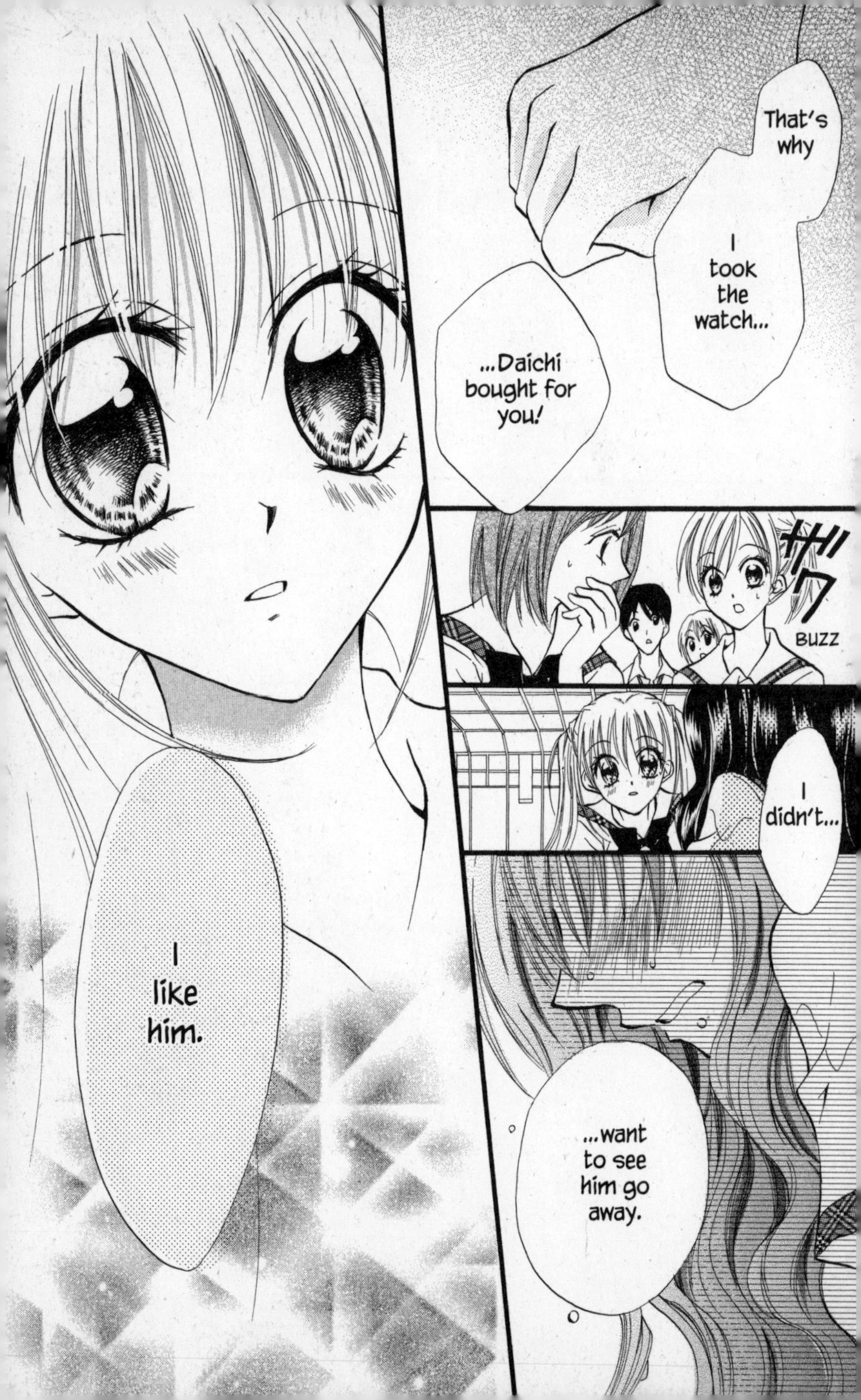

That's why
I took the watch...
...Daichi bought for you!
ザワ
BUZZ
I didn't...
...want to see him go away.
I like him.

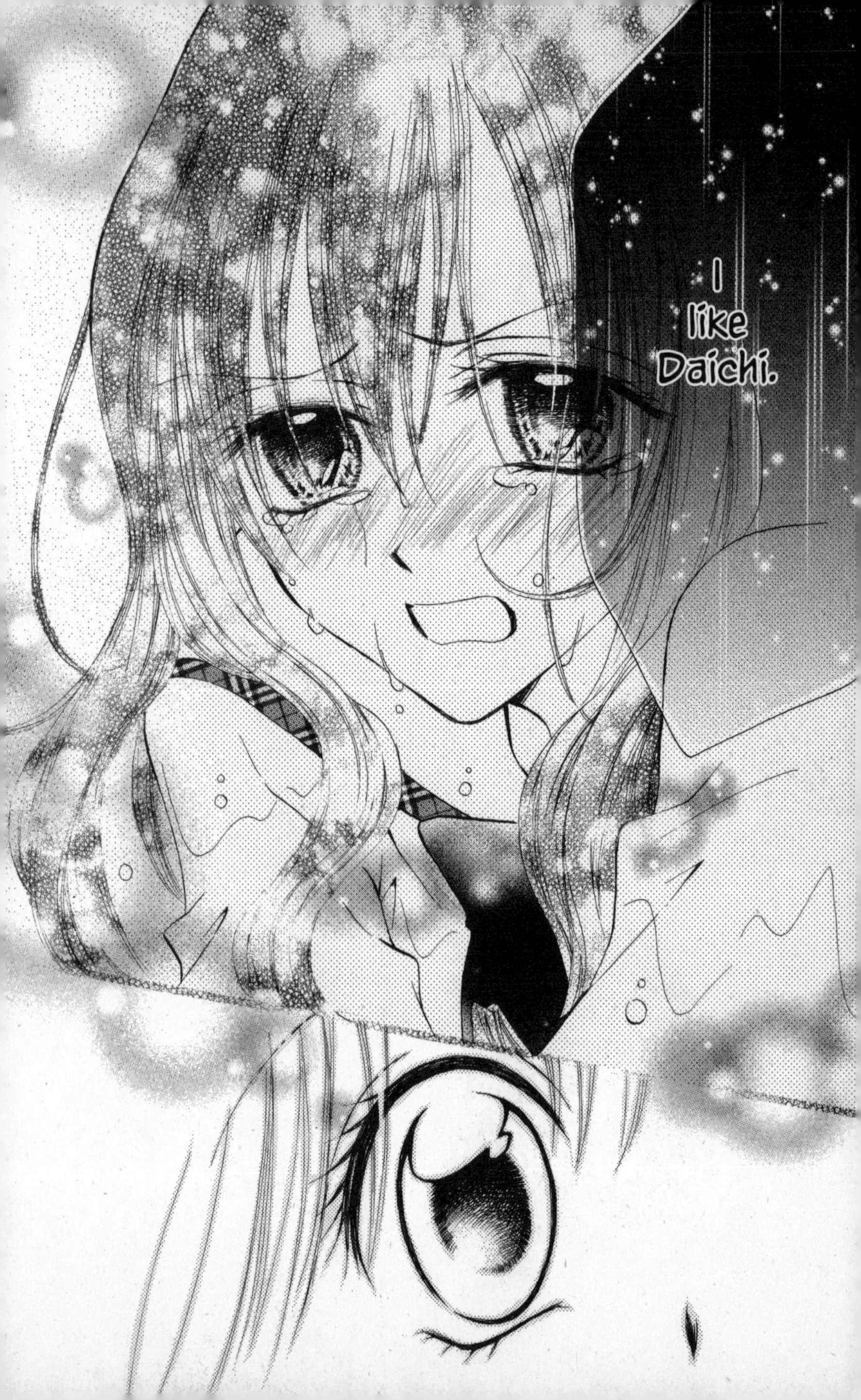
I like Daichi.

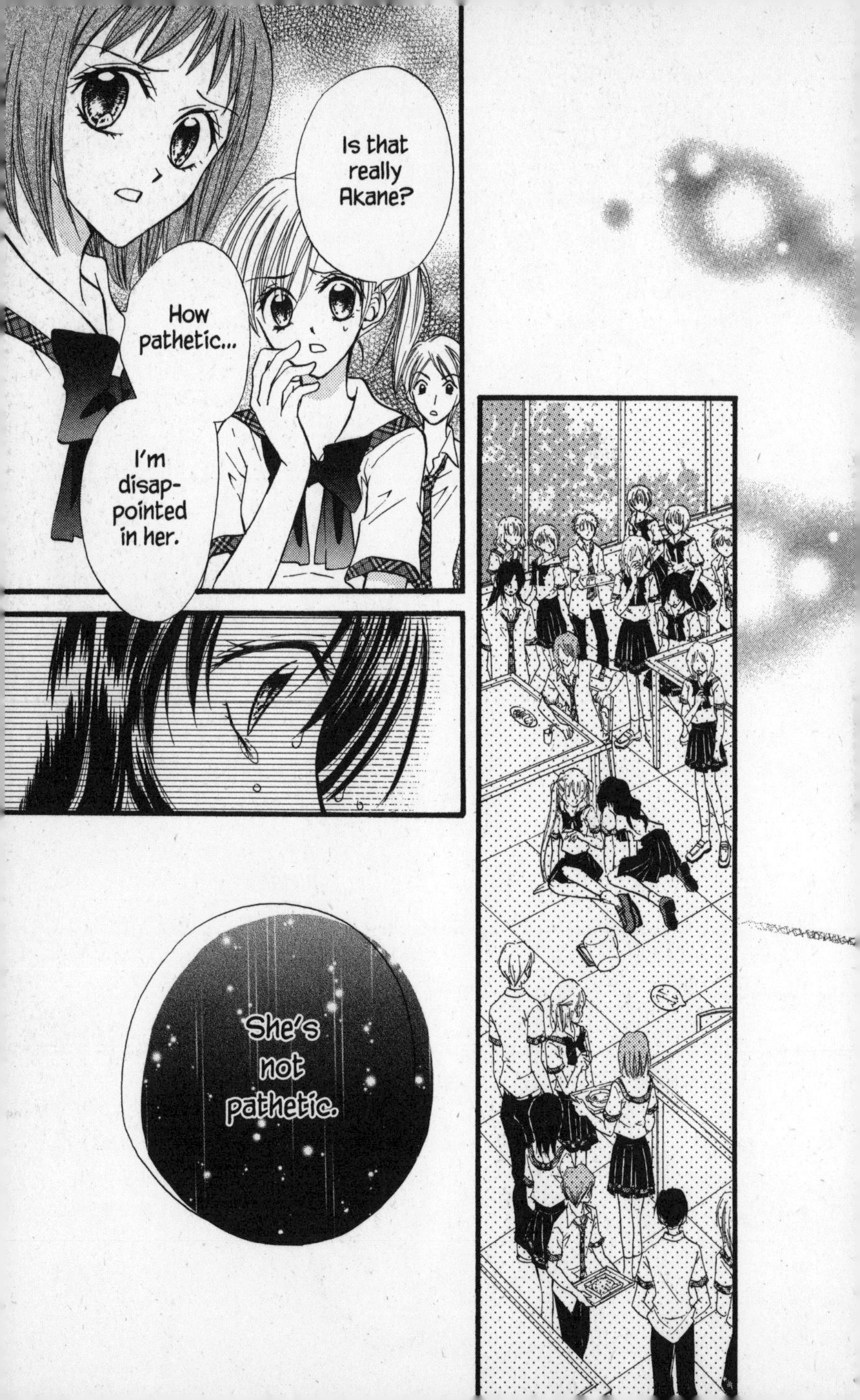
Is that really Akane?
How pathetic...
I'm disap- pointed in her.
She's not pathetic.

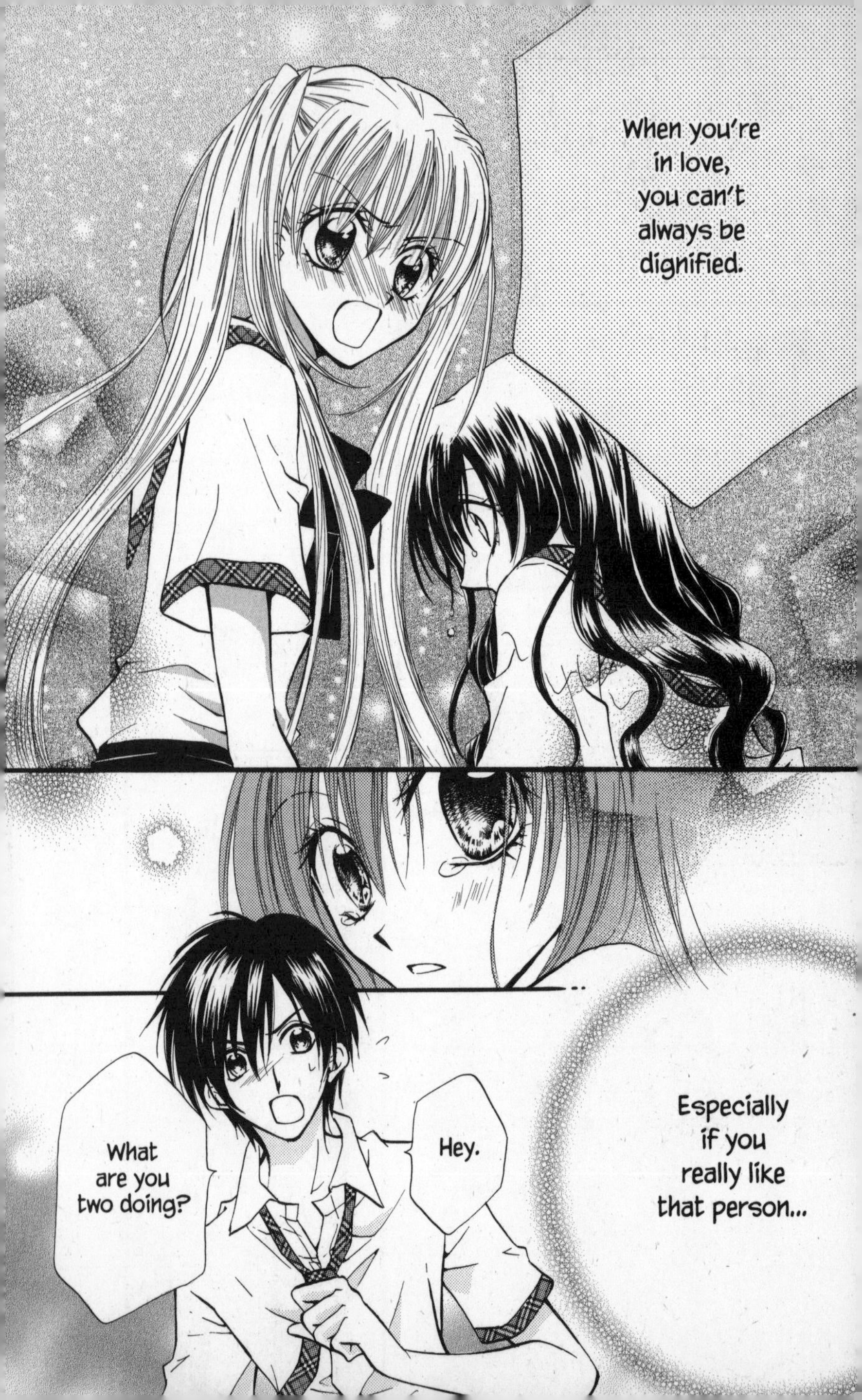
When you're in love, you can't always be dignified.
Especially if you really like that person...
Hey.
What are you two doing?

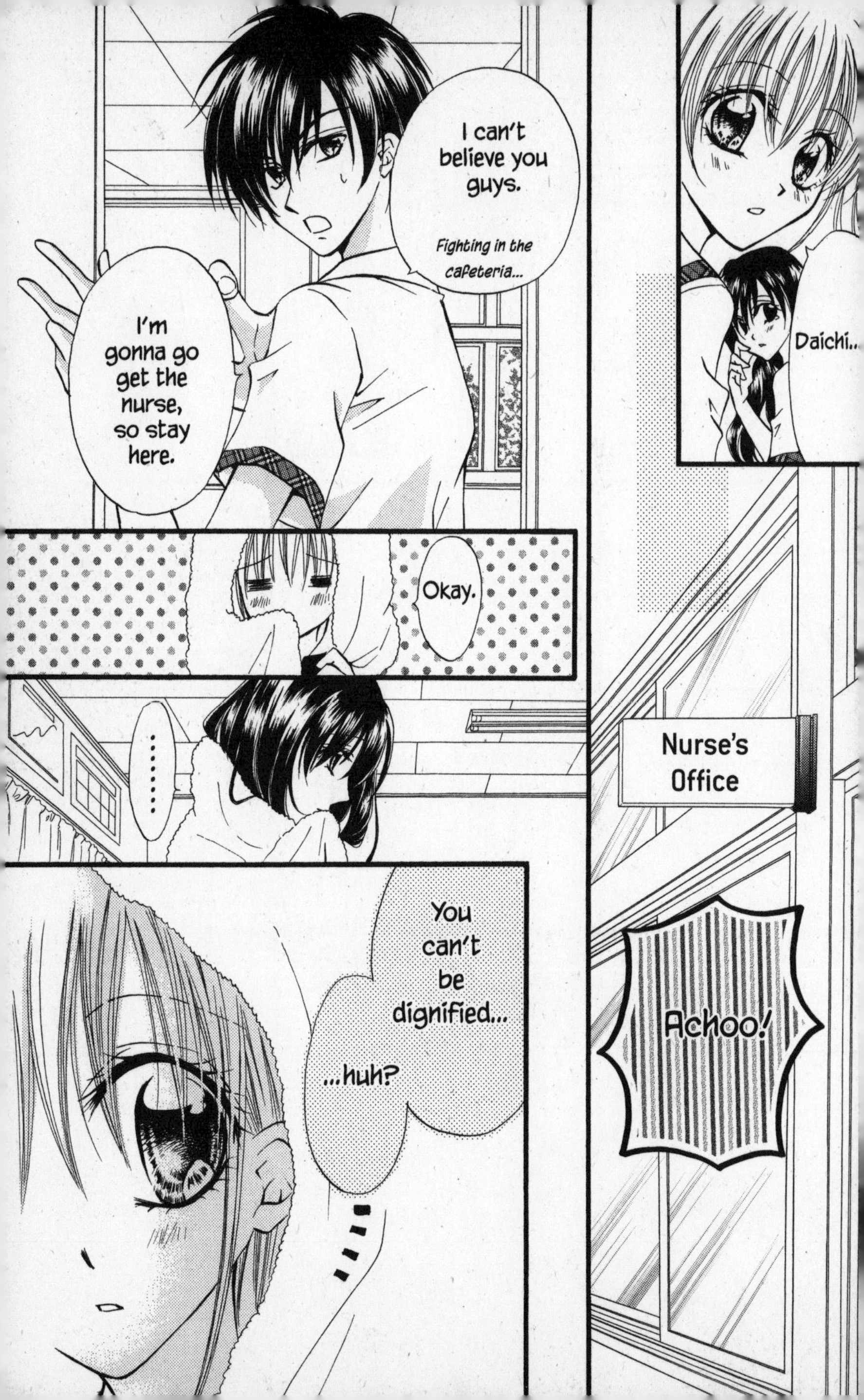
Daichi...
Nurse's Office
Achoo!
I can't believe you guys.
Fighting in the cafeteria...
I'm gonna go get the nurse, so stay here.
Okay.
......
You can't be dignified...
...huh?

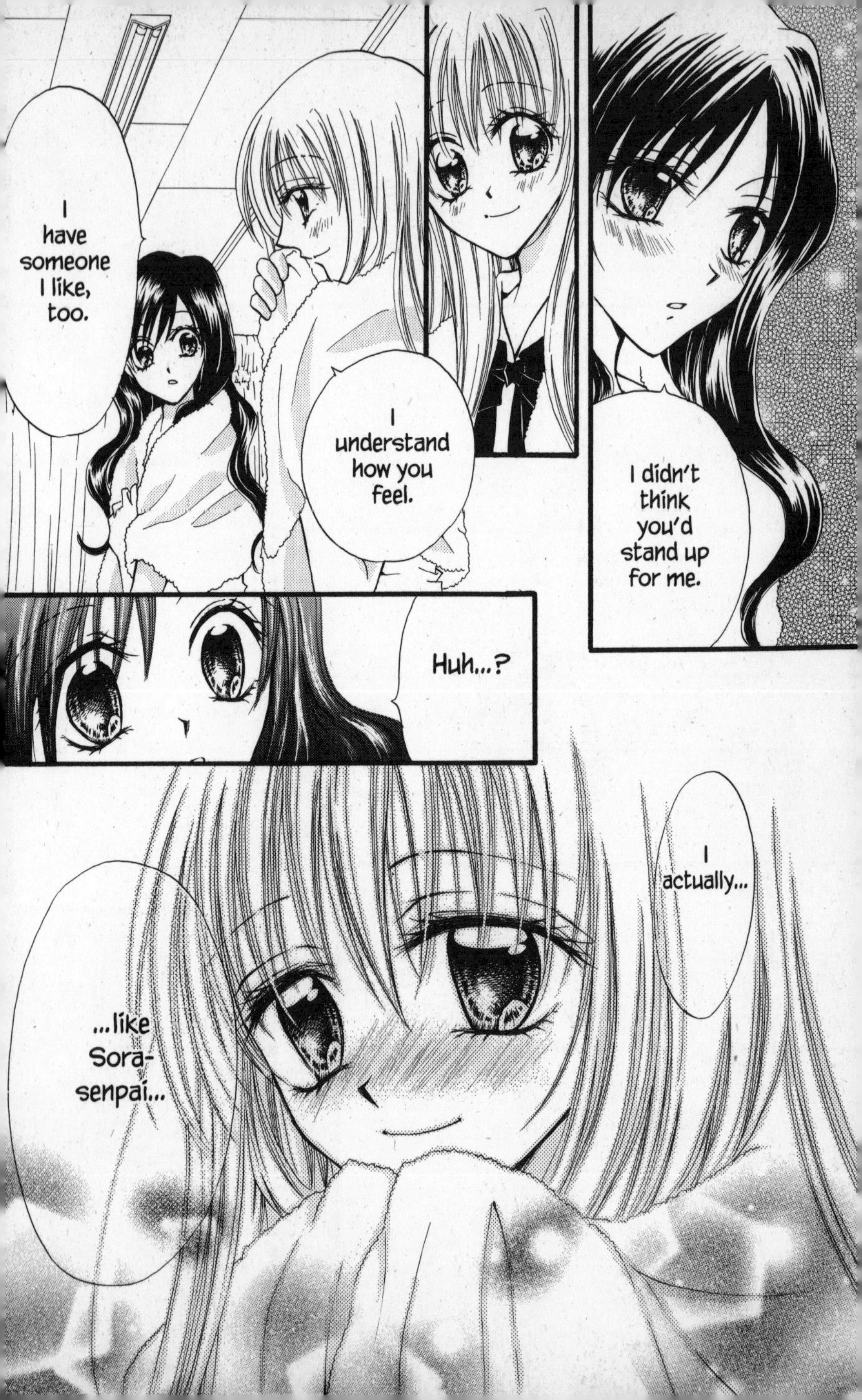
I didn't think you'd stand up for me.
I understand how you feel.
I have someone I like, too.
Huh...?
I actually...
...like Sora-senpai...

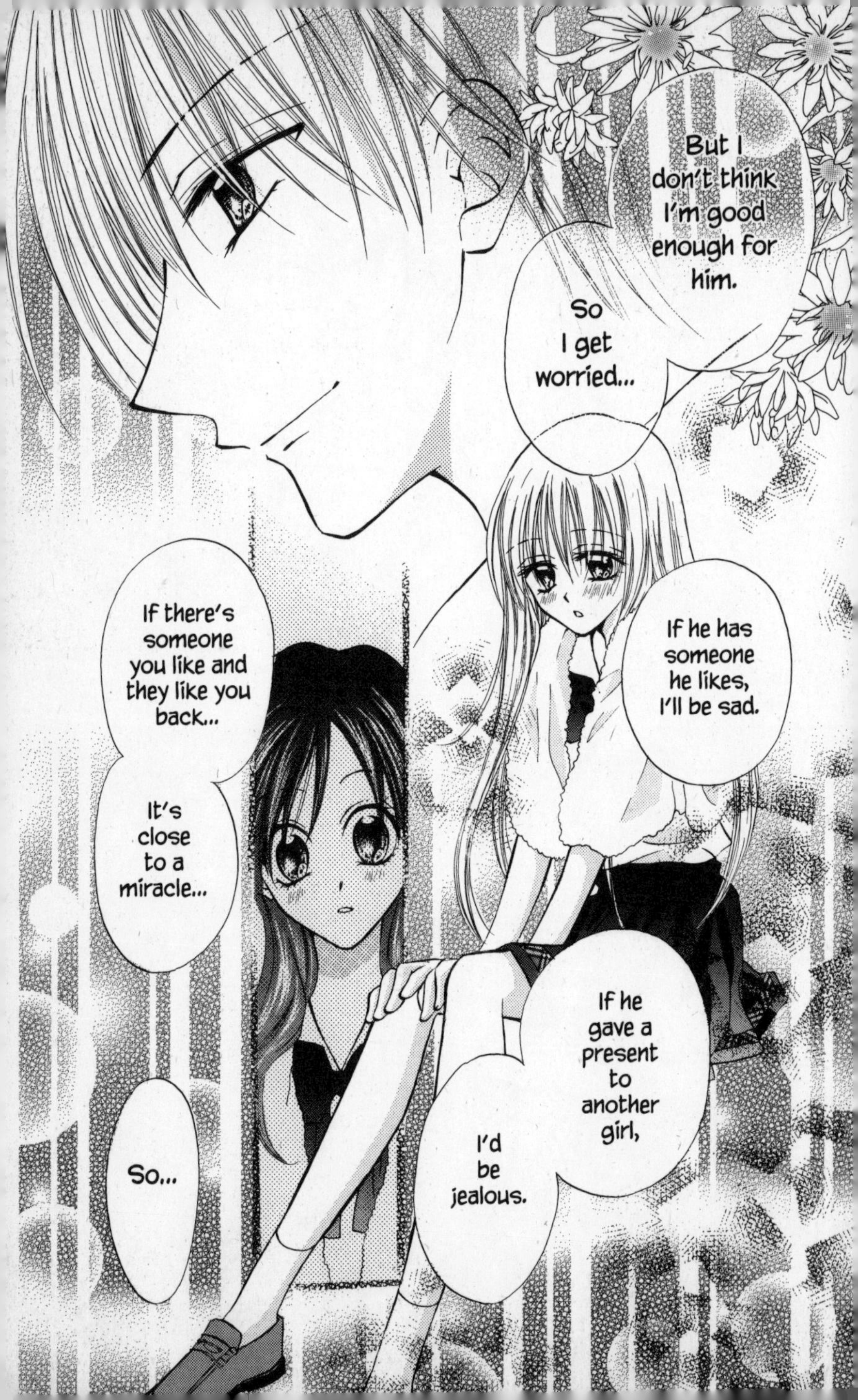
But I don't think I'm good enough for him.
So I get worried...
If he has someone he likes, I'll be sad.
If he gave a present to another girl,
I'd be jealous.
If there's someone you like and they like you back...
It's close to a miracle...
So...

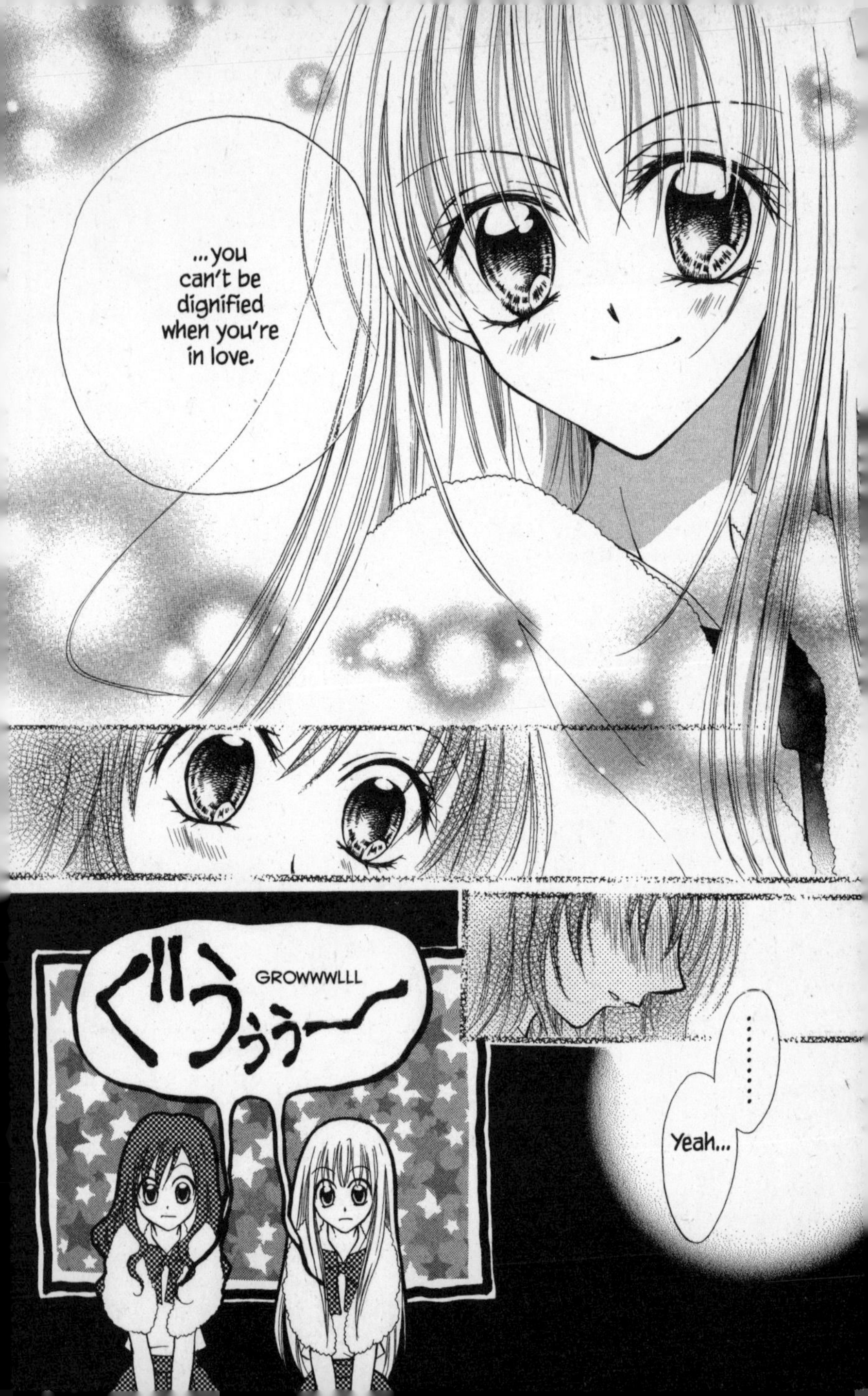
...you can't be dignified when you're in love.
......
Yeah...
くうううー
GROWWWLLL

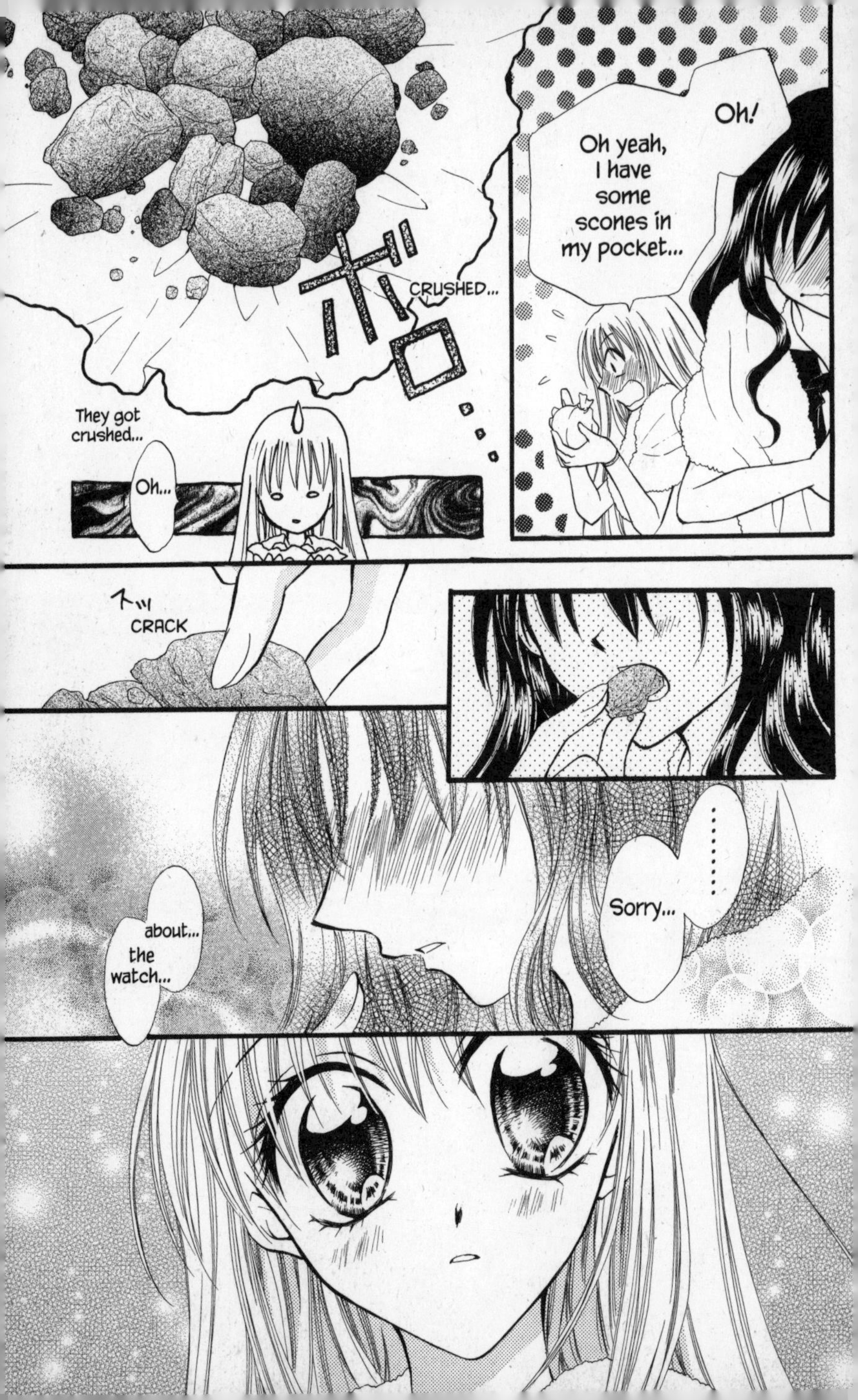
Oh!
Oh yeah, I have some scones in my pocket...
ボロ
CRUSHED...
They got crushed...
Oh...
スッ
CRACK
......
Sorry...
about... the watch...

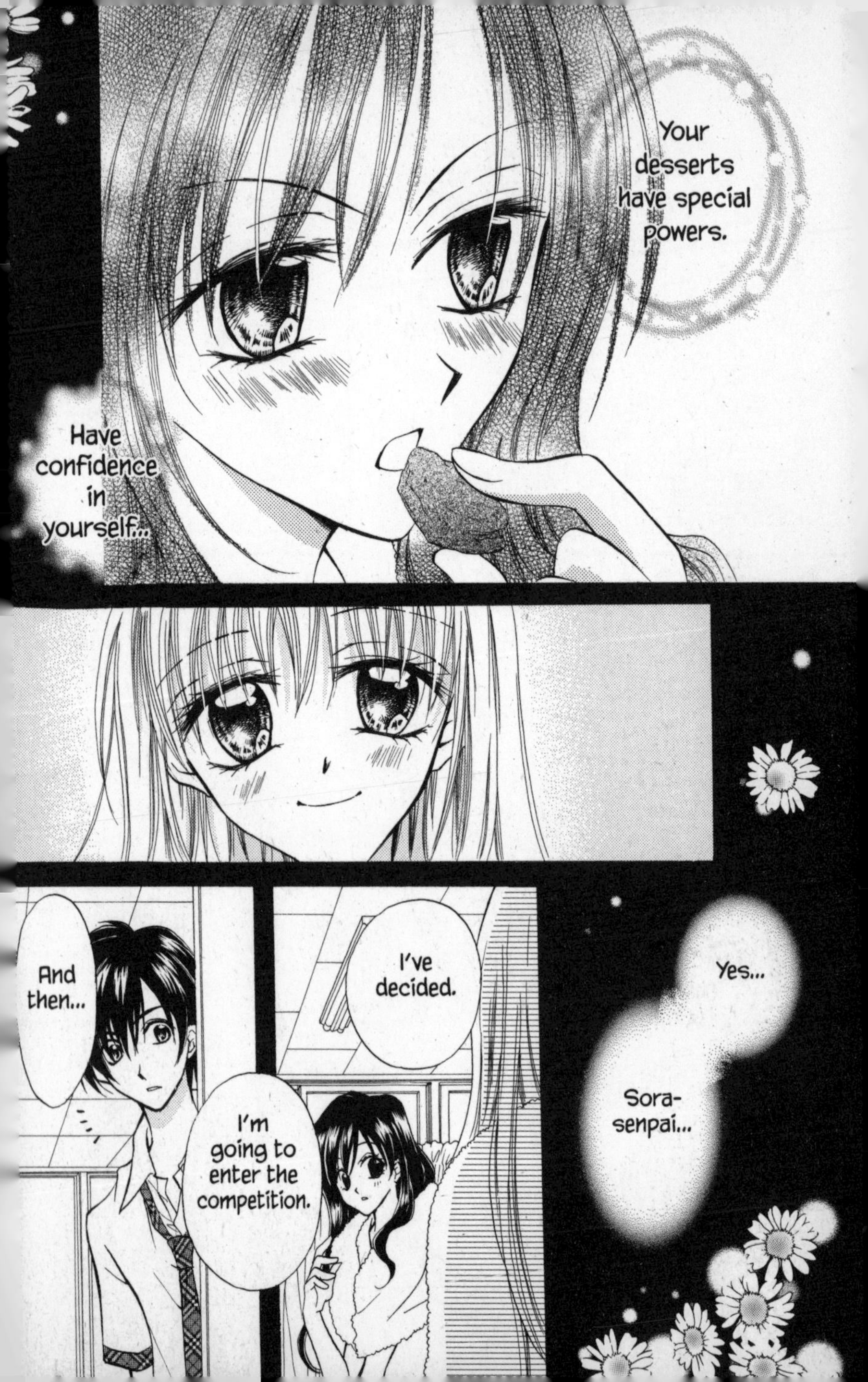
Your desserts have special powers.
Have confidence in yourself...
Yes...
Sora-senpai...
I've decided.
I'm going to enter the competition.
And then...

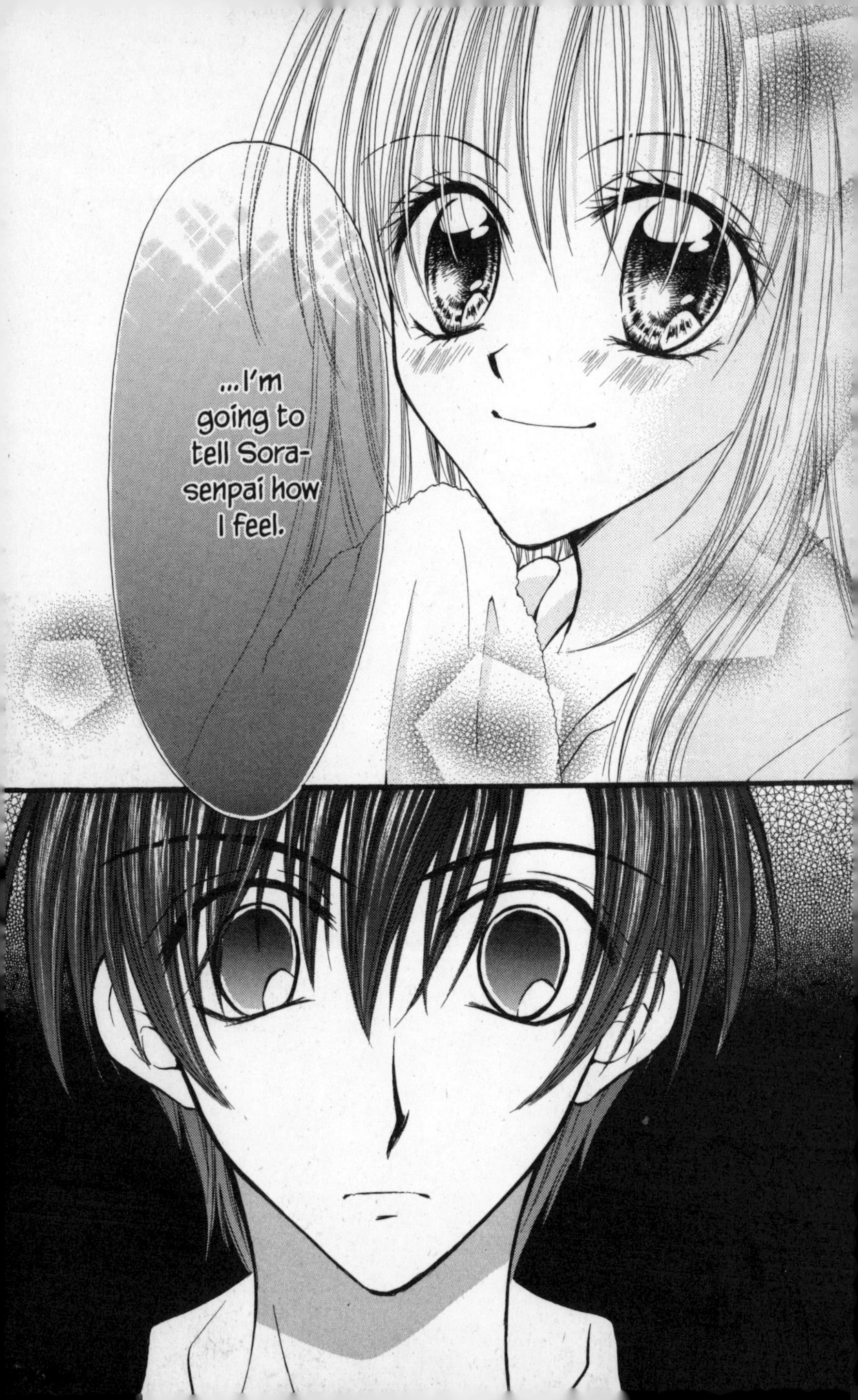
...I'm going to tell Sora-senpai how I feel.

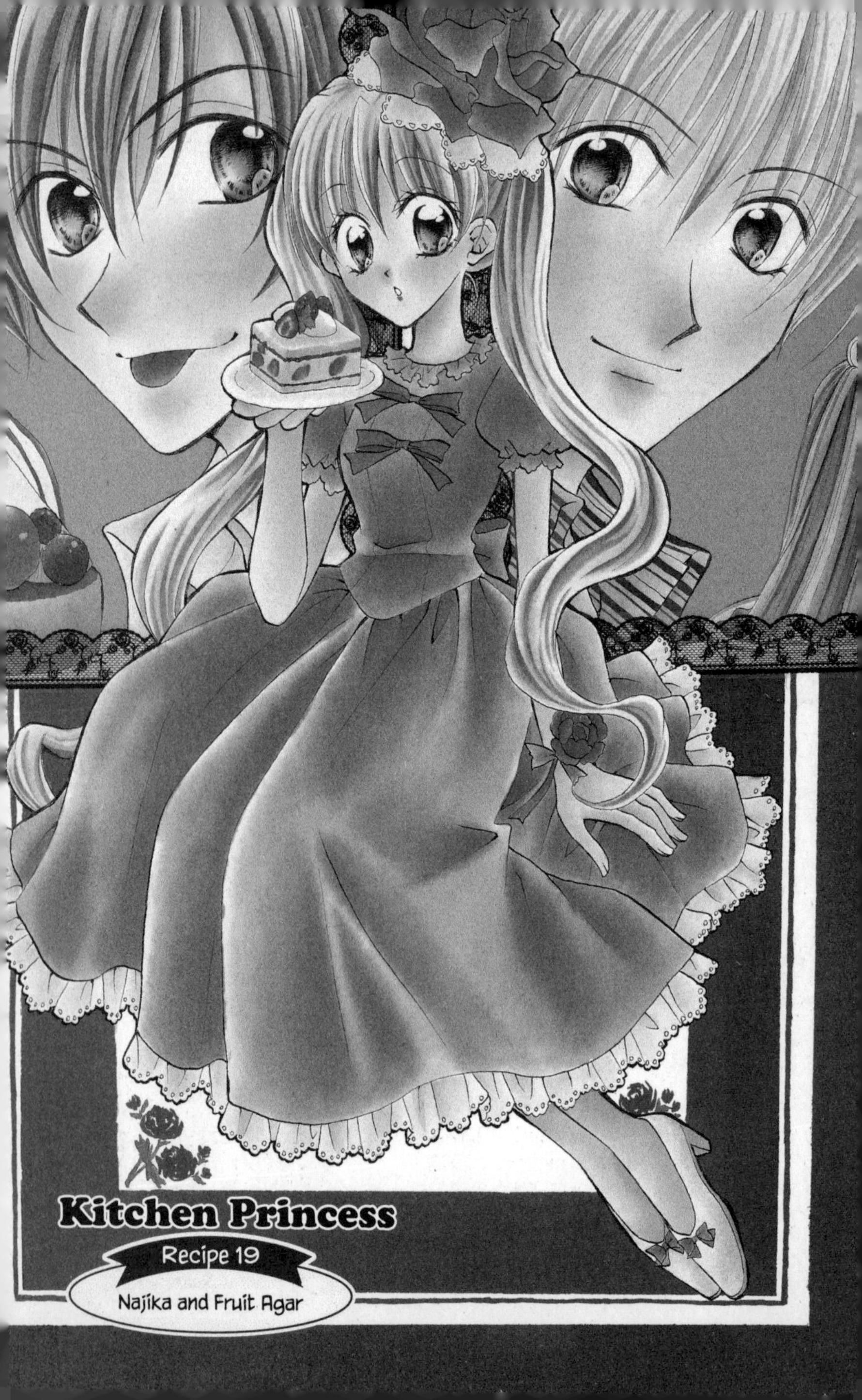
Kitchen Princess
Recipe 19
Najika and Fruit Agar

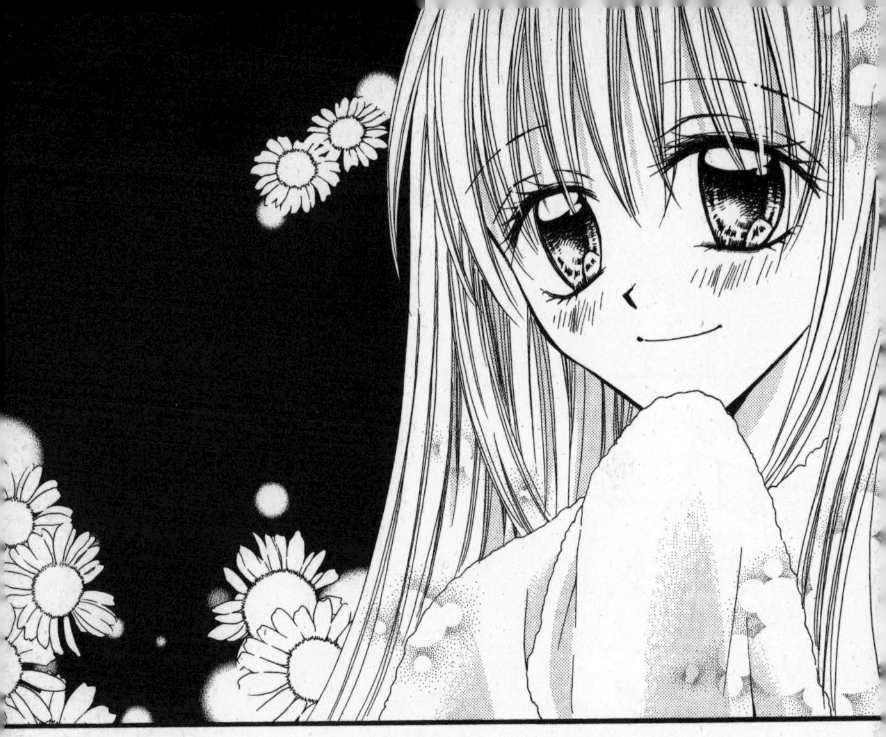

About Recipe 19's Splash Page

I wanted to have Najika dress up a little like a celebrity. You can't tell in the comics, but I wanted to use a deep red for the background, so I chose pink for Najika's dress to match it... Now that I think about it, there are many images of Daichi sticking out his tongue. Whenever I have him next to Sora, it just turns out that way.

About the Special's Splash Page

This splash page is probably second in my list of favorites in *Kitchen Princess*. The background, Najika's hair, and the cake all blend nicely because of the pink. I was happy the printing came out looking so pretty, too! The pastel polka dots (in the ribbon) also came out well. ♫

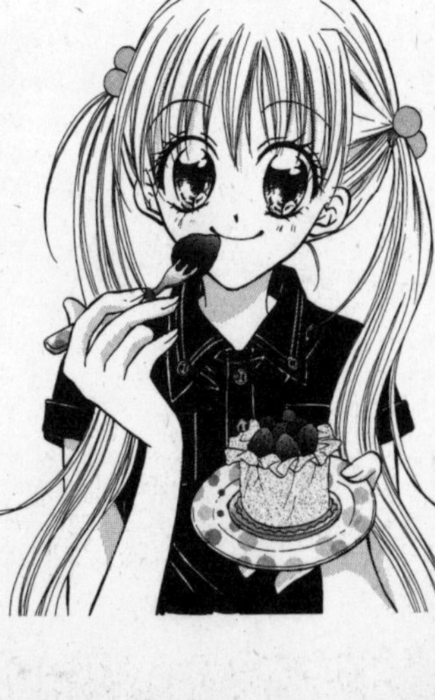

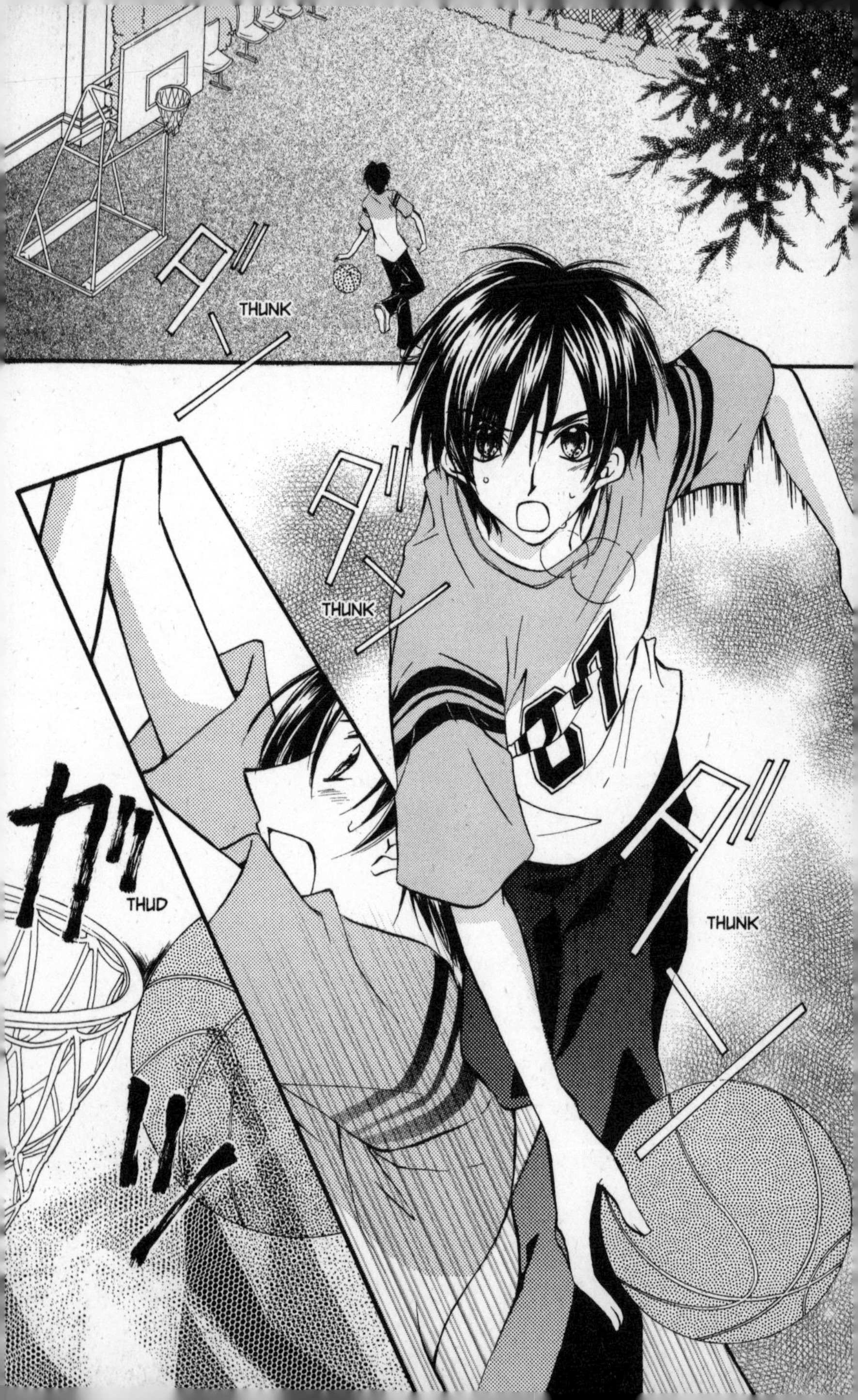
THUNK
THUNK
THUNK
THUD

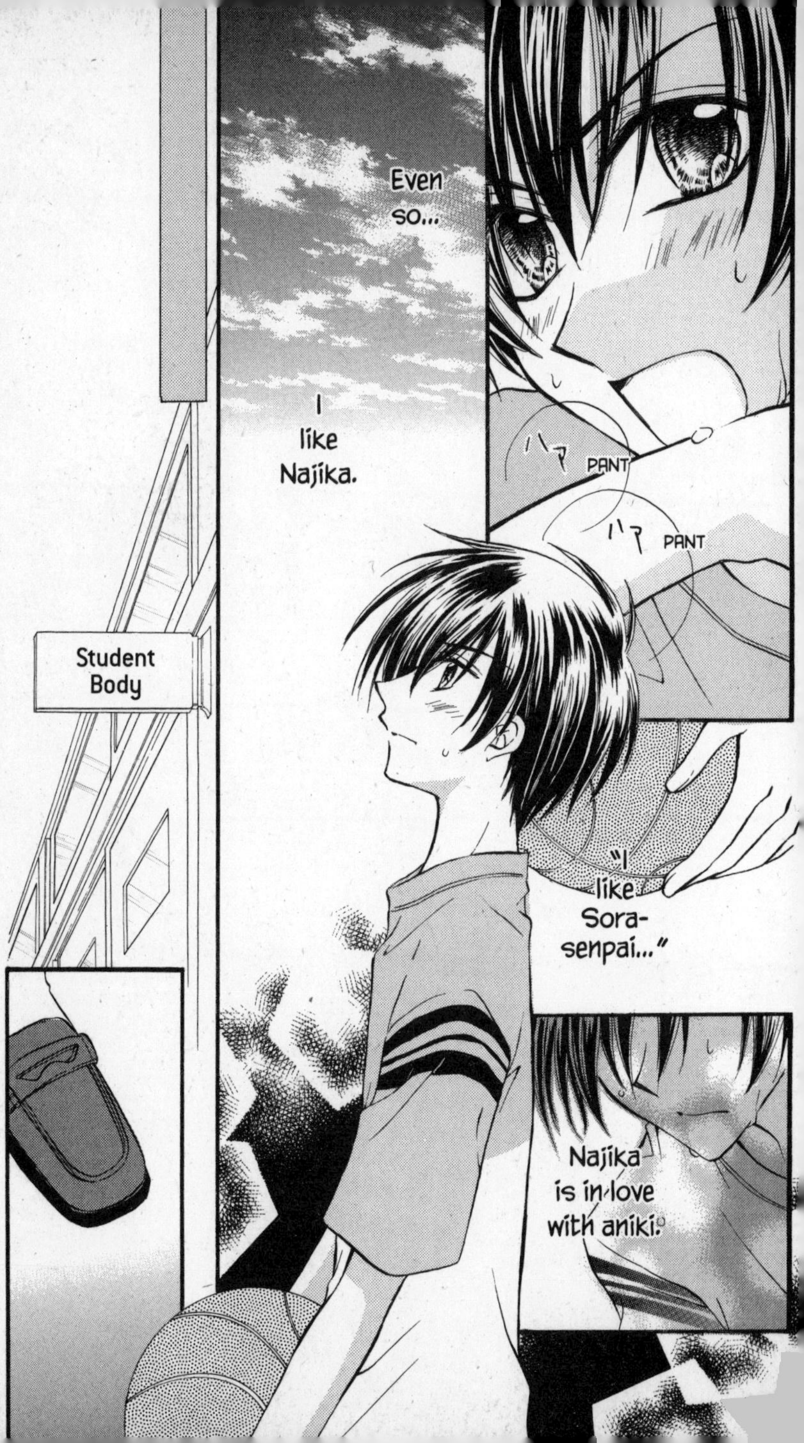
ハァ PANT
ハァ PANT
"I like Sora-senpai..."
Najika is in love with aniki.
Even so...
I like Najika.
Student Body

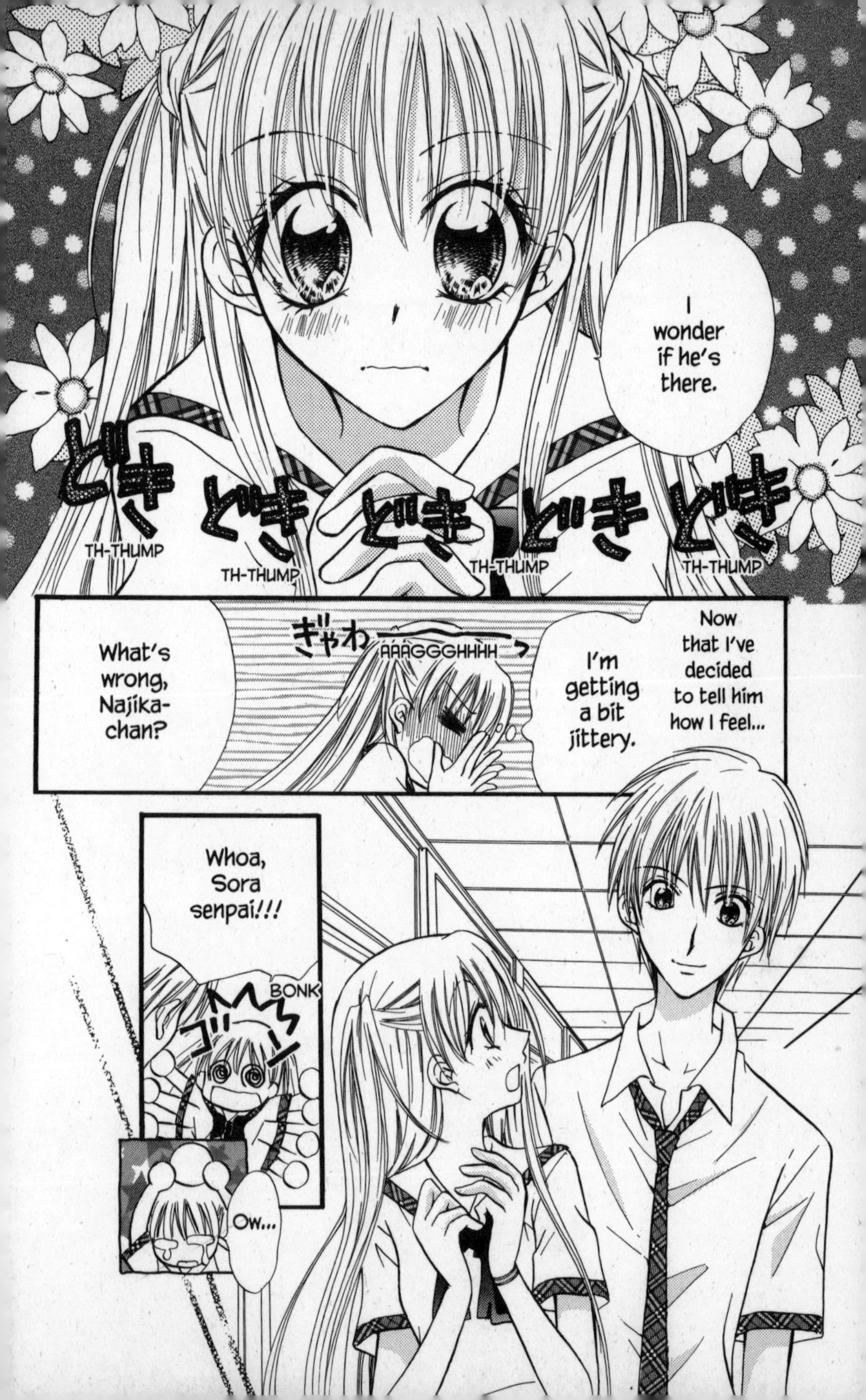
I wonder if he's there.
どきどきどきどきどき
TH-THUMP
TH-THUMP
TH-THUMP
TH-THUMP
Now that I've decided to tell him how I feel...
I'm getting a bit jittery.
ぎゃわー
AAAGGGHHHH
What's wrong, Najika-chan?
Whoa, Sora senpai!!!
ゴン
BONK
Ow...

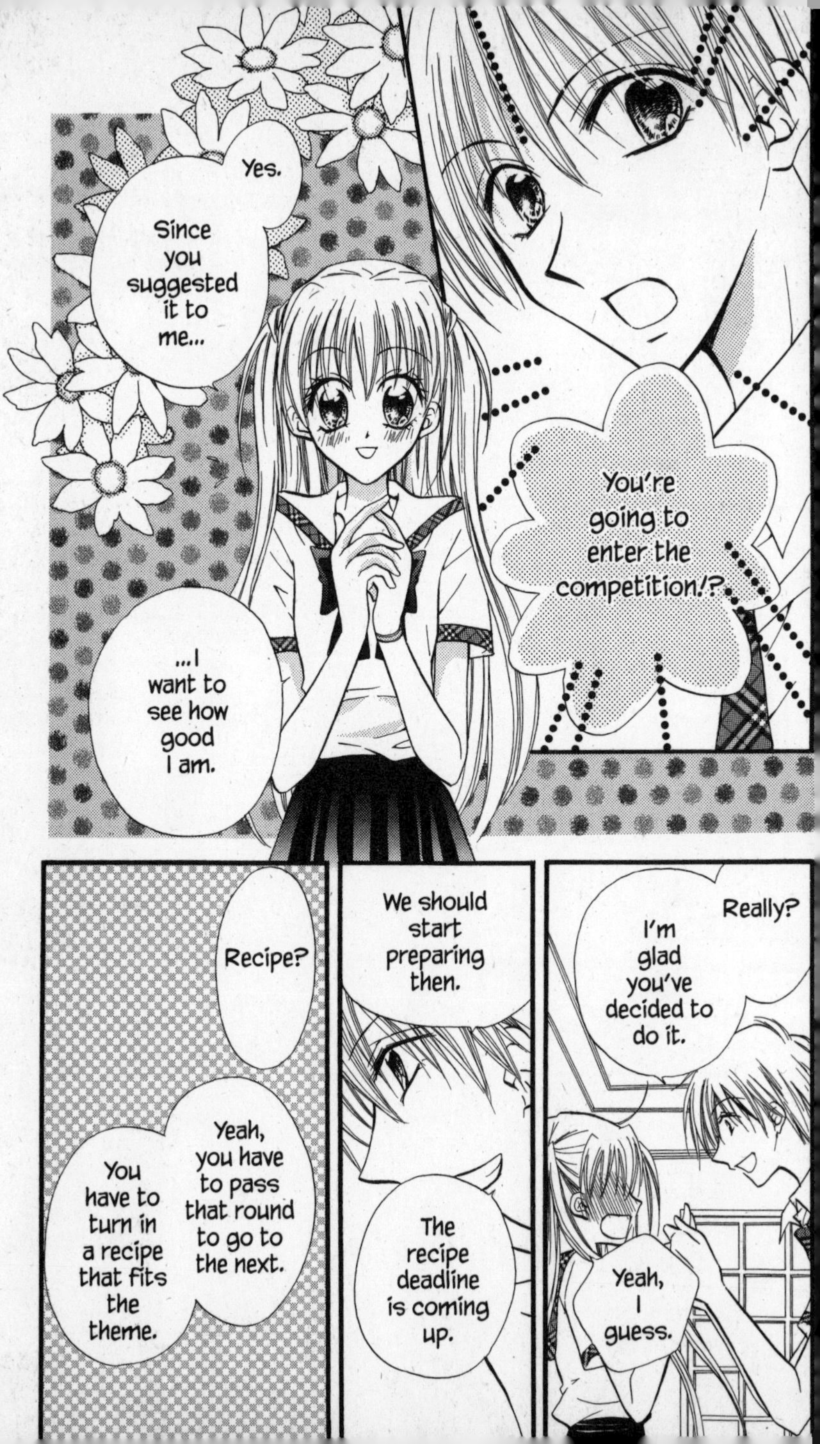
You're going to enter the competition!?
Yes.
Since you suggested it to me...
...I want to see how good I am.
Really?
I'm glad you've decided to do it.
Yeah, I guess.
We should start preparing then.
The recipe deadline is coming up.
Recipe?
Yeah, you have to pass that round to go to the next.
You have to turn in a recipe that fits the theme.

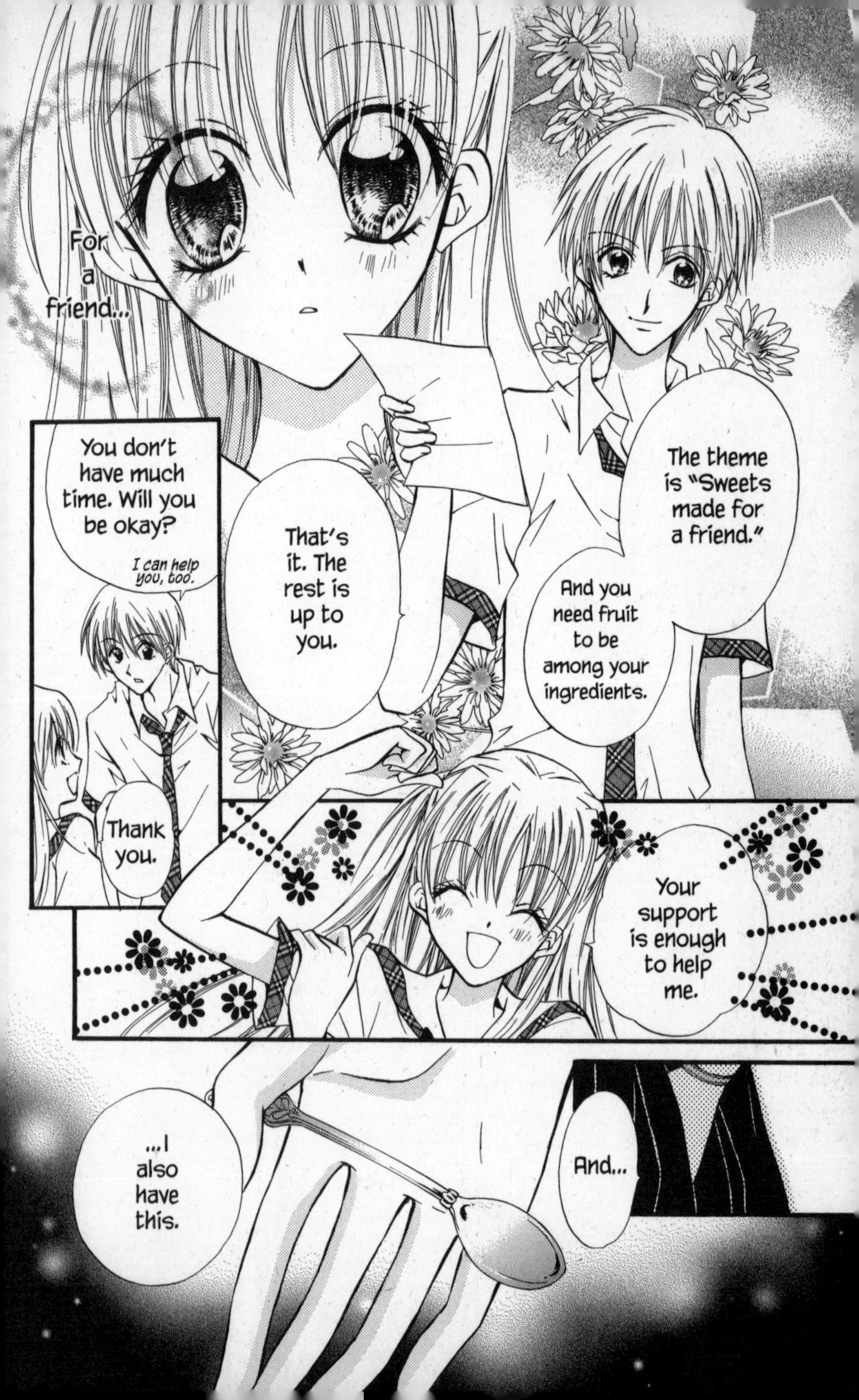

The theme is "Sweets made for a friend."
And you need fruit to be among your ingredients.
That's it. The rest is up to you.
For a friend...
You don't have much time. Will you be okay?
I can help you, too.
Thank you.
Your support is enough to help me.
And...
...I also have this.

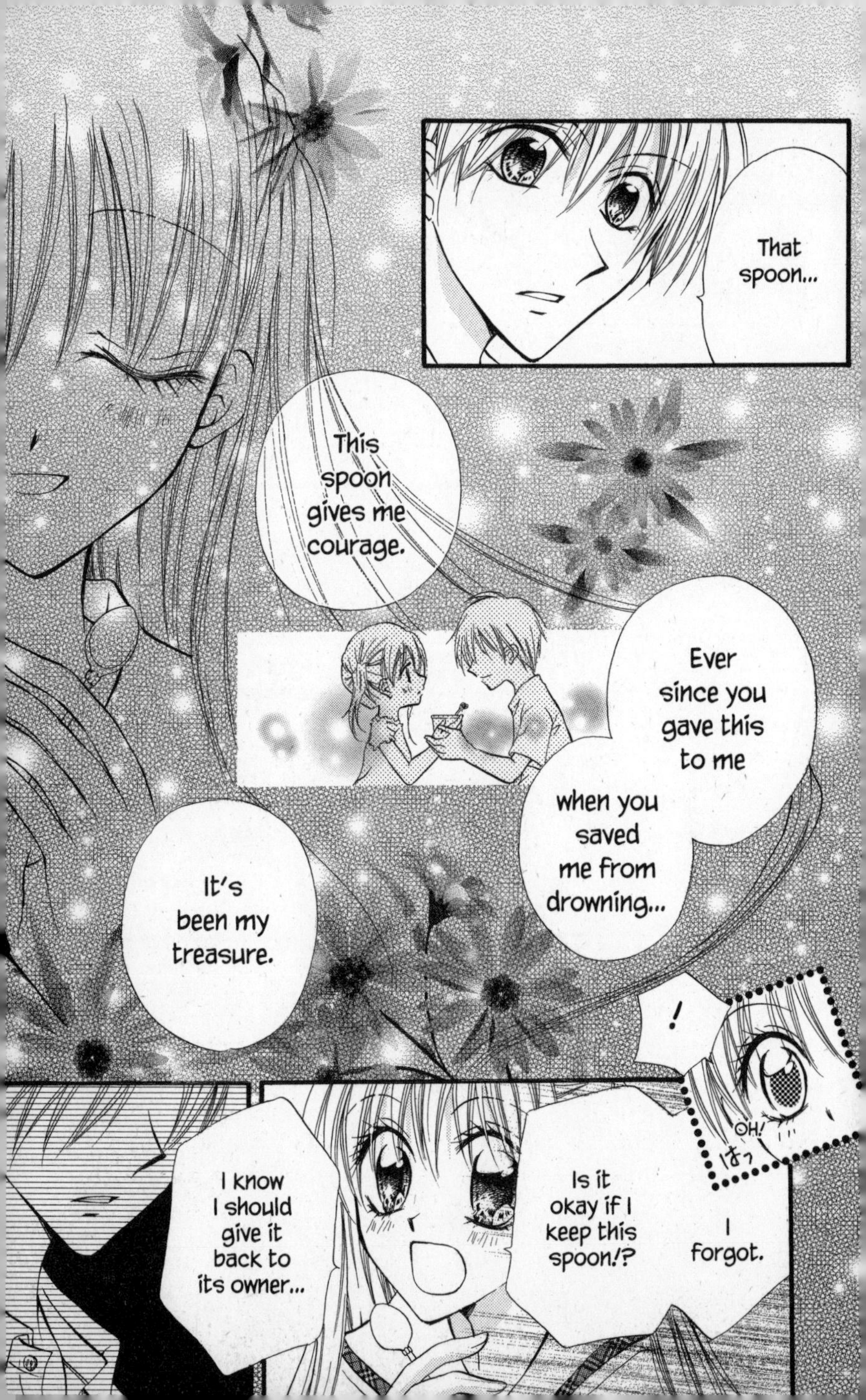
That spoon...
This spoon gives me courage.
Ever since you gave this to me
when you saved me from drowning...
It's been my treasure.
!
OH!
はっ
I forgot.
Is it okay if I keep this spoon!?
I know I should give it back to its owner...

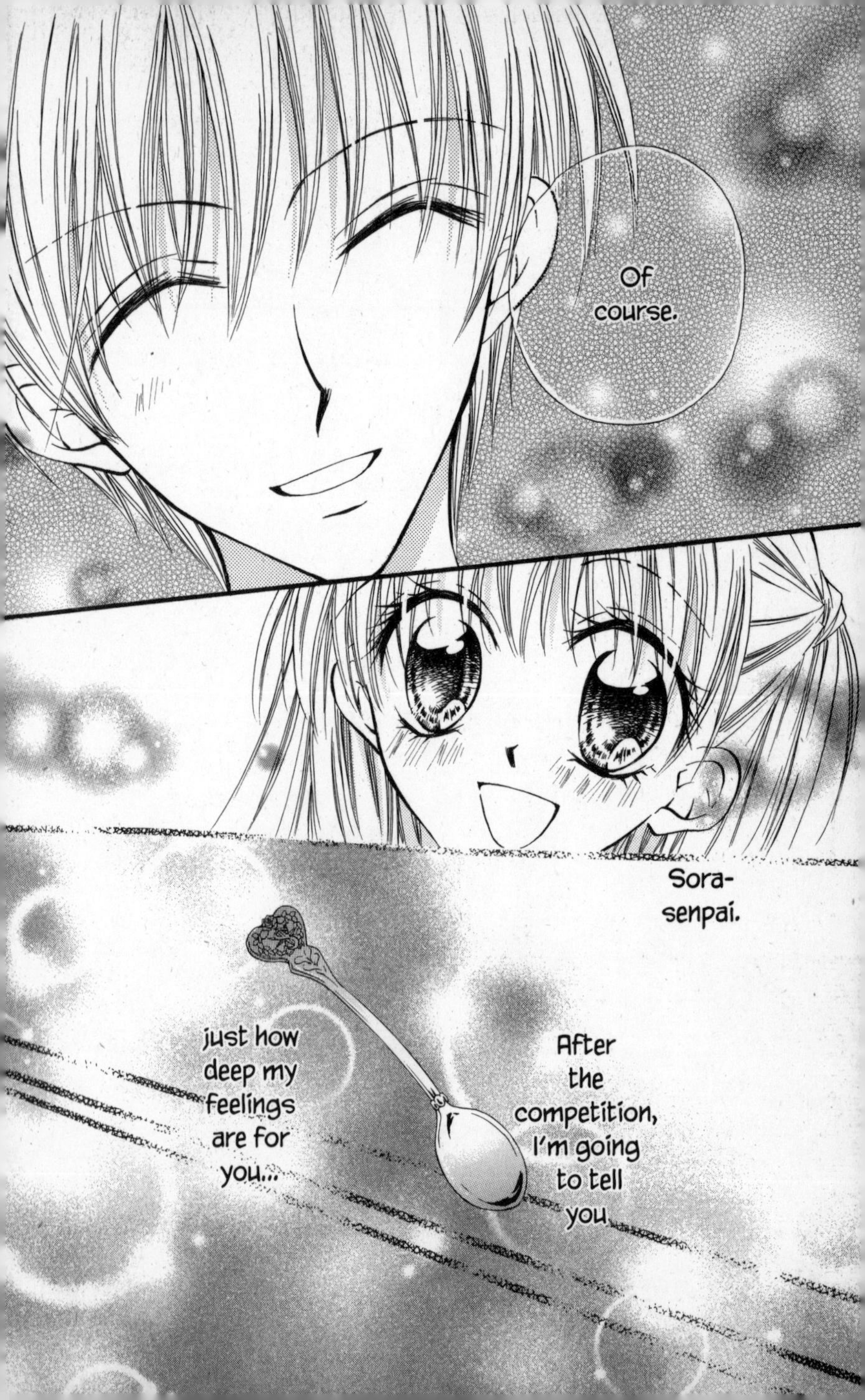
Of course.
Sora-senpai.
After the competition, I'm going to tell you
just how deep my feelings are for you...

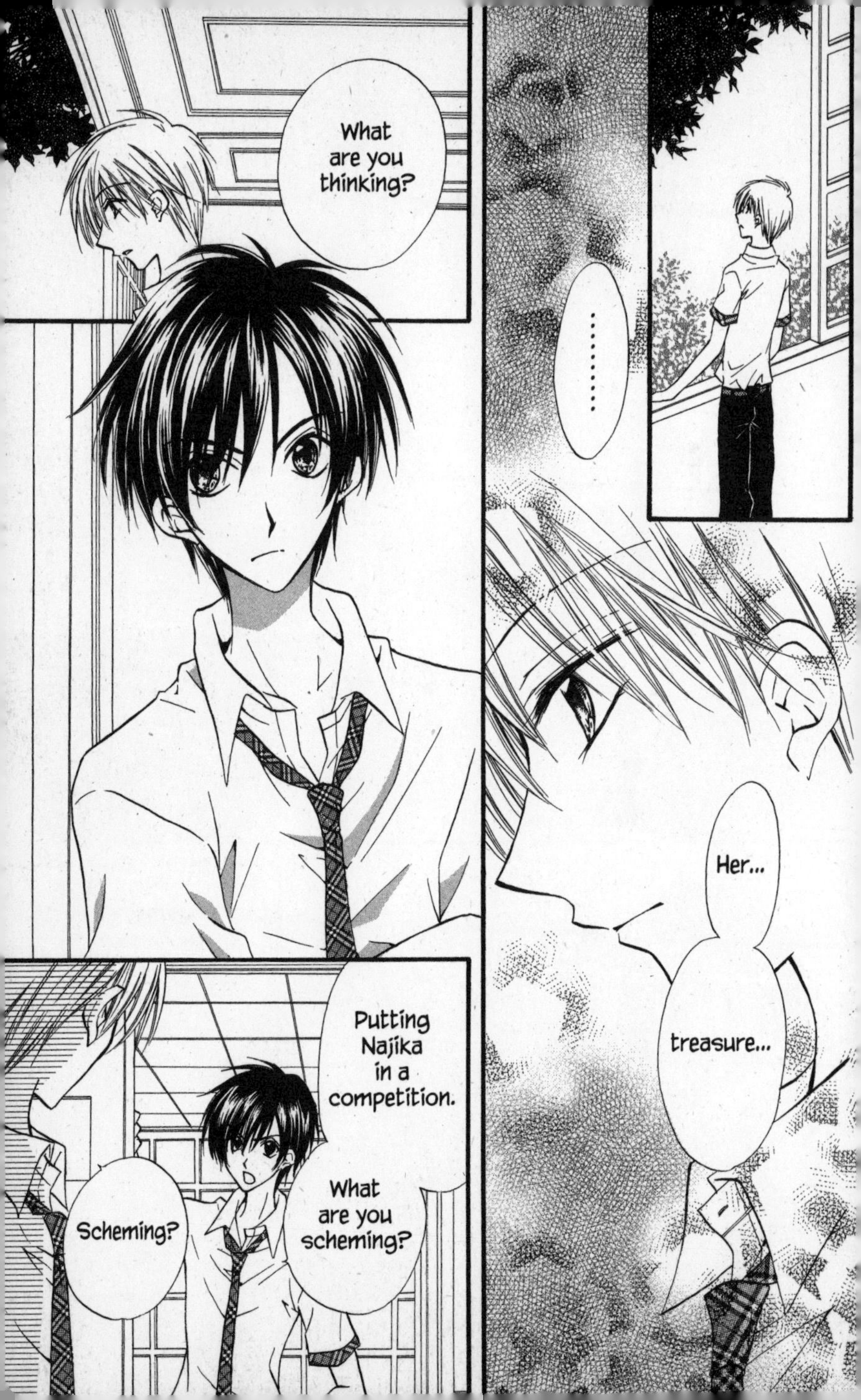
......
Her...
treasure...
What are you thinking?
Putting Najika in a competition.
What are you scheming?
Scheming?

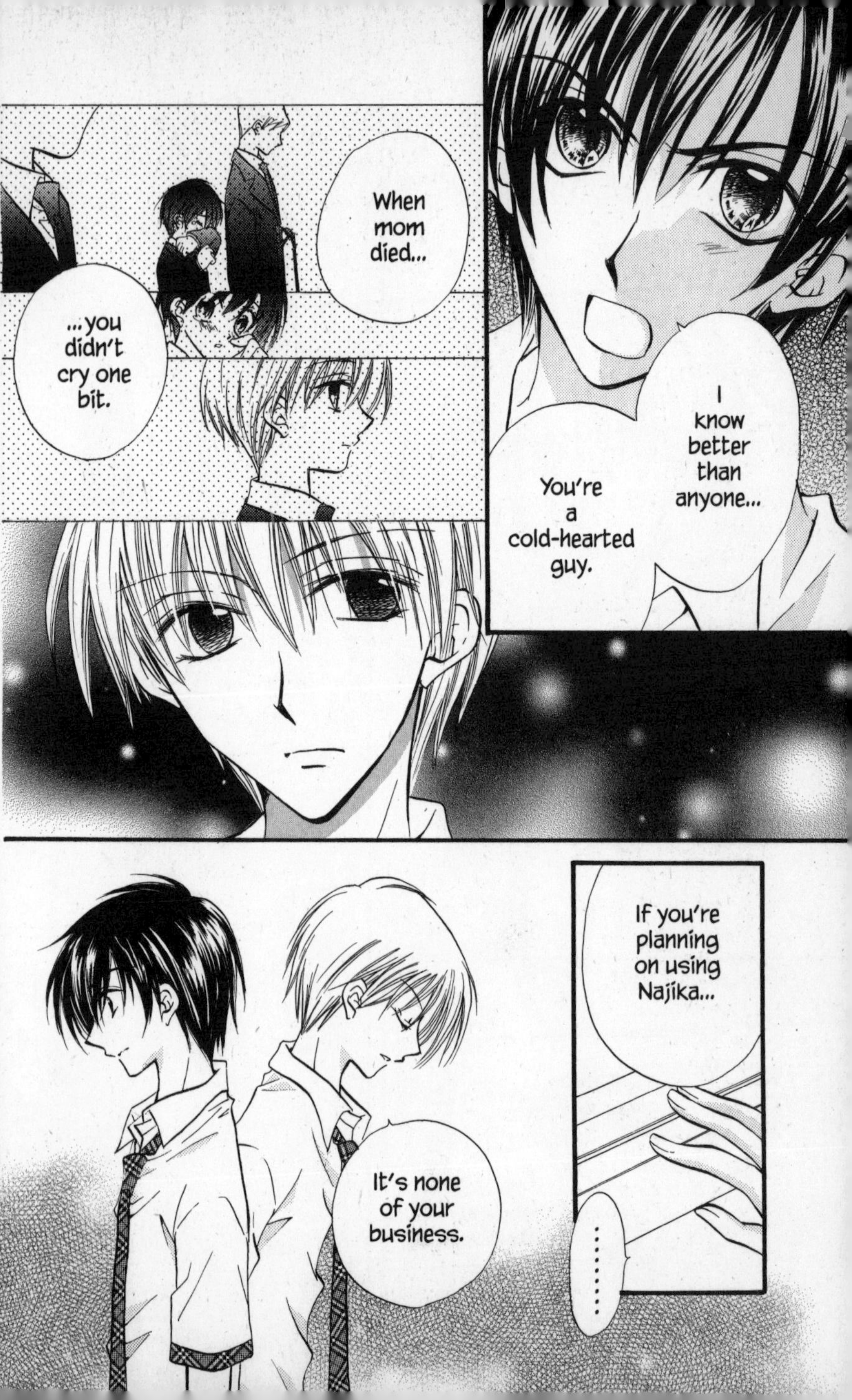
I know better than anyone...
You're a cold-hearted guy.
When mom died...
...you didn't cry one bit.
If you're planning on using Najika...
......
It's none of your business.

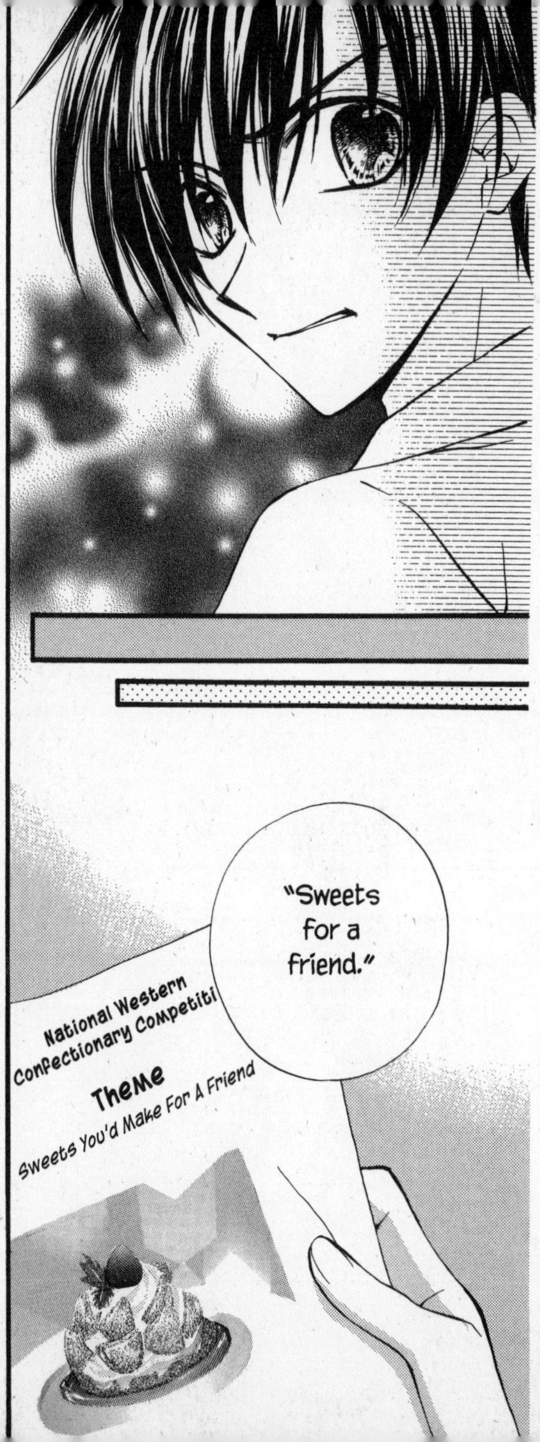
"Sweets for a friend."
National Western Confectionary Competiti
Theme
Sweets You'd Make For A Friend

Recipe 19

I had a month of vacation right before this chapter, and since it was during New Year's, I took it easy. Although I did go to my favorite place, Disneyland, for the countdown, and my schedule was pretty hectic. And I spent the rest of my days playing games... The vacation went by quickly... Fujita-san's stubble is back, too.

Special

I drew this chapter a while ago, but since we couldn't fit it into the last volume, it's featured in this volume. It was fun drawing people other than the regular cast. And the name "Komugi-chan" was so cute. ♥ (Miyuki sensei named her.) It was a feature on "touching stories," so I drew many pictures where people were crying. I do like bittersweet illustrations.

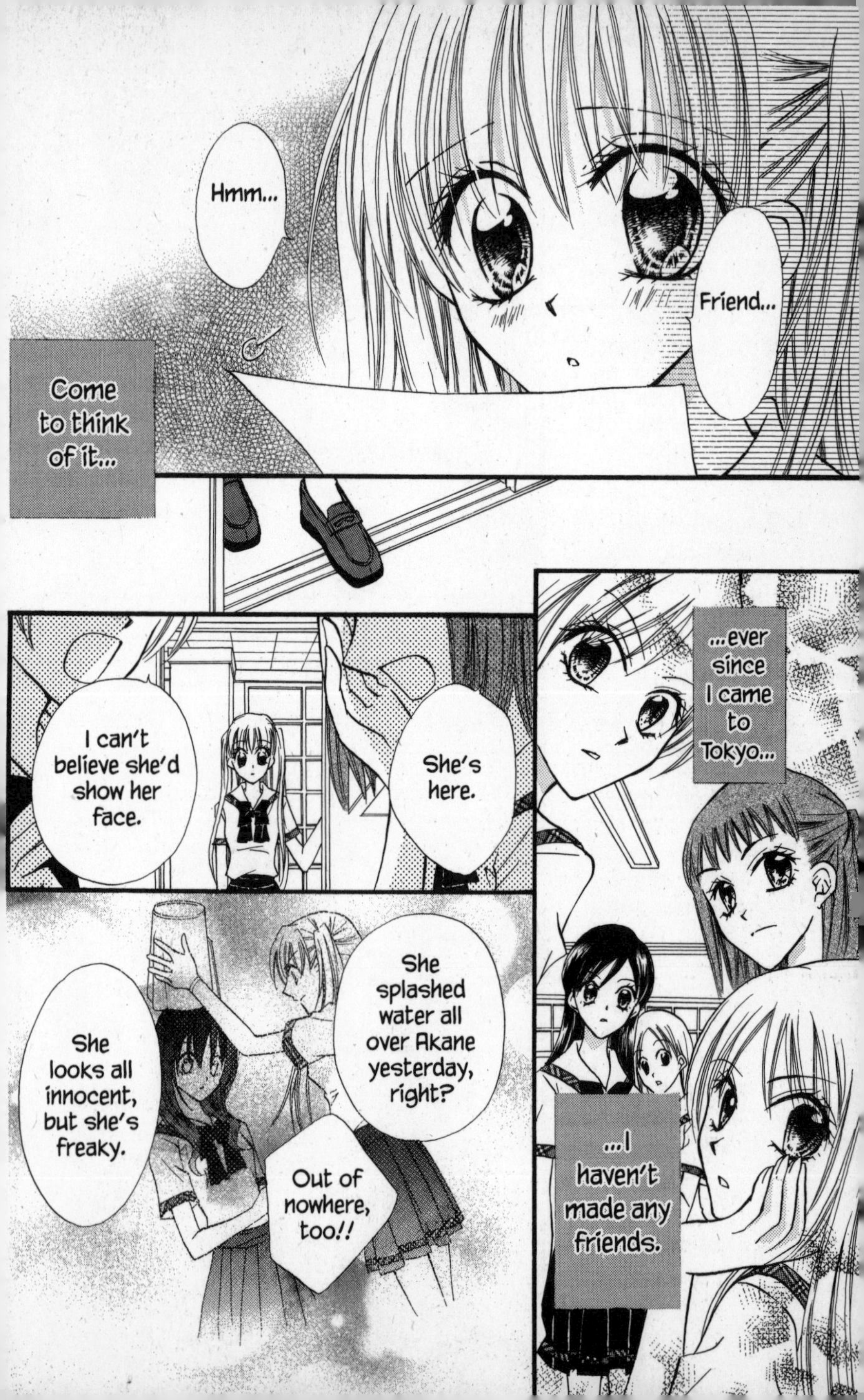
Friend...
Hmm...
Come to think of it...
...ever since I came to Tokyo...
...I haven't made any friends.
She's here.
I can't believe she'd show her face.
She splashed water all over Akane yesterday, right?
She looks all innocent, but she's freaky.
Out of nowhere, too!!

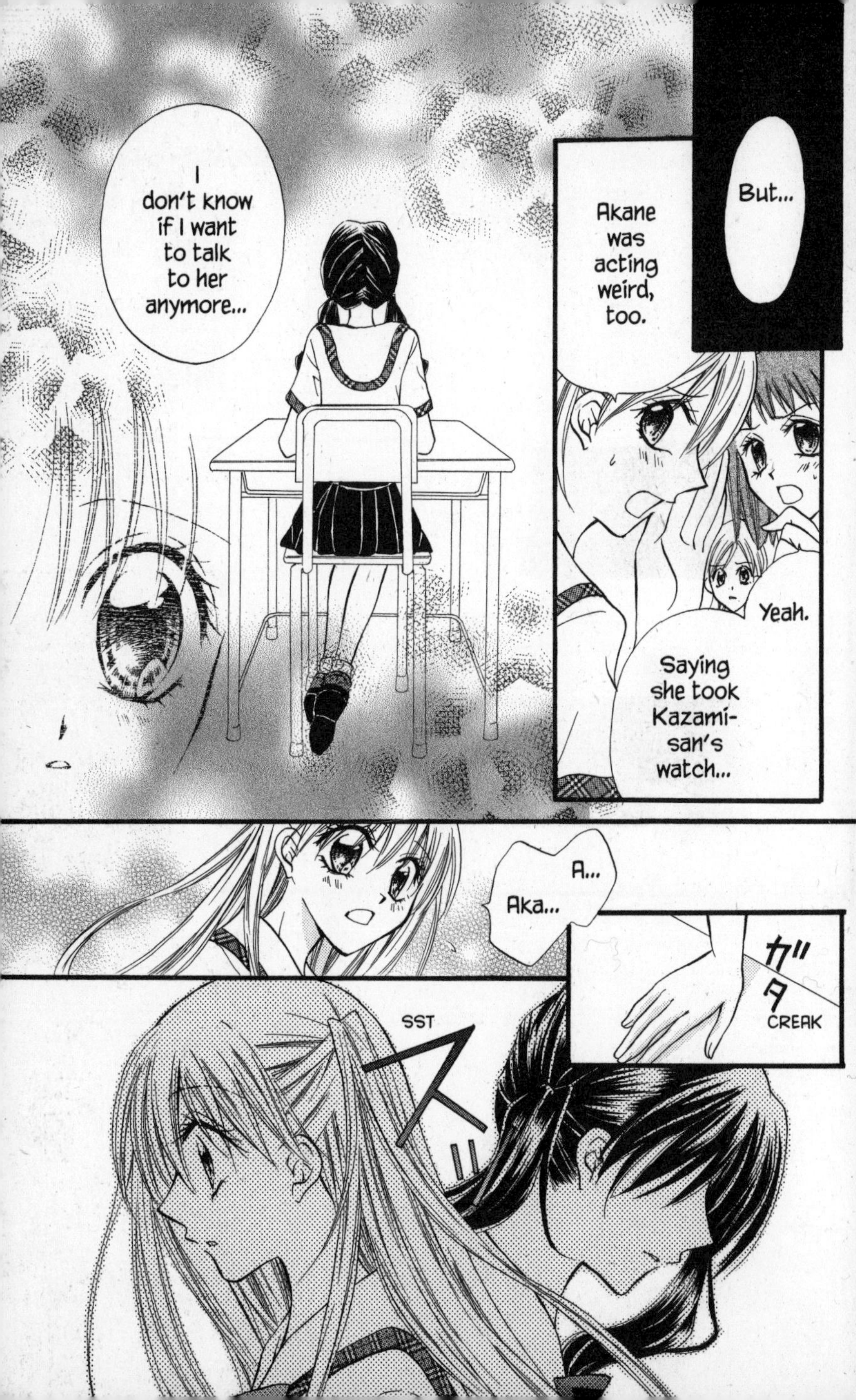
But...
Akane was acting weird, too.
Yeah.
Saying she took Kazami-san's watch...
I don't know if I want to talk to her anymore...
A...
Aka...
ガタ
CREAK
SST

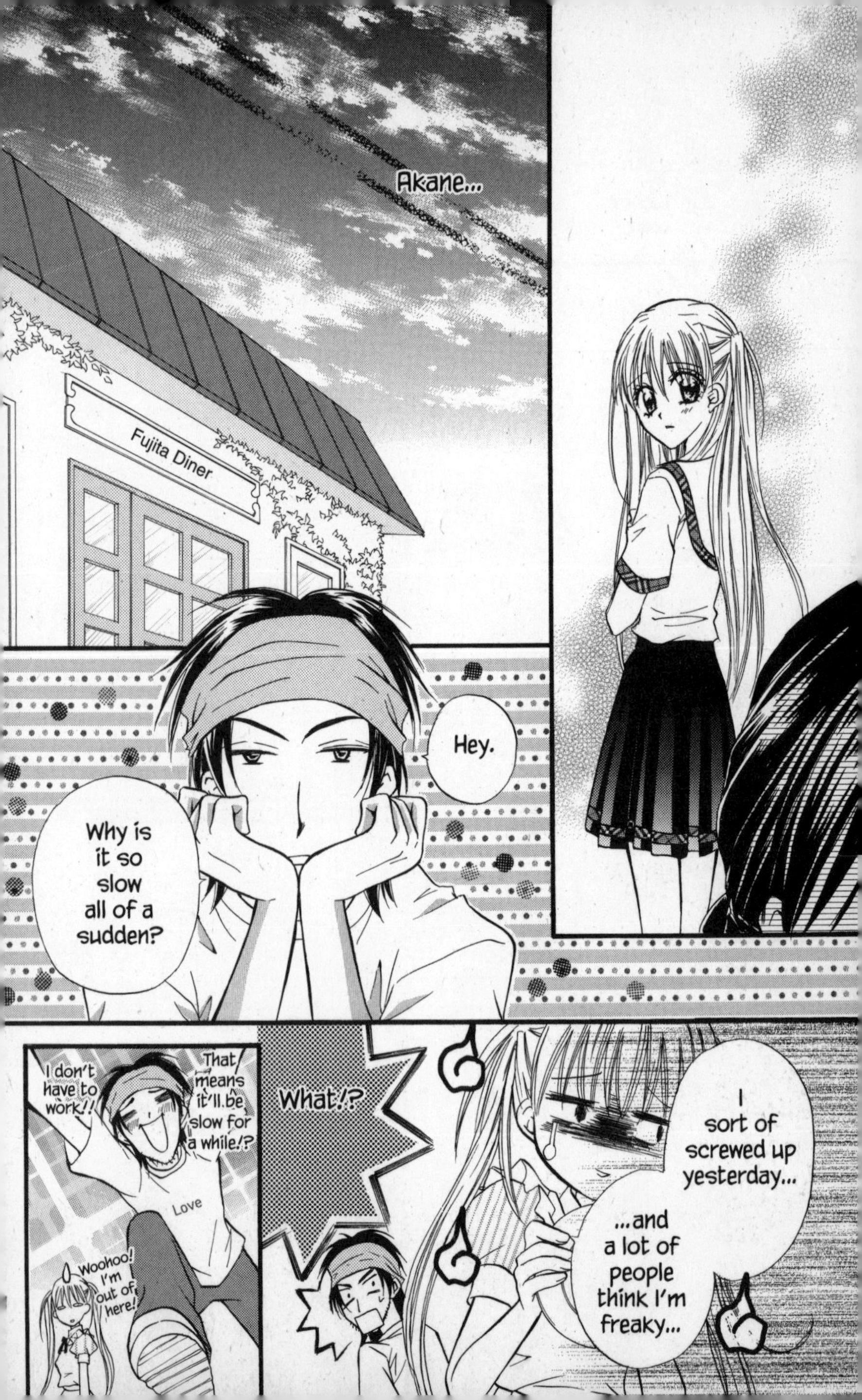

Akane...
Fujita Diner
Hey.
Why is it so slow all of a sudden?
I sort of screwed up yesterday...
...and a lot of people think I'm freaky...
What!?
That means it'll be slow for a while!?
I don't have to work!!
Love
Woohoo! I'm out of here!

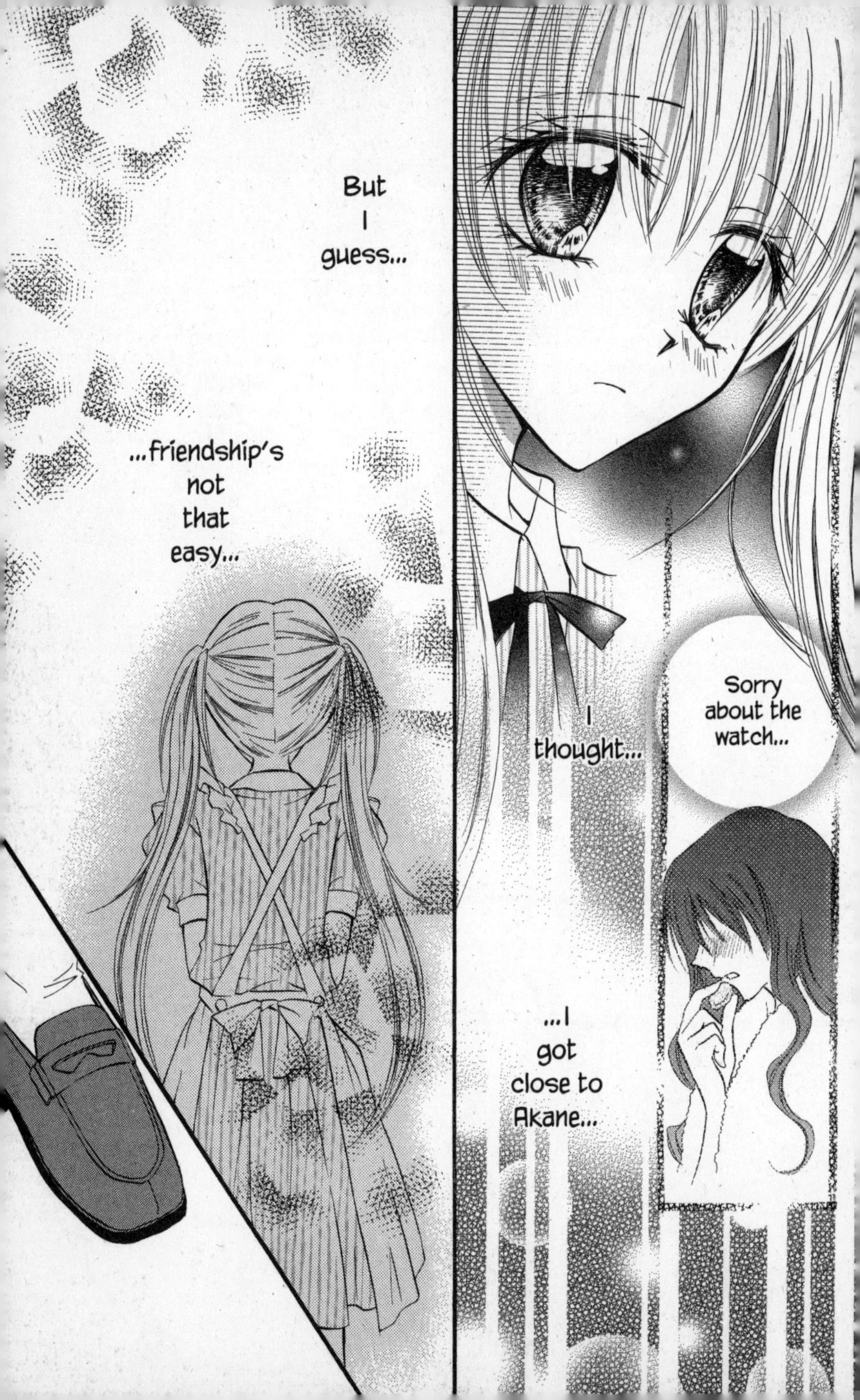
Sorry about the watch...
I thought...
...I got close to Akane...
But I guess...
...friendship's not that easy...

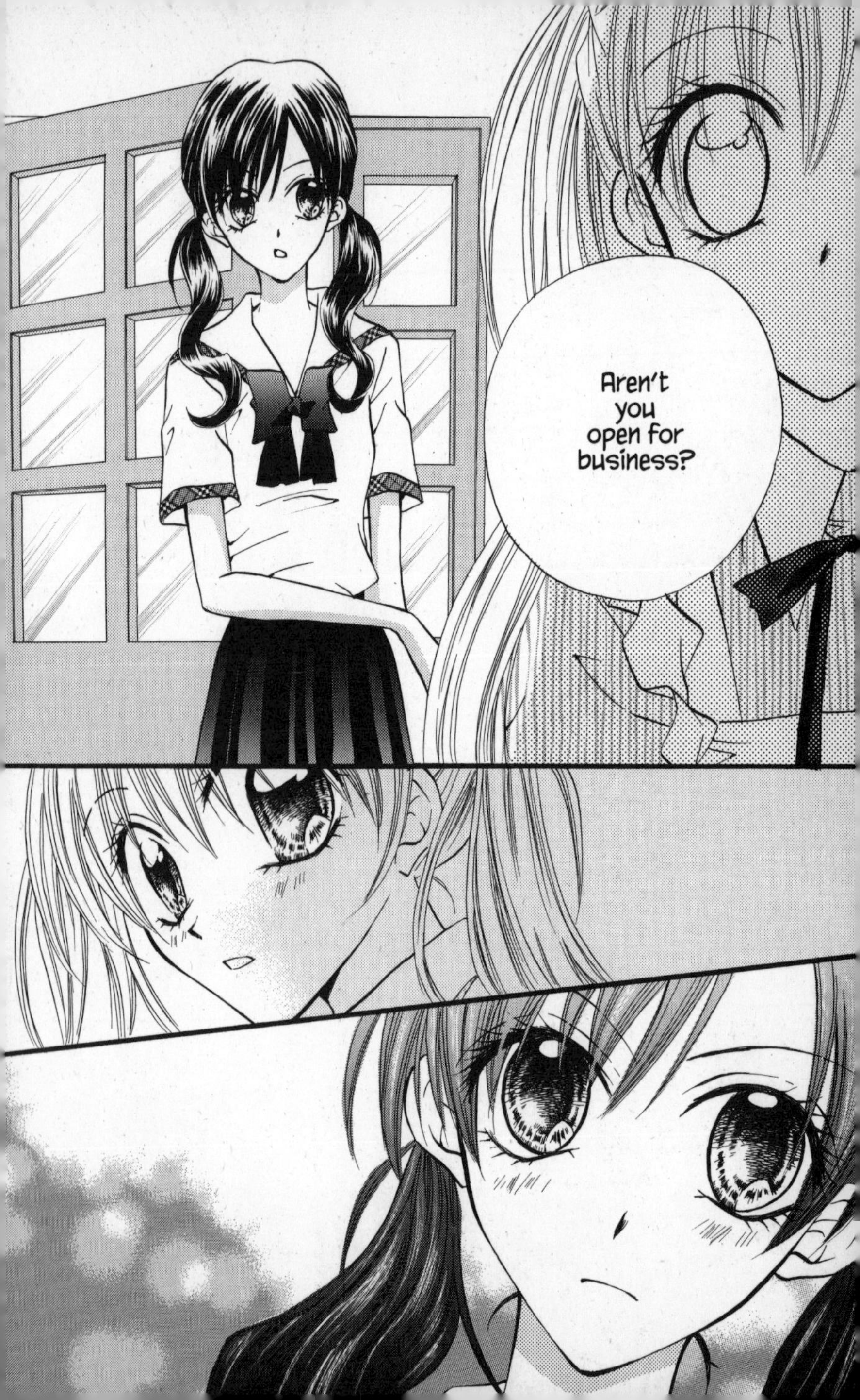
Aren't you open for business?

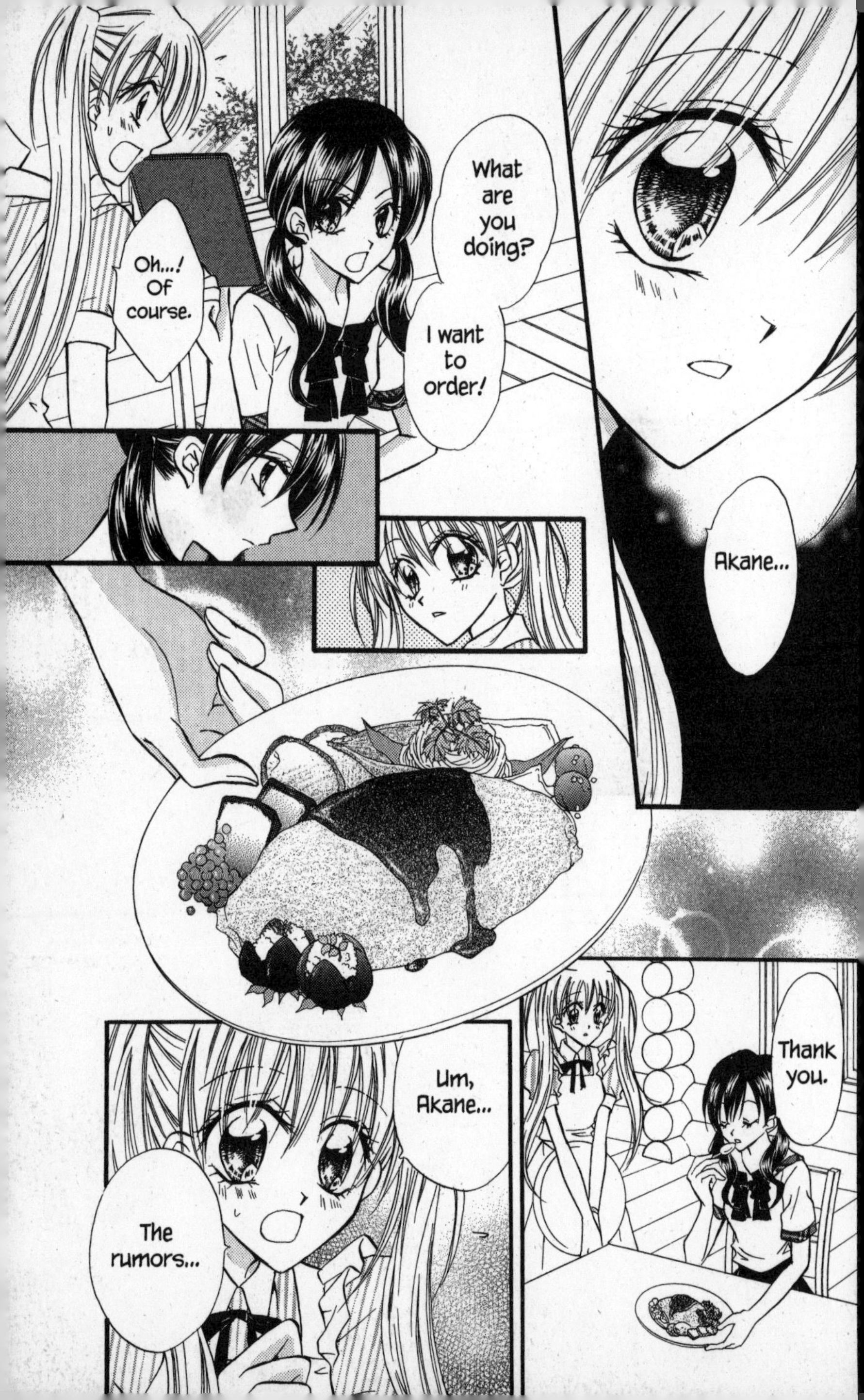
Akane...
What are you doing?
I want to order!
Oh...! Of course.
Thank you.
Um, Akane...
The rumors...

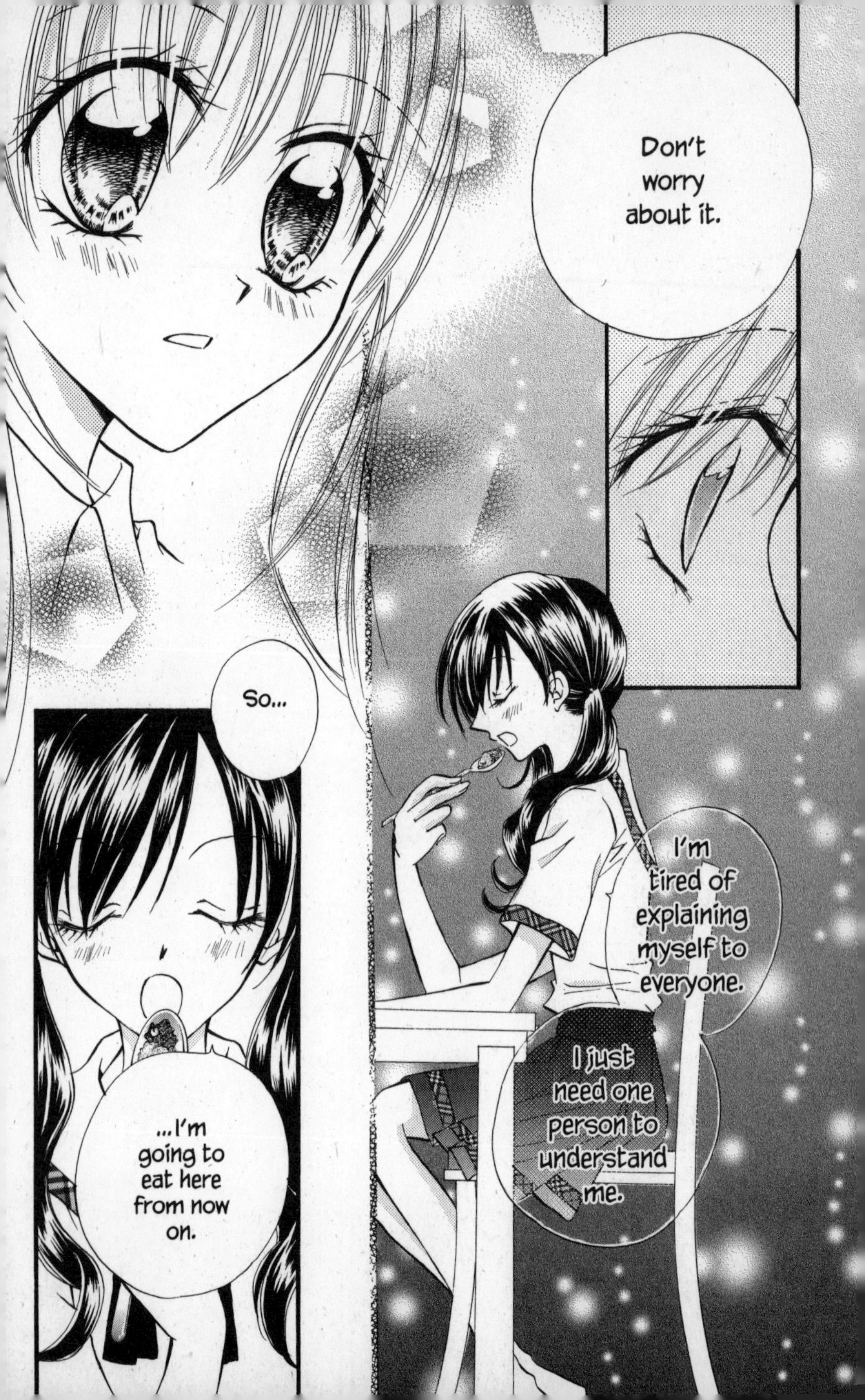
Don't worry about it.
I'm tired of explaining myself to everyone.
I just need one person to understand me.
So...
...I'm going to eat here from now on.

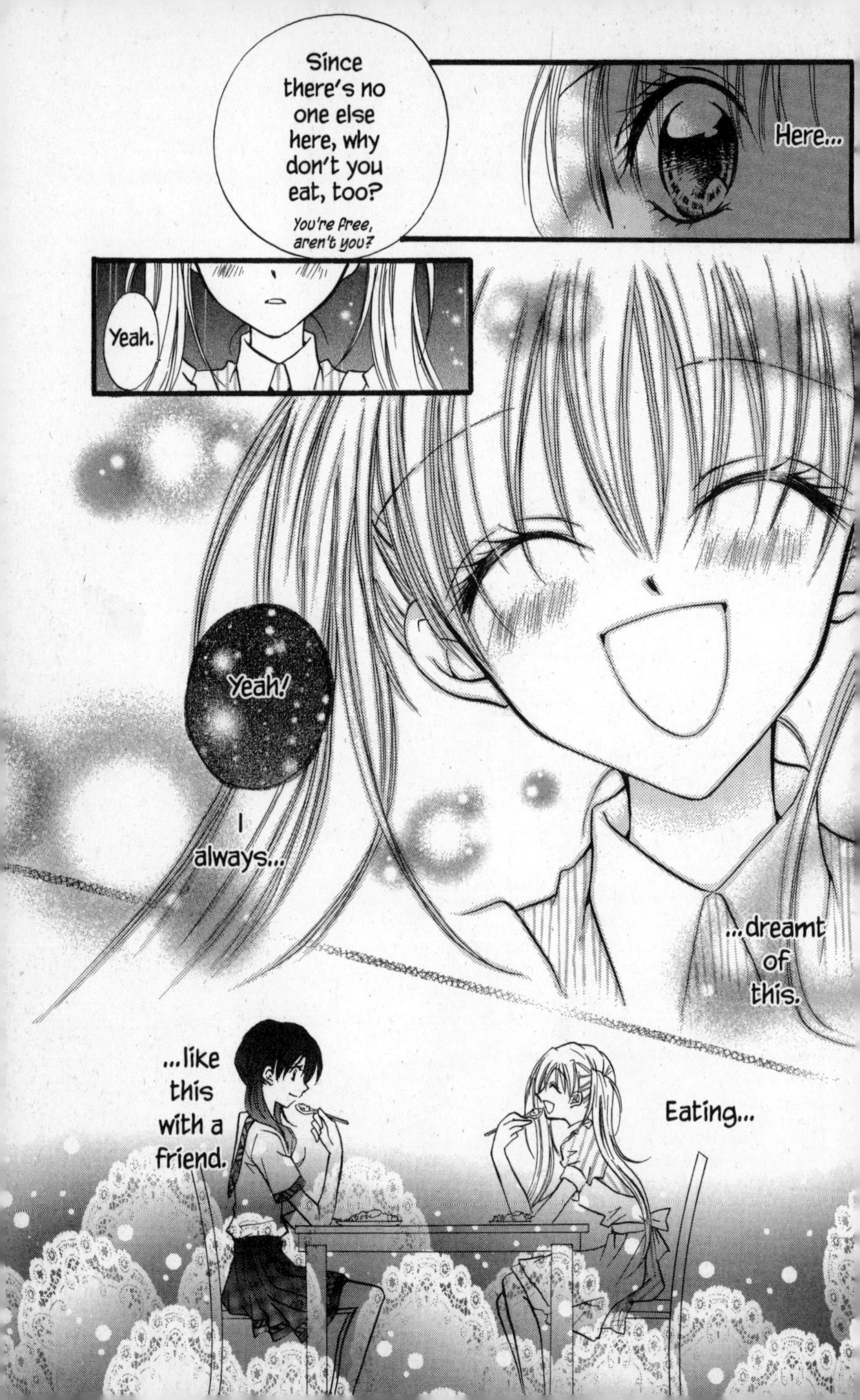
Here...
Since there's no one else here, why don't you eat, too?
You're free, aren't you?
Yeah.
Yeah!
I always...
...dreamt of this.
Eating...
...like this with a friend.

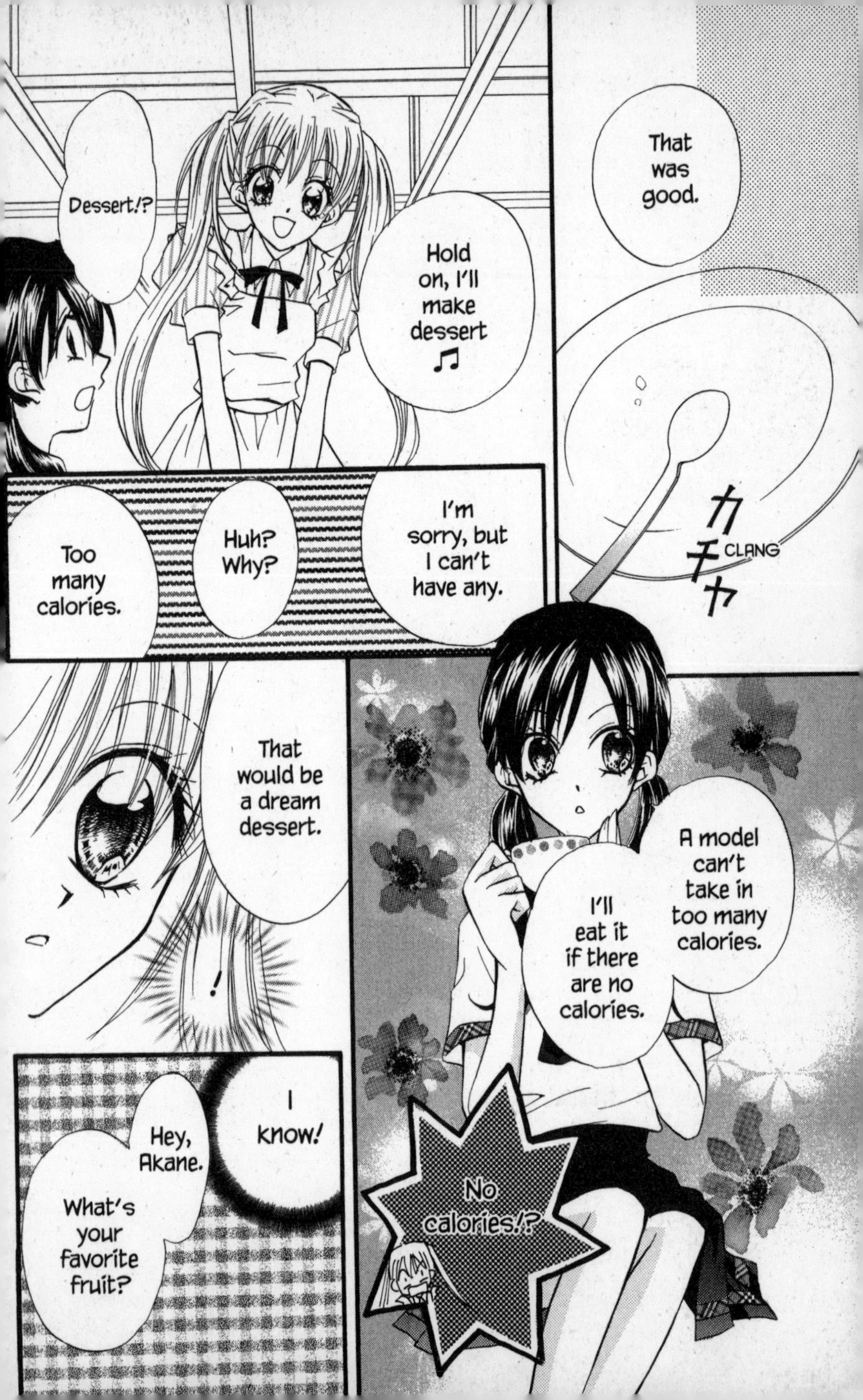

That was good.
カチャ
CLANG
Hold on, I'll make dessert ♫
Dessert!?
I'm sorry, but I can't have any.
Huh? Why?
Too many calories.
A model can't take in too many calories.
I'll eat it if there are no calories.
No calories!?
That would be a dream dessert.
!
I know!
Hey, Akane.
What's your favorite fruit?

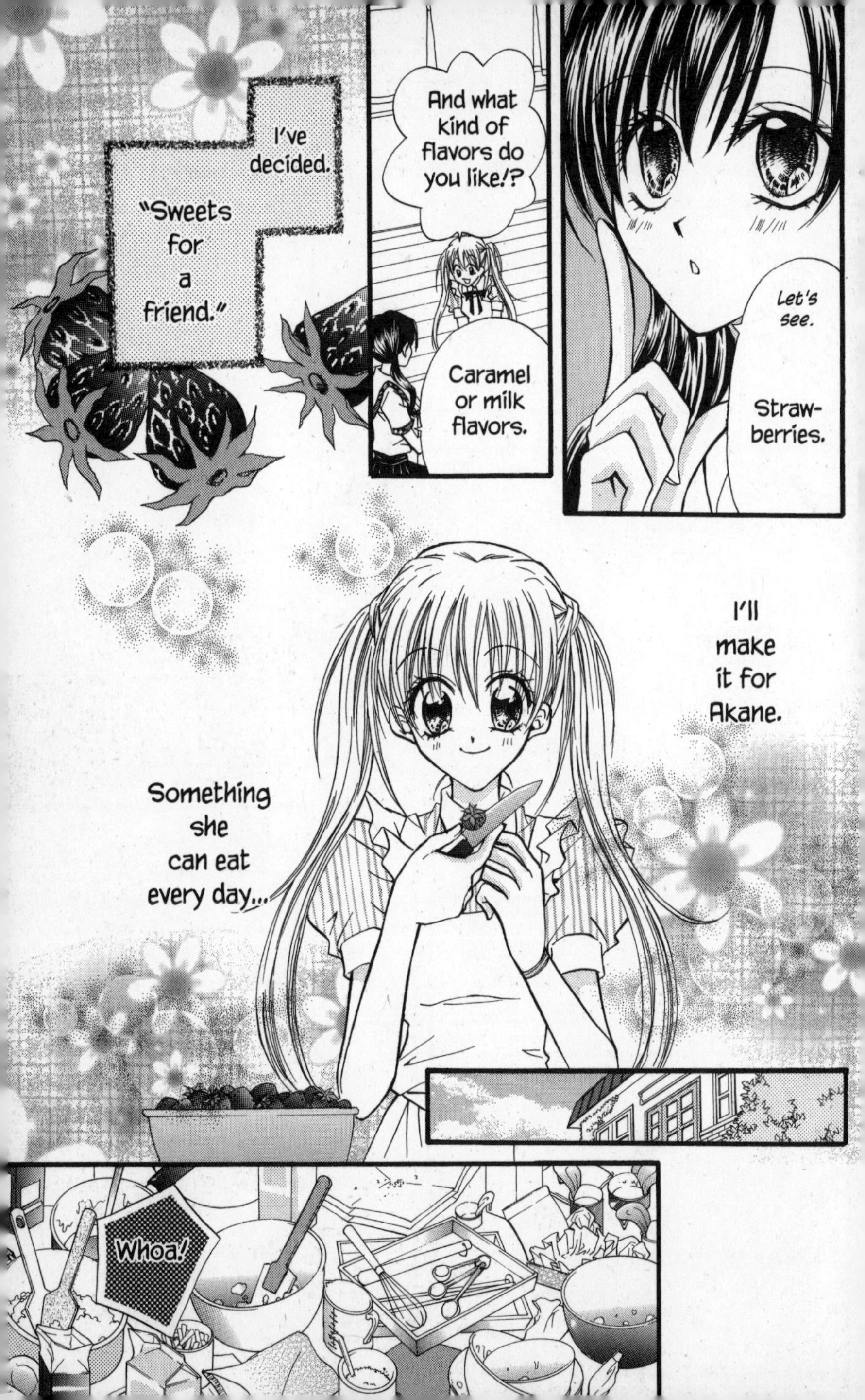
Let's see.
Straw-berries.
And what kind of flavors do you like!?
Caramel or milk flavors.
I've decided.
"Sweets for a friend."
I'll make it for Akane.
Something she can eat every day...
Whoa!

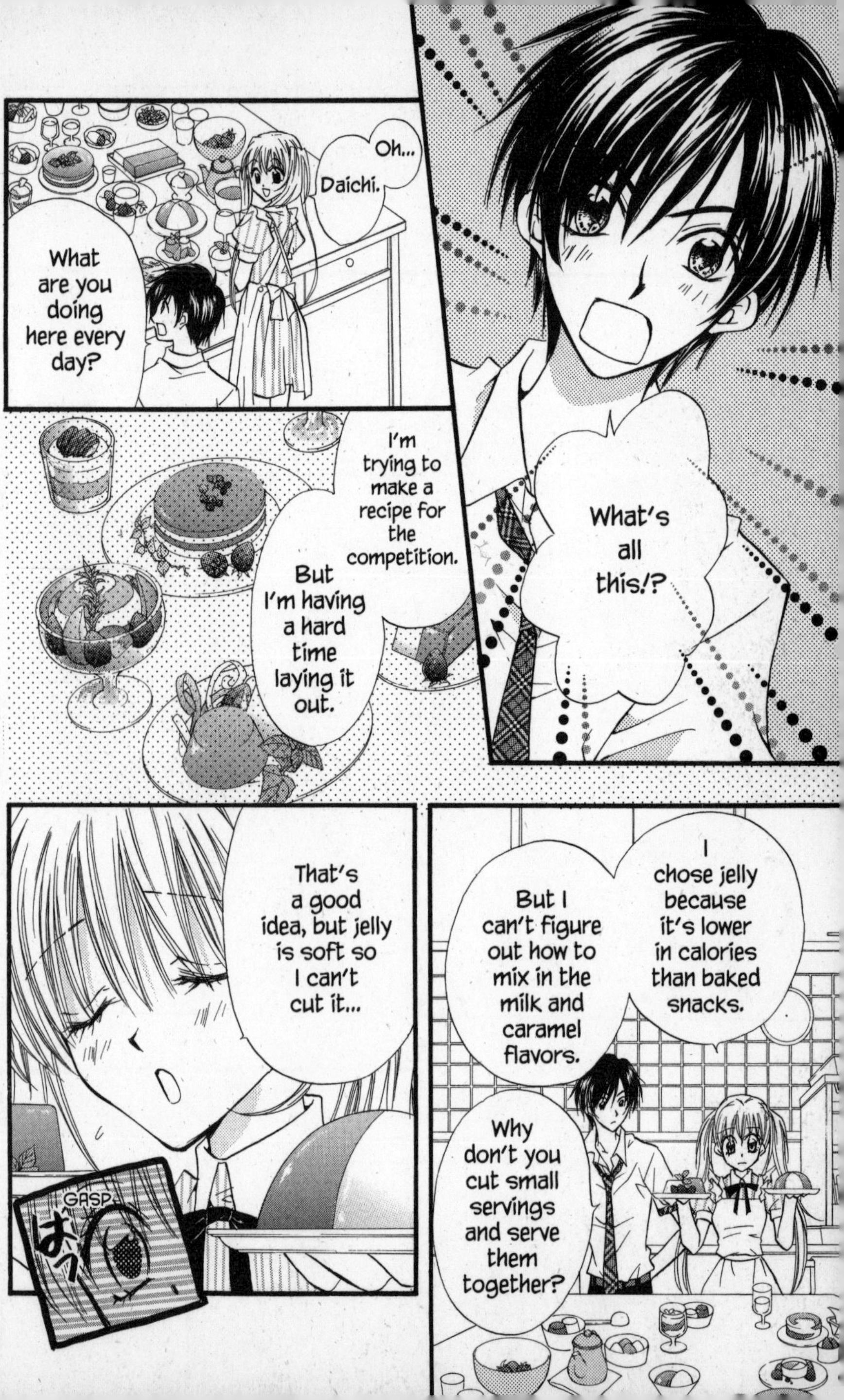
What's all this!?
Oh... Daichi.
What are you doing here every day?
I'm trying to make a recipe for the competition.
But I'm having a hard time laying it out.
I chose jelly because it's lower in calories than baked snacks.
But I can't figure out how to mix in the milk and caramel flavors.
Why don't you cut small servings and serve them together?
That's a good idea, but jelly is soft so I can't cut it...
GASP

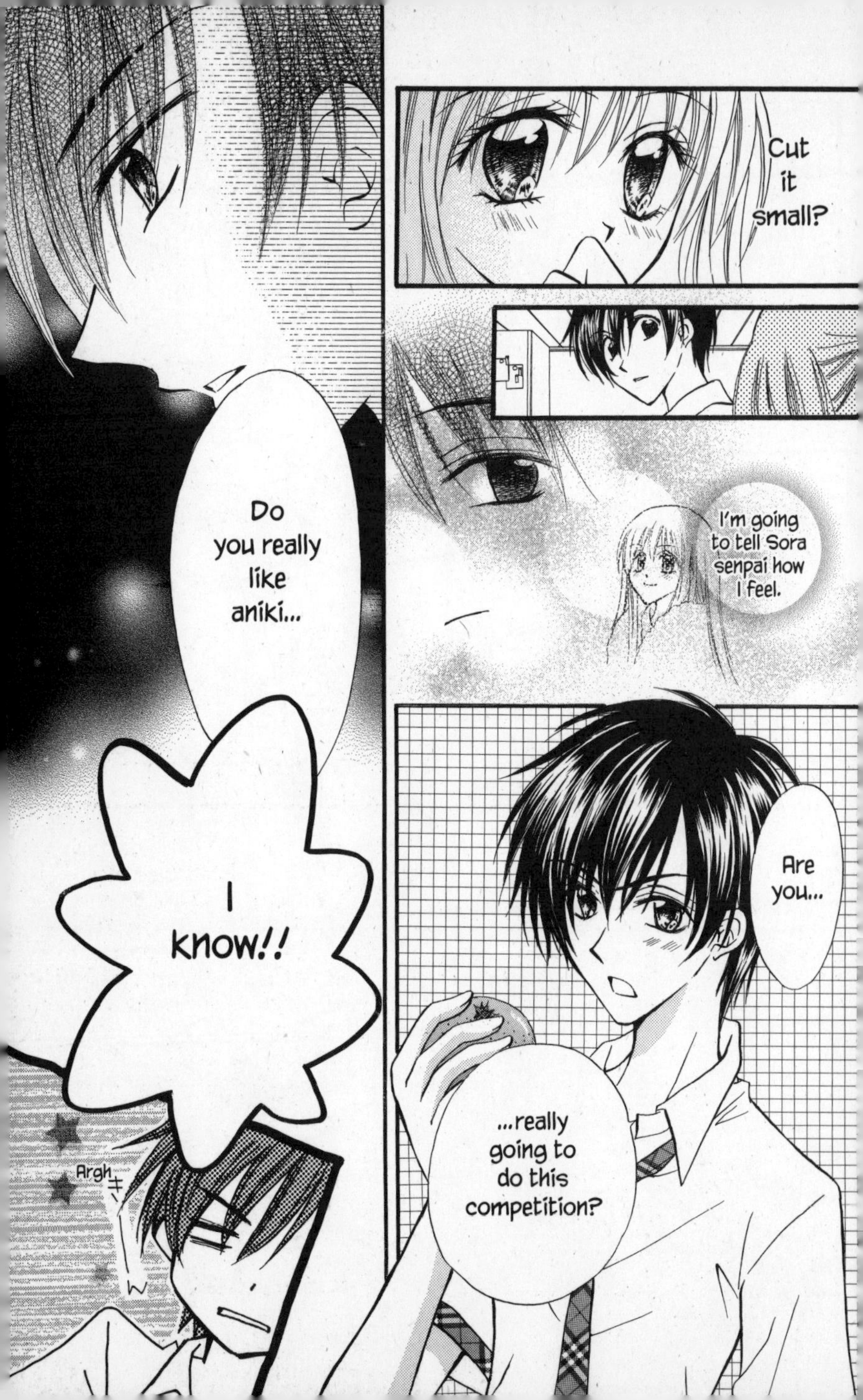
Cut it small?
I'm going to tell Sora senpai how I feel.
Are you...
...really going to do this competition?
Do you really like aniki...
I know!!
Argh

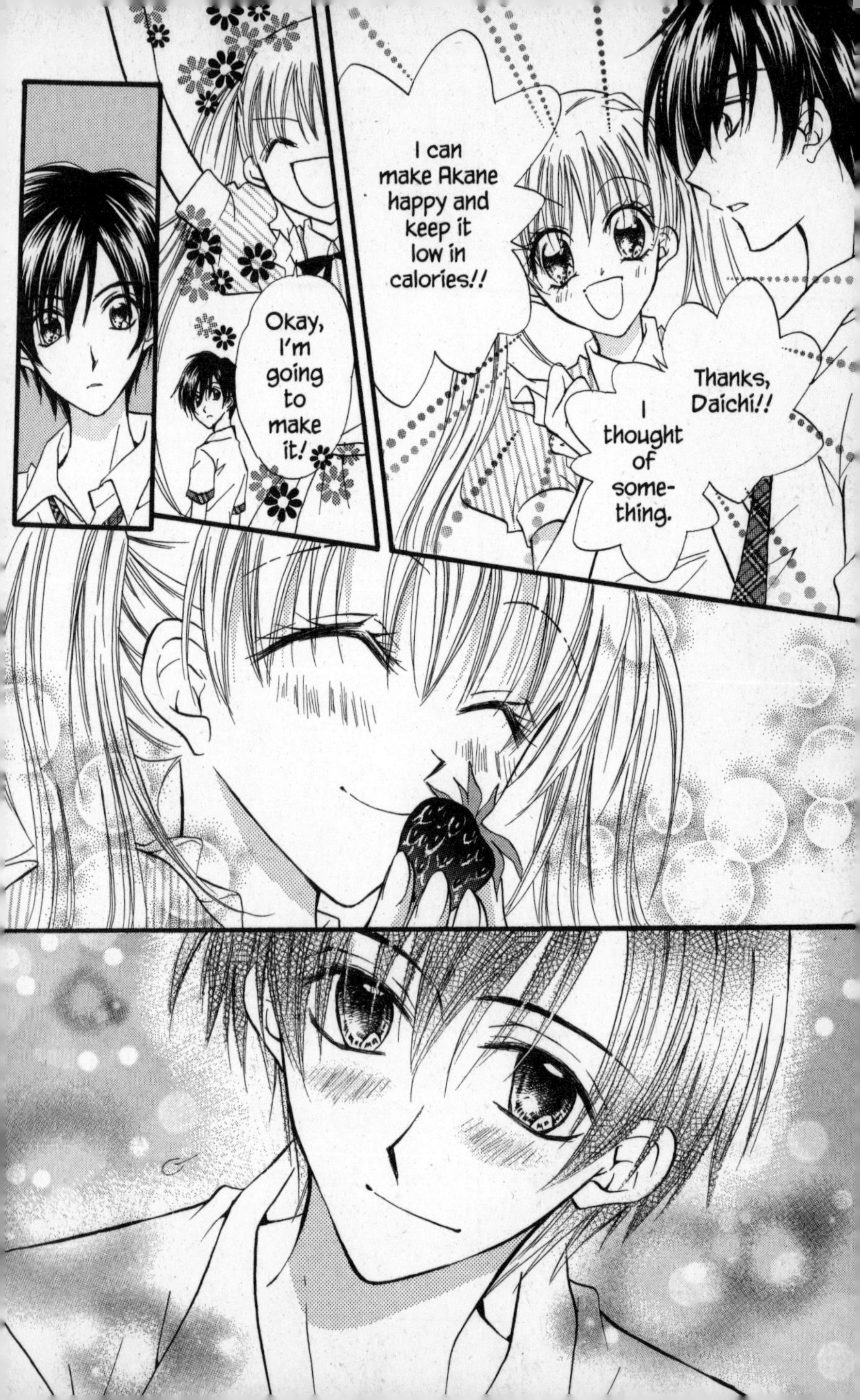
Thanks, Daichi!!
I thought of some-thing.
I can make Akane happy and keep it low in calories!!
Okay, I'm going to make it!

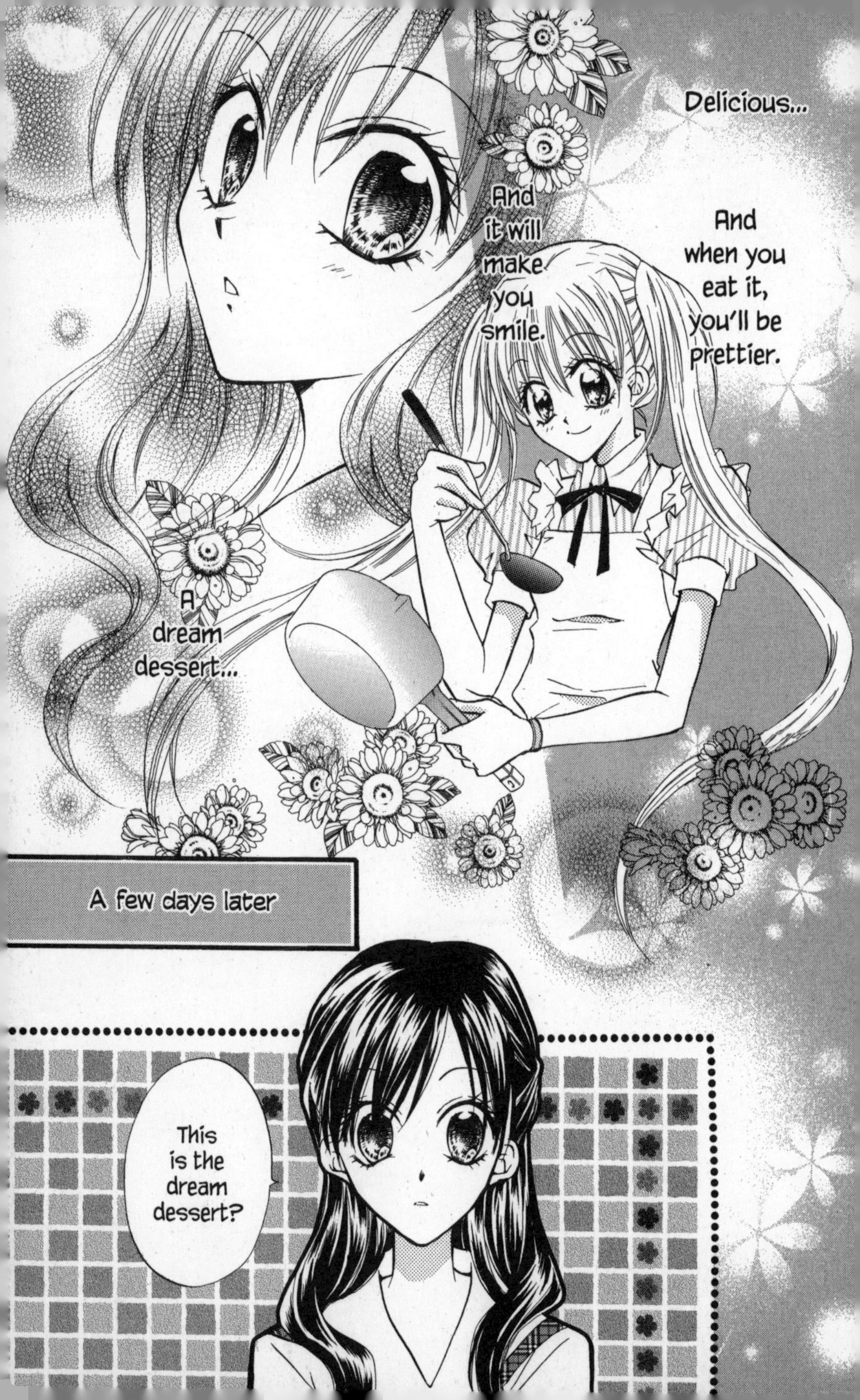
Delicious...
And when you eat it, you'll be prettier.
And it will make you smile.
A dream dessert...
A few days later
This is the dream dessert?

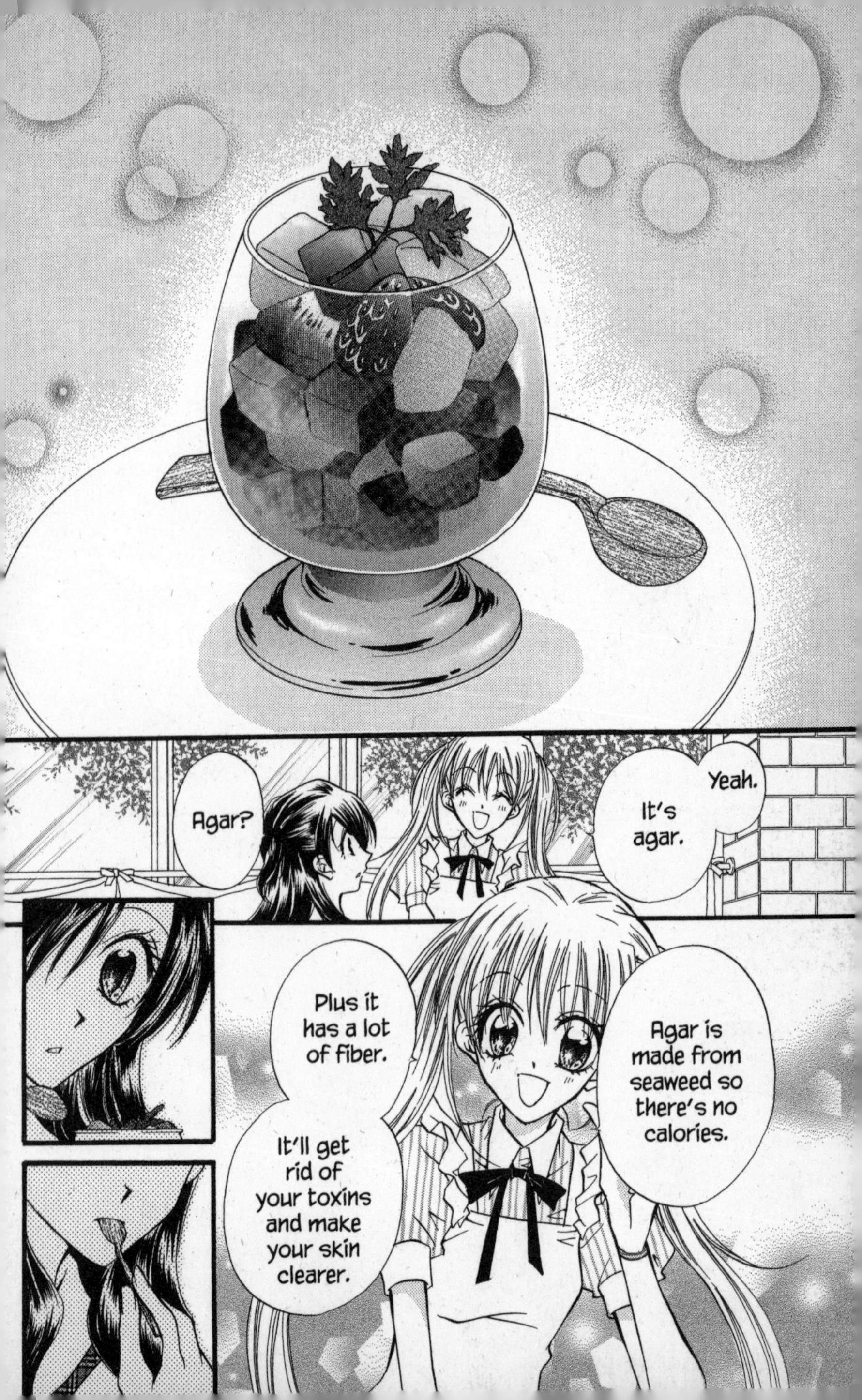
Yeah.
It's agar.
Agar?
Agar is made from seaweed so there's no calories.
Plus it has a lot of fiber.
It'll get rid of your toxins and make your skin clearer.

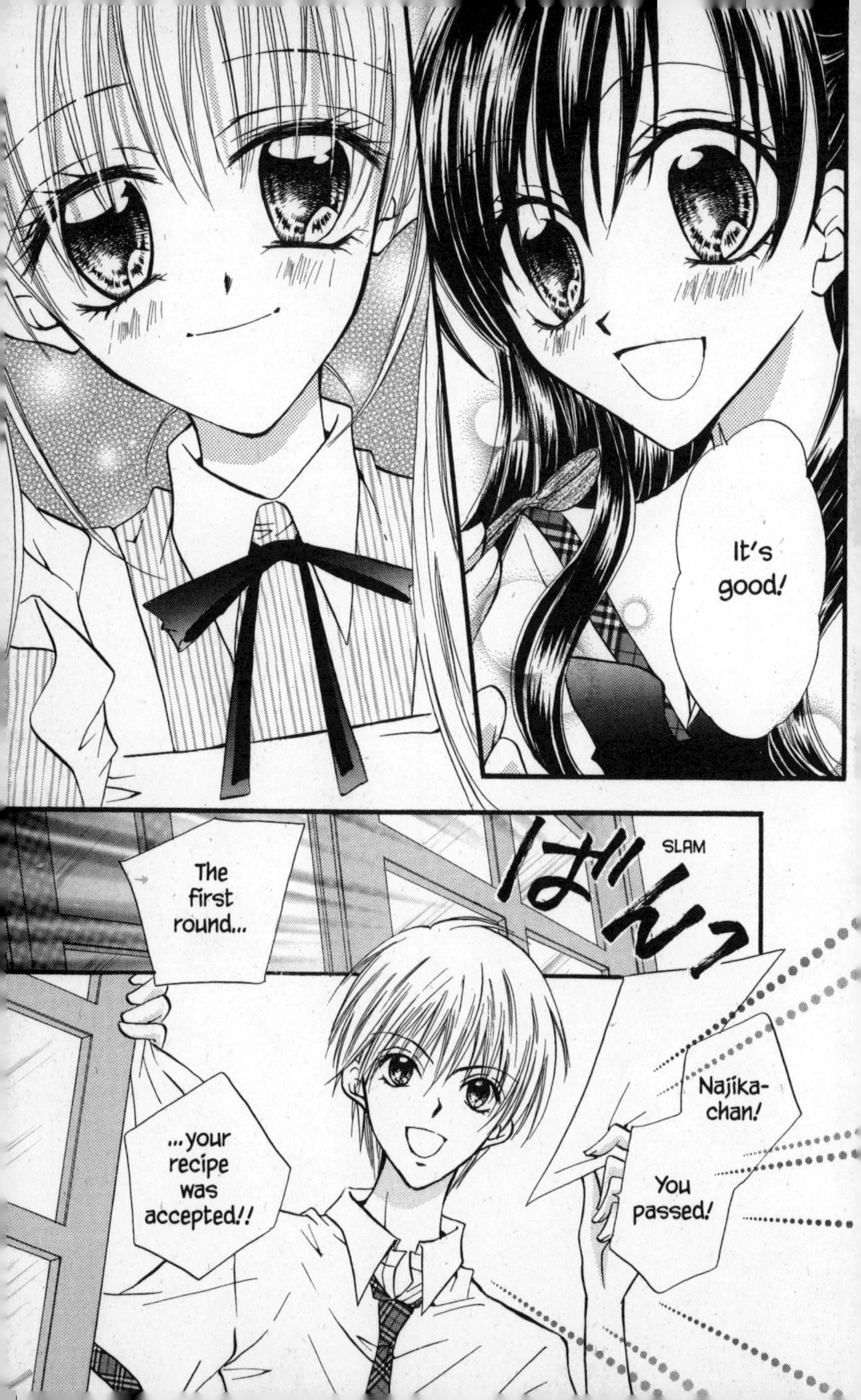
It's good!
ばんっ
SLAM
Najika-chan!
You passed!
The first round...
...your recipe was accepted!!

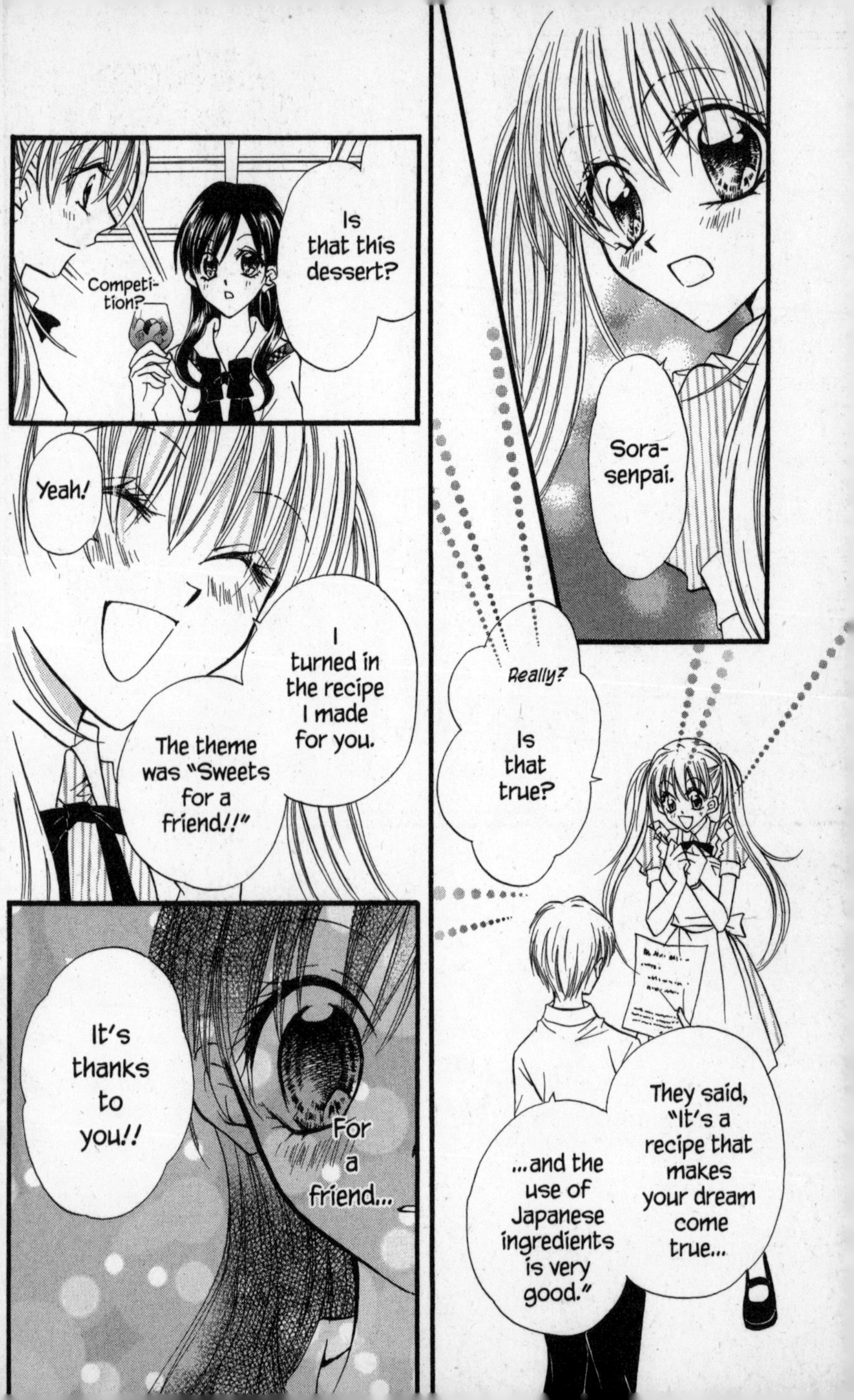
Sora-senpai.
Really?
Is that true?
They said, "It's a recipe that makes your dream come true...
...and the use of Japanese ingredients is very good."
Is that this dessert?
Competition?
Yeah!
I turned in the recipe I made for you.
The theme was "Sweets for a friend!!"
For a friend...
It's thanks to you!!

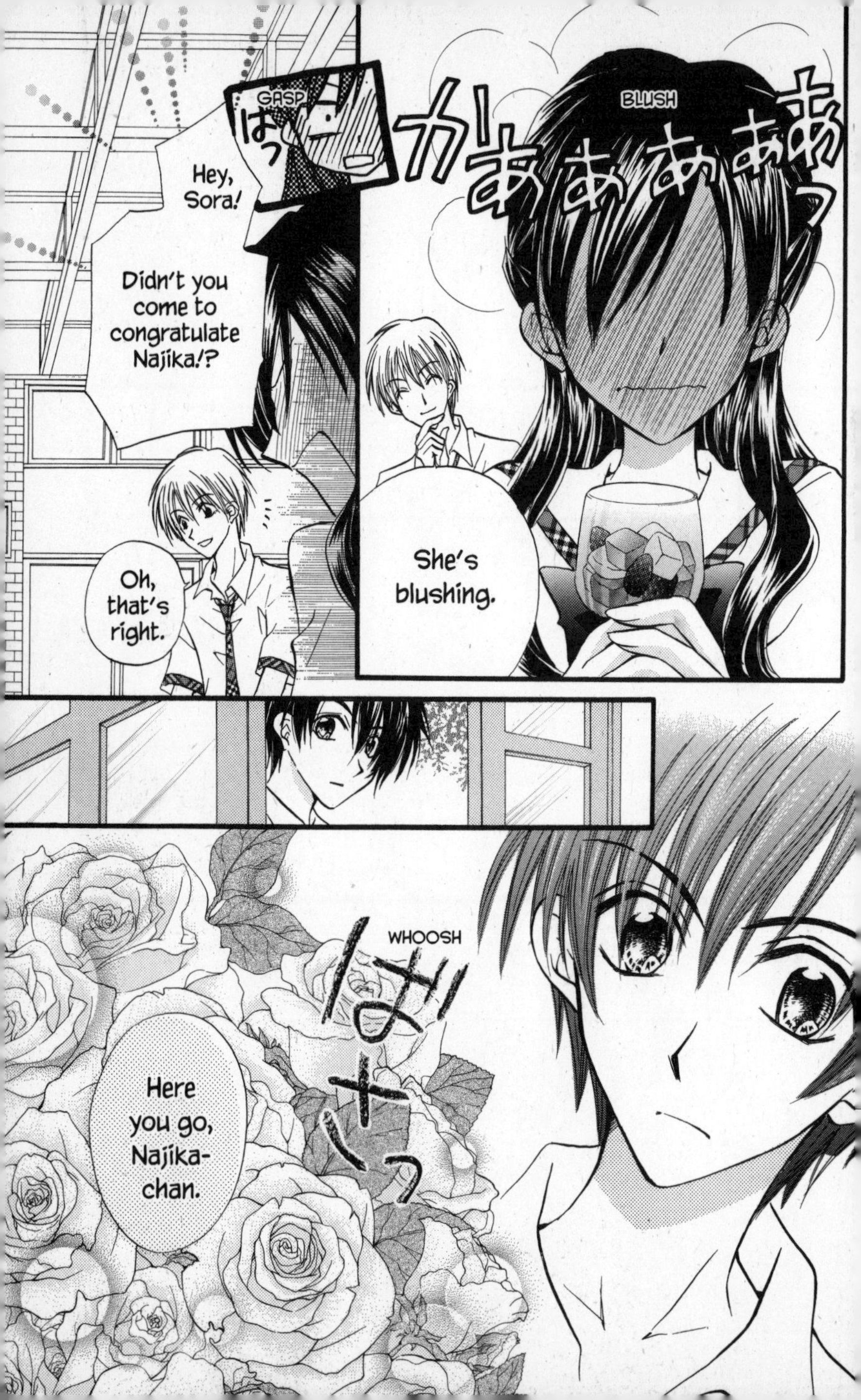
BLUSH
She's blushing.
GASP
はっ
Hey, Sora!
Didn't you come to congratulate Najika!?
Oh, that's right.
WHOOSH
ばさっ
Here you go, Najika-chan.

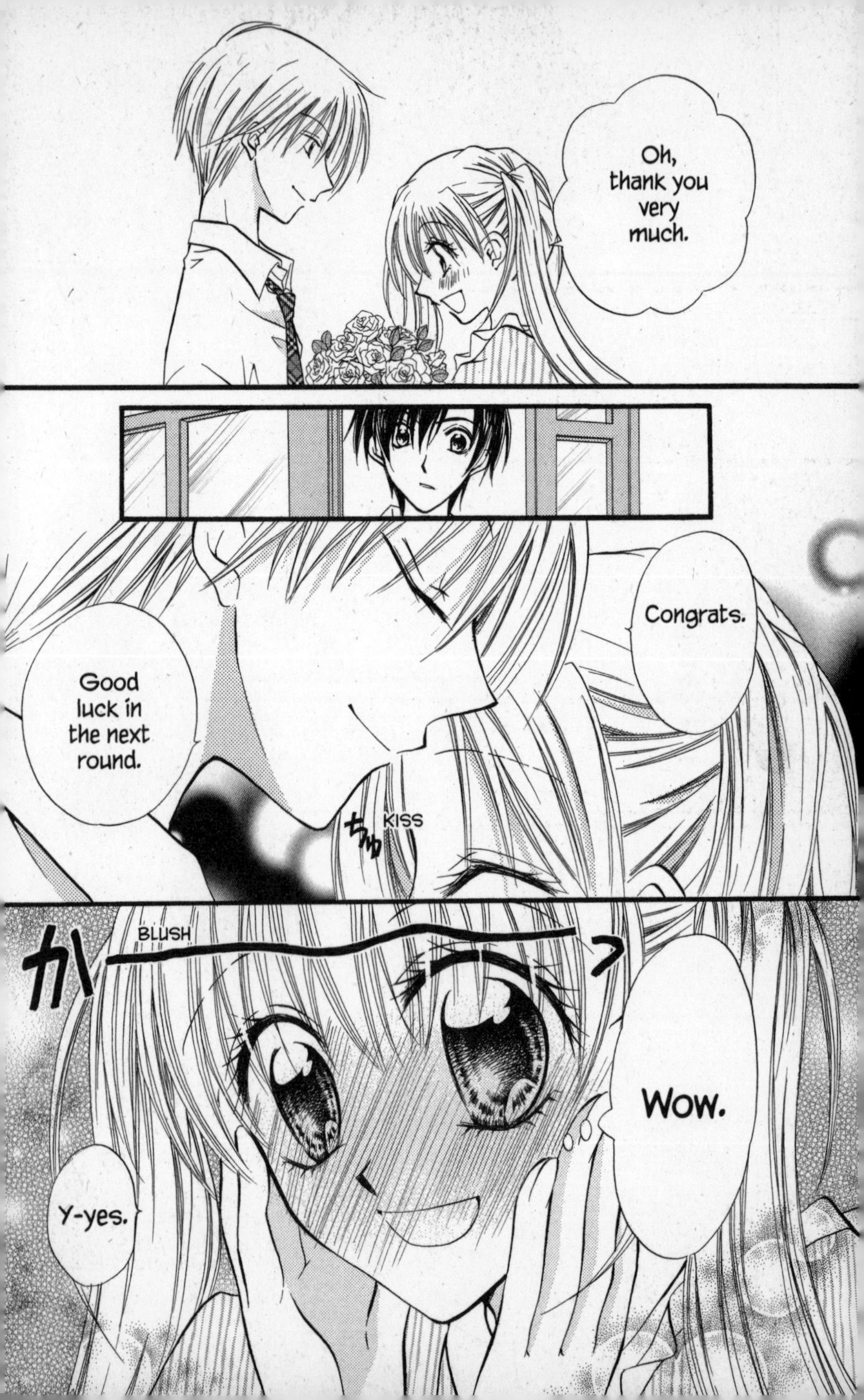
Oh, thank you very much.
Congrats.
Good luck in the next round.
ちゅ KISS
カー BLUSH
Wow.
Y-yes.

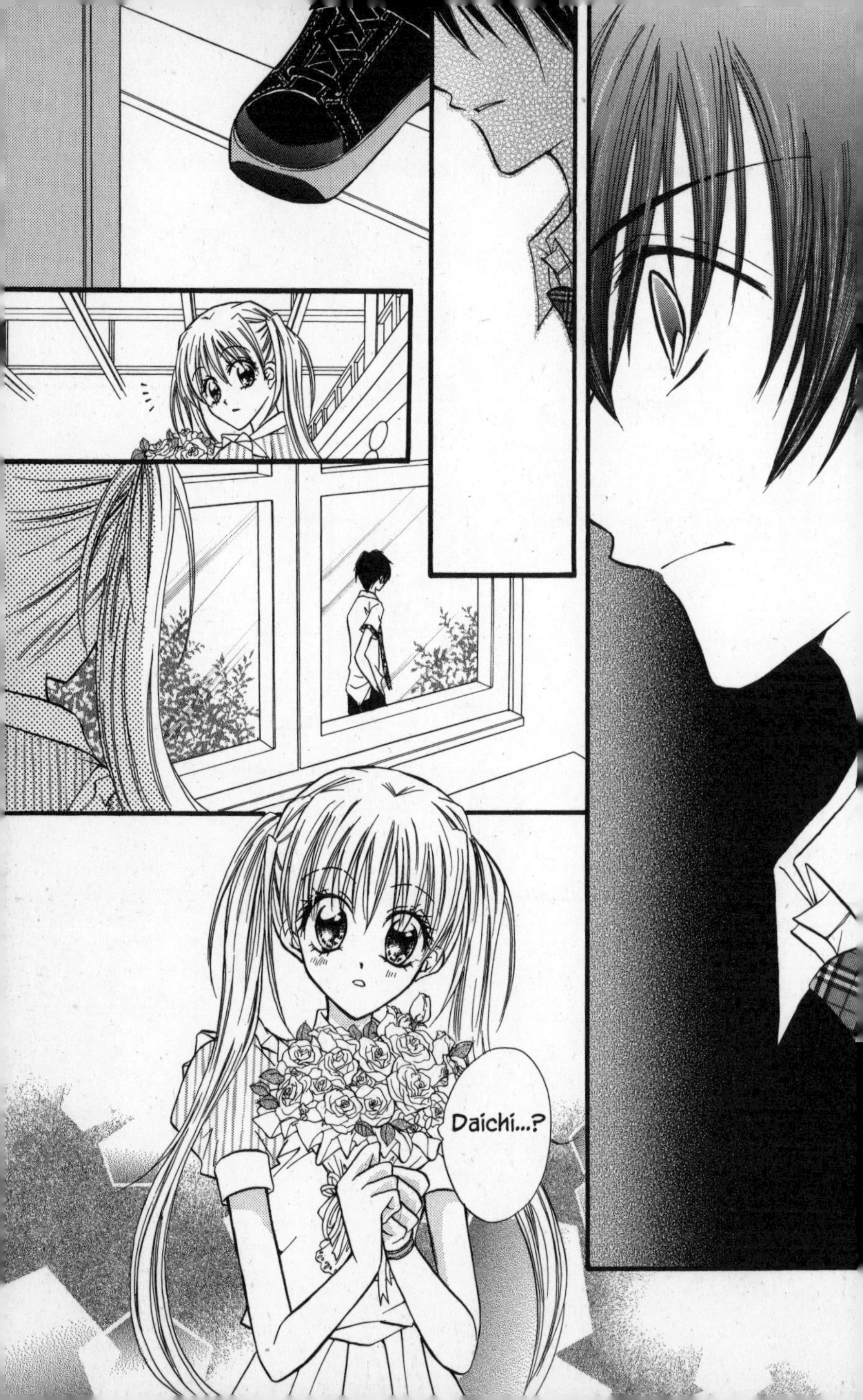
Daichi...?

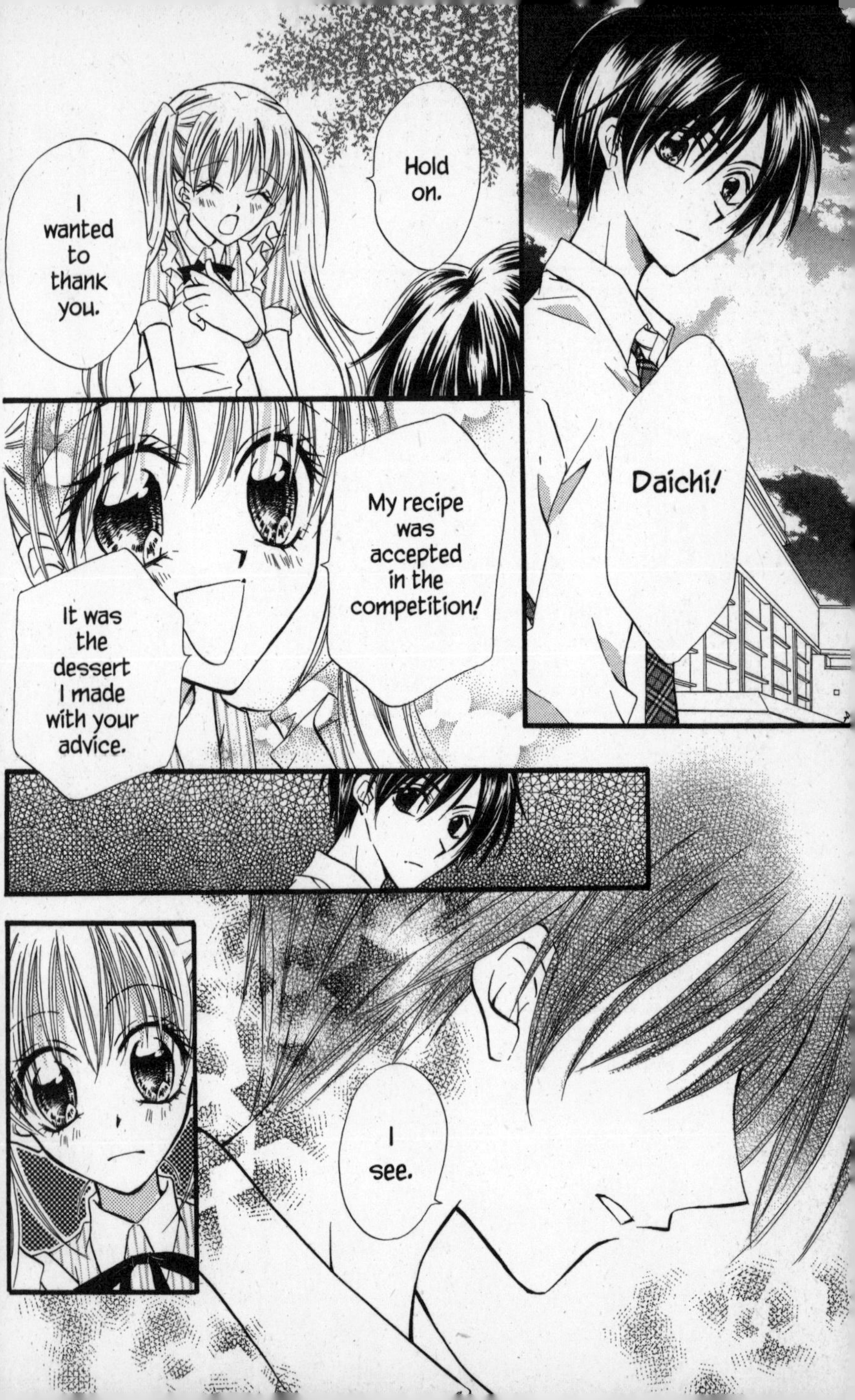
Daichi!
Hold on.
I wanted to thank you.
My recipe was accepted in the competition!
It was the dessert I made with your advice.
I see.

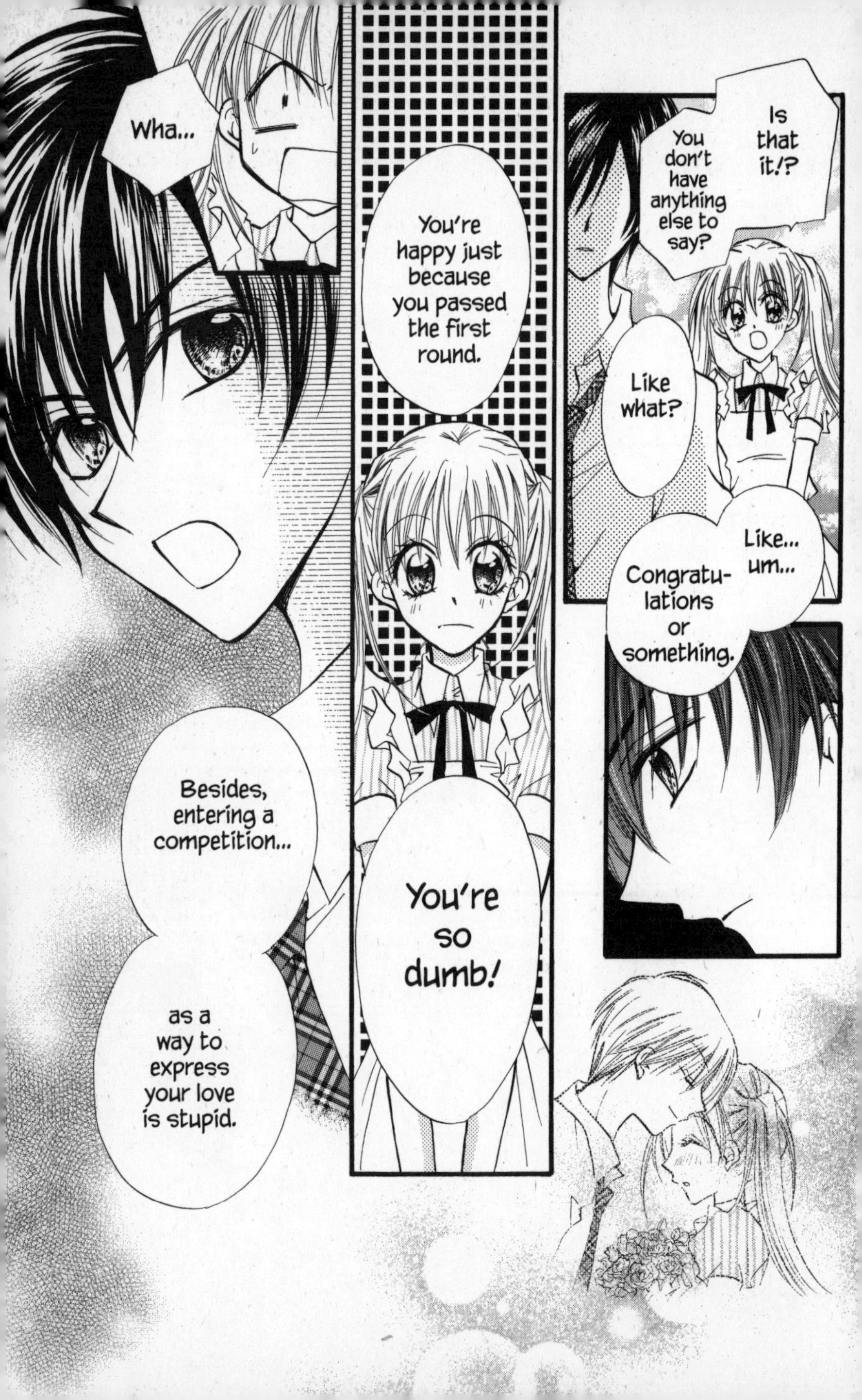
Is that it!?
You don't have anything else to say?
Like what?
Like... um...
Congratulations or something.
You're happy just because you passed the first round.
You're so dumb!
Wha...
Besides, entering a competition...
as a way to express your love is stupid.

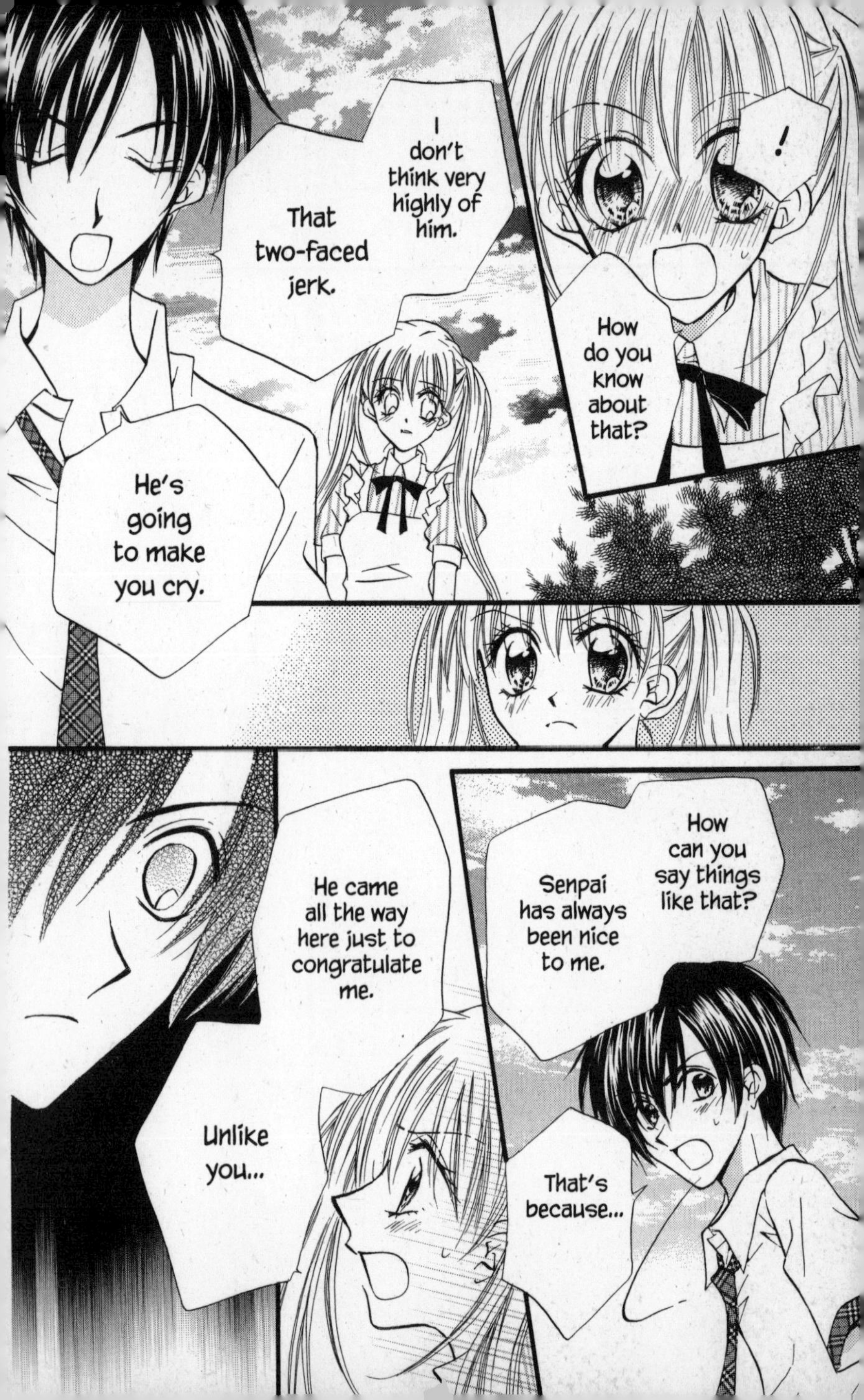
!
How do you know about that?
I don't think very highly of him.
That two-faced jerk.
He's going to make you cry.
How can you say things like that?
Senpai has always been nice to me.
He came all the way here just to congratulate me.
Unlike you...
That's because...

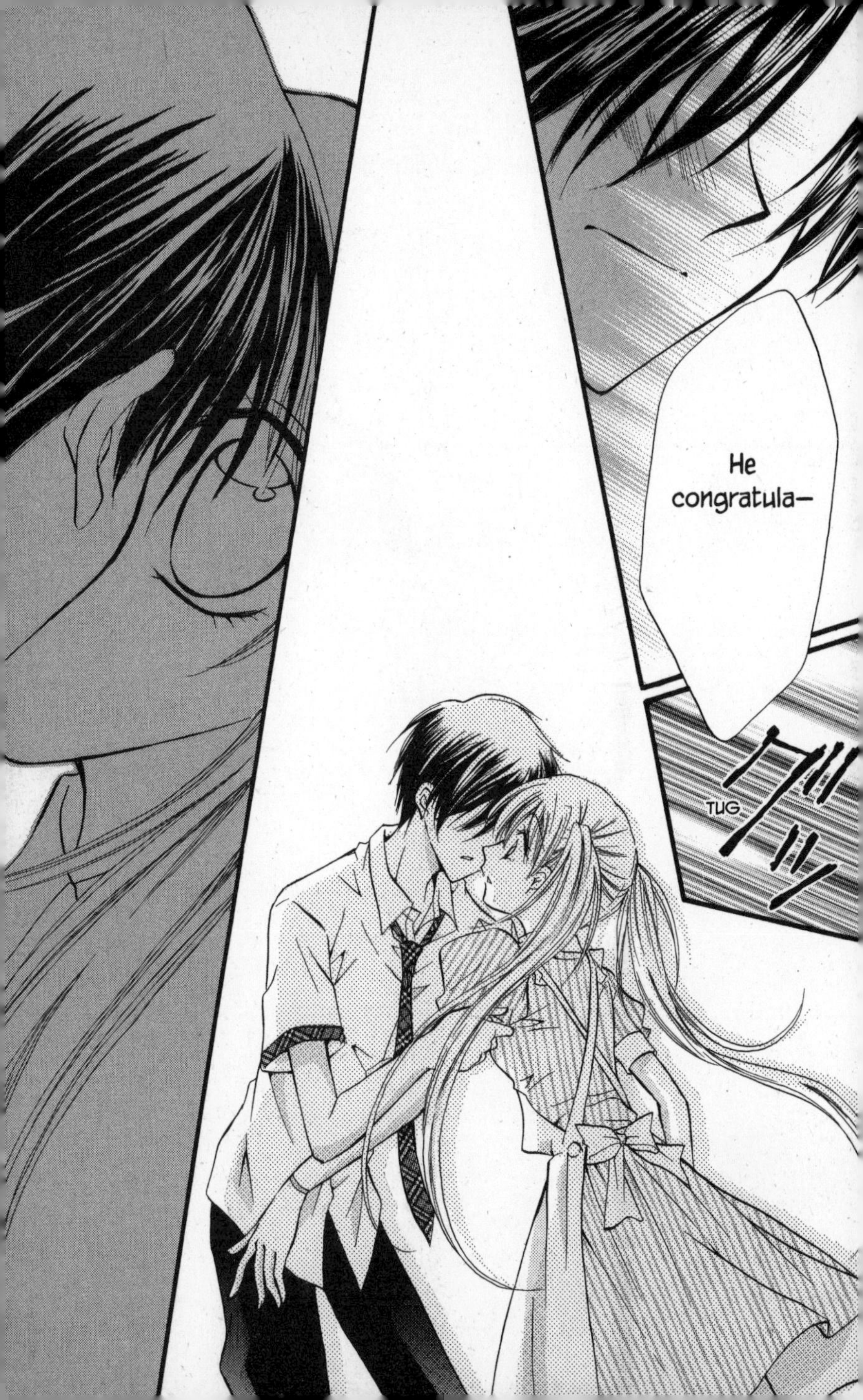
He congratula—
TUG

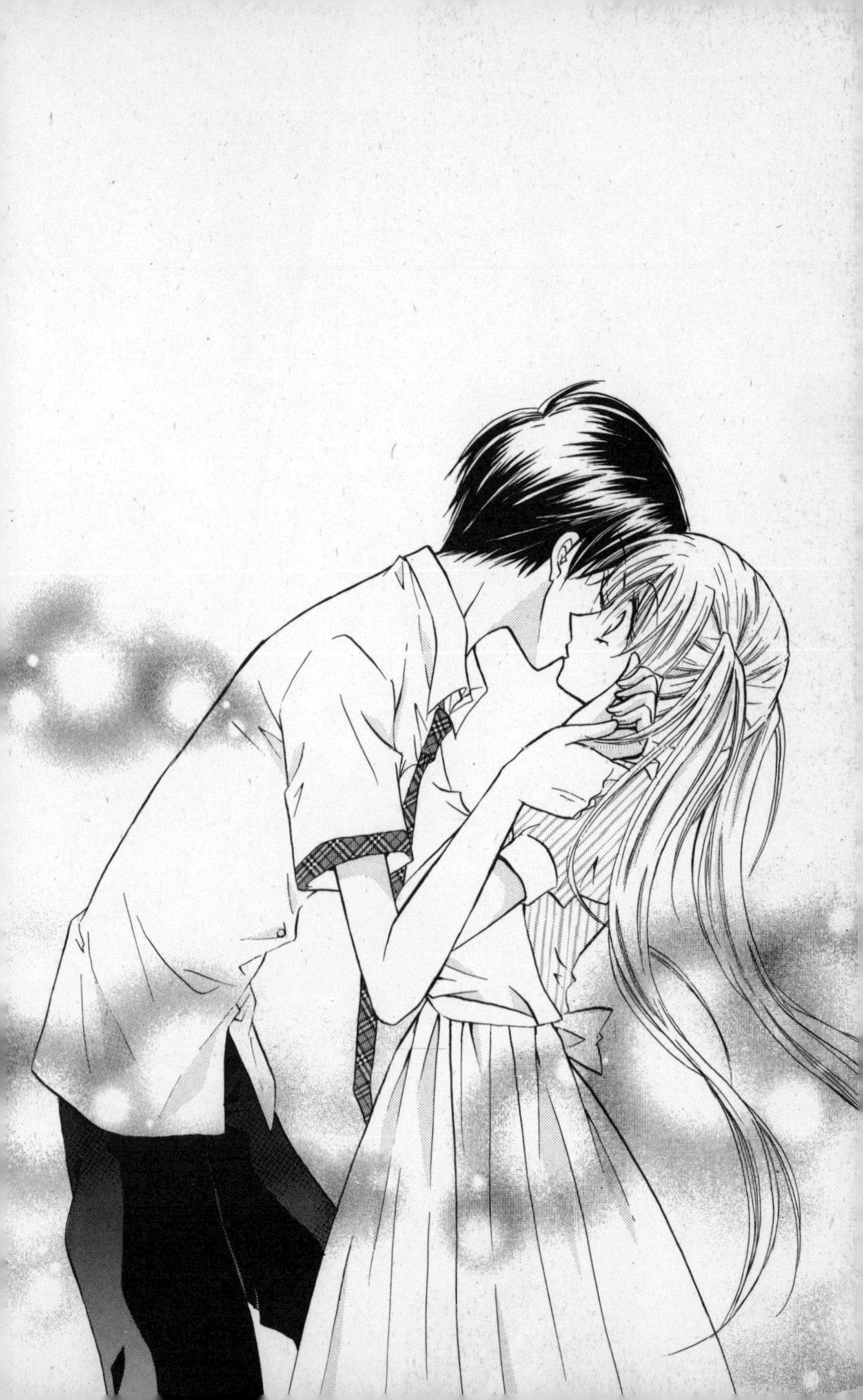

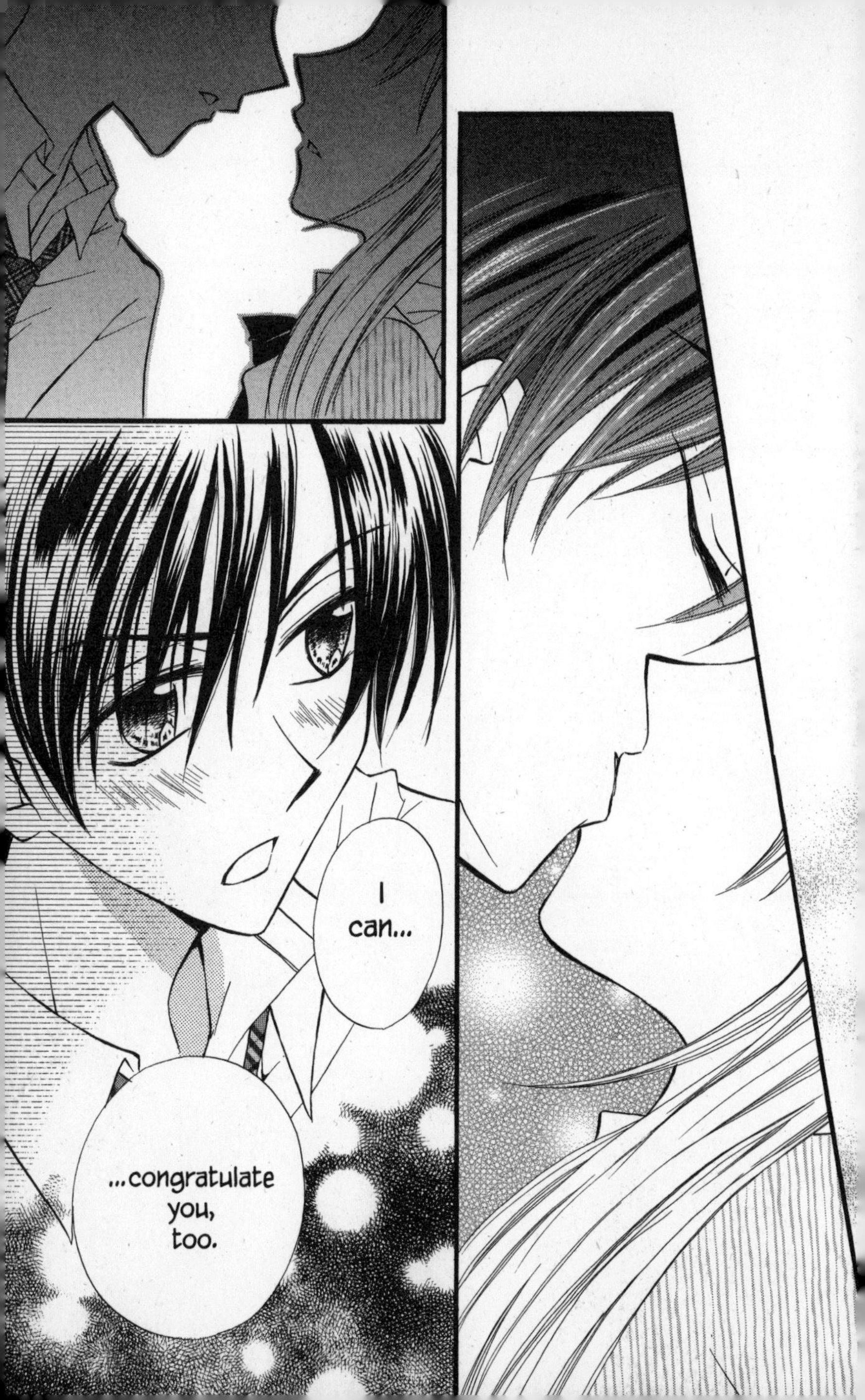
I can...
...congratulate you, too.

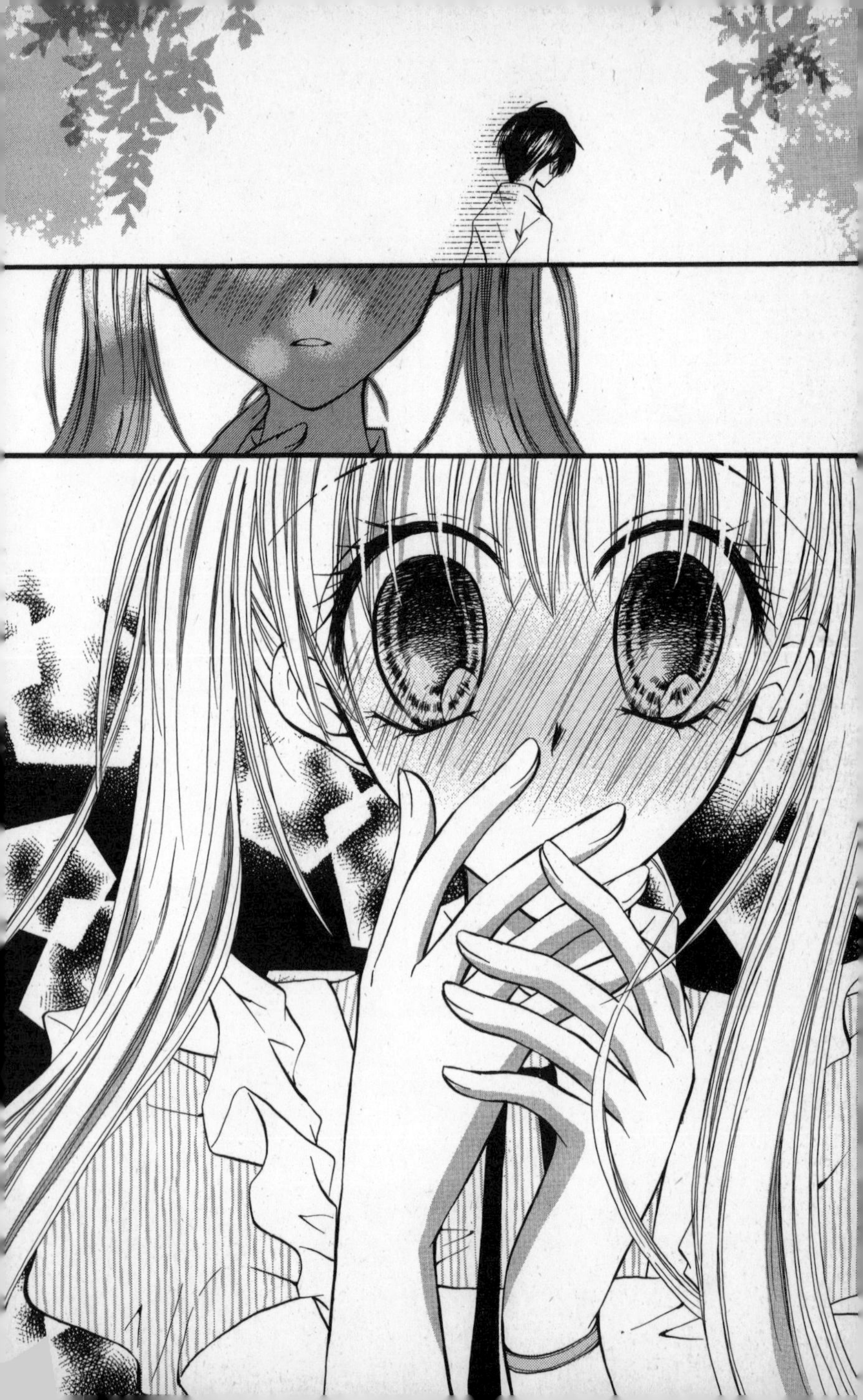

Kitchen Princess

4 Panel Manga #3

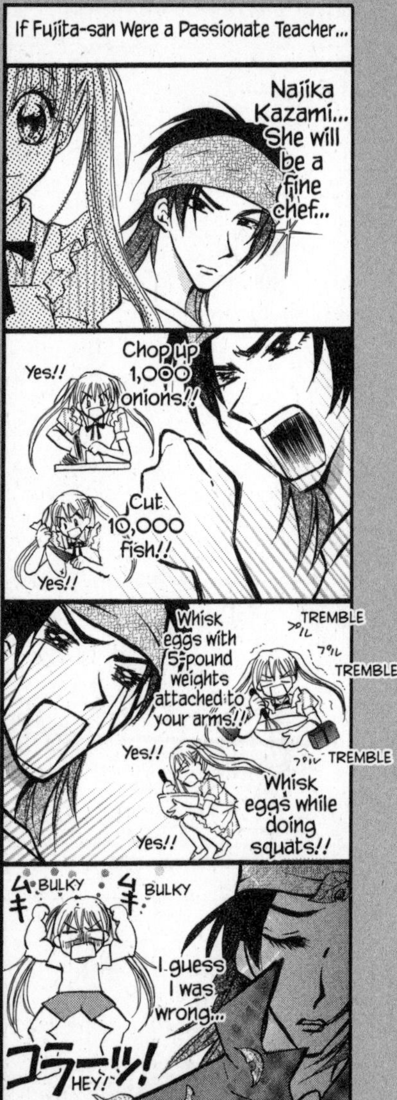

If Fujita-san Were a Passionate Teacher...
Najika Kazami... She will be a fine chef...
Chop up 1,000 onions!!
Yes!!
Cut 10,000 fish!!
Yes!!
TREMBLE
Whisk eggs with 5-pound weights attached to your arms!!
TREMBLE
TREMBLE
Yes!!
Whisk eggs while doing squats!!
Yes!!
BULKY
BULKY
I guess I was wrong...
コラーッ!
HEY!

Kitchen Princess

4 Panel Manga #4

If it were *Kitchen Prince*...
I am Najio Kazami
I just transferred to Seika Academy.
Kazami-kun, you can ask me anything.
Sorako-san... she's pretty and smart.
Your food is good.
...
Daiko-chan... she's also cute.
And she has a crush on me.
Dear Hagio sensei.
Which one should I choose...?
I don't care.

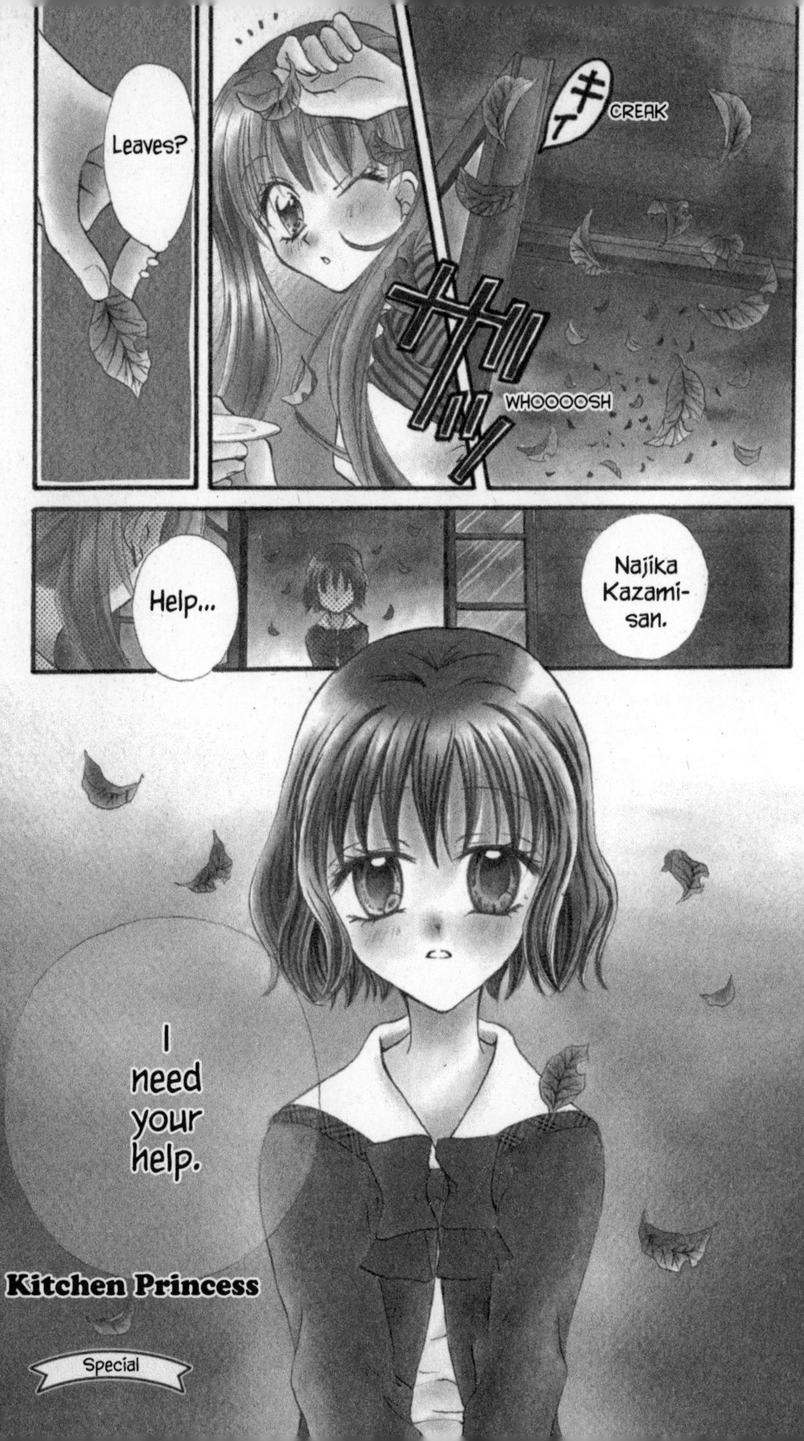
CREAK
WHOOOOSH
Leaves?
Najika Kazami-san.
Help...
I need your help.
Kitchen Princess
Special

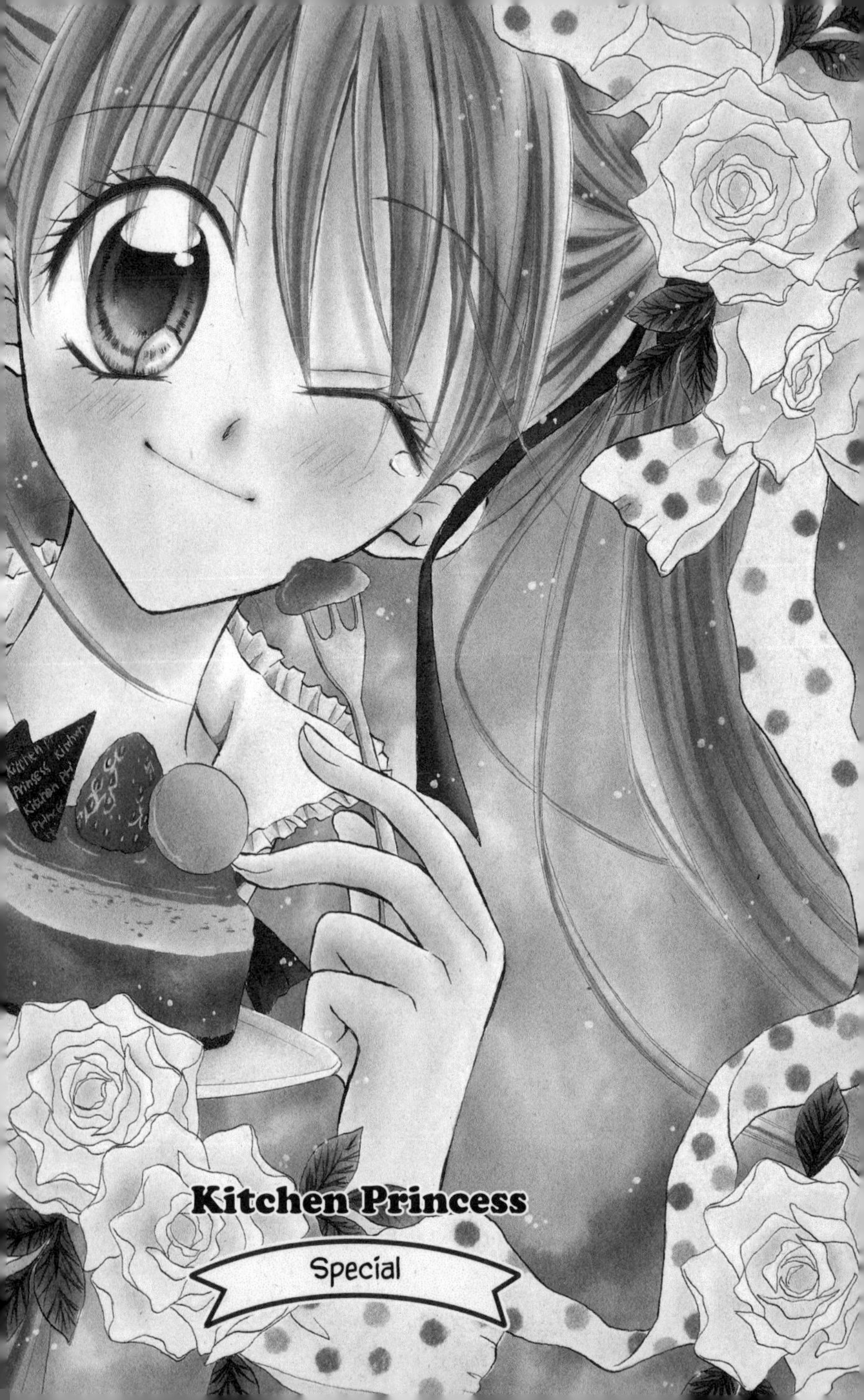
Kitchen Princess
Special

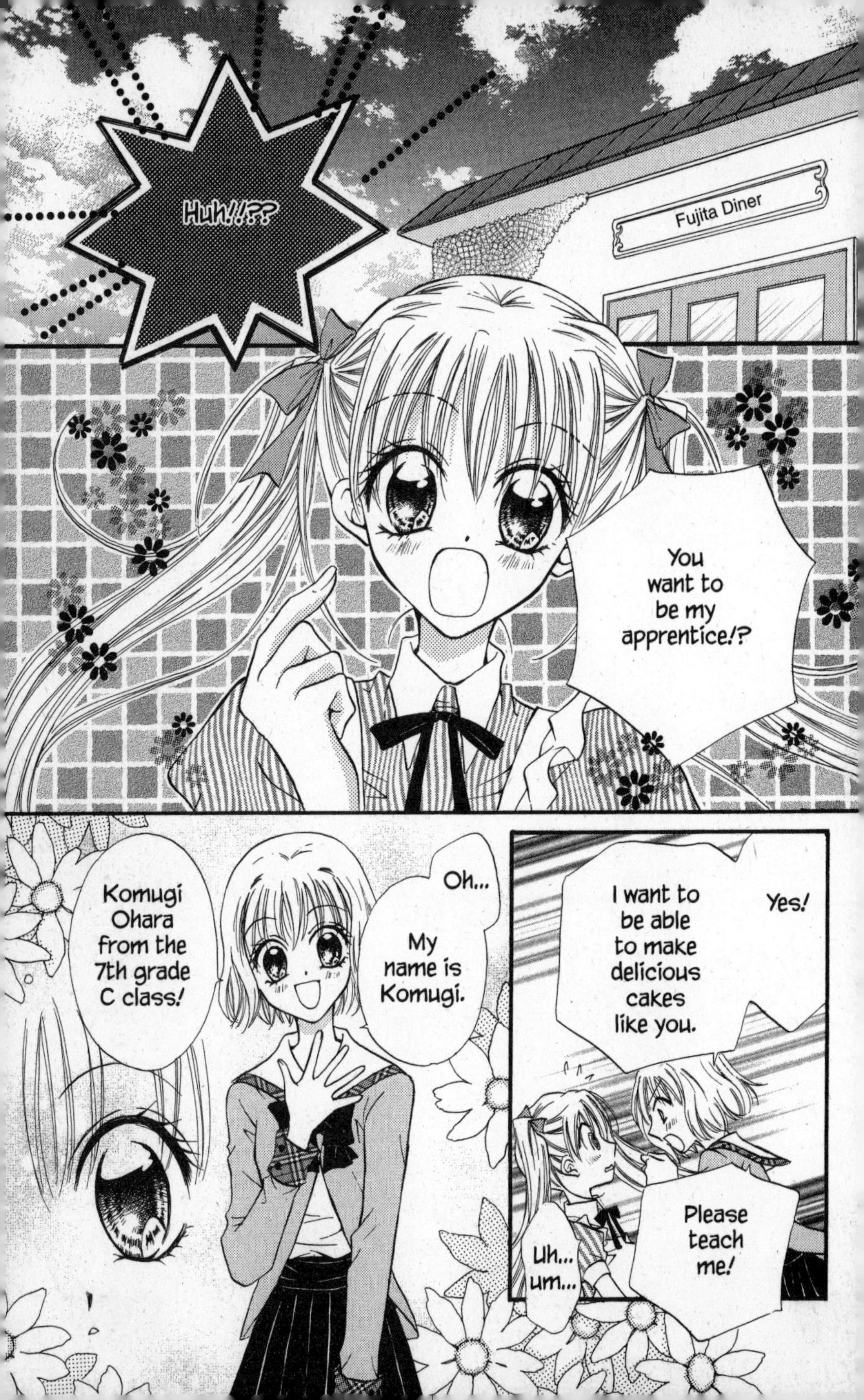
Fujita Diner
Huh!!??
You want to be my apprentice!?
Yes!
I want to be able to make delicious cakes like you.
Please teach me!
Uh... um...
Oh...
My name is Komugi.
Komugi Ohara from the 7th grade C class!

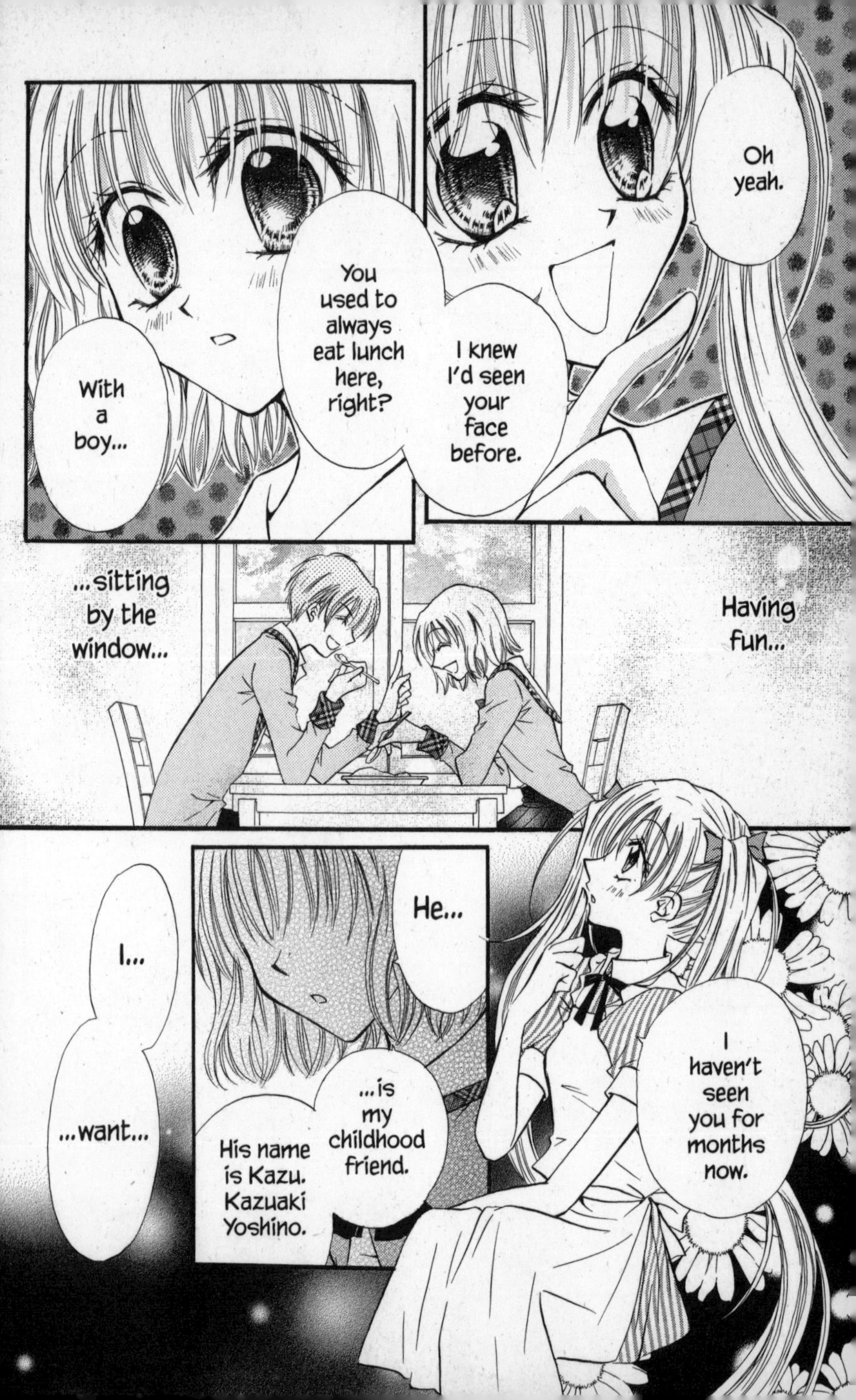
Oh yeah.
I knew I'd seen your face before.
You used to always eat lunch here, right?
With a boy...
Having fun...
...sitting by the window...
I haven't seen you for months now.
He...
...is my childhood friend.
His name is Kazu. Kazuaki Yoshino.
I...
...want...

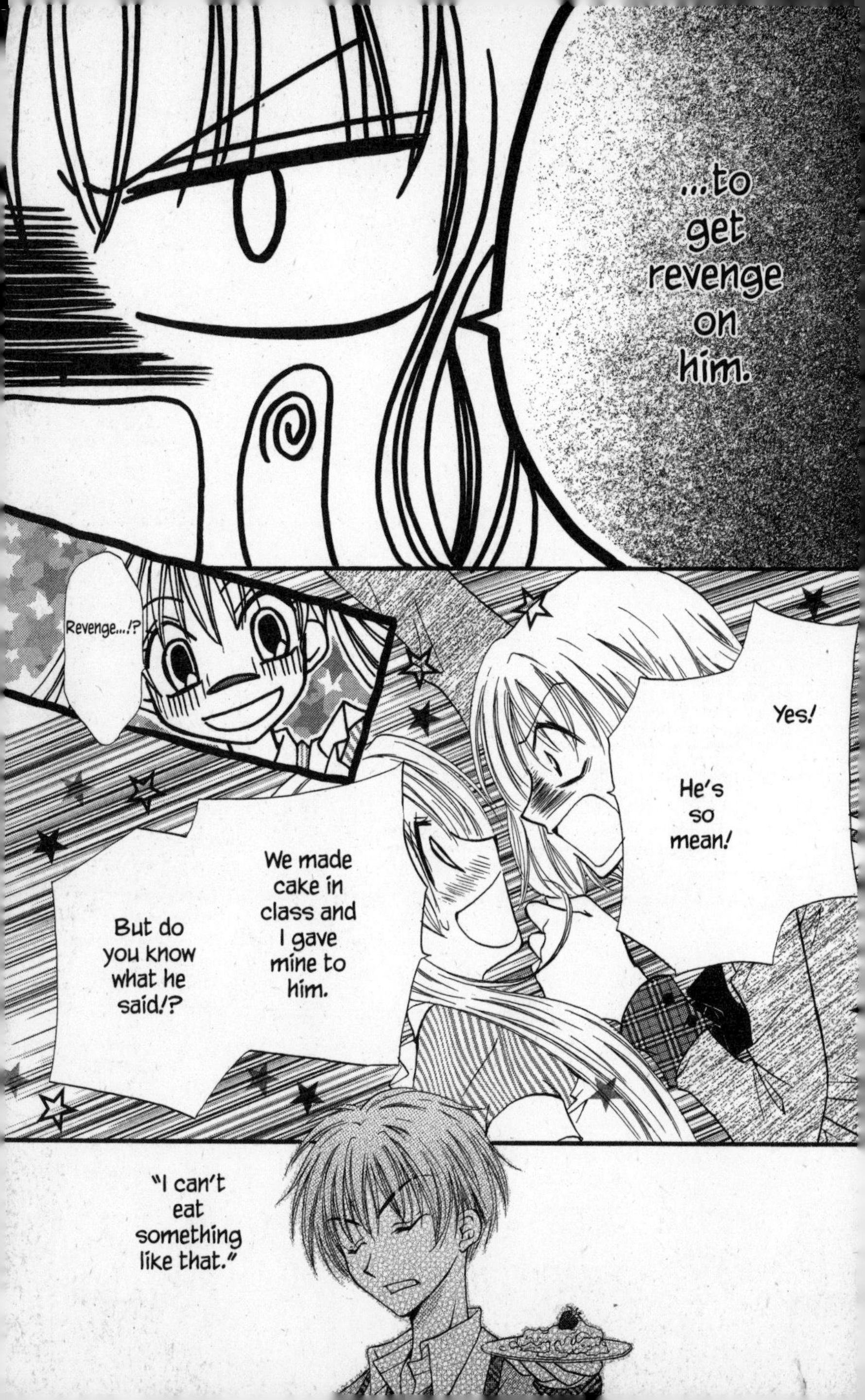
...to get revenge on him.
Revenge...!?
Yes!
He's so mean!
We made cake in class and I gave mine to him.
But do you know what he said!?
"I can't eat something like that."

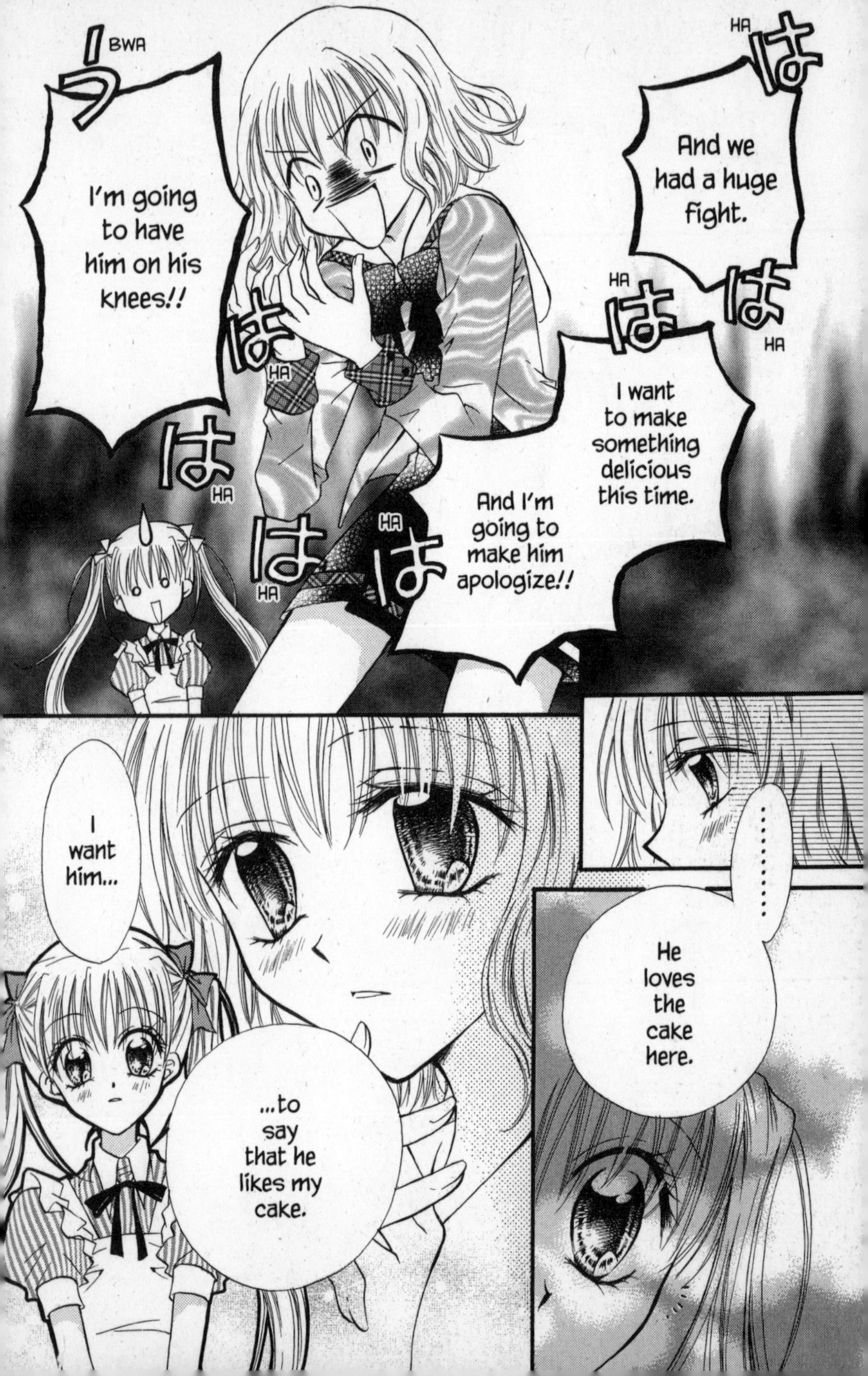

HA は
And we had a huge fight.
HA は
は HA
I want to make something delicious this time.
And I'm going to make him apologize!!
う BWA
I'm going to have him on his knees!!
は HA
は HA
は HA
は HA
......
He loves the cake here.
I want him...
...to say that he likes my cake.

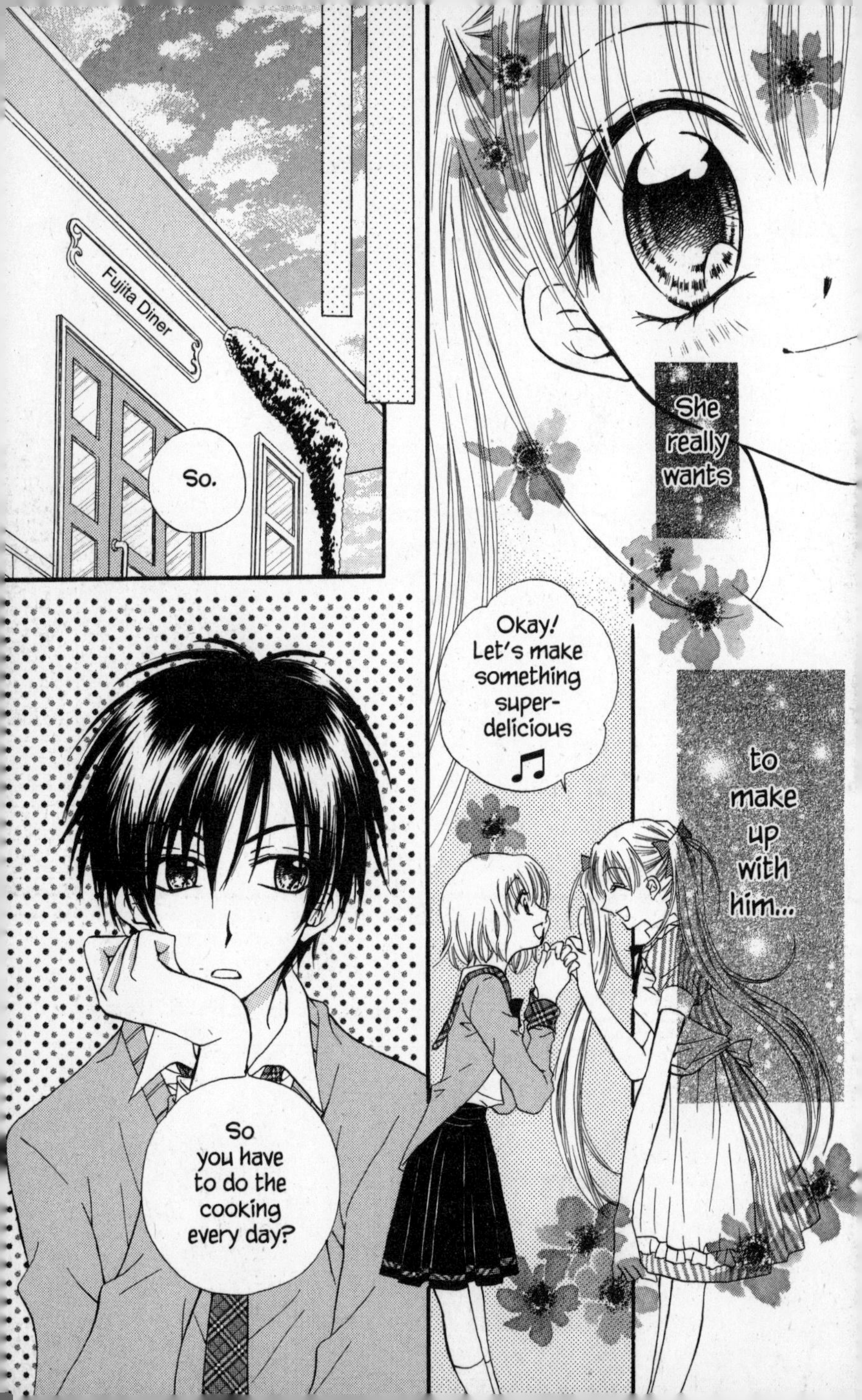
She really wants
to make up with him...
Okay! Let's make something super-delicious ♫
Fujita Diner
So.
So you have to do the cooking every day?

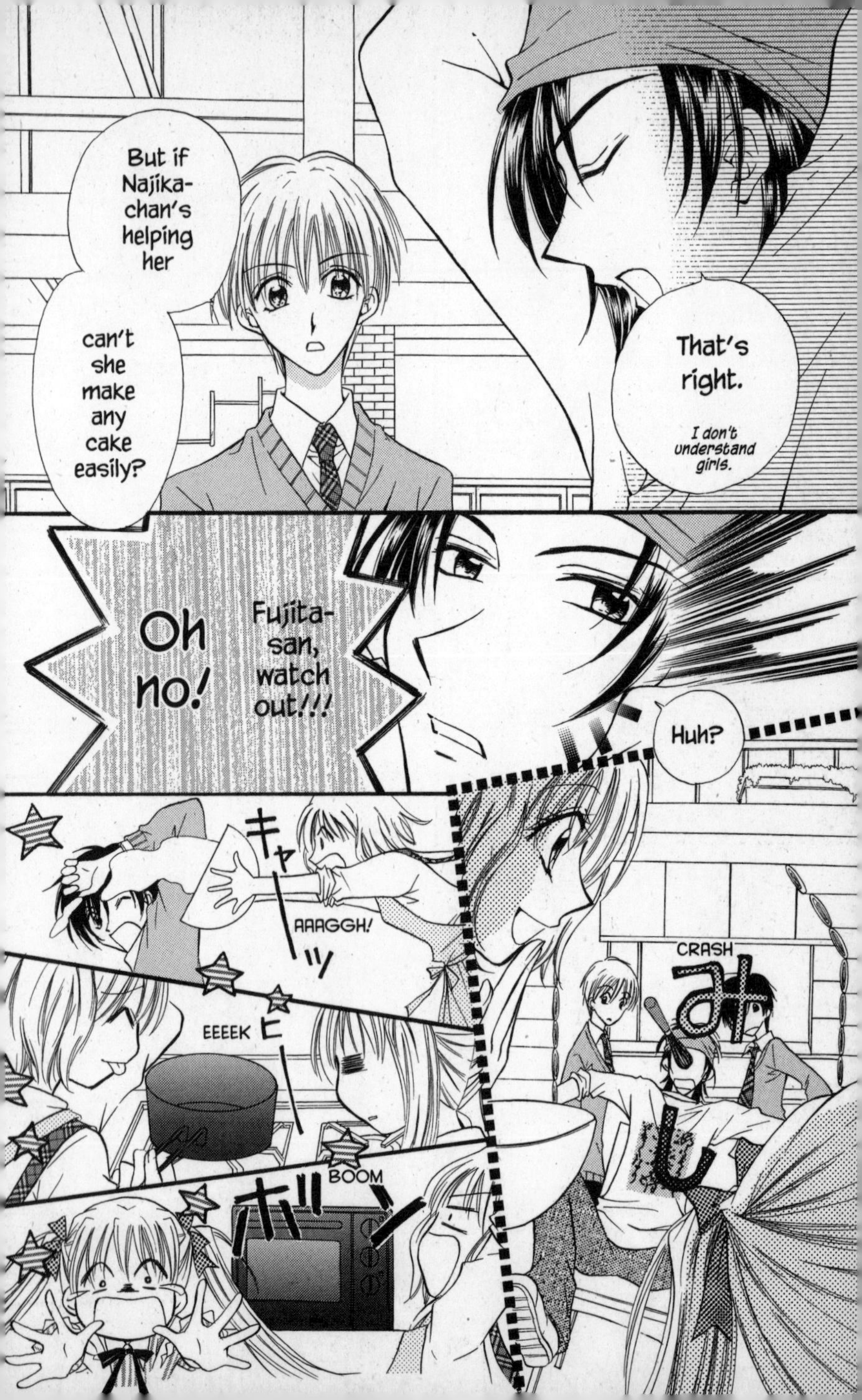
But if Najika-chan's helping her
can't she make any cake easily?
That's right.
I don't understand girls.
Oh no!
Fujita-san, watch out!!!
Huh?
キャーッ
AAAGGH!
ヒー
EEEEK
BOOM
CRASH

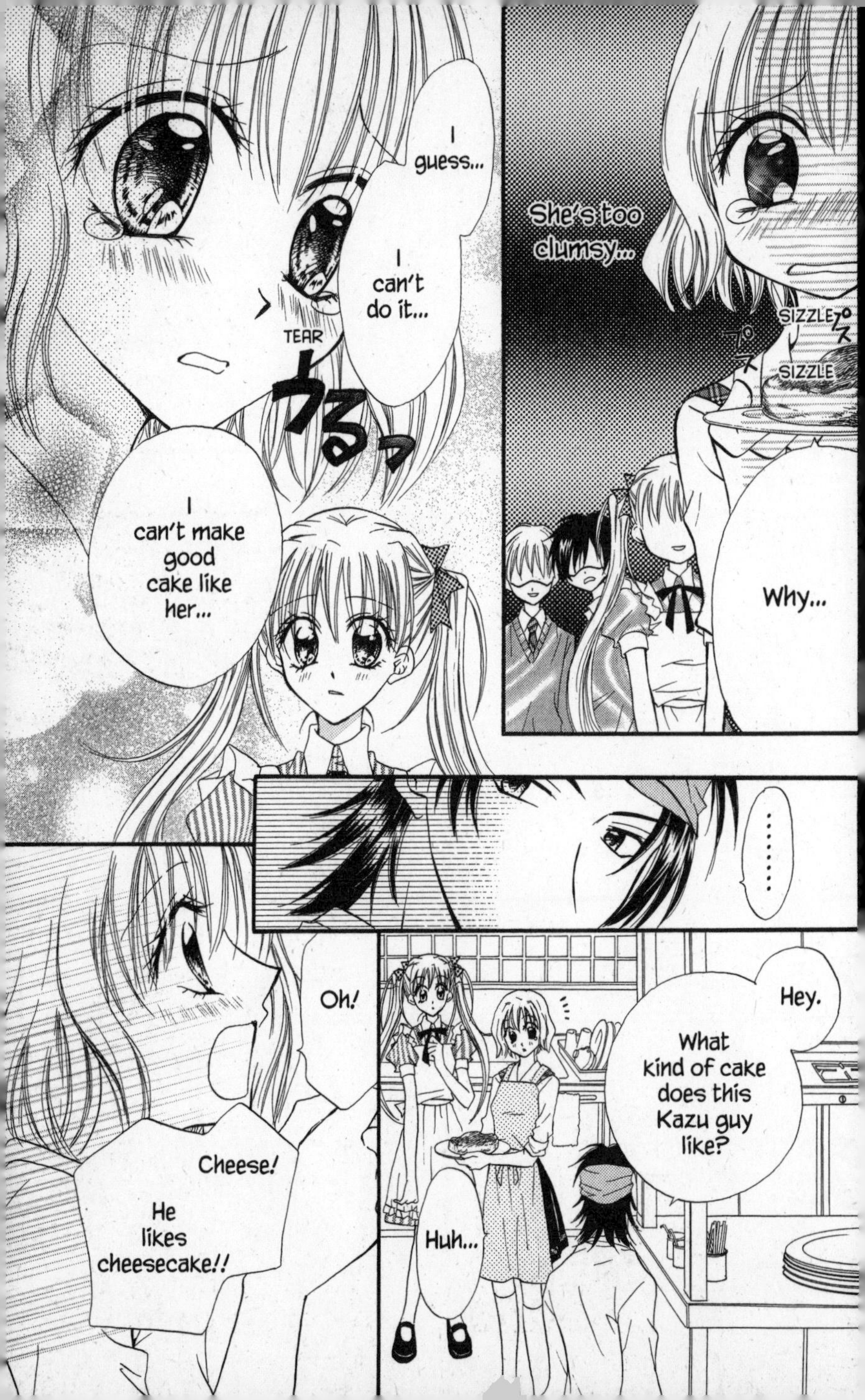
She's too clumsy...
SIZZLE
SIZZLE
Why...
I guess...
I can't do it...
TEAR
うるっ
I can't make good cake like her...
......
Hey.
What kind of cake does this Kazu guy like?
Huh...
Oh!
Cheese!
He likes cheesecake!!

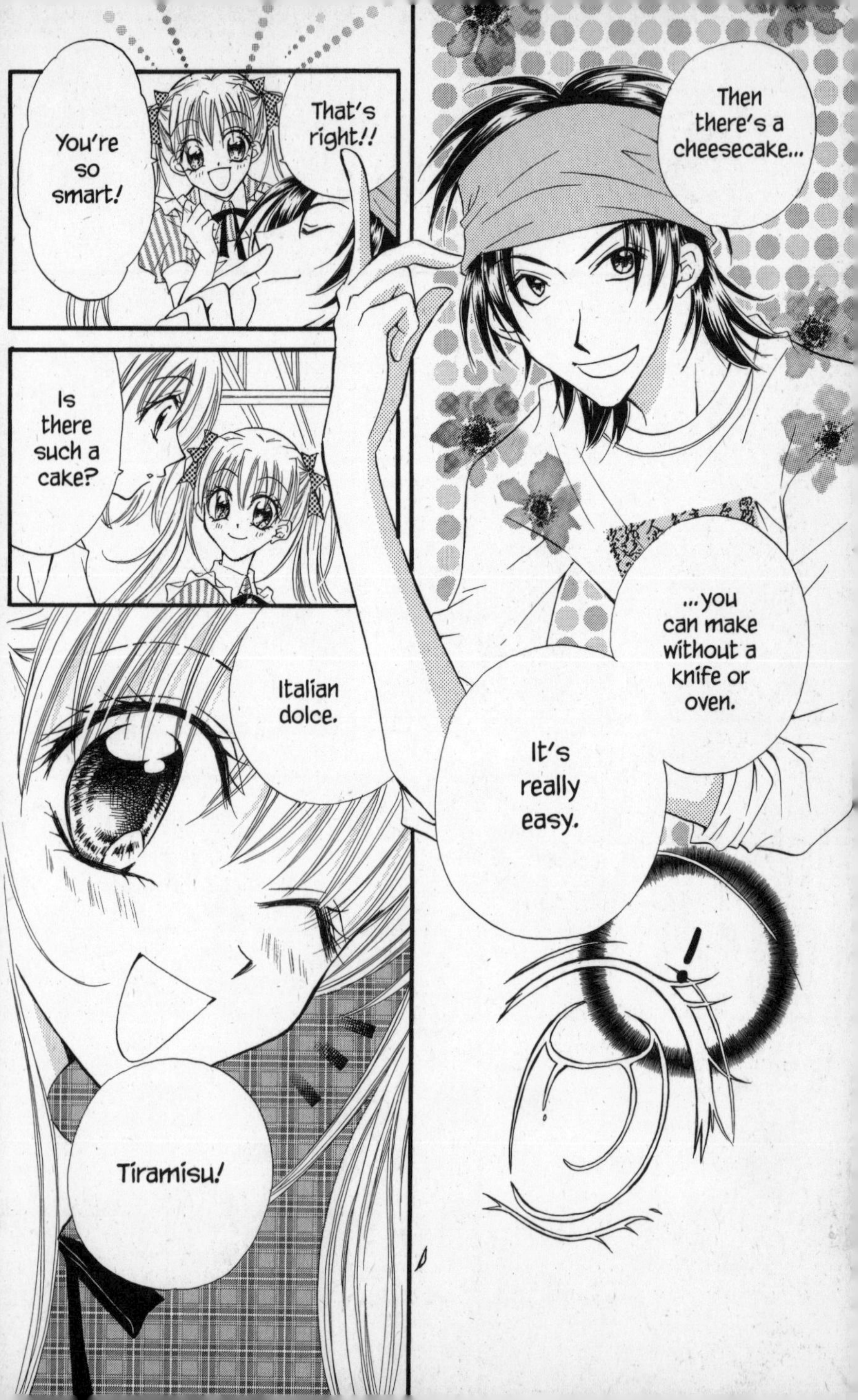
Then there's a cheesecake...
...you can make without a knife or oven.
It's really easy.
!
That's right!!
You're so smart!
Is there such a cake?
Italian dolce.
Tiramisu!

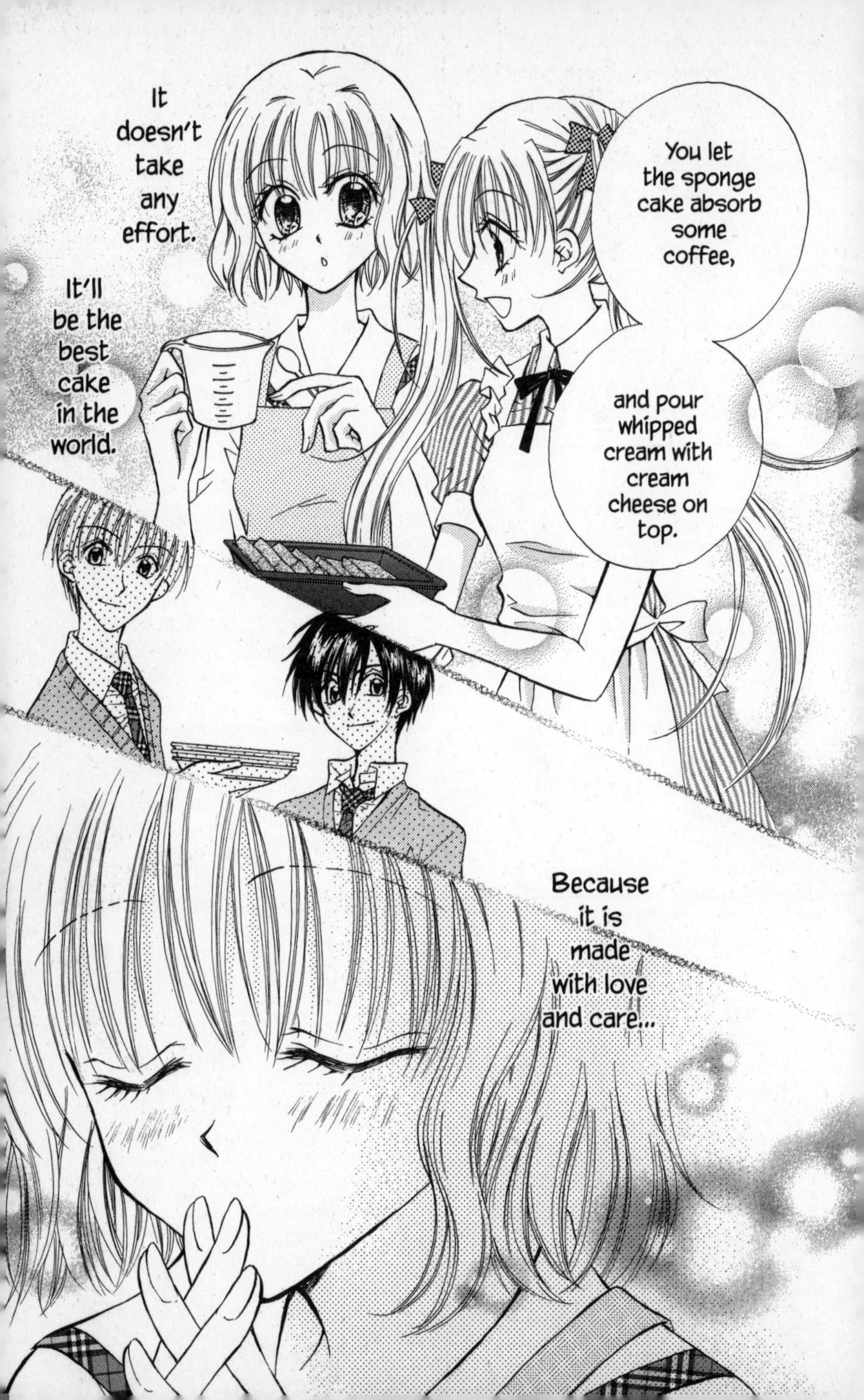
You let the sponge cake absorb some coffee,
and pour whipped cream with cream cheese on top.
It doesn't take any effort.
It'll be the best cake in the world.
Because it is made with love and care...

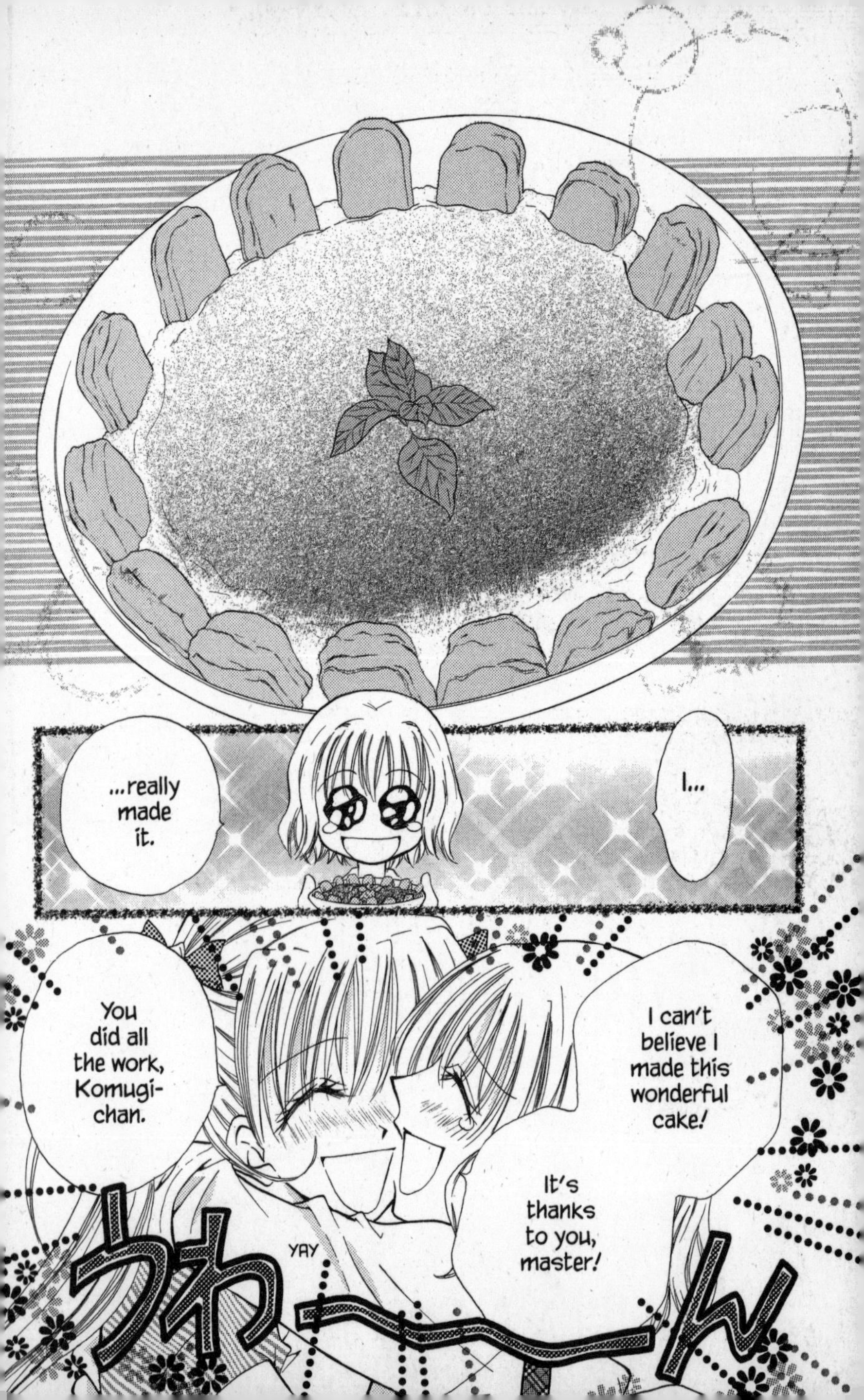
I...
...really made it.
I can't believe I made this wonderful cake!
You did all the work, Komugi-chan.
It's thanks to you, master!
YAY
うわーーん

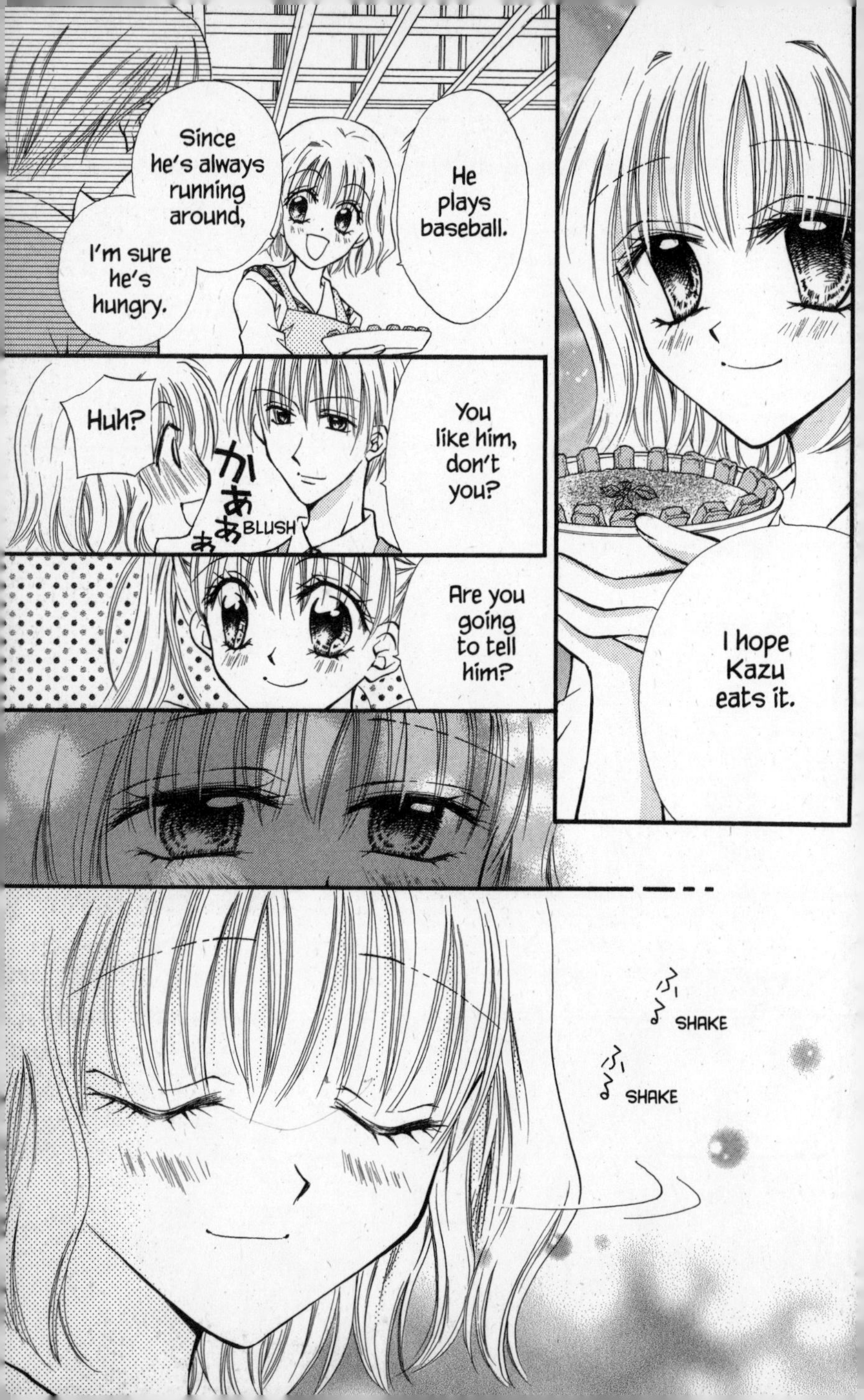
I hope Kazu eats it.
He plays baseball.
Since he's always running around,
I'm sure he's hungry.
You like him, don't you?
Huh?
かあああ BLUSH
Are you going to tell him?
ふる SHAKE
ふる SHAKE

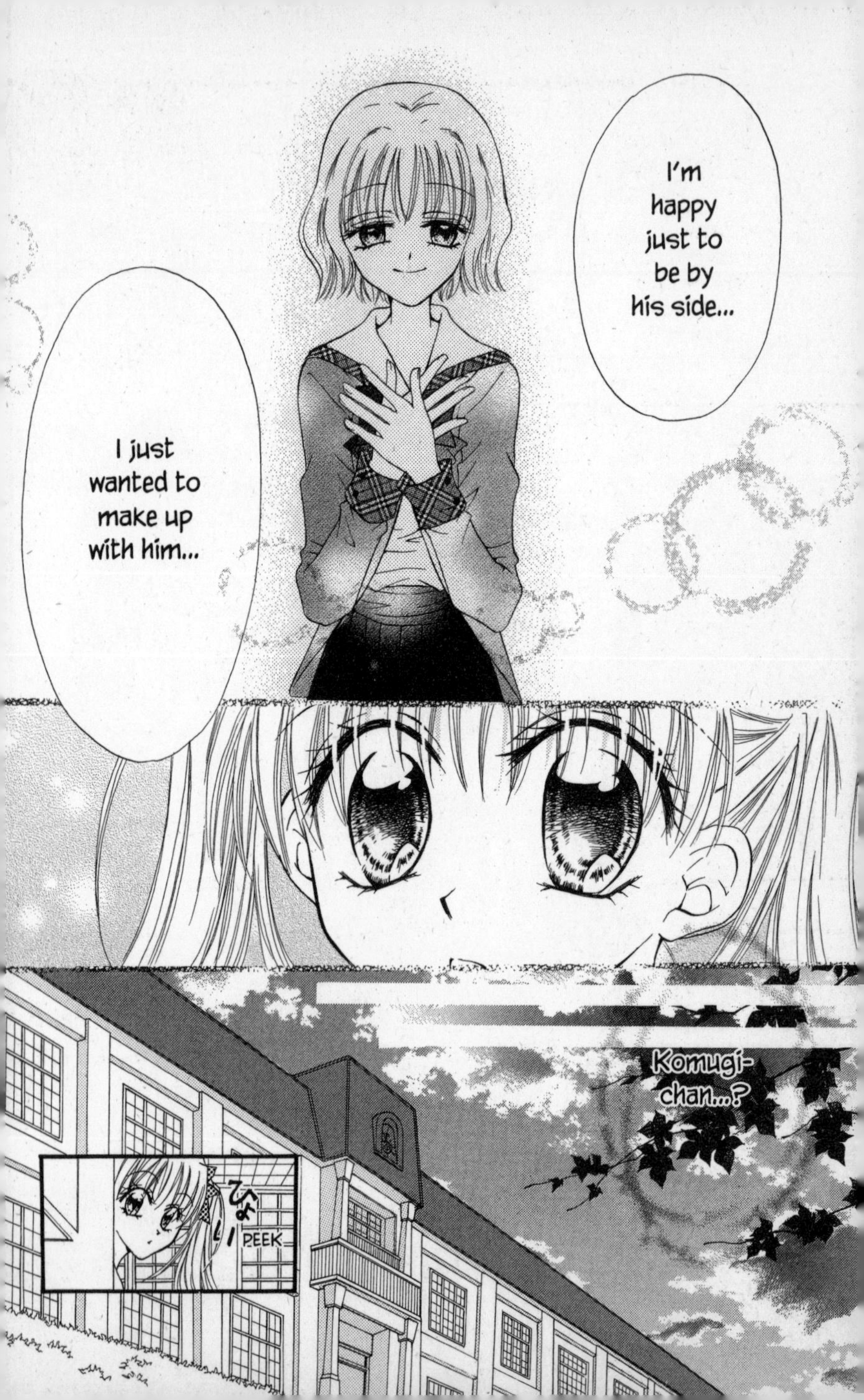
I'm happy just to be by his side...
I just wanted to make up with him...
Komugi-chan...?
ひょい
PEEK

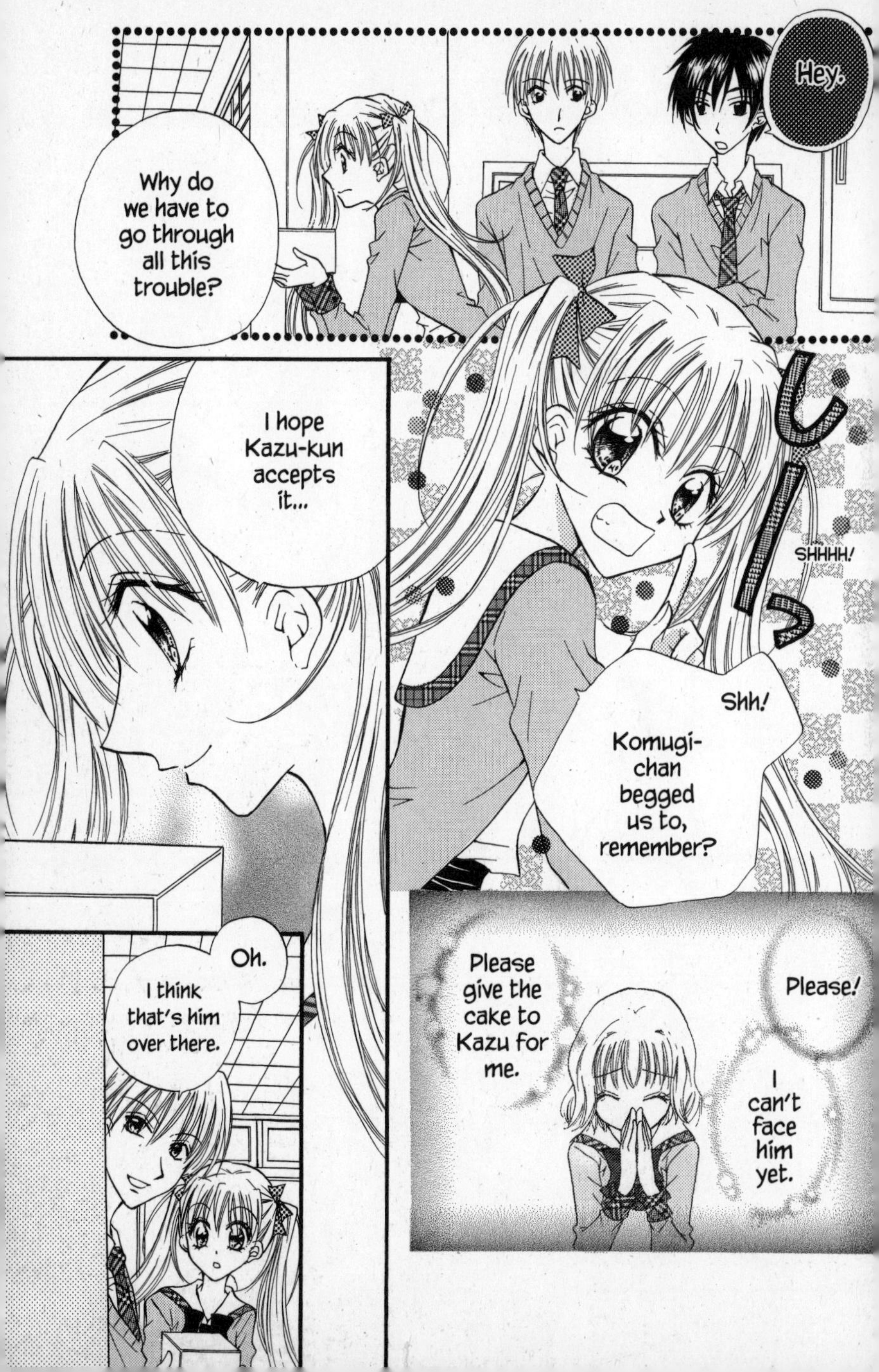
Hey.
Why do we have to go through all this trouble?
SHHHH!
Shh!
Komugi-chan begged us to, remember?
I hope Kazu-kun accepts it...
Please!
I can't face him yet.
Please give the cake to Kazu for me.
Oh.
I think that's him over there.

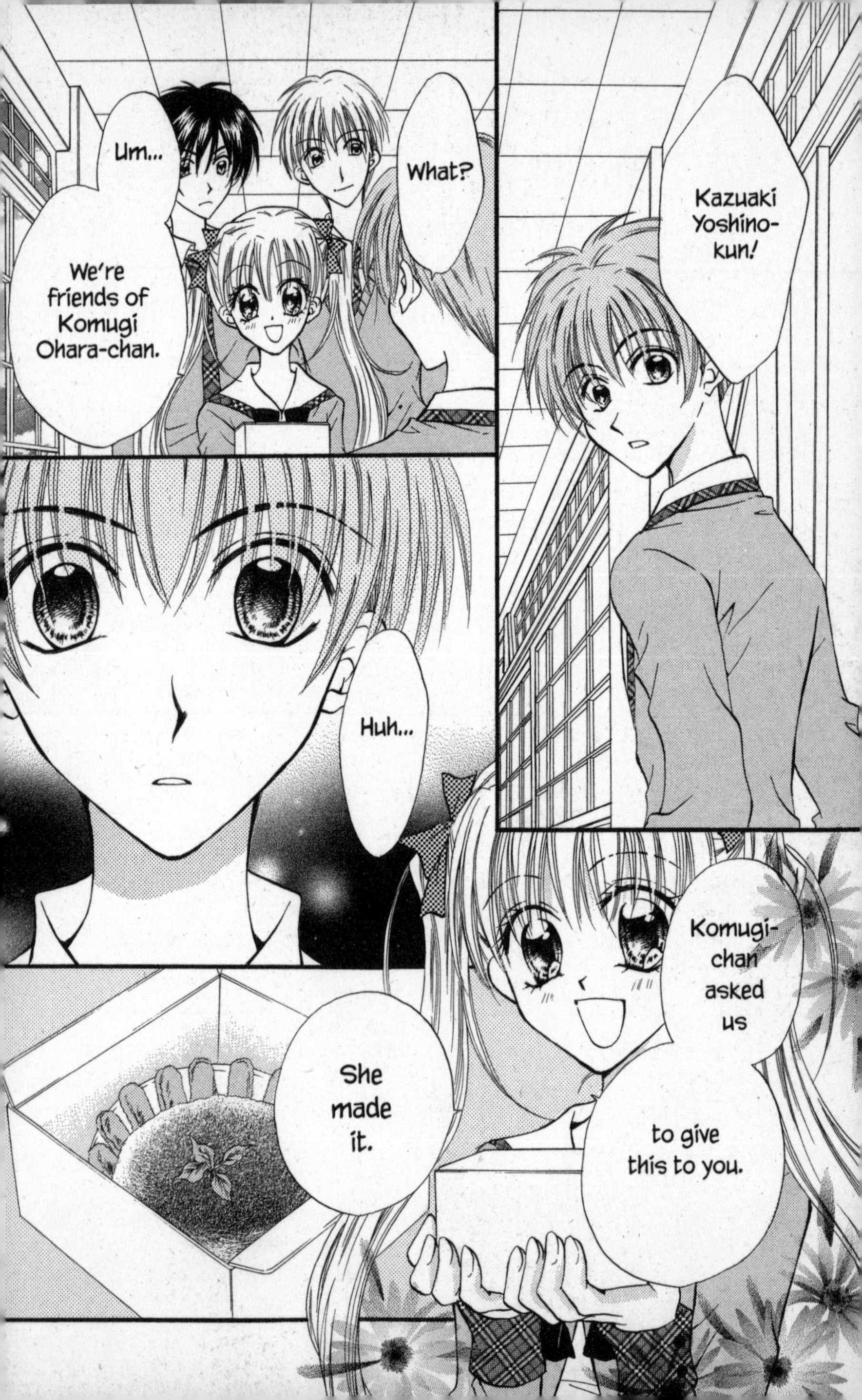
Kazuaki Yoshino-kun!
What?
Um...
We're friends of Komugi Ohara-chan.
Huh...
Komugi-chan asked us
to give this to you.
She made it.

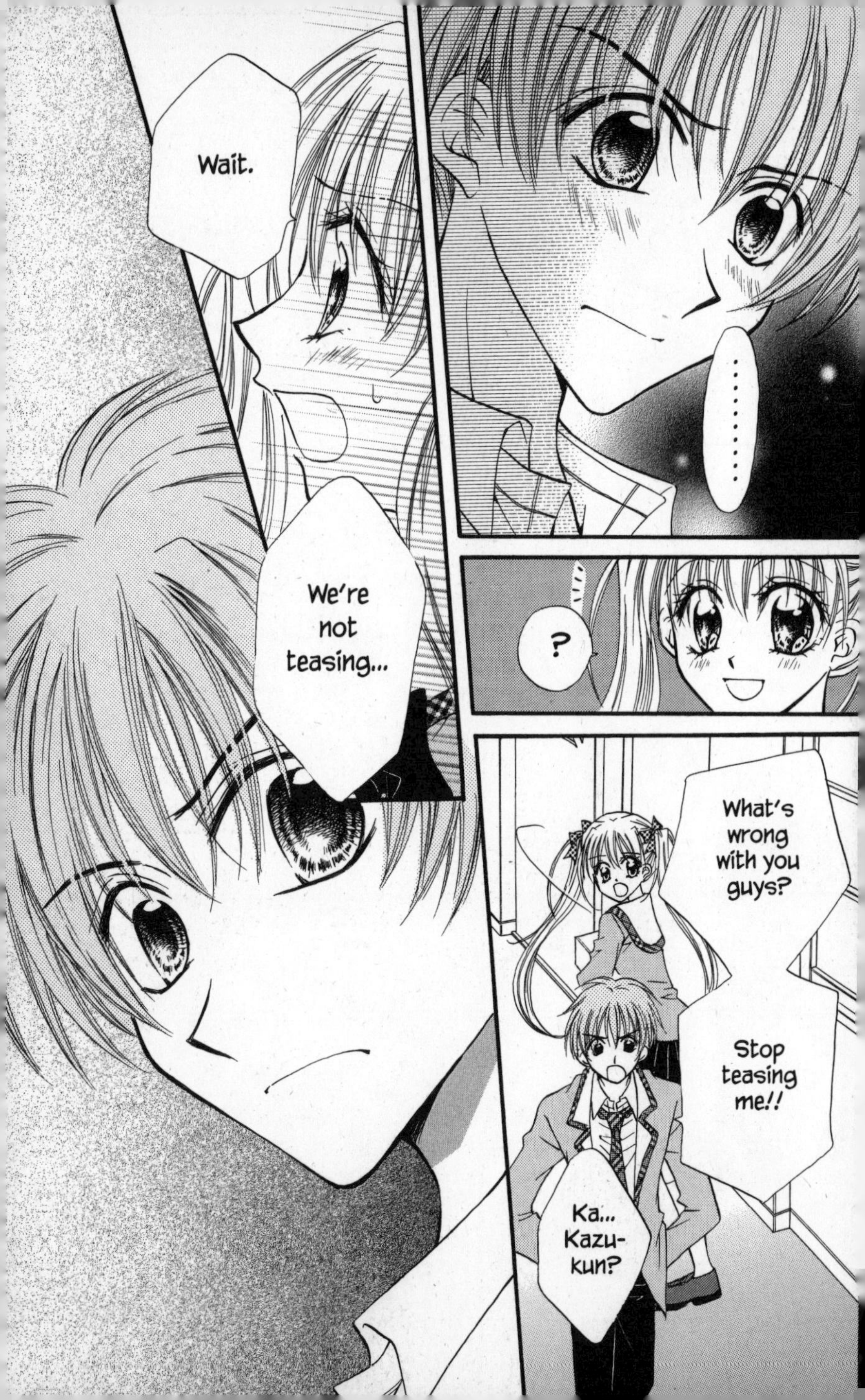
......
?
What's wrong with you guys?
Stop teasing me!!
Ka... Kazu-kun?
Wait.
We're not teasing...

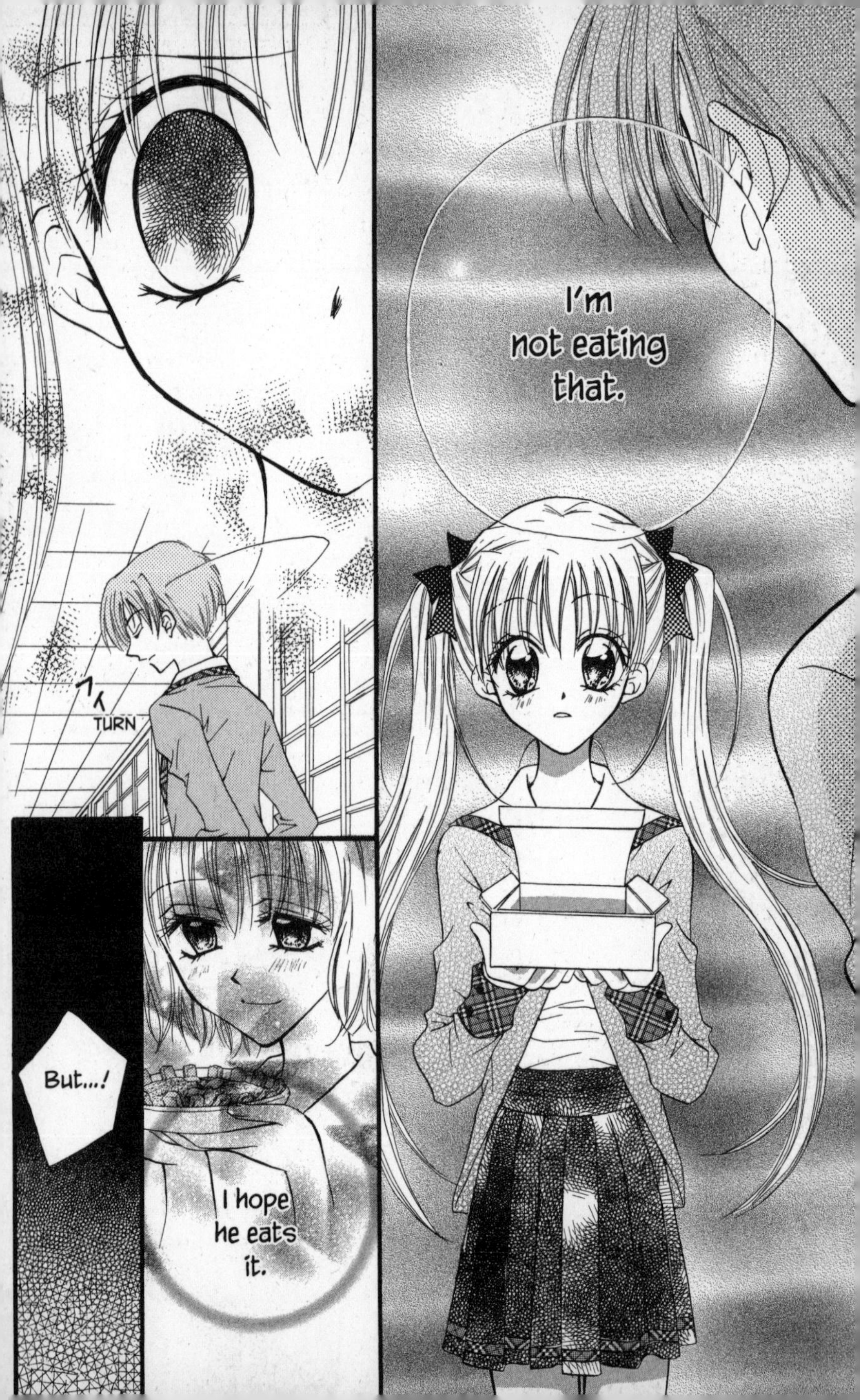

I'm not eating that.
TURN
But...!
I hope he eats it.

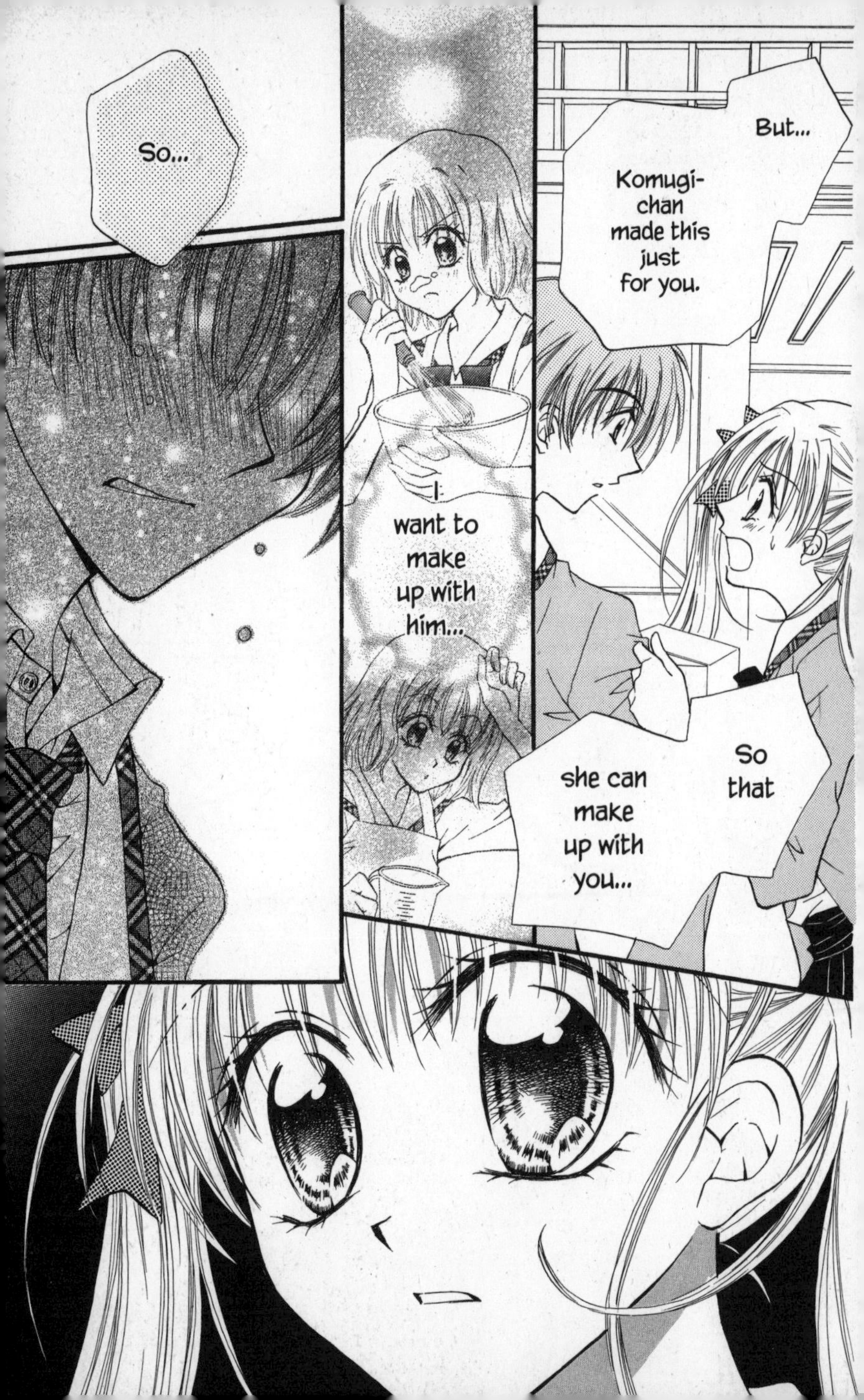
But...
Komugi-chan made this just for you.
So that she can make up with you...
I want to make up with him...
So...

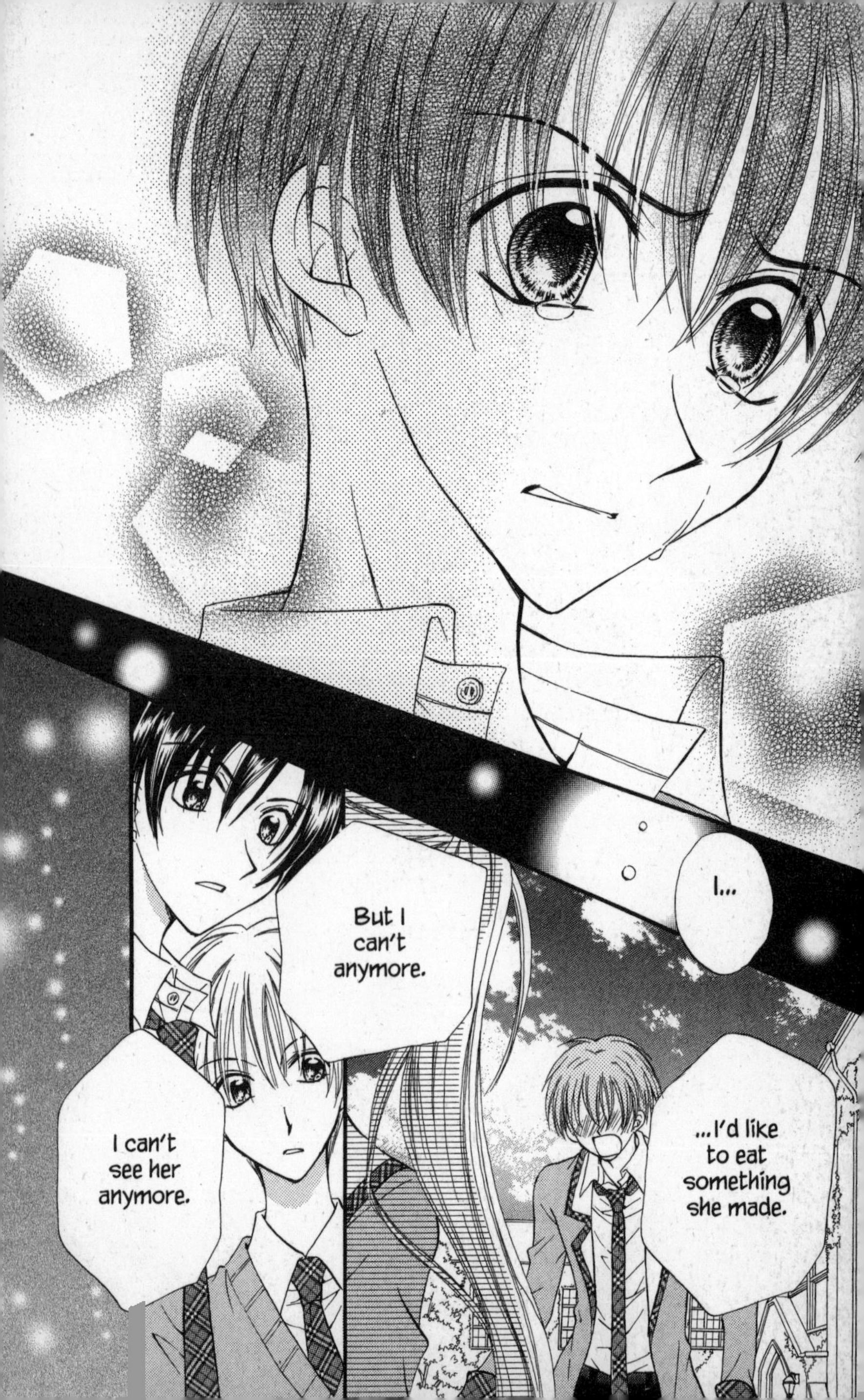
I...
...I'd like to eat something she made.
But I can't anymore.
I can't see her anymore.

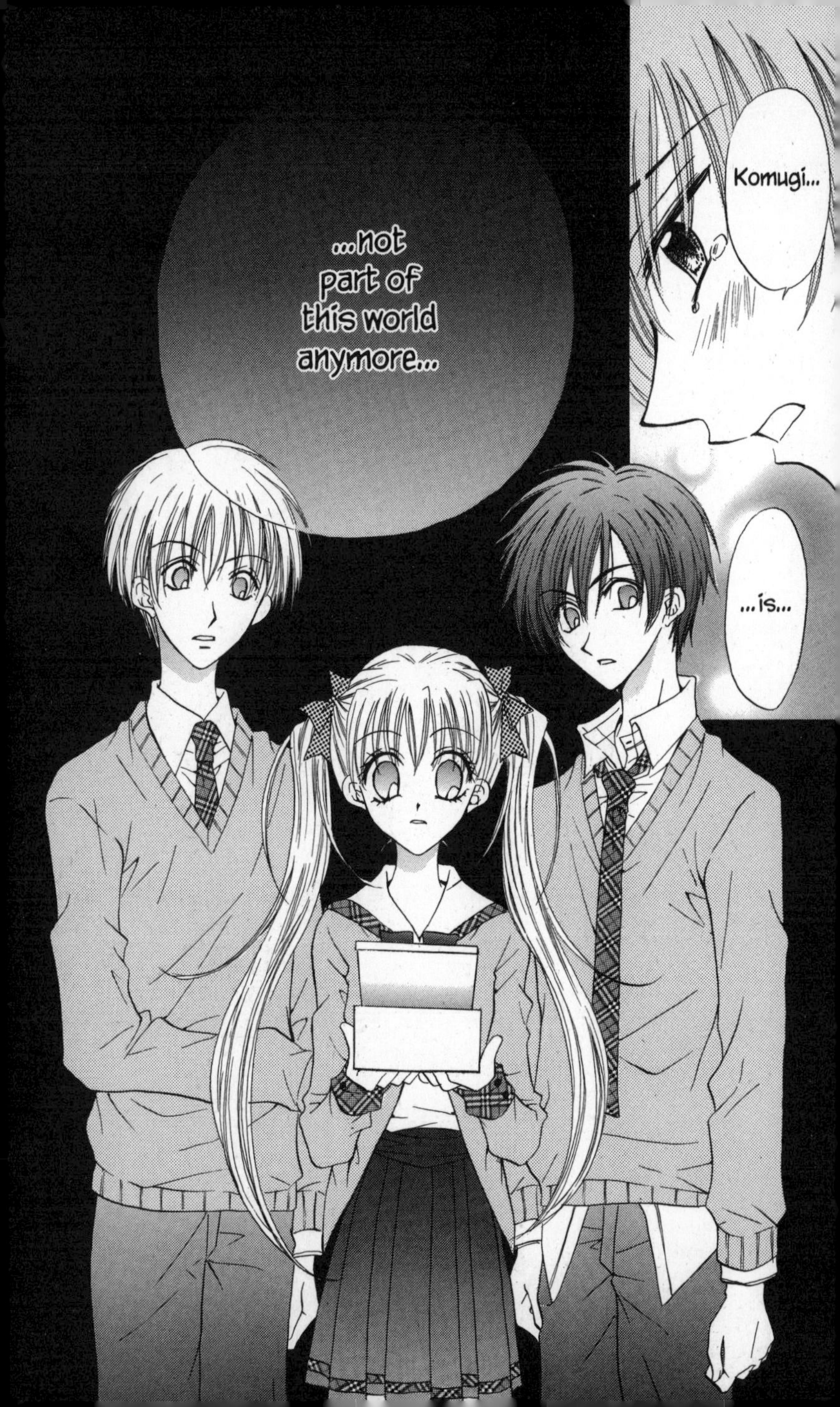
Komugi...
...is...
...not part of this world anymore...

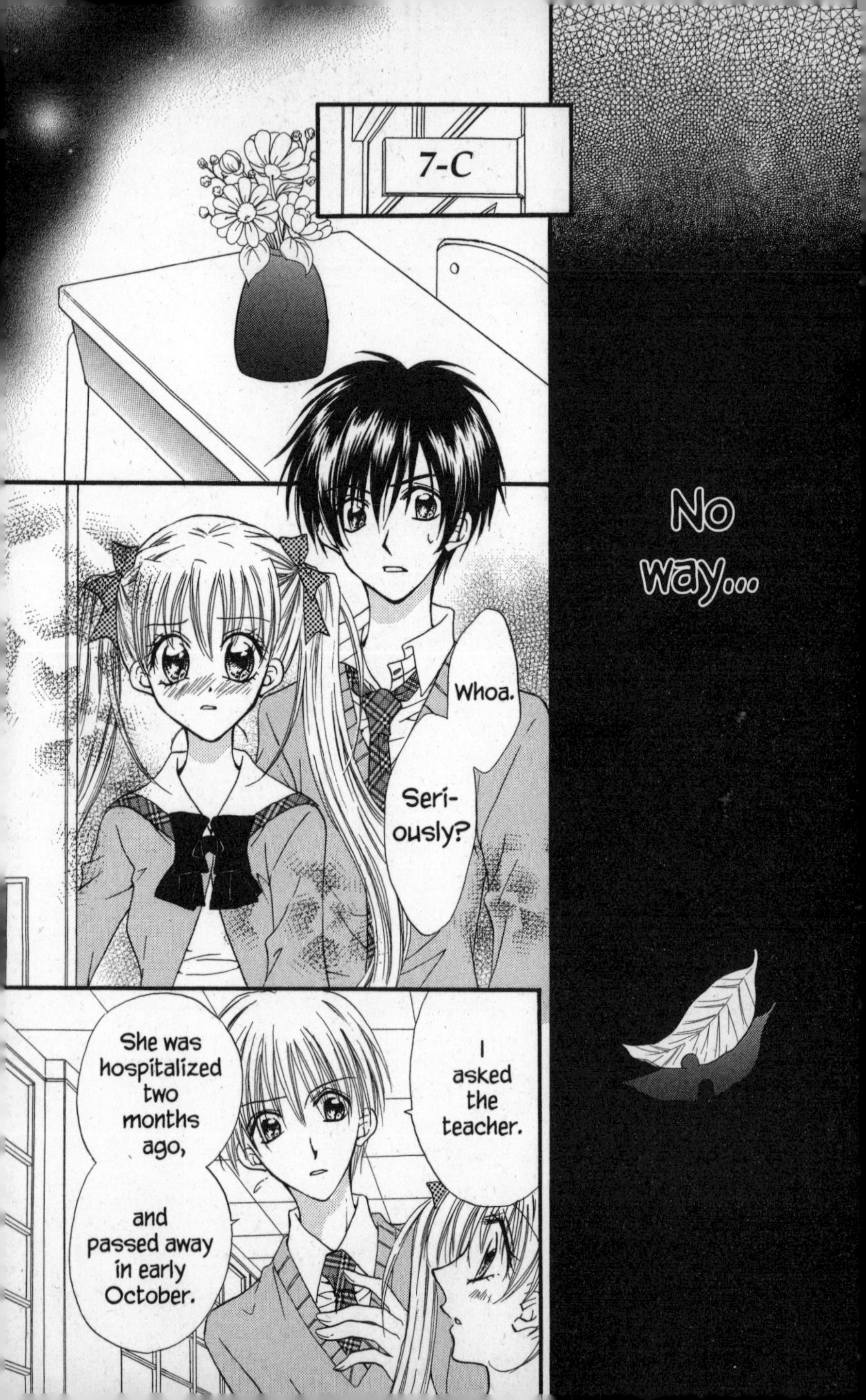
No way...
7-C
Whoa.
Seri-ously?
I asked the teacher.
She was hospitalized two months ago,
and passed away in early October.

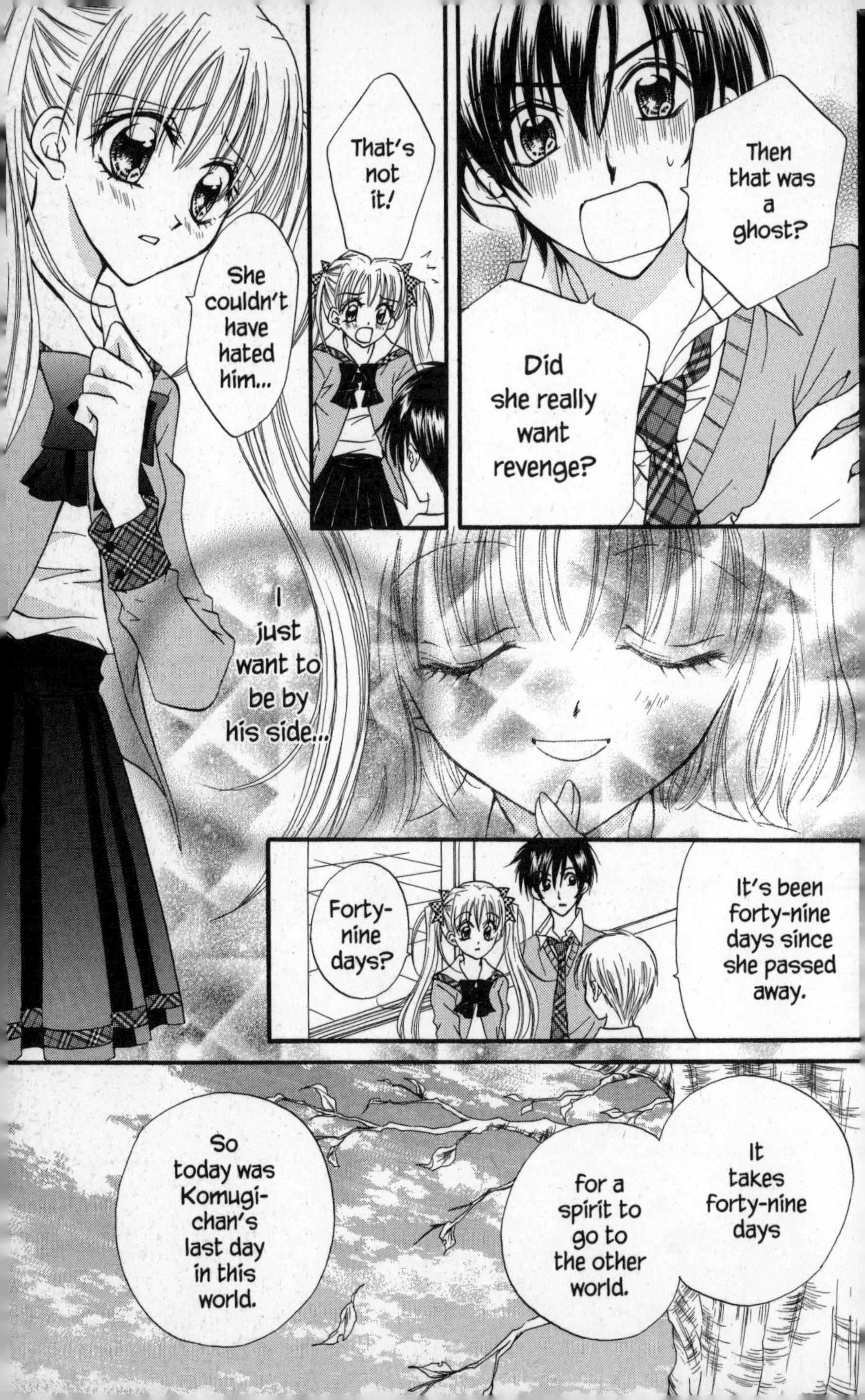
Then that was a ghost?
Did she really want revenge?
That's not it!
She couldn't have hated him...
I just want to be by his side...
It's been forty-nine days since she passed away.
Forty-nine days?
It takes forty-nine days
for a spirit to go to the other world.
So today was Komugi-chan's last day in this world.

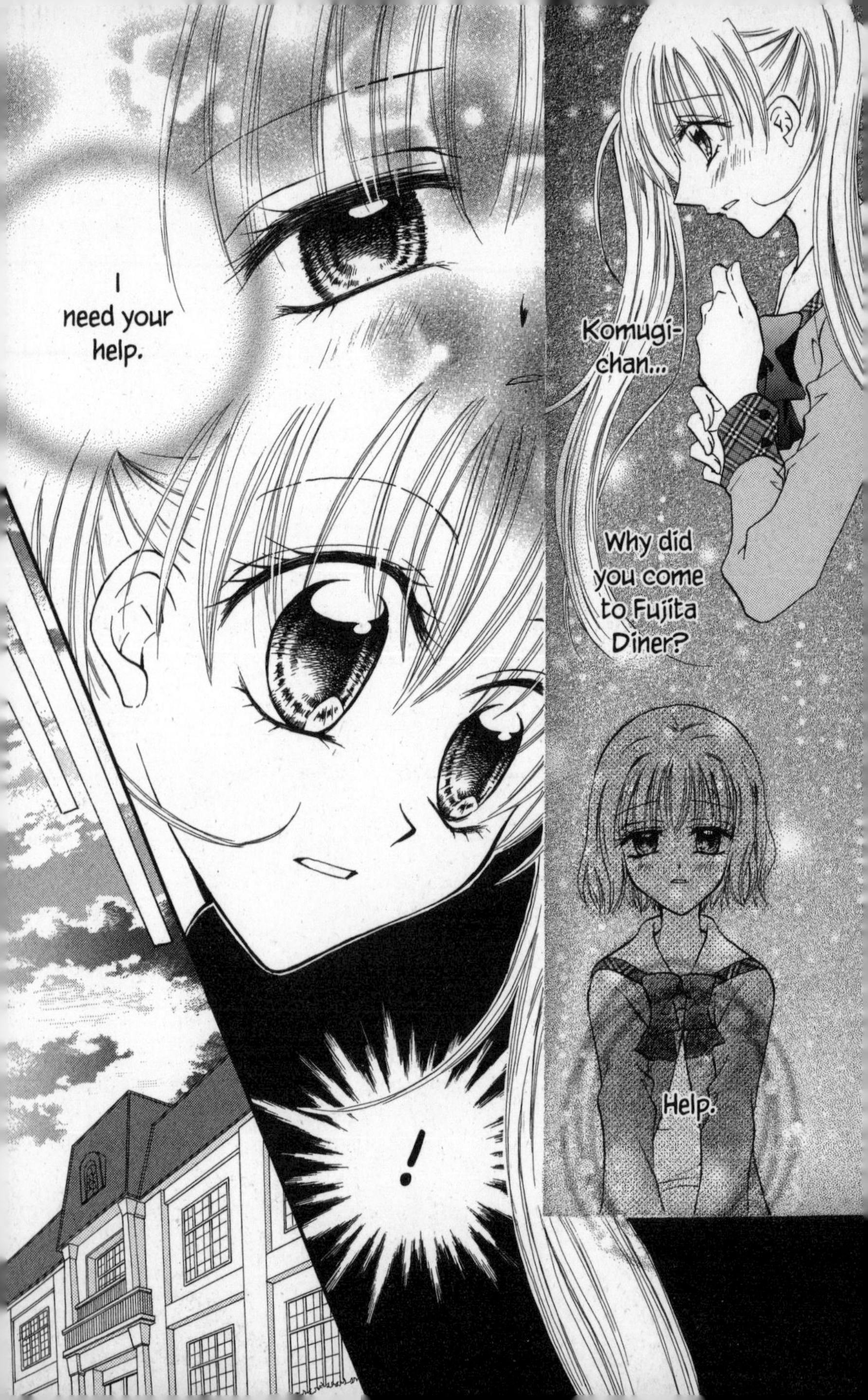
Komugi-chan...
Why did you come to Fujita Diner?
Help.
I need your help.
!

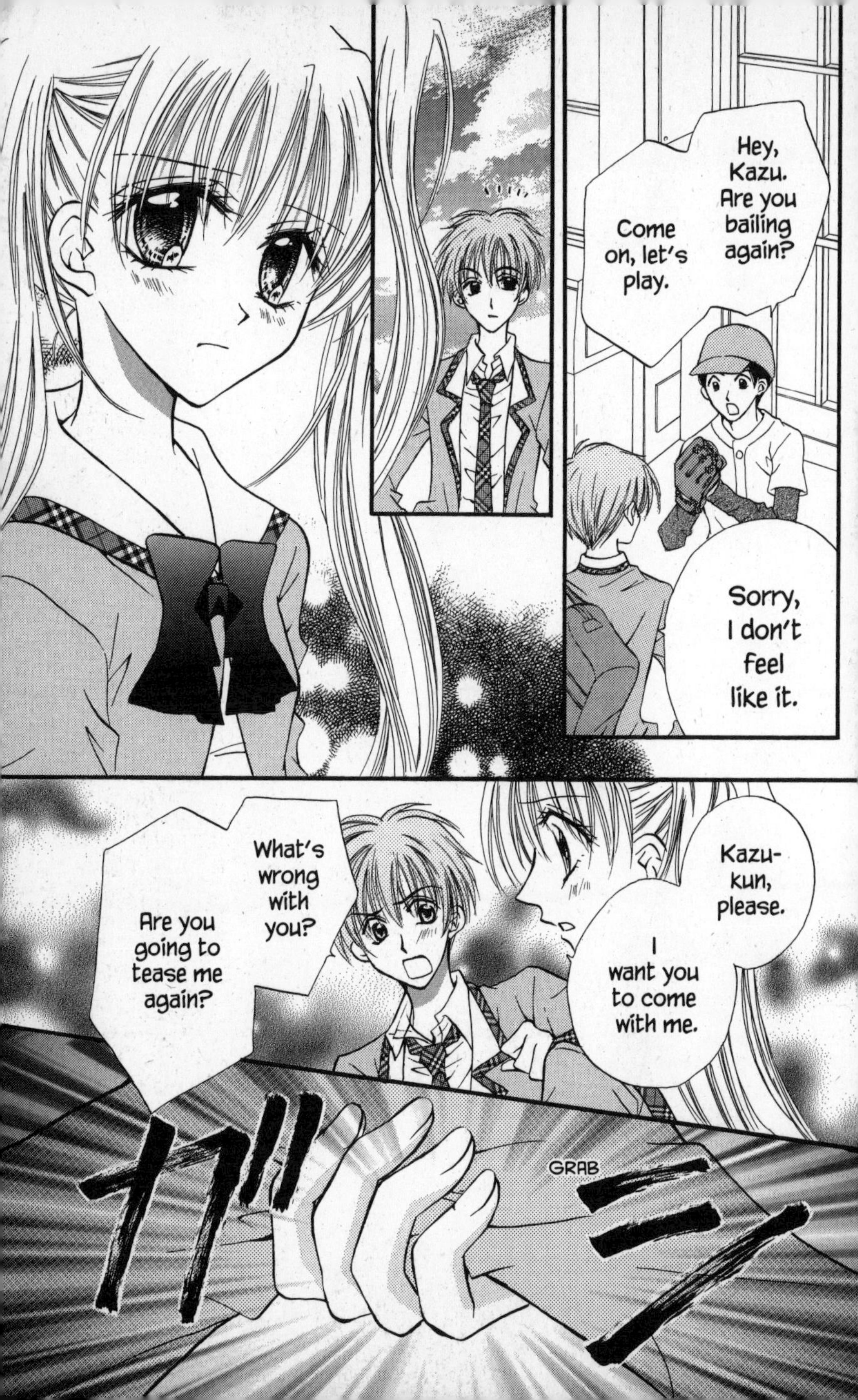
Hey, Kazu. Are you bailing again?
Come on, let's play.
Sorry, I don't feel like it.
Kazu-kun, please.
I want you to come with me.
What's wrong with you?
Are you going to tease me again?
GRAB

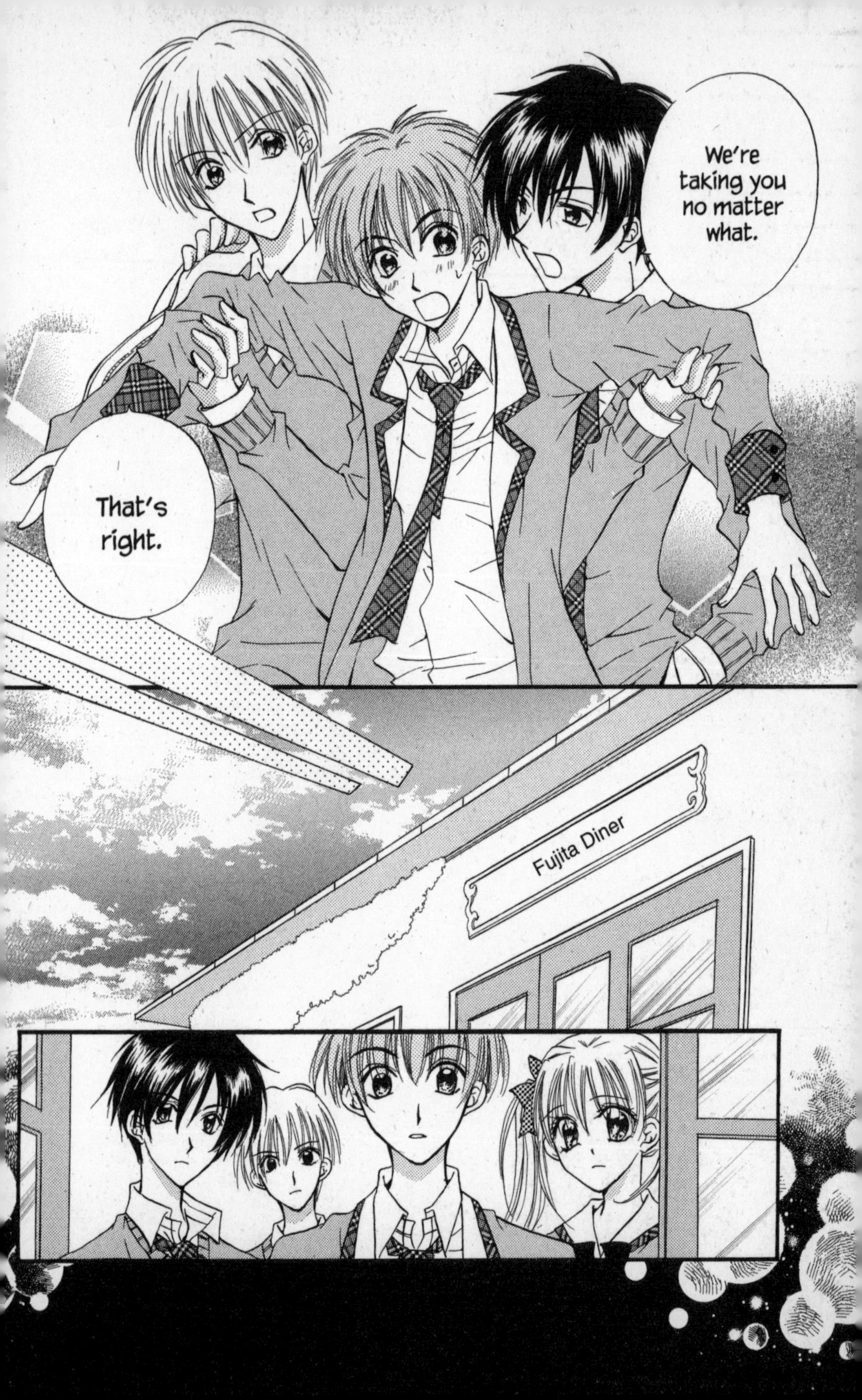
We're taking you no matter what.
That's right.
Fujita Diner

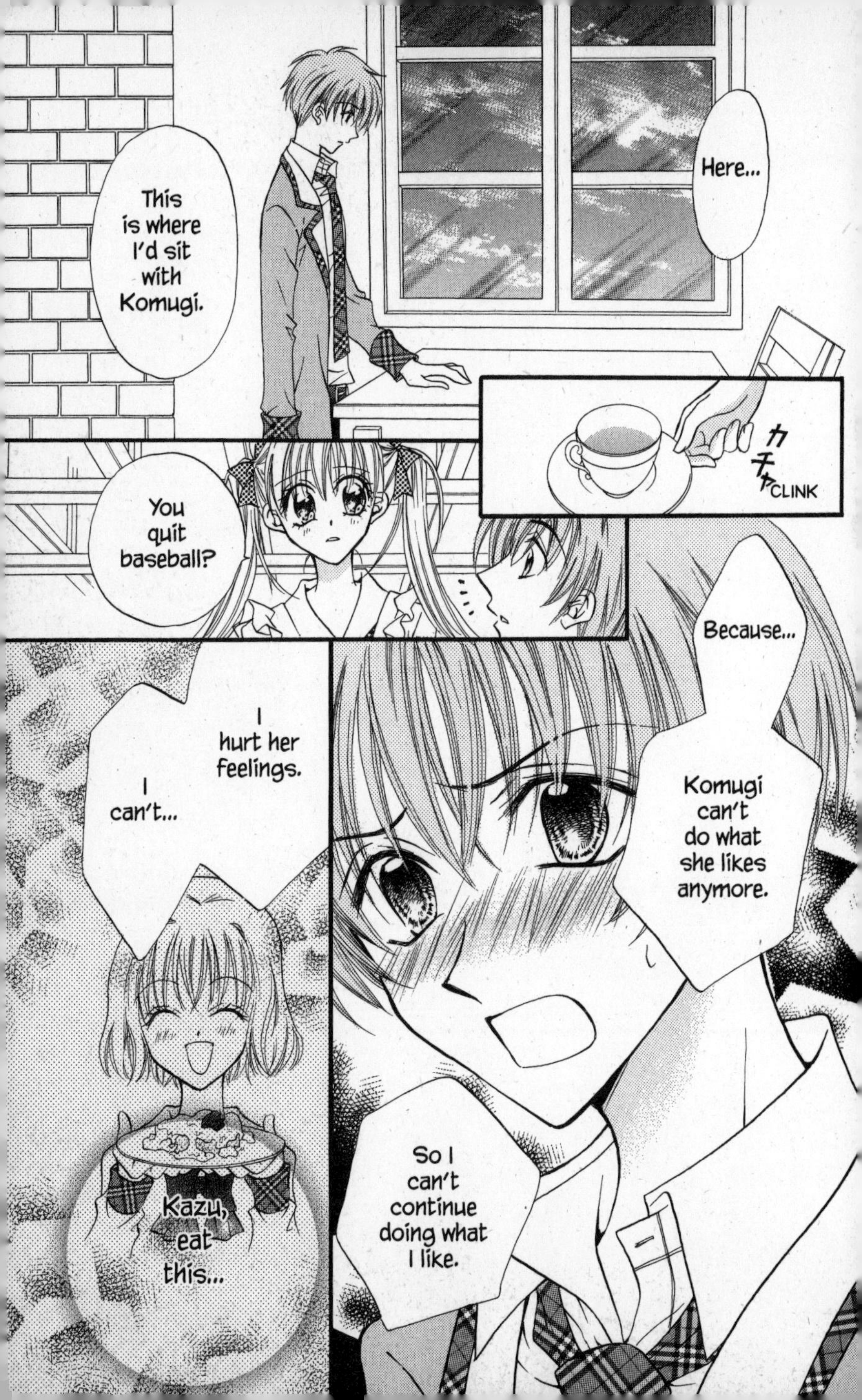
Here...
This is where I'd sit with Komugi.
カチャ CLINK
You quit baseball?
Because...
Komugi can't do what she likes anymore.
So I can't continue doing what I like.
I hurt her feelings.
I can't...
Kazu, eat this...

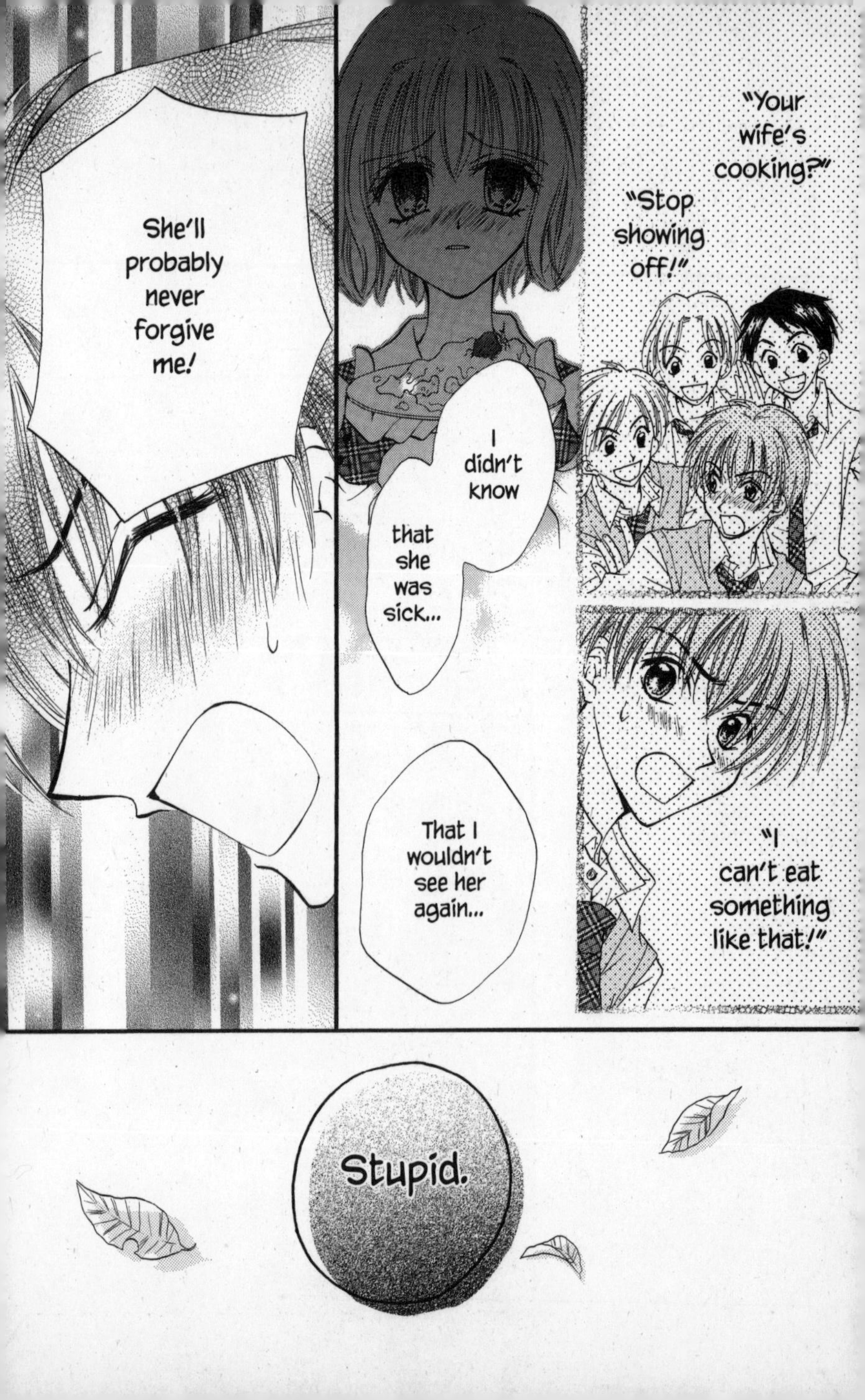
"Your wife's cooking?"
"Stop showing off!"
"I can't eat something like that!"
I didn't know that she was sick...
That I wouldn't see her again...
She'll probably never forgive me!
Stupid.

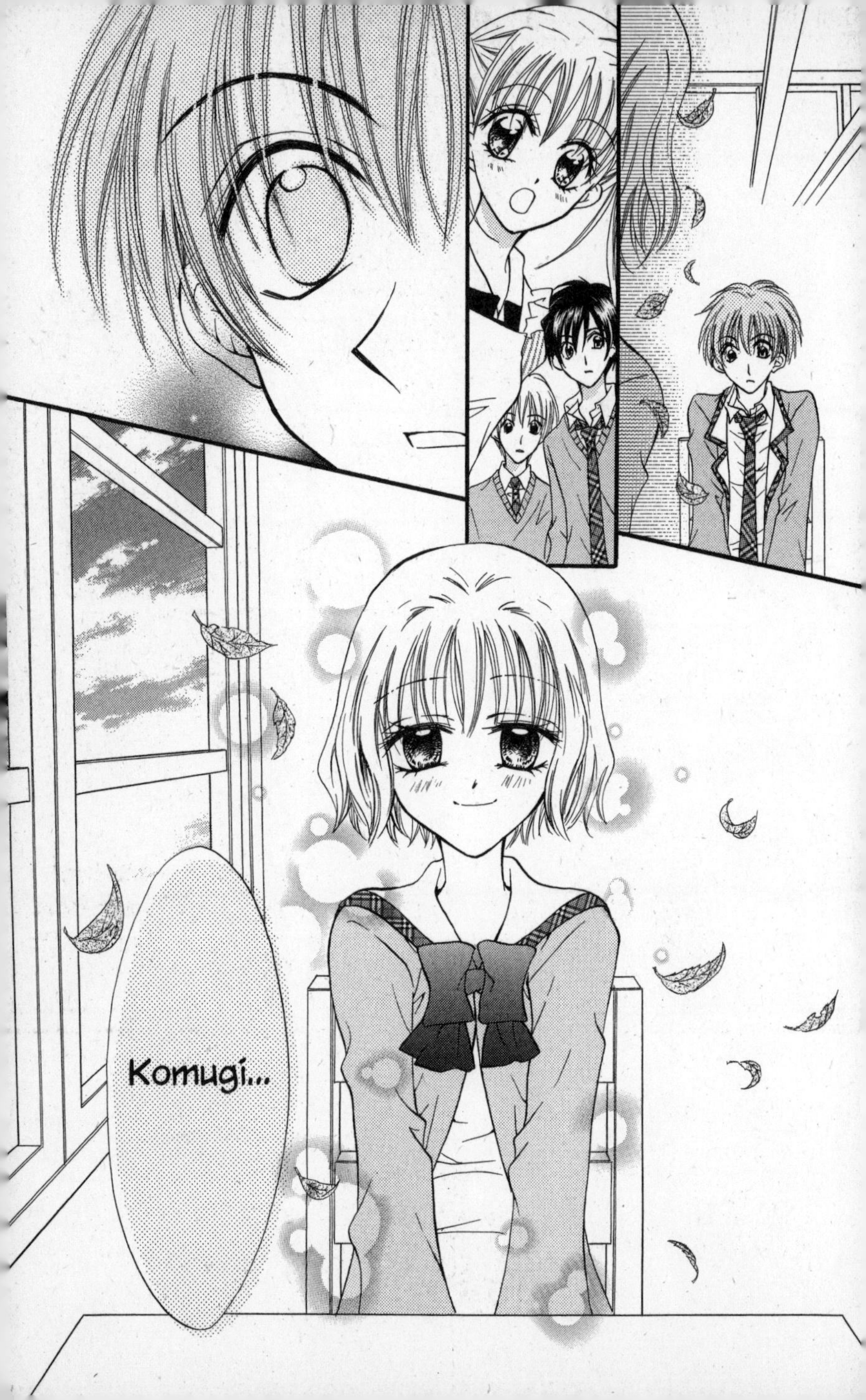
Komugi...

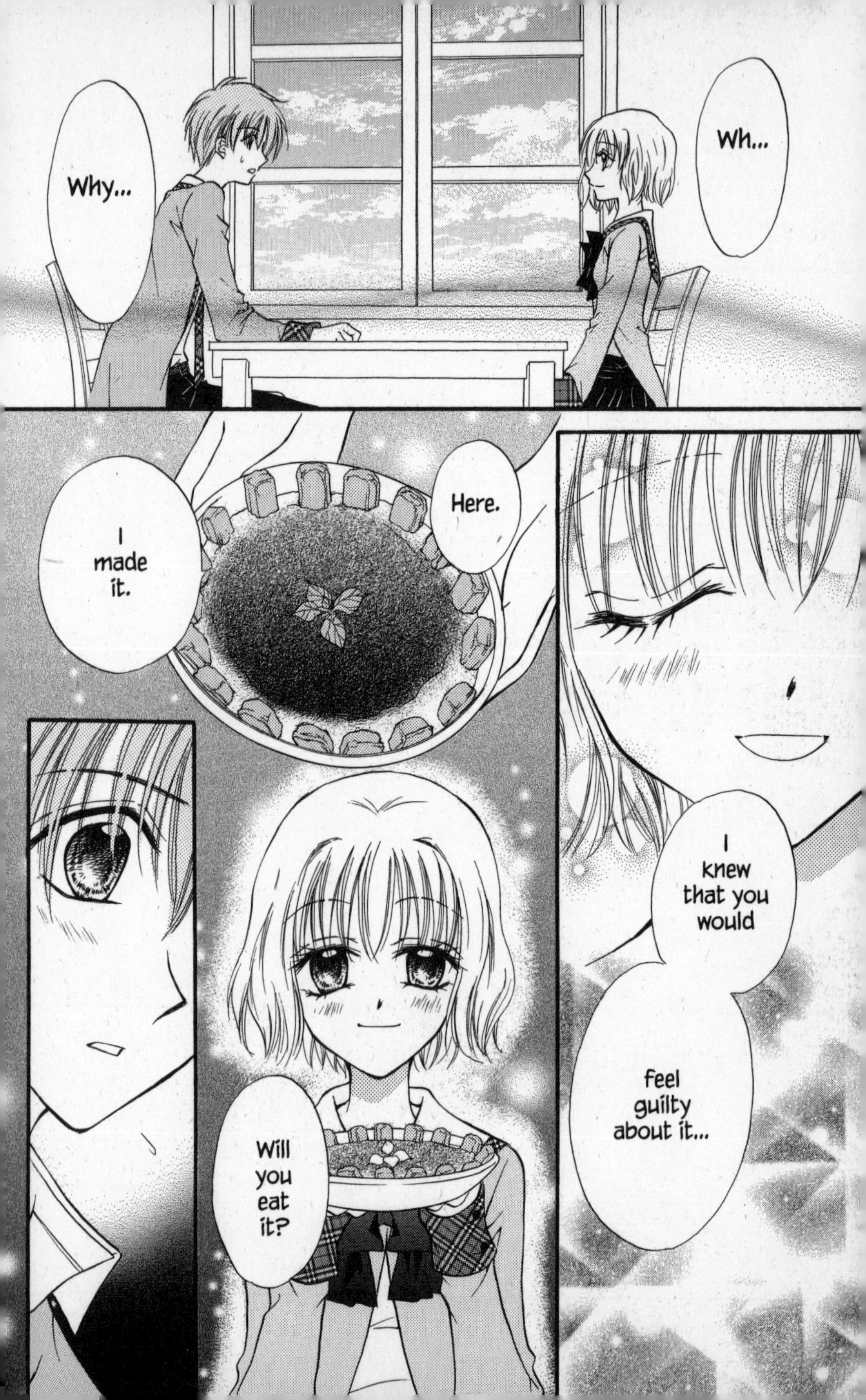
Wh...
Why...
I knew that you would
feel guilty about it...
Here.
I made it.
Will you eat it?

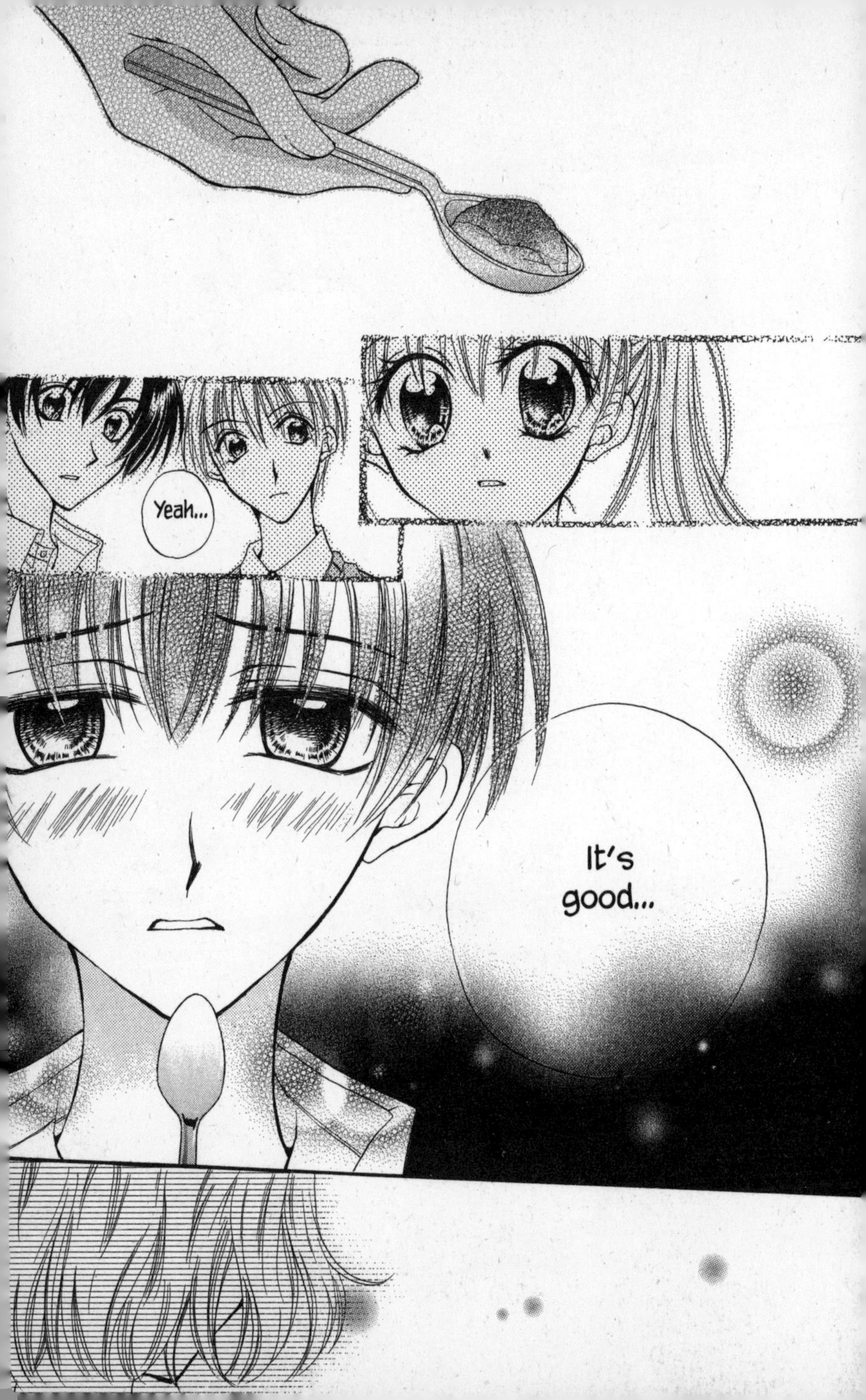
Yeah...
It's good...

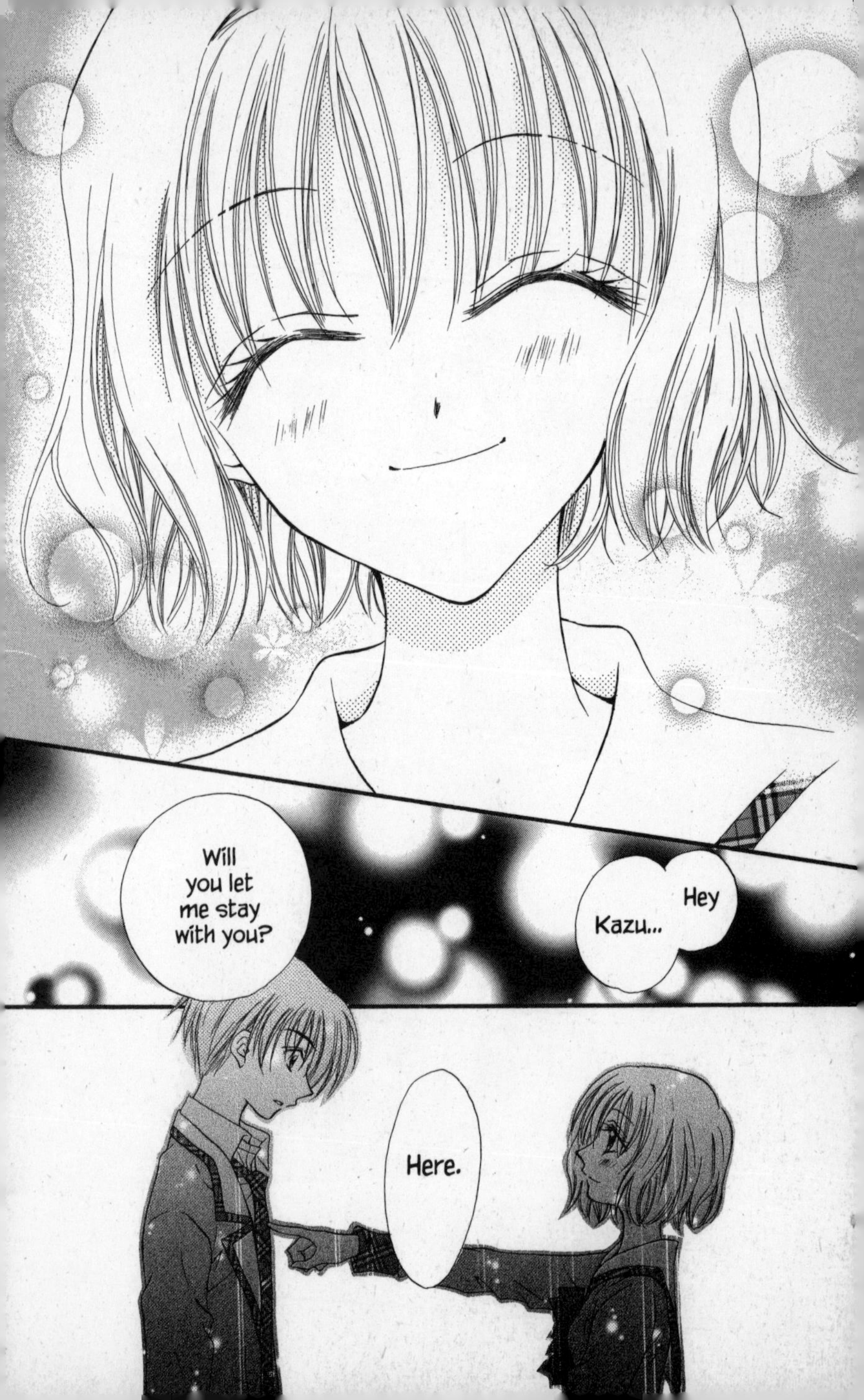
Hey Kazu...
Will you let me stay with you?
Here.

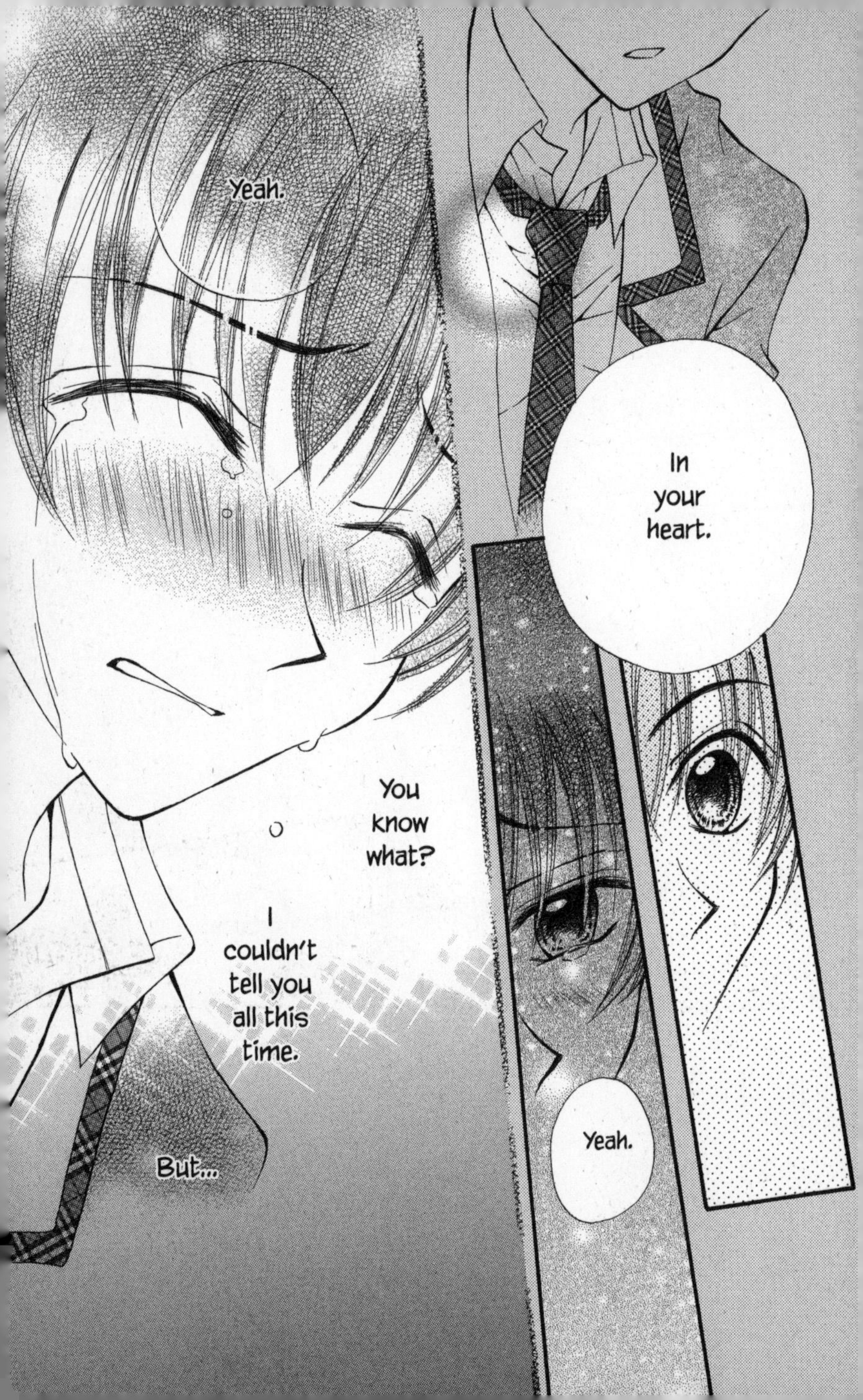
In your heart.
Yeah.
Yeah.
You know what?
I couldn't tell you all this time.
But...

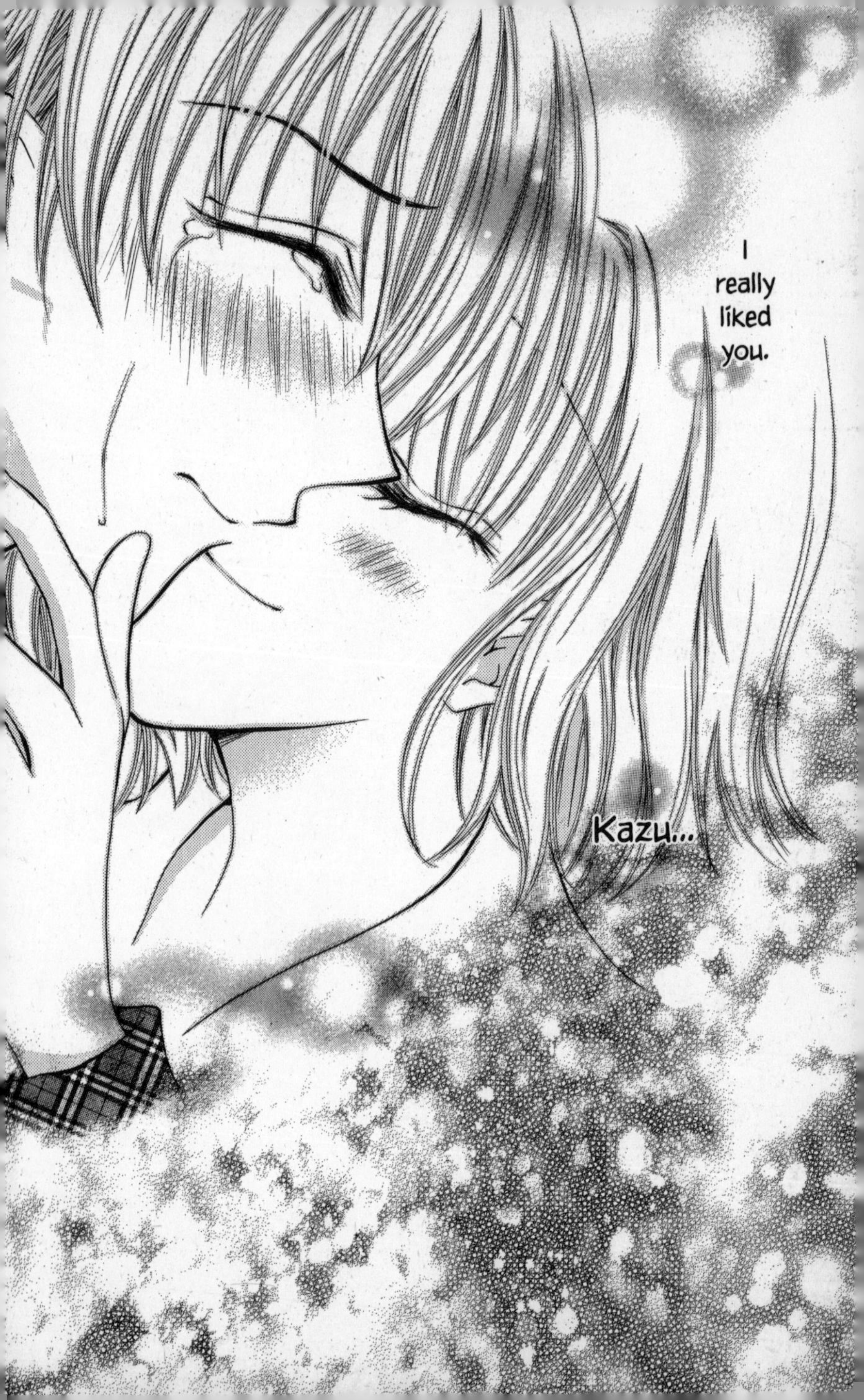
I really liked you.
Kazu...

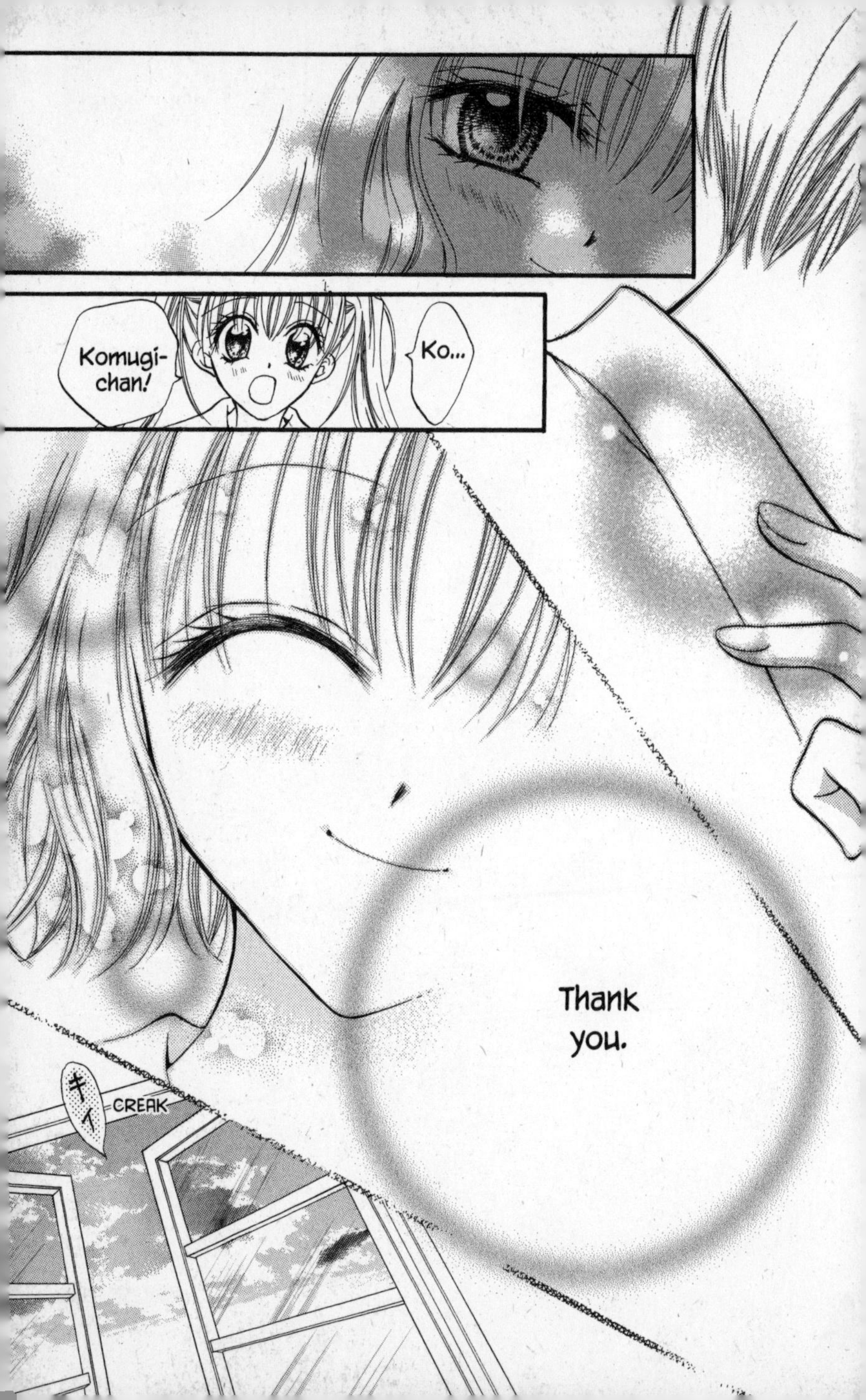
Ko...
Komugi-chan!
Thank you.
キィ
CREAK

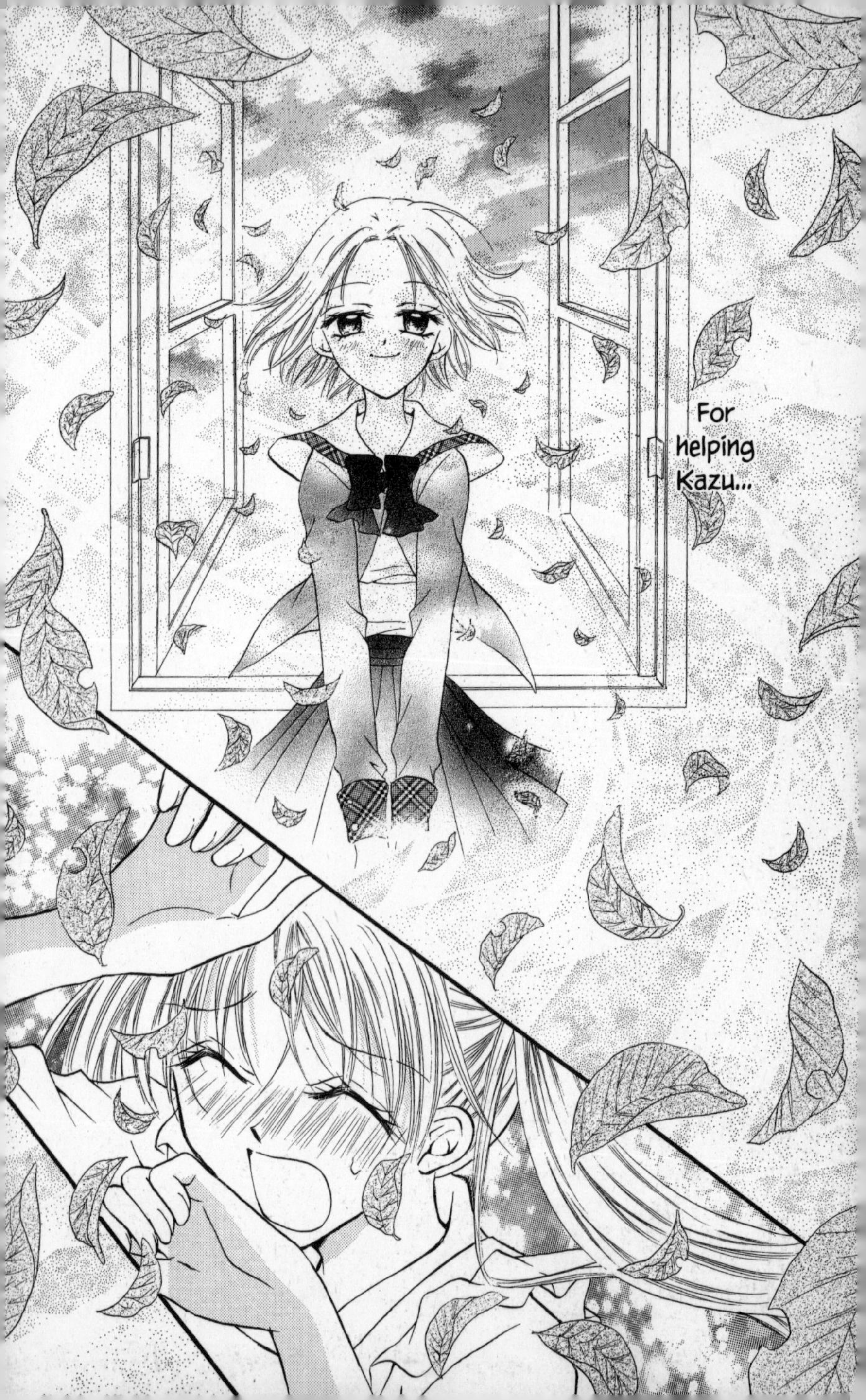
For helping Kazu...

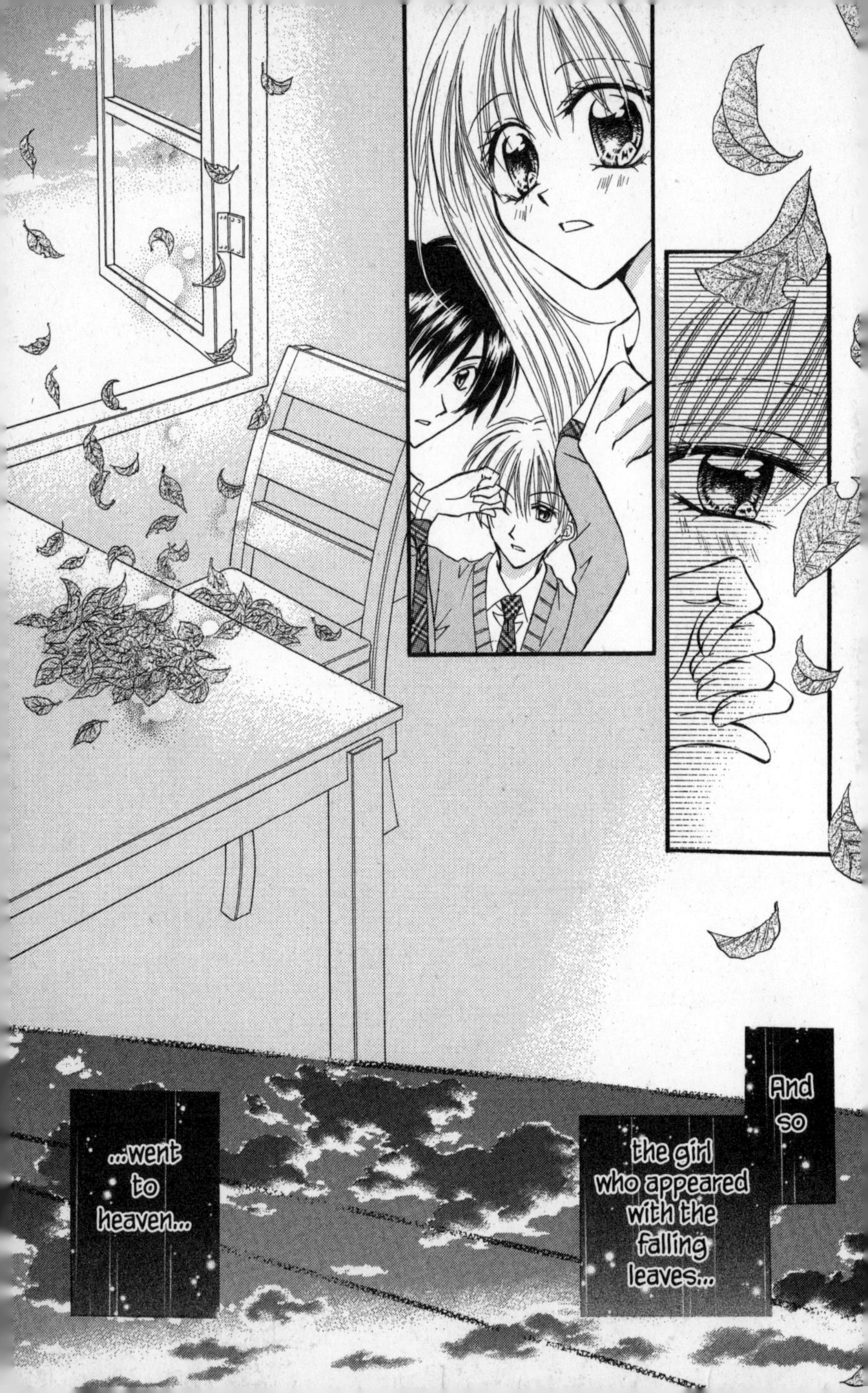
And so
the girl who appeared with the falling leaves...
...went to heaven...

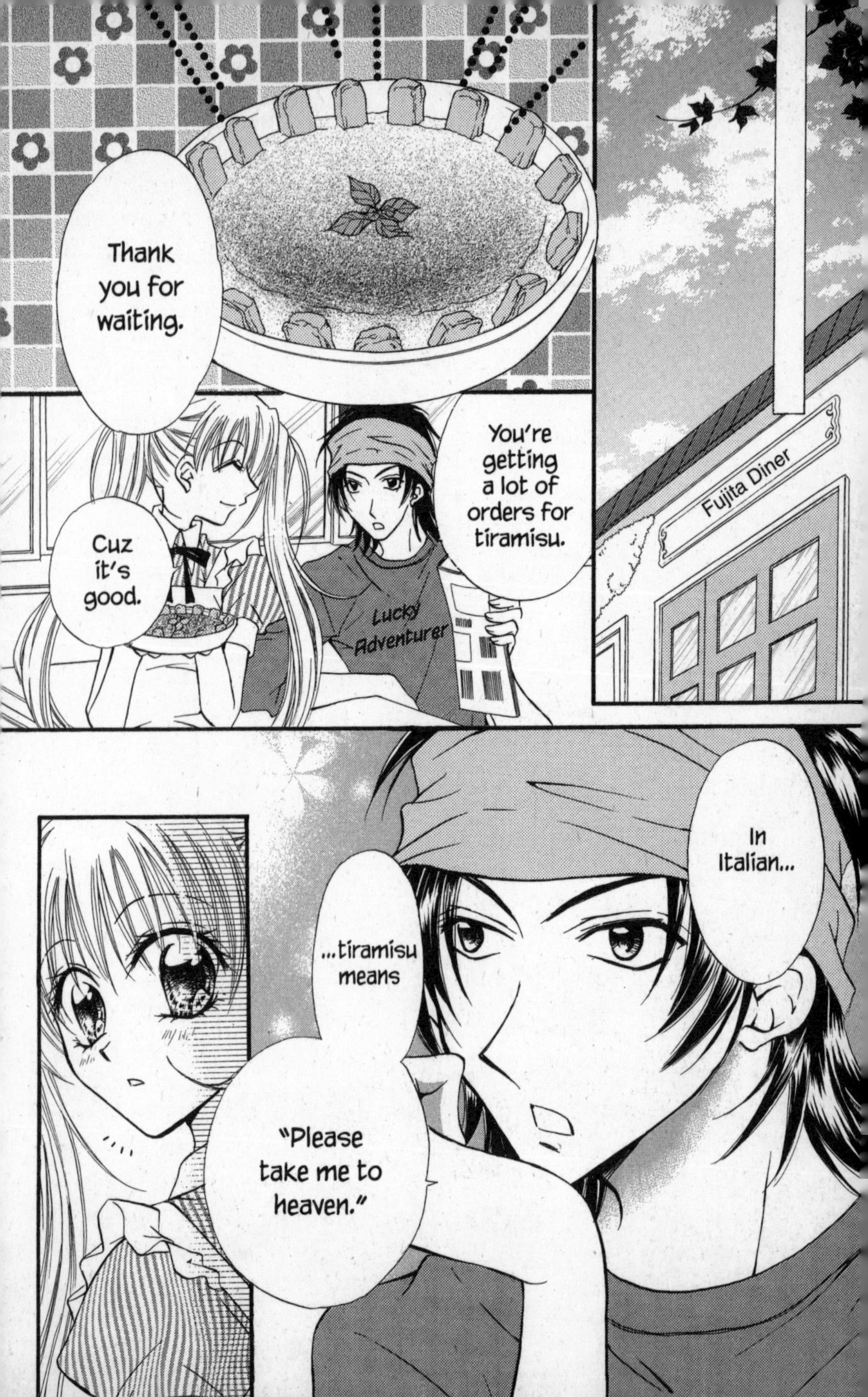
Fujita Diner
Thank you for waiting.
You're getting a lot of orders for tiramisu.
Cuz it's good.
Lucky Adventurer
In Italian...
...tiramisu means
"Please take me to heaven."

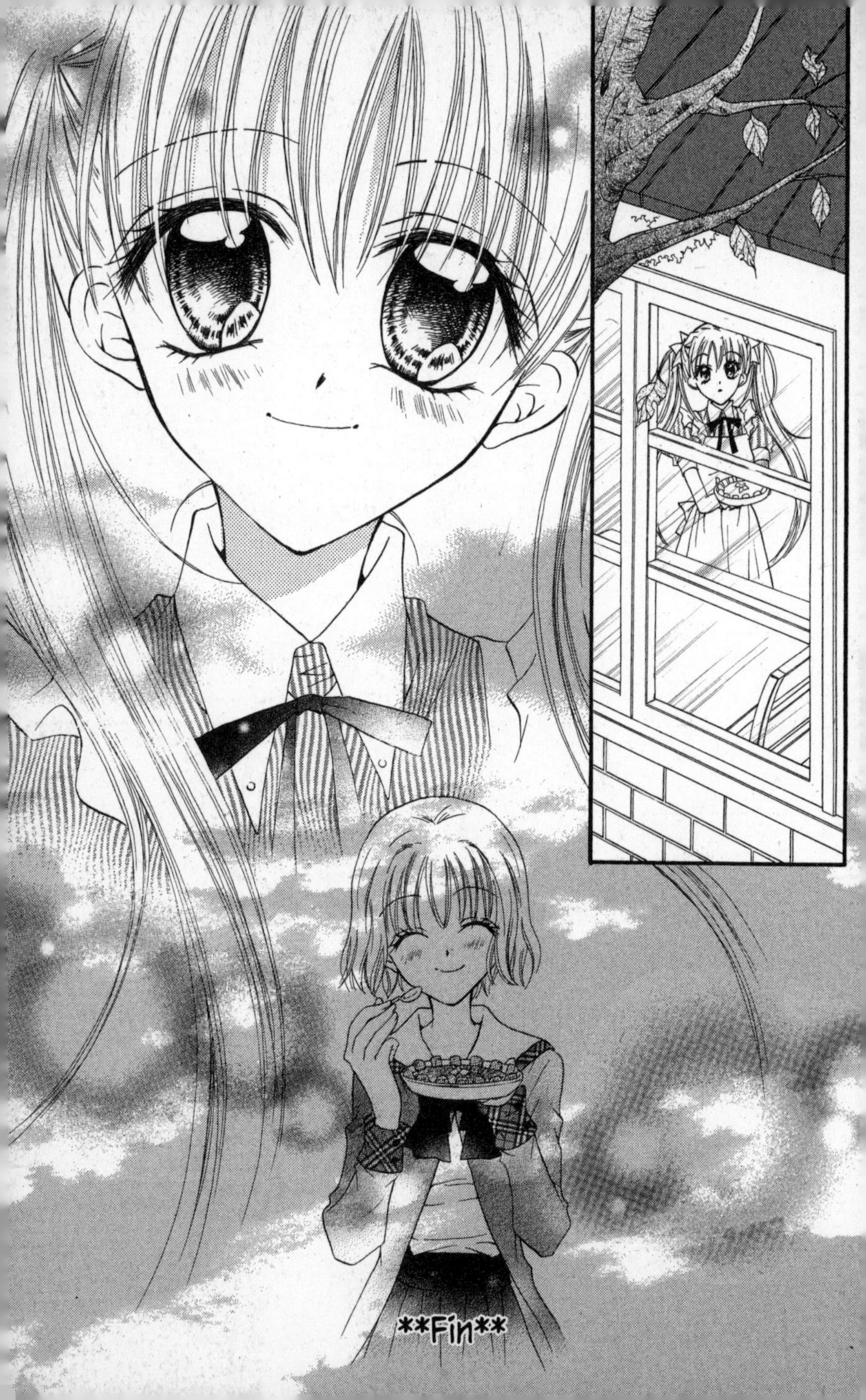
Fin

Thank you

The four panel comics were something I drew for the *Nakayoshi* Funny Feature. Since it was an opportunity to draw the characters in different situations, I went really different! And so that's why they turned out like that... I hope you liked them. I personally like the "If it were Kitchen Prince!!" Please tell me what you think. ♥

Nakayoshi Editorial Team
PO BOX 91
Akasaka, Tokyo 107-8652

Natsumi Ando
Shobayashi-sama
Yamada-sama & Kishimoto-sama &
Miyuki sensei Haruse-sama

Thank you for all your help!!

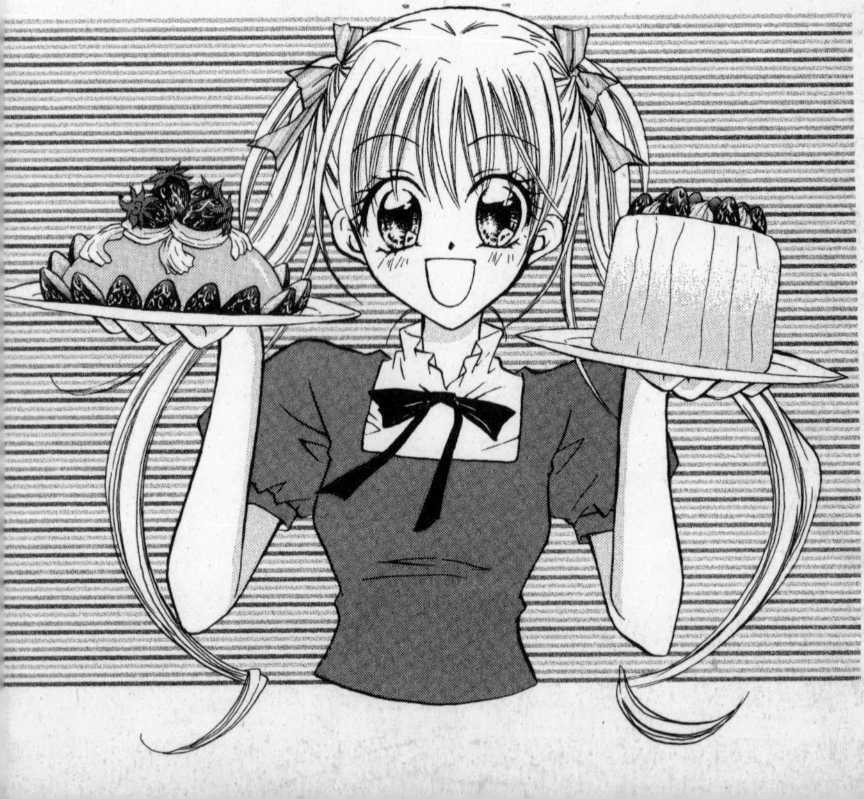

Kitchen Palace

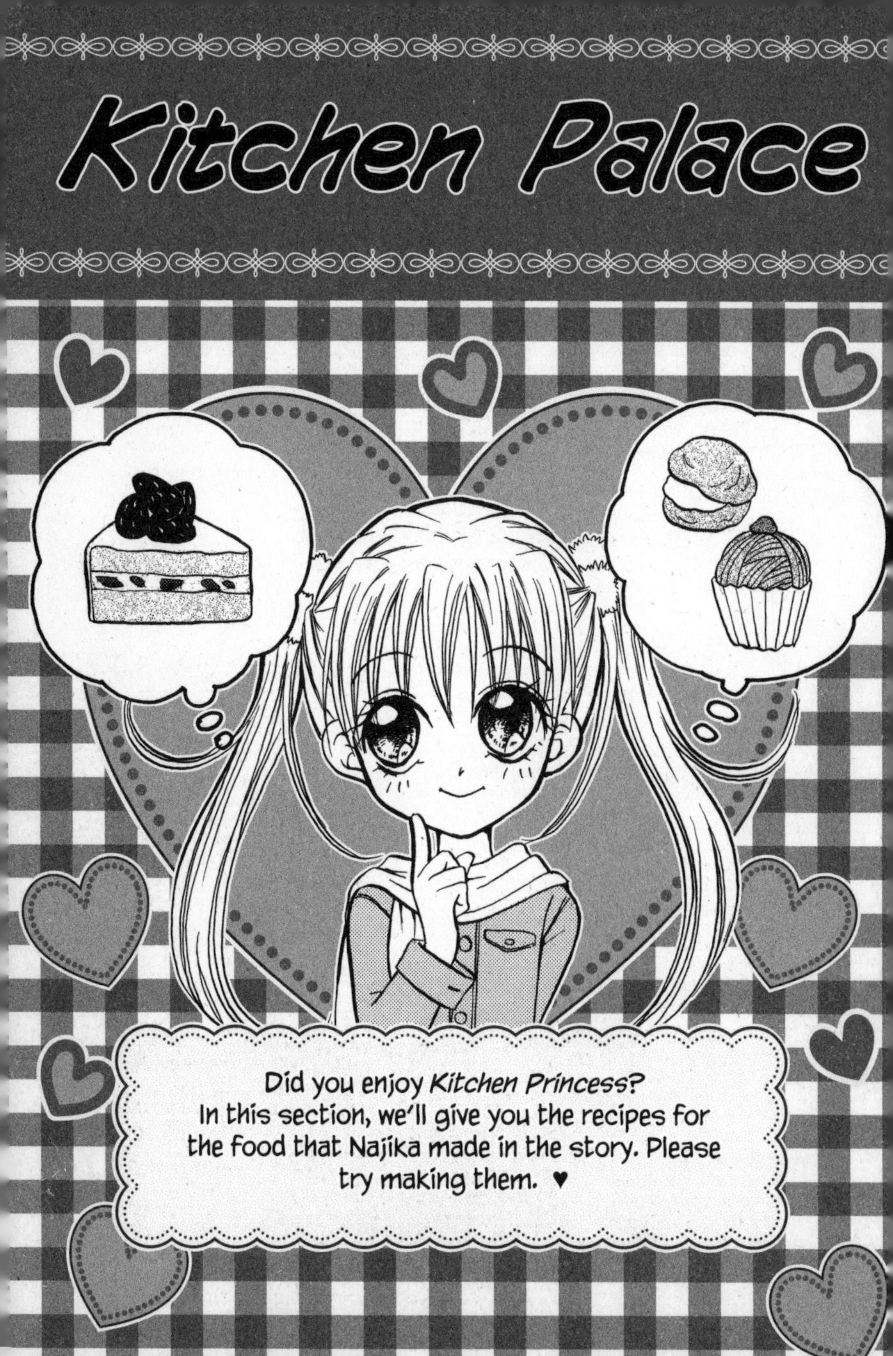

Did you enjoy *Kitchen Princess*?
In this section, we'll give you the recipes for the food that Najika made in the story. Please try making them. ♥

Omrice

Tip from Najika.

It's a simple recipe, because all you do is put the ingredients in the rice cooker! You can make a lot at once, so it's perfect for parties.

Chicken Rice

Chicken Rice: Makes 2 cups

1/3 of a carrot, onion, 1/4 lb. chicken thighs, 2 tablespoons oil, 2 teaspoons consommé soup powder, 2 cups rice, 4 tablespoons ketchup, some salt and pepper, some green peas, 1 teaspoon butter. Flat and Thin Baked Eggs: Makes 1 serving 2 eggs, 1 teaspoon salt, 1 teaspoon sugar, 1 teaspoon oil, 1 teaspoon butter

How to Make

Consommé

1. Cut up the carrot, onion, and chicken into small bits. The chicken pieces should be bite-sized. Pour oil in a frying pan and stir-fry the onion and carrots. When the onion becomes transparent, add the chicken and fry until it becomes white.

2. Dissolve the consommé powder in hot water. Put the rinsed rice in the pot, add the dissolved consommé, and 4 cups water. Add ketchup and stir.

3. Add the stir-fried chicken and vegetables to the pot. Add salt, pepper, and butter to taste. Cook the rice. Once the rice is cooked, add green peas and mix it together.

4. Make the omrice egg one serving at a time. Break the eggs into a bowl and add salt and sugar. Stir well. Put a frying pan on medium heat and add oil and butter. When the butter starts to melt, pour in the egg. When the egg is half cooked, turn off the heat. In the middle of the egg, place 1/4 of the chicken rice. Wrap up the rice with the egg and you're done! Two cups of rice will make 4 servings.

Flat and Thin Baked Eggs

1. Now we make the egg that will wrap the rice balls. Break the eggs into a bowl and add salt and sugar. Stir and drain it through a strainer.

2. Pour oil in a frying pan (you won't use butter) and when it gets hot, take it off the heat and put the pan on top of a wet towel to cool. If you do this, it doesn't burn as much.

3. Pour in the egg and put it back on low heat. When the surface becomes dry, use chopsticks to flip it over. Make sure it doesn't rip. Cook the other side and when it is cool, cut it according to the size of the rice ball. Wrap the rice ball and you're done.

DONE ♥

If you top it off with ketchup, it'll taste much better!!

You can place scrambled eggs on top of the chicken rice, or make chicken rice balls. Arrange it any way you like!

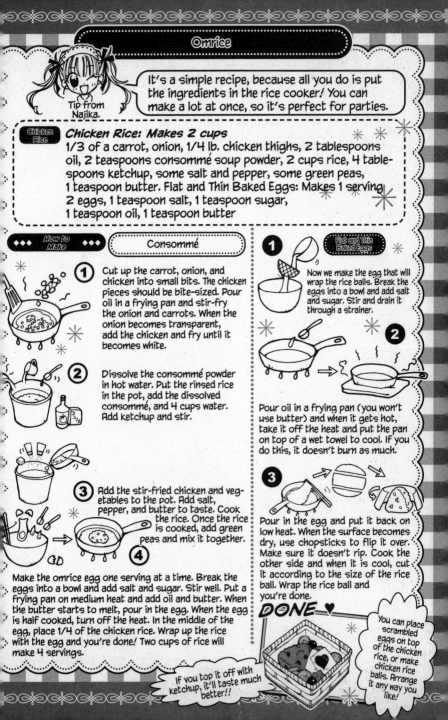

Apple Cake

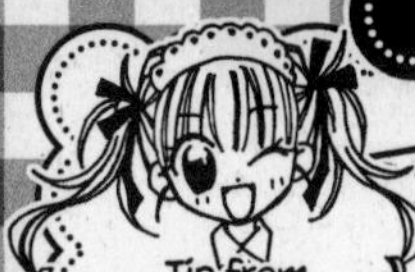

Tip from Najika.

You should use a slightly sour apple to make it good when cooked!

Apple Cake

Apple Cake: 1 cake 5 or 6" squared

5 tablespoons unsalted butter, 1/2 cup sugar, 2 eggs, 3/4 cup flour, 1 teaspoon baking powder,1 apple

How to Make

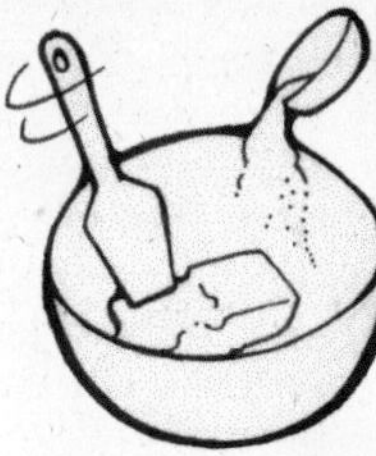

1 Leave the butter out to soften. After it's soft, put it in a bowl with the sugar and stir.

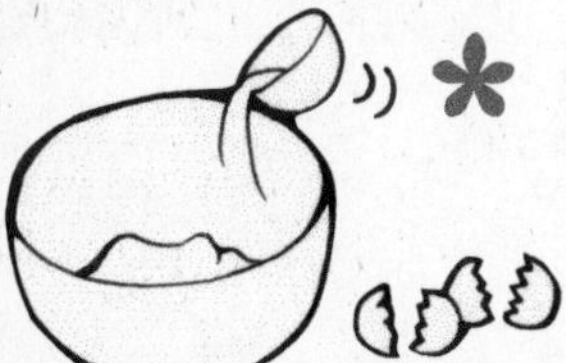

2 Break the eggs into a separate bowl and add them a little at a time to the bowl from step 1.

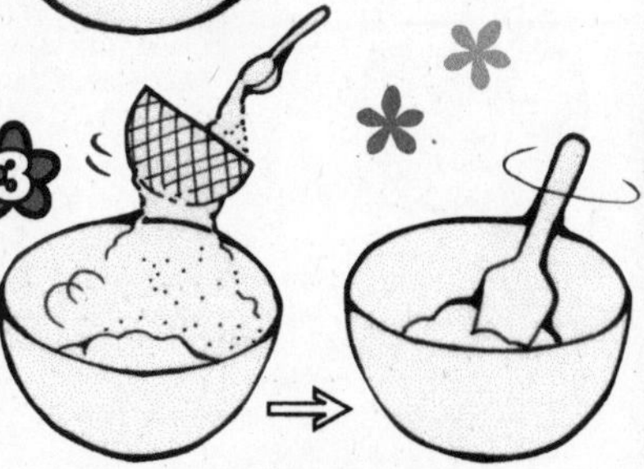

3 Sift the flour and the baking powder in the bowl from step 1 and stir.

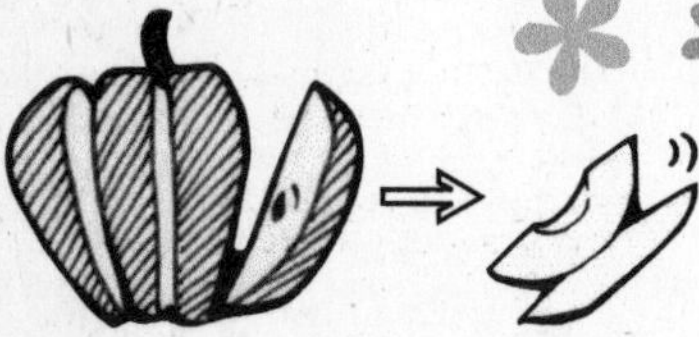

4 Cut the apple into 8 pieces. Peel off the skin and take out the core.

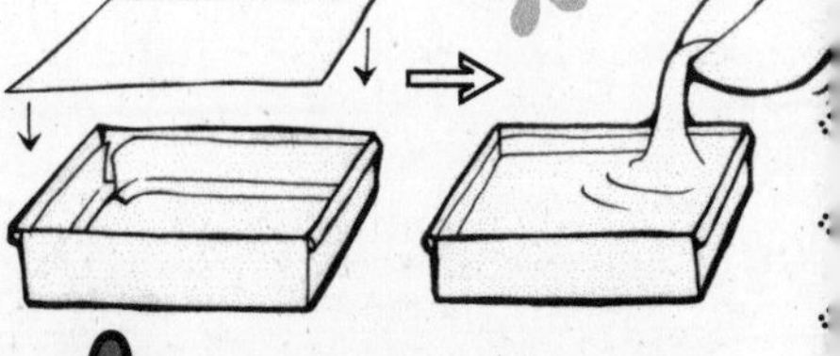

5 Lay wax paper in a cake pan and pour the mixture from step 3.

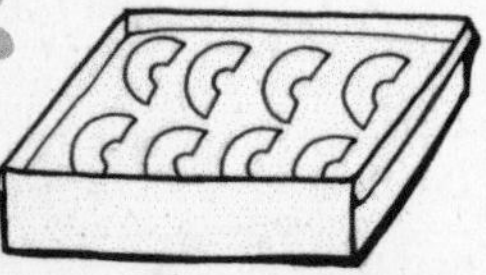

6 Flatten the surface and lay out the apple slices on top. Bake it in an oven preheated to 350 degrees F for 25-30 minutes. It's done if you poke a toothpick in it and it comes out clean!

If you don't have a square cake pan, you can use a round one or even a pound cake pan.

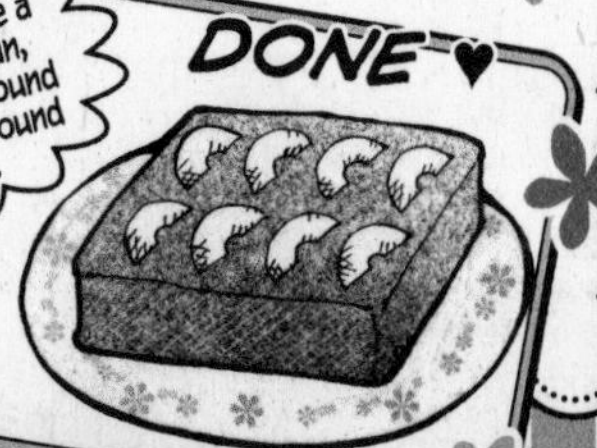
DONE ♥

Cocoa Scone

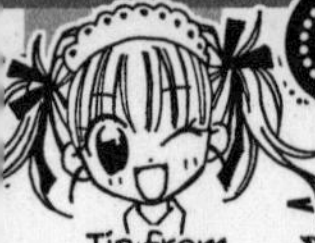

Tip from Najika.

Adding cocoa makes it perfect for Valentine's Day. ♥ If you don't add cocoa, it'll be plain- flavored, which is good, too!

How to Make

Preheat the oven to 400 degrees F

Cocoa Scone

Cocoa Scone: Makes about 6

3/4 cup flour, 1 teaspoon baking powder, 3 tablespoons unsweetened cocoa, 1 tablespoon sugar, some salt, 2 tablespoons butter, 3 tablespoons milk

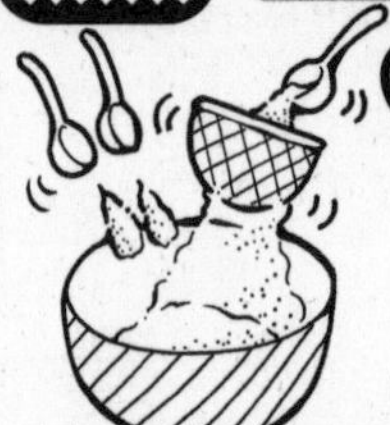

1. Sift the flour, baking powder, and cocoa into a bowl. Add sugar and salt and mix.

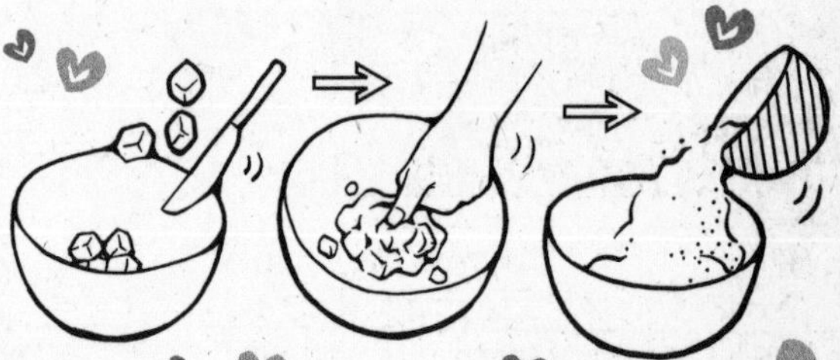

2. Cut the butter into small pieces with a butter knife and smash them in a bowl with your fingers. Add the mix from step 1.

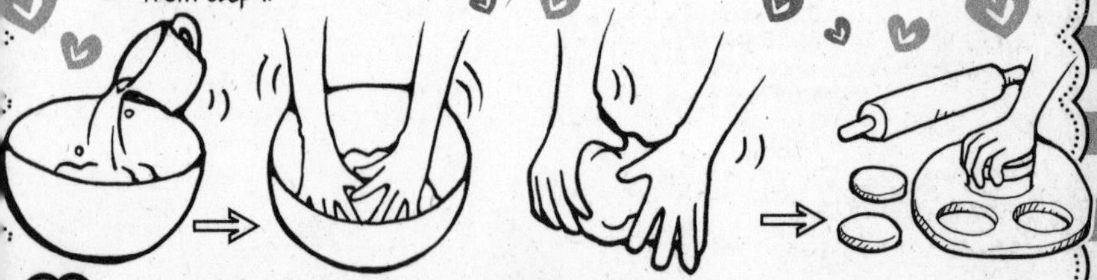

3. Add milk into the bowl from step 2 and mix.

4. Sprinkle some flour onto a cutting board and place the dough on top of it. Use a rolling pin to roll out the dough. The dough should be about 3/4 inch high. Use a round cookie cutter that is about 2 inches in diameter and cut out the dough. If you don't have a cookie cutter, you can use an upside- down cup.

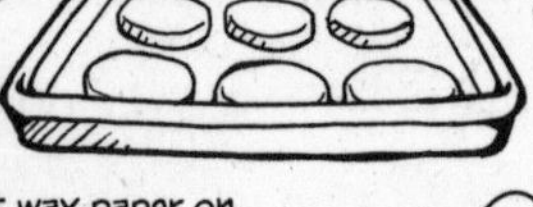

5. Lay out wax paper on a cookie sheet and place the cut pieces of dough. Bake in the oven for about 12 minutes, and you're done!

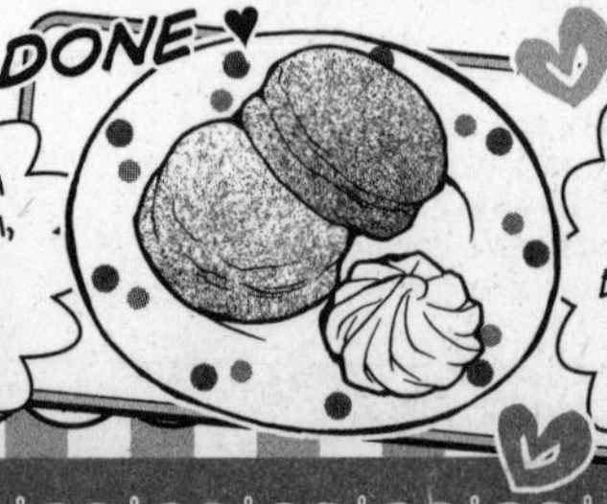
DONE ♥

You can serve them with whipped cream, jam, or honey to make them even more delicious!

Scones are a popular snack to enjoy with tea in England.

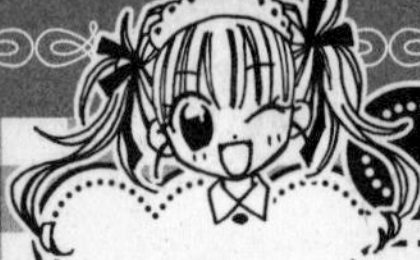

Fruit Agar

Agar has a lot of fiber and is good for your digestion. Eat a lot and stay healthy ♥

Tip from Najika.

Syrup

3/4 cup water, 6 tablespoons sugar, some syrup from mixed canned fruit. Caramel Agar: Makes a 6-inch x 6-inch piece. 1 3/4 cups water, 1/8 cup powdered agar mix, 3 tablespoons sugar, 1/4 cup water to add to the caramel sauce. Milk Agar: Makes a 6-inch x 6-inch piece. 1 1/3 cups water, 1/8 cup powdered agar mix, 1 cup milk, 3 tablespoons sugar, a little vanilla (It's okay if you don't have any). Fruit for decoration, some canned mixed fruit, some strawberries and kiwi.

How to Make

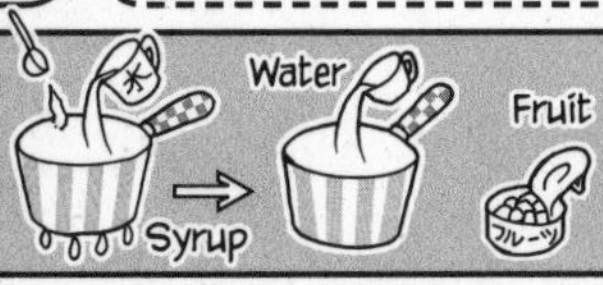
Water
Fruit
Syrup
フルーツ

Put water and sugar in a saucepan and cook over low heat for 5 minutes. Once the sugar dissolves, take it off the heat and add the syrup from the canned fruit. Cool and put in the refrigerator.

Caramel Agar

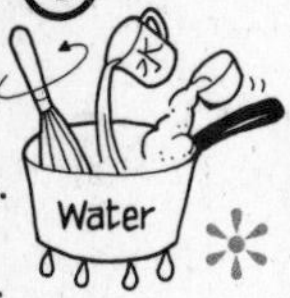
Water

1. Pour water and the powdered agar mix into a saucepan and cook it over medium heat. Mix it well and when it comes to a boil, lower the heat and simmer for 2 minutes.

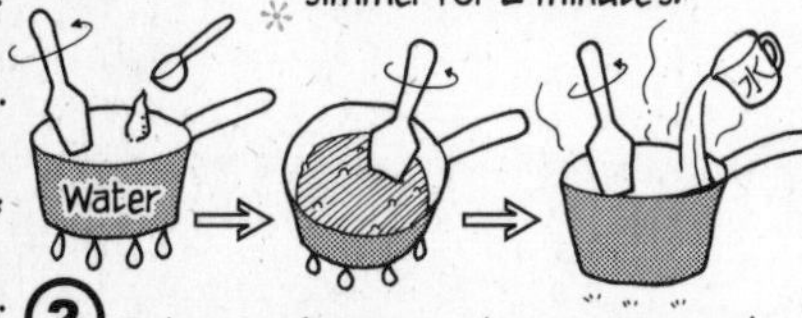
Water

2. Put sugar in a separate saucepan and cook it over low heat. Stir until the sugar melts and becomes brown. When it starts to boil, turn off the heat and add water. Stir well. *When you add water, it will sizzle so be careful.

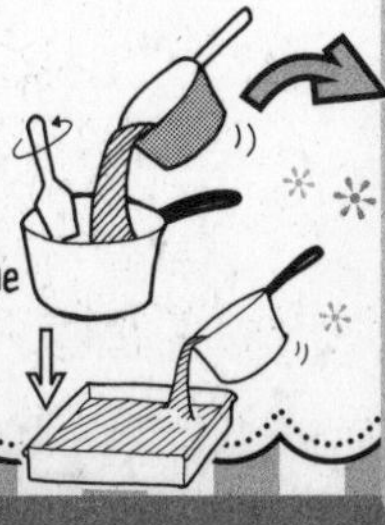

3. Add the mix from step 2 into step 1. Pour it into a shallow container and chill in the refrigerator for about an hour.

Milk Agar

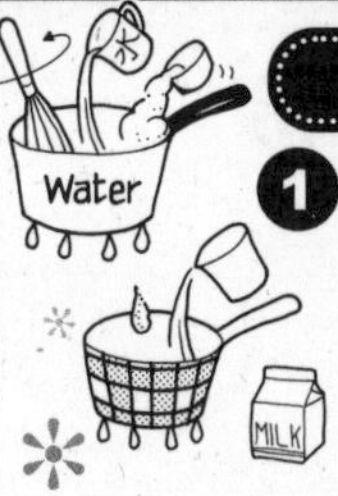
Water
MILK

1. Pour water and the powdered agar mix into a saucepan and cook it over medium heat. Mix it well and when it comes to a boil, lower the heat and simmer for 2 minutes.

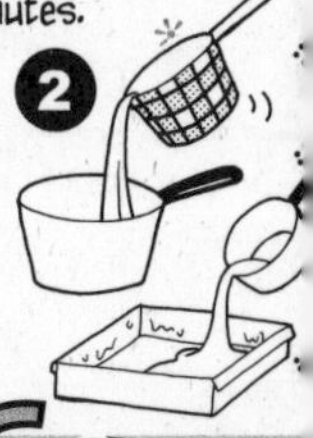

2. Put the milk, sugar, and vanilla into another small saucepan and cook over medium heat. When it becomes lukewarm, pour it into the saucepan from step 1 and mix. Pour it into a shallow container and chill it in the refrigerator for about an hour.

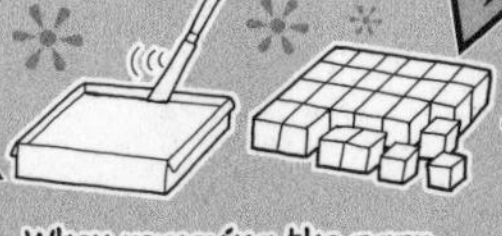

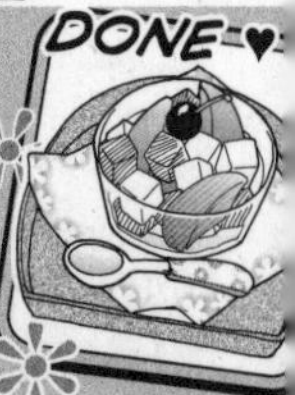
DONE ♥

When removing the agar from the container, first loosen the sides and then pop the whole thing out. Then you can cut it into smaller cubes of about 3/4 inch. Make sure to cut up the fruit i bite-sizes, too. ***Put the cubes into a glass c with some of the syrup from the mixed fru and the syrup you made and serve!***

Tiramisu

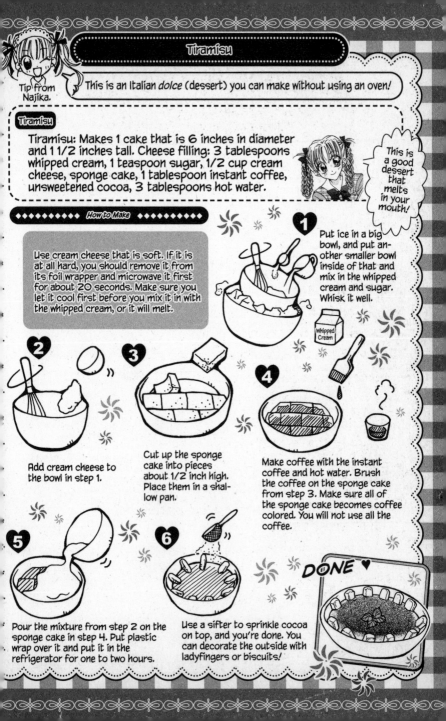

Tip from Najika.

This is an Italian *dolce* (dessert) you can make without using an oven!

Tiramisu

Tiramisu: Makes 1 cake that is 6 inches in diameter and 1 1/2 inches tall. Cheese filling: 3 tablespoons whipped cream, 1 teaspoon sugar, 1/2 cup cream cheese, sponge cake, 1 tablespoon instant coffee, unsweetened cocoa, 3 tablespoons hot water.

This is a good dessert that melts in your mouth!

♦♦♦♦♦♦♦♦♦♦ How to Make ♦♦♦♦♦♦♦♦♦♦

Use cream cheese that is soft. If it is at all hard, you should remove it from its foil wrapper and microwave it first for about 20 seconds. Make sure you let it cool first before you mix it in with the whipped cream, or it will melt.

1 Put ice in a big bowl, and put another smaller bowl inside of that and mix in the whipped cream and sugar. Whisk it well.

Whipped Cream

2 Add cream cheese to the bowl in step 1.

3 Cut up the sponge cake into pieces about 1/2 inch high. Place them in a shallow pan.

4 Make coffee with the instant coffee and hot water. Brush the coffee on the sponge cake from step 3. Make sure all of the sponge cake becomes coffee colored. You will not use all the coffee.

5 Pour the mixture from step 2 on the sponge cake in step 4. Put plastic wrap over it and put it in the refrigerator for one to two hours.

6 Use a sifter to sprinkle cocoa on top, and you're done. You can decorate the outside with ladyfingers or biscuits!

DONE ♥

Kitchen Princess

From the Writer

Hello! I am Miyuki Kobayashi, the writer and the one in charge of the recipes. Besides writing manga stories, I also write novels. Kodansha just released my newest novel, *I'm About to Cry*, so please check it out. And thank you for all your letters. I will use this area to answer some of the questions I've gotten.

Question 1: "What is your favorite dessert?"

Answer: I like cream puffs and flan. Ando-sensei likes green tea-flavored things, but I like things with custard in them. The one thing I fell in love with was a dessert called Rose Macaroon Cake made by a French pastry chef.

Question 2: "What kind of snacks do you like to eat?"

Answer: I've liked cheese-flavored Karl ever since I was a kid. I like the TV commercials, too. And I also like to eat Kaki no Tane (laugh)!

I would like to answer more questions, so please feel free to send me letters. Lastly, I would like to thank Natsumi Ando sensei, our editor Kishimoto-san, Saito-san from the editing team, and our editor-in-chief Nouchi-san. I'll see you again in Volume 5!

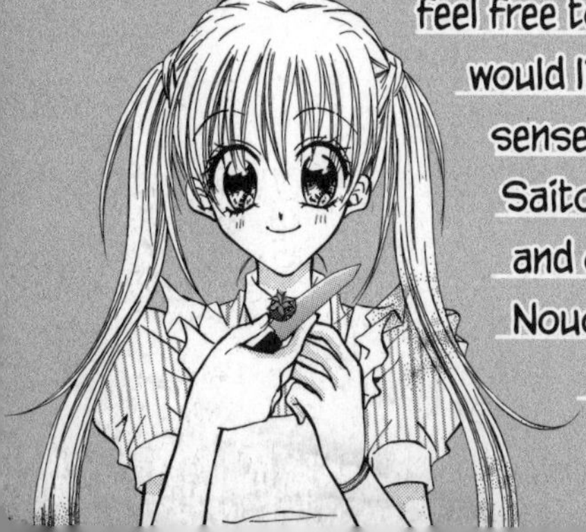

About the Creator

Natsumi Ando

She was born January 27th in Aichi prefecture. She won the 19th Nakayoshi Rookie Award in 1994 and debuted as a manga artist. The title she drew was *Headstrong Cinderella*. Her other known works are *Zodiac P.I., Wild Heart,* and others. Her hobbies include reading, watching movies, and eating delicious food.

Translation Notes

Japanese is a tricky language for most Westerners, and translation is often more art than science. For your edification and reading pleasure, here are notes on some of the places where we could have gone in a different direction in our translation of the work, or where a Japanese cultural reference is used.

Omrice, page 5

Omrice is a Japanese dish that is similar to an omelette. It is stir-fried rice wrapped inside eggs. The rice has chicken and vegetables and is flavored with ketchup. After it is wrapped in a sheet of egg, it is topped with more ketchup.

Aniki, page 107

Aniki is a term for "older brother," usually used by boys (or girls who are tomboys) in their younger teens. It is less honorific than "onii-chan" and "onii-san."

Najika is in love with aniki.

Najio, Sorako, and Daiko, page 144

Adding "o" to the end of the name usually indicates that it is a name for a boy. Likewise, adding "ko" to the end of the name indicates that it is a name for a girl. This is usually done as a joke in manga; for example, the names Najiko, Sorako, or Daiko are completely made up.

Flowers on the desk, page 166

When a student passes away, it is customary to place flowers on his or her desk. Since Japanese students do not change classrooms, the students have assigned seating. Daichi and Najika are therefore able to tell as soon as they see the flowers that Komugi has passed away.

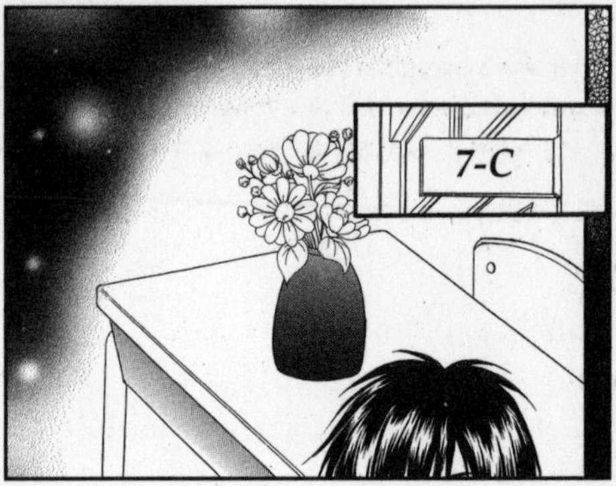
7-C

Forty-nine days, page 167

This is a Buddhist belief. Just as Sora says, when a person passes away, it is said that the spirit wanders in this world for seven weeks (forty-nine days) while it is preparing for reincarnation.

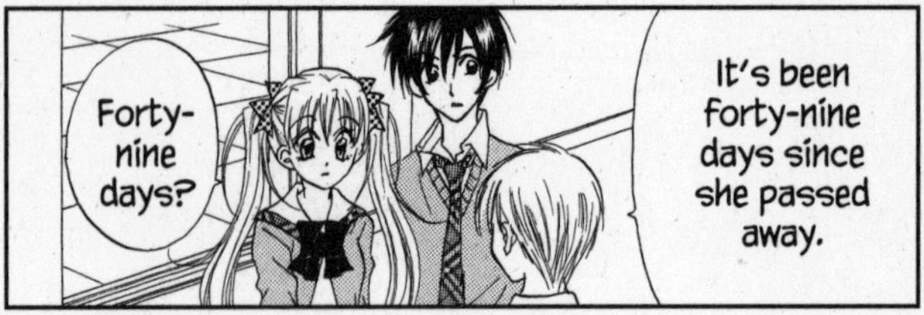
It's been forty-nine days since she passed away.
Forty-nine days?

Karl, page 191

Karl is a Japanese snack that is made by the Meiji Seika Company. It was released in 1967 with two flavors—cheese and chicken soup. Their mascot is "Karl," a middle-aged farmer with facial hair who wears a straw hat. The snack is fried and puffed, similar to cheese puffs in the United States.

Kaki no Tane, page 191

Kaki no Tane is a Japanese snack of rice crackers and peanuts. The name means "persimmon seed," and comes from the shape of the crackers. They are thinly sliced in quarter moon shapes.

Preview of Volume 5

We are pleased to present you a preview from volume 5. Please check our website (www.delreymagna.com) to see when this volume will be available in English. For now you'll have to make do with Japanese!

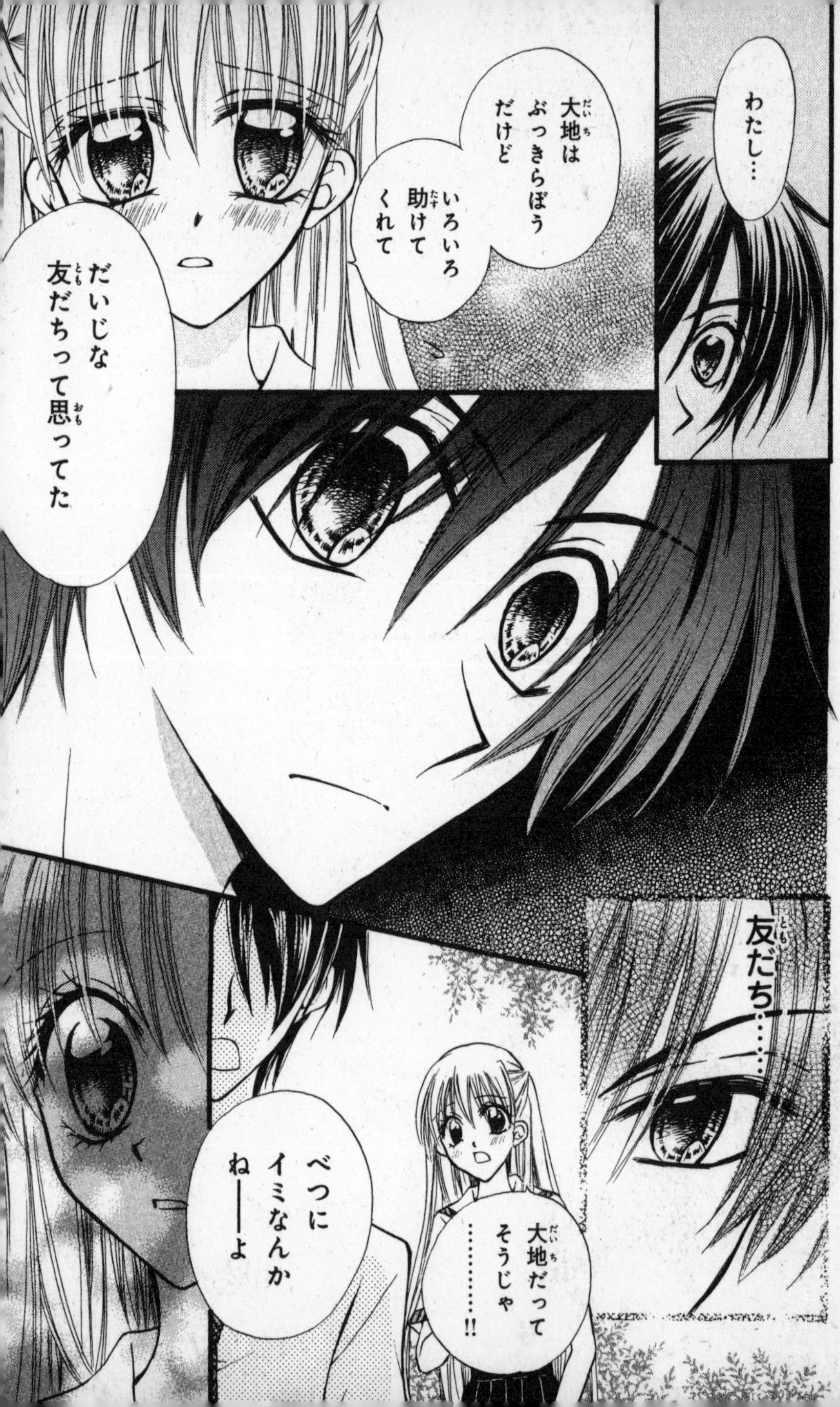

わたし…
大地はぶっきらぼうだけど
いろいろ助けてくれて
だいじな友だちって思ってた
友だち……
大地だってそうじゃ……!!
べつにイミなんかねー―よ

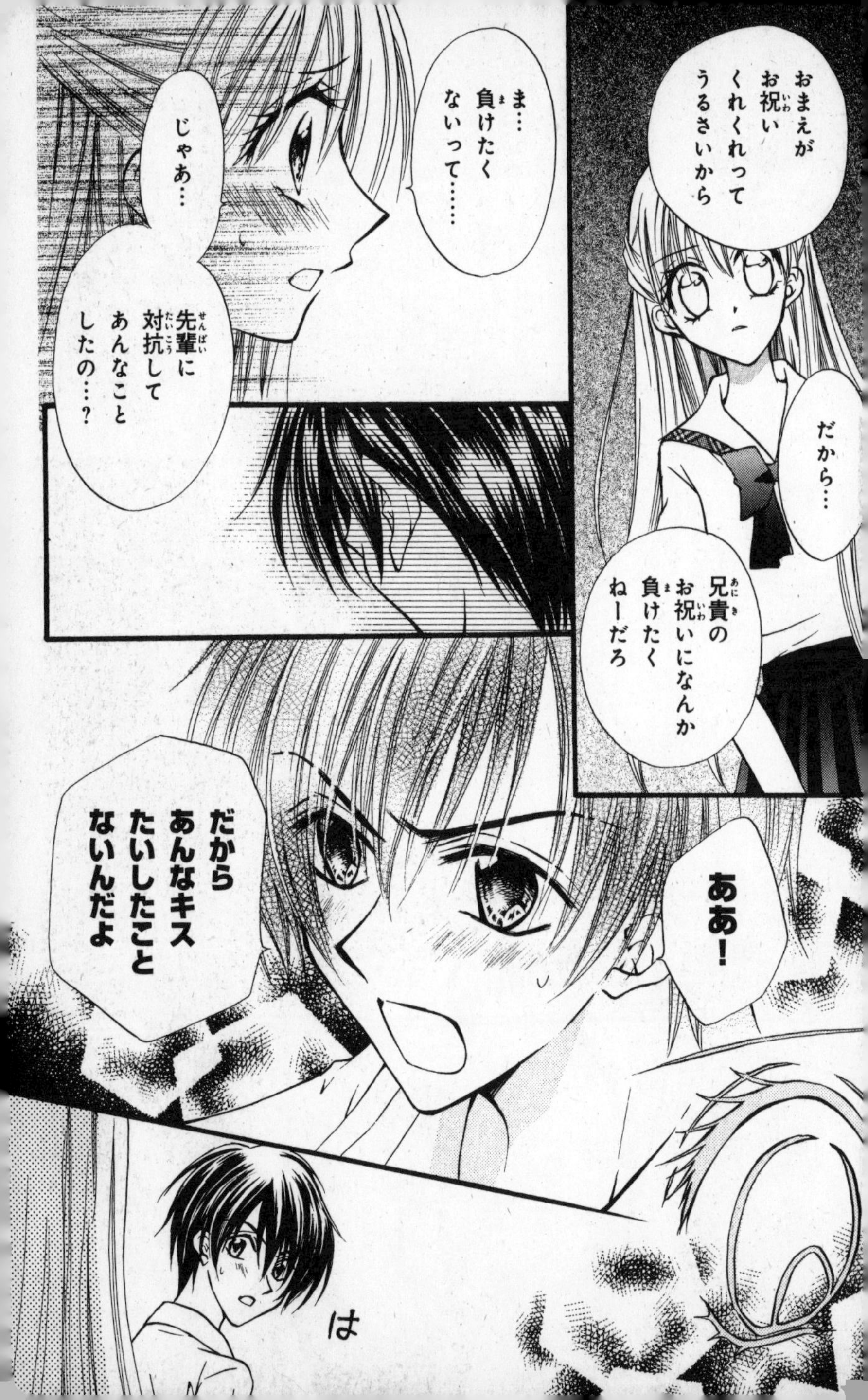
おまえがお祝いくれくれってうるさいから
だから…
兄貴のお祝いになんか負けたくねーだろ
ま…負けたくないって……
じゃあ…
先輩に対抗してあんなことしたの…?
ああ!
だからあんなキスたいしたことないんだよ
は

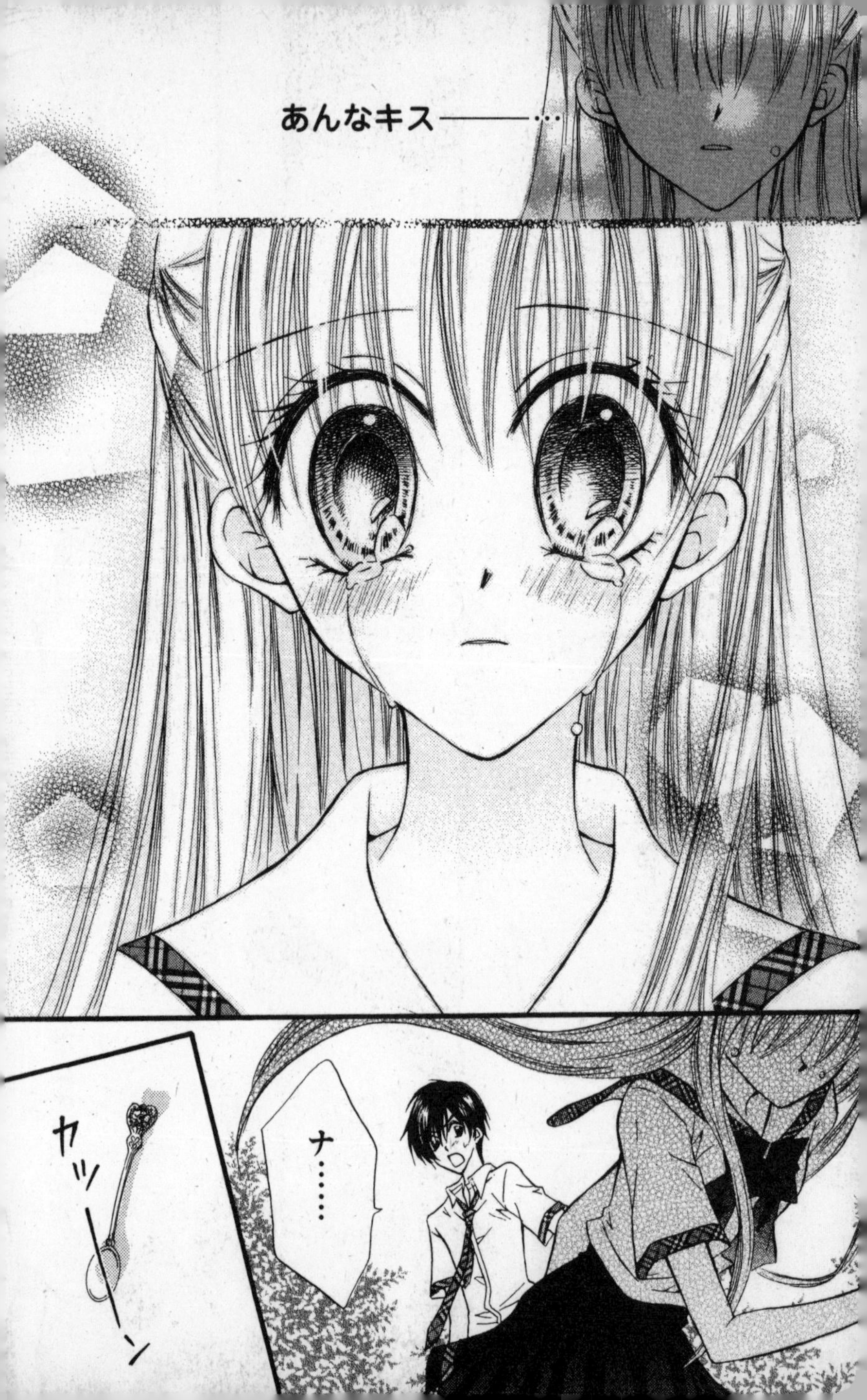
あんなキス――…
ナ……
カツーーン

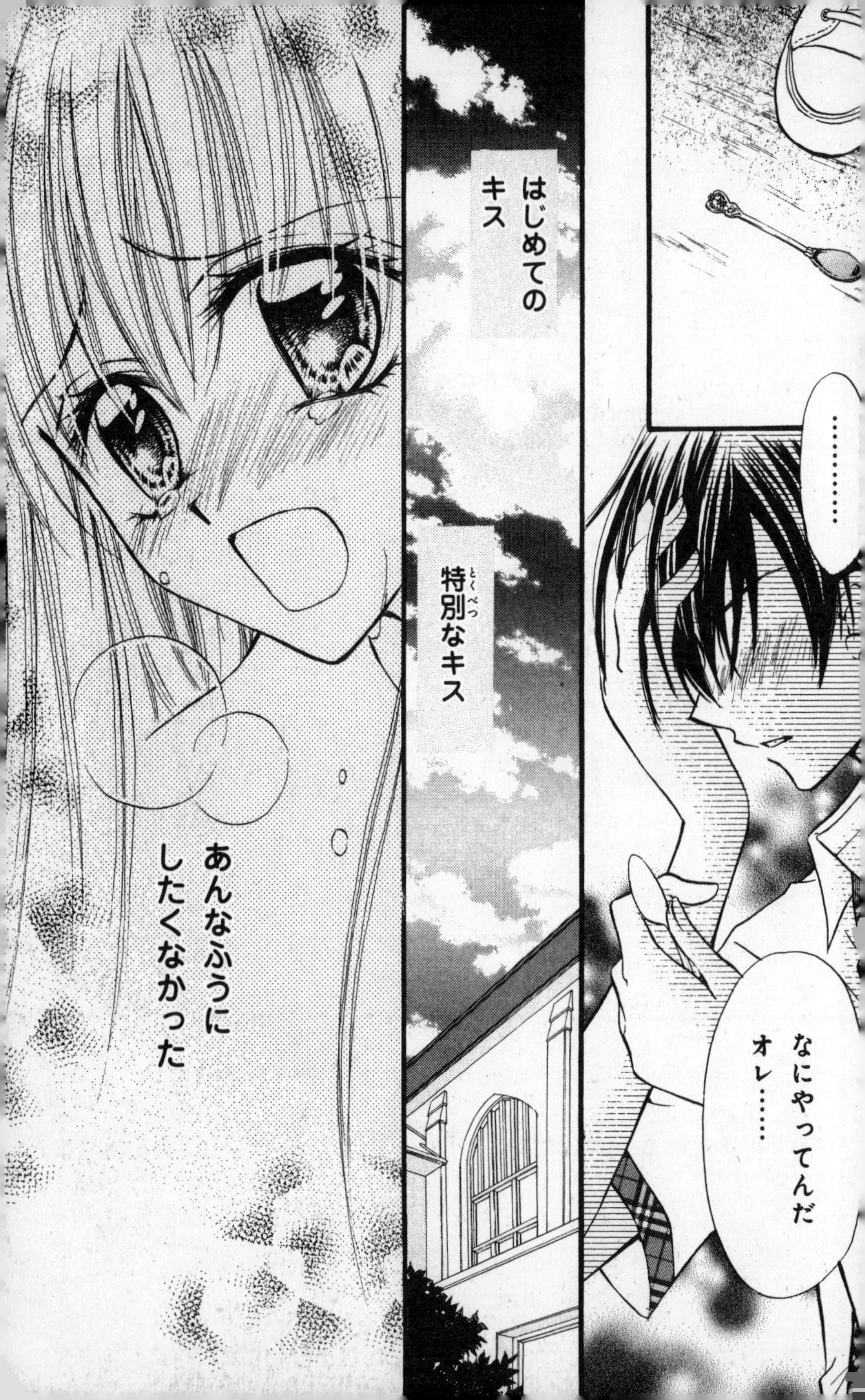
…………
なにやってんだ オレ……
はじめての キス
特別なキス
あんなふうに したくなかった

PEACH-PIT

Creators of *Dears* and *Rozen Maiden*

Everybody at Seiyo Elementary thinks that stylish and super-cool Amu has it all. But nobody knows the *real* Amu, a shy girl who wishes she had the courage to truly be herself. Changing Amu's life is going to take more than wishes and dreams—it's going to take a little magic! One morning, Amu finds a surprise in her bed: three strange little eggs. Each egg contains a Guardian Character, an angel-like being who can give her the power to be someone new. With the help of her Guardian Characters, Amu is about to discover that her true self is even more amazing than she ever dreamed.

Special extras in each volume! Read them all!

DEL REY MANGA デルレイ

The Otaku's Choice